ED ATKINS

ED ATKINS

Edited by
Polly Staple, Nathan Ladd and Ed Atkins

TATE

Using the word (God) openly
Eating an apple at Thy house
Making a feather while on Thy day
Denying that I made it
Making a mousetrap on Thy day
Contriving of the chimes on Thy day
Squirting water on Thy day
Making pies on Sunday night
Swimming in a kimnel on Thy day
Putting a pin in Iohn Keys hat on Thy day
to pick him
Carelessly hearing and committing
many sermons
Refusing to go to the close at my
mothers command
Threatning my father and mother Smith
to burne them and the house over them
Wishing death and hoping it to some
Striking many
Having uncleane thoughts words and actions
and dreamese
Stealing cherry cobs from Eduard Storer
Denying that I did so
Denying a crossbow to my mother and
grandmother though I knew of it
Setting my heart on money learning pleasure
more than Thee
A relapse
A relapse
A breaking again of my covenant renued
in the Lords Supper
Punching my sister
Robbing my mothers box of plums and sugar
Calling Dorothy Rose a jade
Glutiny in my sickness
Peevishness with my mother
With my sister
Falling out with the servants
Divers commissions of alle my duties
Idle discourse on Thy day and at other times
Not turning nearer to Thee for my affections
Not living according to my belief
Not loving Thee for Thy self
Not loving Thee for Thy goodness to us
Not desiring Thy ordinances
Not long [longing] for Thee in [illegible]
Fearing man above Thee
Using unlawful means to bring us
out of distresses
Caring for worldly things more than God
Not craving a blessing from God
on our honest endeavors
Missing chapel
Beating Arthur Storer
Peevishness at Master Clarks for a piece
of bread and butter
Striving to cheat with a brass halfe crowne
Twisting a cord on Sunday morning
Reading the history of the Christian
champions on Sunday

Isaac Newton, 'Isaac Newton's List of Sins', *Fitzwilliam Notebook* 1 Jan 1662

CONTENTS

FOREWORD

Ed Atkins is one of the most influential artists of his generation. This ambitious solo exhibition at Tate Britain is the first UK institutional presentation of his work in over ten years and the largest survey exhibition of his work to date.

This exhibition marks Atkins's return to Tate Britain, having exhibited at the gallery as part of the Art Now programme in 2011. Held two years after he graduated from the Slade School of Art and Design, the show helped cement his reputation as a leading contemporary artist early in his career. The following year Atkins exhibited at Chisenhale Gallery and was part of the 55th Venice Biennale, returning there again in 2019. He went on to have solo presentations at major institutions around the world, including Stedelijk Museum, Amsterdam; Palais de Tokyo, Paris; Kunsthalle Zürich; and Serpentine Galleries, London. More recently Atkins has had significant solo exhibitions at Kunsthaus Bregenz; Martin-Gropius-Bau, Berlin; K21 Kunstsammlung Nordrhein-Westfalen, Düsseldorf; New Museum, New York; and Tank Qiao Space, Shanghai. In that time Atkins has also undertaken professorships at Goldsmiths, University of London and HFBK University of Fine Arts Hamburg, and is currently a professor at Kunstakademie at Düsseldorf. Writing is an important facet of Atkins's artistic practice and he has published numerous books including an epic soliloquy, *Old Food* and a collection of his writings, *A Primer for Cadavers*. Atkins's practice is defined by his work with high-definition video which manipulate the conventions of moving image, literature and theatre. This exhibition assembles an expansive body of works made over the last fifteen years. Atkins critically reflects on the fundamental changes in technology and what it has done to images and our sense of self.

Atkins's computer-generated figures are unnervingly intimate and lifelike self-portraits. His CGI imagery brings an uncanny semblance of life to what is irreducibly real in human experience, both emotionally and corporeally: fragility, loss, injury, illness, decay and the inevitability of death. In an era in which we are daily asked online to prove whether we are human or 'bot', Atkins's deepfakes of himself pursue existential questions. Such questions are descended from a modern canon of literature, philosophy and psychoanalysis, whose veracities are progressively eroded by computer technology. Presented as video installations within gallery spaces, often within and against object-like props and elements of architecture, visitors find themselves immersed in the works duplicitous renderings of the real. In this exhibition Atkins extends these motifs through a multitude of works in other mediums: drawings, paintings, photography, writing and embroideries.

The exhibition at Tate Britain is curated by Polly Staple, formerly Director of Collection, British Art, and Nathan Ladd, Curator, Contemporary British Art, with Hannah Marsh, Assistant Curator, Contemporary British Art, in close dialogue with Atkins. Emilia Will is the project editor of this publication and it was designed by HIT. The making of an exhibition is a collective endeavour, and we would like to warmly thank colleagues across Tate for their essential contributions.

Published on the occasion of Ed Atkins's exhibition at Tate Britain, this book captures the complexity of Atkins's work and the exhibition itself. It begins with a conversation between Polly Staple and Atkins that walks us through the show, giving direct insight into the artist's practice and the process of bringing this first UK survey of his work to fruition. Art critic and historian Hal Foster undertakes a close reading of Atkins's 2021 video *The worm*, asking 'what kind of realism is at stake here?' Novelist and critic Ben Lerner responds to Atkins's *Pianowork 2* 2023 through the concepts of pain and its representation, authenticity and the politics of feeling. Author Kathryn Scanlan's new text 'Play's the Thing' carefully scrutinises Atkins's Post-it note drawings, the film *Nurses Come and Go, But None for Me* 2024 and the oscillation between our inner and outer realities. Curator and psychotherapist Jamie Stevens develops a psychoanalytic enquiry into Atkins's work as he explores the presence of 'internal monologue' and how this may relate to our own discernment of reality and an active, critical consciousness. Finally, Nathan Ladd takes the body as subject, both the artist's and the implication of our own in an intercorporeal relationship with Atkins's work. The book includes previously unpublished behind-the-scenes production photographs across many years as well as those from *Nurses…*, premiering in the exhibition. Assembled video stills and installation images of the works included in the exhibition are arranged in significant groups, including a special selection of Post-it note drawings compiled for the book.

For their vital support throughout the making of this exhibition, we would like to warmly thank Cabinet Gallery, London; Gladstone Gallery, New York; Galerie Isabella Bortolozzi, Berlin; and dépendance, Brussels. Special thanks are due to the following individuals and institutions for their generosity and support of the exhibition through the loan of important works: Cabinet Gallery, Gladstone Gallery, Galerie Isabella Bortolozzi, Hartwig Art Foundation, Amsterdam, Robert Ramsauer, and those who wish to remain anonymous. We are grateful for the generous support of this exhibition by the Ed Atkins Exhibition Supporters Circle: Danish Arts Foundation and Tate International Council and Tate Patrons. We would also like to extend our thanks to Hartwig Art Foundation who commissioned and produced *Nurses Come and Go, But None For Me* that will premiere in the exhibition.

The exhibition at Tate Britain has been made possible by the provision of insurance through the UK Government Indemnity Scheme. We thank HM Government for providing Government Indemnity, and the Department for Culture, Media and Sport and Arts Council England for arranging the indemnity.

Finally, our deepest thanks go to Ed Atkins for the vision, generosity and commitment that allowed us to bring this exhibition to fruition, which we are proud to share with audiences.

Alex Farquharson
Director, Tate Britain

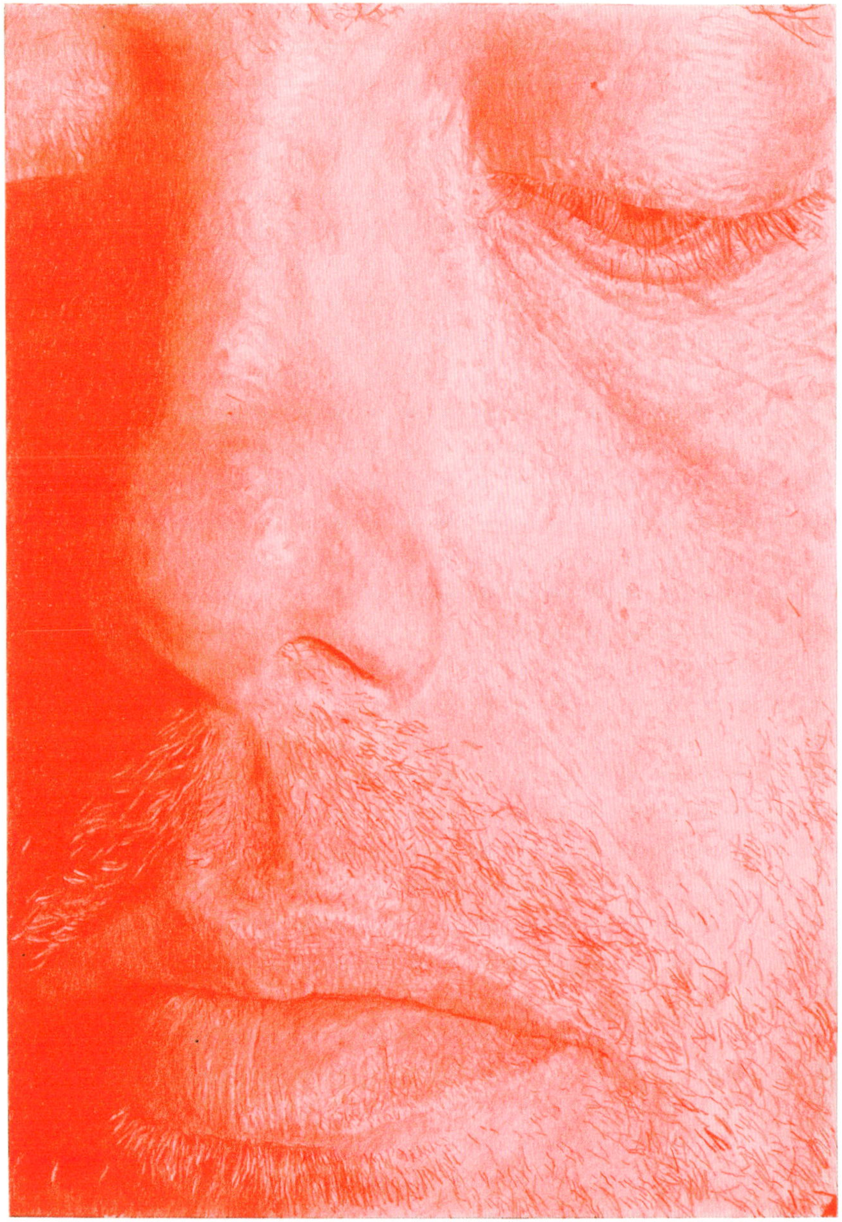

Untitled 2023, coloured pencil on paper, 52.1 × 41.3

AUTOFICTION: INTRODUCING ED ATKINS

Polly Staple and Nathan Ladd

For over a decade Ed Atkins has been making videos and animations that trace the dwindling gap between digital form and human feeling. Using his desires, experiences and his own body as a model, Atkins's works misuse contemporary technologies to critically reflect what they have done to images and a sense of self. His works pit a weightless digital life against a physical world of heft, craft and touch. He uses tropes and techniques from cinema, gaming, literature and theatre in a body of work allegorising loss, intimacy and love.

Ed Atkins at Tate Britain is a retrospective of sorts, spanning the past fifteen years or so of the artist's career. The idea of a 'retrospective', as we have conceived of it with him, was an attempt to find a way of making a survey exhibition feel alive and dynamic rather than simply a repository for the past. For Atkins, allowing the exhibition to capture a sense of digression, thought in motion, mistake, confusion, desire, unintelligibility, incoherence and interruption was essential for this very experience of liveness. Like Atkins's work, the show feels like an accumulation of a life. The more you see, the more complex and less contained it becomes. The work resists presumptions and simple explanations, and the exhibition shares in its partial imagining of the messy reality of a life.

1 Ed Atkins in conversation with Polly Staple, in this publication, p.34.

Ed Atkins assembles paintings, writing, embroideries and drawings alongside the moving-image works for which the artist is most well known. At first glance, the exhibition seems to run chronologically, as videos are encountered in a succession of large-scale installations. However, resisting strict media and temporal discretion, it is also intentionally mixed up: videos are displayed with self-portrait drawings, paintings of mattresses, pillows and limbs, and various embroideries. Several of the videos are split across rooms, have been remastered or are encountered on repeat. Repetition and difference, a recurring theme within Atkins's work, is a structural device within the exhibition itself. There is a constant sense of the familiar being made strange and of a deep enquiry into the oscillating relationship between the real, realism and fiction.

Early experiments in moving image reveal a conspicuous development in the video technology Atkins uses. Works such as *Cur* and *Death Mask II: The Scent*, both from 2010, are influenced by analogue, structuralist film but preoccupied with the then relatively new world of prosumer desktop video editing and the ambiguous notion of High Definition. Later works such as *Refuse.exe* 2019—employing the Unreal Engine, a software engine for making 3D video games and experiences—grapple with the mechanics of simulating reality, while *The worm* 2021 and *Pianowork 2* 2023 depict digital avatars of the artist that appear almost human. The exhibition culminates with the premiere of Atkins's most recent work, *Nurses Come and Go, But None for Me* 2024, a feature-length, live-action film made in collaboration with Steven Zultanski.

Atkins's experience of loss, specifically the death of his father, Philip Atkins, from cancer in 2010, has had a significant influence on his work, which he has described as being 'steeped in an involuted figuring with death'.[1] Connecting works across the exhibition made between 2010 and 2025, loss is profoundly felt and forensically analysed in the media Atkins uses. We encounter an emotional reckoning with the technologies of reproduction and obsolescence that shape our image world. Atkins rhymes his artistic methodology and intellectual enquiry with experiences of loss and the often overwhelming and intuitive excess of feeling surrounding it. Encountering Atkins's work throughout the exhibition a perverse kind of visual pleasure emerges, at once repulsive and attractive.

With works such as *Hisser* 2015, followed by *Old Food* 2017–19, *The worm* and *Pianowork 2*, we observe Atkins turning to the digitally rendered body, initially through the purchase of 'off the shelf' 3D models, ultimately to the use of a double of himself in *Pianowork 2*. We encounter many wretched white male bodies, surrogates of the artist: isolated, and some in emotional crisis, grappling with shame and grief. These figures play out all kinds of loss in digitally rendered and troubling environments where everything—however flawlessly reproduced—is irretrievably absent. Whether strikingly generic or his own image made digital, Atkins's surrogates are familiarly human, yet they consistently expose their own artifice with uncanny effect as technology ultimately fails in its capacity to replicate reality.

The exhibition also includes a series of highly detailed drawings of Atkins's own face and limbs alongside paintings of mattresses and pillows that bear traces of bodies. Self-portraiture and a striving towards a certain corporeal visibility is a consistent theme within the exhibition. The self-portraits are marvellous in their precision but also on occasion—as with his 'spider self-portraits'—horrifying, corpse-like. Atkins's neurotic picturing of his own body reminds us of the anxiety of contemporary self-identity and self-expression: the desire to control one's image and how others may see you is a contemporary psychological crisis played out through social media and a world of selfies.

Over the past twenty years or so the dominance of screens and online life has shifted traditional perceptions of spatiality and temporality in ever more unsettling and seductive ways.[2] Public platforms of surveillance capitalism and the attention economy have created new forms of perception: distinctions between on- and off-screen realities blur; extreme modes of engagement and distraction play out while the erosion of memory, a sense of digital dissonance and self-alienation in turn create an increasing desire for real, offline, visceral, human connection. Atkins's work strategically encapsulates and demonstrates this digitally mediated experience and the libidinal behaviours it channels. This is most obvious, for example, in the raw intimacy and liveness of recent works such as *The worm*, in which Atkins calls his mother on the phone, or *Pianowork 2*, where he painfully labours over a piece of piano music.

In Atkins's videos, sound takes on its own materiality, adding weight that contrasts with the immaterial artifice of computer-generated imagery (CGI). Like the fidelity to the real in the artist's reproduction of skin and hair, each tic and twitch, the sound in his work pulls us towards the real in a collision with the ultimate failure of digital tools to render it on screen. Musical extracts such as a Polovtsian dance by Borodin or Elton John and Kiki Dee's 'Don't Go Breaking My Heart' allow Atkins to exploit music's capacity to manipulate our emotions, triggering emotional reactions, sentimentality and familiar memories.

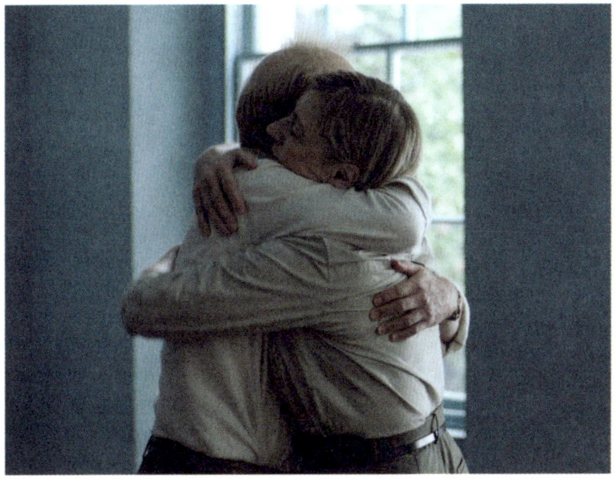

Production still from *Nurses Come and Go, But None for Me* 2024, with Steven Zultanski, video with sound

In contrast with the more traceless, digital form of Atkins's videos, his embroideries, self-portrait and Post-it note drawings belong to a traditional vernacular order. Conventional homemade embroidery requires hours of careful domestic labour. However, Atkins employs machines to make his on a grand scale, akin to the 4:3 projection screen. They

2
The first widely available consumer touchscreen smartphones were launched in 2007.

are instilled with the cool distance afforded by a mechanised process, just as the used linen, stained with marks of its previous ownership, is embroidered with texts processed by artificial intelligence. Like the costumes of *Old Food*, the embroideries bear witness to bodies, absent now save for their residues or indexes on the material's surface.

You do feel the painstaking labour in the series of highly detailed self-portraits and fragmented body parts. They are all meticulously observed and carefully hand-drawn and painted by Atkins, poring over every detail of the skin. These works are no less interested in technology and technologies of representation, however, than Atkins's recent video installations employing CGI software. Across a variety of media, be they analogue or digital, Atkins grapples with questions of representation, indexical cataloguing and psychological crisis.

At the heart of the exhibition is a mass of Post-it note drawings originally made by Atkins for his children. The artist has described them as 'miniature images of seemingly infinite invention'.[3] Each drawing's creation is full of love and as such they are 'tiny, laboured, inscrutable attempts to communicate feeling'.[4] The cartoonish tone and hysterical exaggeration of the drawings brings us into an easier relationship with violence and bodily anxiety, and acts as a recuperative, cathartic tool that draws parallels with the film *Nurses*.... The drawings contain an excess of sentiment that is productively frustrated by the limits of their own representation. As Atkins conceives it, this gesture might be understood as the central movement in all his works; the loss felt in the exhibition is not only sorrowful but a precondition of all experience.

The Post-it note drawings are joyful and playful. Running through all of Atkins's work is an absurd, confessional humour, scatological slapstick, gore and physical theatre. You can see this used with queasy effect in *Old Food* or *Refuse.exe*, but also in the sense of wonder—and the wonderful—conjured in the array of opera costumes displayed with *Old Food* and the Post-it note drawings. Atkins has said of the Post-it note drawings that he wanted them to be 'the legend at the bottom of the map, to teach a way of looking and accepting and feeling that might be useful for everything else. A productive not-knowing where knowledge acquisition is in its proper place, and not forced into an interrogative mode.'[5]

In Atkins's work what usually may be considered as unspectacular actions, banal expressions and prosaic gestures are presented as significant. The contrast between the expected spectacle of the mediums he uses and the peripheral aspects of experience he tasks them with representing creates a disjuncture familiar in our lives. The exhibition presents an entanglement of reality and artifice, familial inheritance, the obscene norms of media culture and the psychopathology of everyday technological life. Atkins's works prompt a heightened awareness of our own interiority within our fragile bodies. Our significance to ourselves is at odds with what we know of the world. As Atkins describes, the intention when we encounter his work 'is that we might be afforded access to otherwise unavailable feelings'.[6]

3 Ed Atkins, correspondence with Polly Staple and Nathan Ladd, via email, Feb. 2024.

4 Ibid.

5 Ed Atkins in conversation with Polly Staple, in this publication, p.42.

6 Ed Atkins, correspondence with Polly Staple and Nathan Ladd, Sept. 2024.

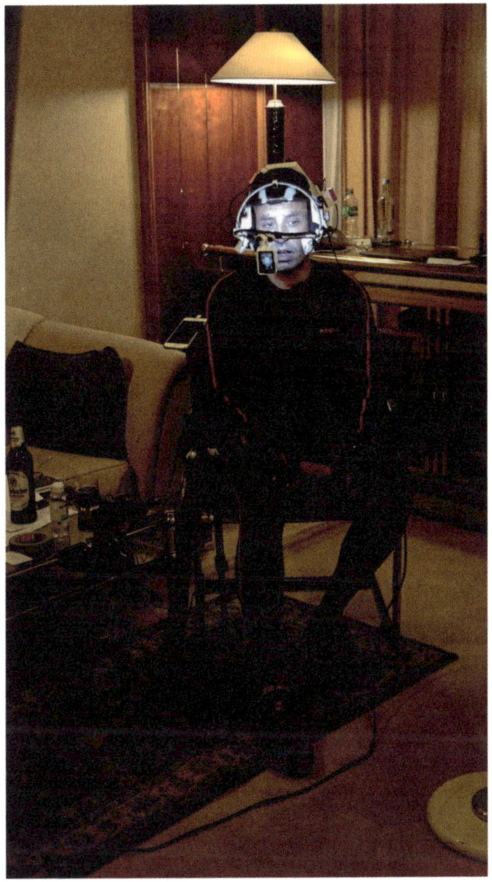

The artist rigged with performance capture equipment in a hotel room in Berlin in 2021, ready to call his mother for *The worm*.

LOSS

Ed Atkins in conversation with Polly Staple

POLLY STAPLE:

The Tate exhibition is your largest to date, spanning the past fifteen years or so of your practice, starting with *Death Mask II: The Scent* from 2010 and ending with your new work *Nurses Come and Go, But None for Me* from 2024. To a certain extent the exhibition runs chronologically and the video works are experienced in progression, but the overall presentation is also intentionally mixed up: video projections are displayed with paintings and drawings, for example, and several works are split or encountered on repeat. What was your approach to the challenge of making a retrospective exhibition?

ED ATKINS:

I needed to work out what the show would *not* be first. I definitely didn't want a chronology of discrete works. I didn't want to make coherent or unselfconscious what was surely not. I wanted the opposite. Something more liberal with the conceptual, narrative situation—and to perform that in the space via the exhibition design. I wanted to confuse works, sully works by exposure to others, reveal recursive, inadvertent, obsessive aspects, denigrate works maybe. Elevate others. I wanted to mishandle things in a manner to reveal my hand and chisel off any historical plaque too.

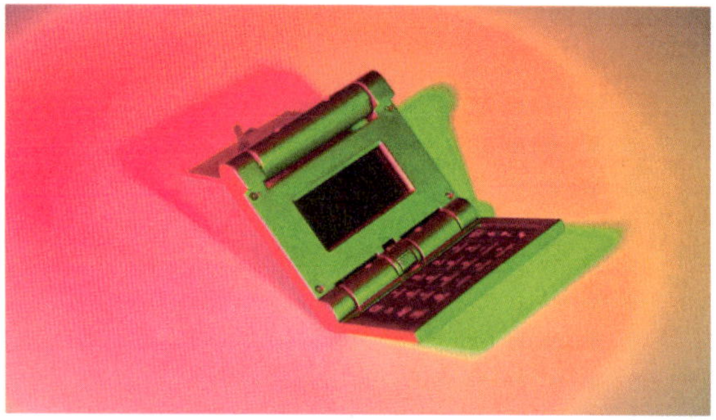

Death Mask II: The Scent 2010, video and sound

I've always made works live, so to speak. In order, from start to finish. Most works are first shown still wet, warm, alive and flawed. Retrospection means the works aren't this, but the show itself takes over the role of the live thing happening in the now. For me, the signifiers of that liveness are a tangible sense of thought in motion, replete with digression, mistake, confusion, desire, unintelligibility, incoherence, interruption, and of course loss. I want the show to lose my work so it might be found and prevailed upon anew.

My life and the work I make are more or less inextricable to me. At least in terms of choice. How do I convey the life-ness that made those works—my life—through the exhibition? I mean my life not in some factual, chronological, biographical way—but sensationally, in a way to mirror the making and my own unlicensed wants. To treat the show holistically. Not cumulatively or historiographically, but like how a body or a life is holistic. I don't feel—and I don't want an audience to feel—that the more you see of my work, the more the work describes an oeuvre. Instead, I want it so the more you see, the richer and more complex, less authored, less gettable things become. With an idea that 'getting it' is the de facto reductive coherency of convenient interpretation and ostensibly violent.

PS:

Death Mask II: The Scent is presented in the first room with an embroidery work containing your father, Philip Atkins's, cancer diary, but alphabetised to unintelligibility. The diary has also become the focus of the final work in the show, *Nurses Come and Go, But None for Me*. When we were grappling with how to open the show, it made sense to use *Death Mask II: The Scent* but also to both prefigure the final act of the show with the embroidery and assert a material register—the non-digital—in your work from the beginning. Perhaps then we could also start at the end with *Nurses*...?

EA:

Absolutely. I've actually been working with Dad's death diary—which he called *Sick Notes*—since he died. It's a diary he kept from cancer diagnosis until his death in June 2009. Six months or so. But despite the obvious hold my Dad's death has on my work, I've always felt conflicted about speaking of it explicitly through the work. Not because of some prohibitive moral quandary but because the experience of his death suffuses everything, and in ways that are foundational to how the work itself functions. Maybe more

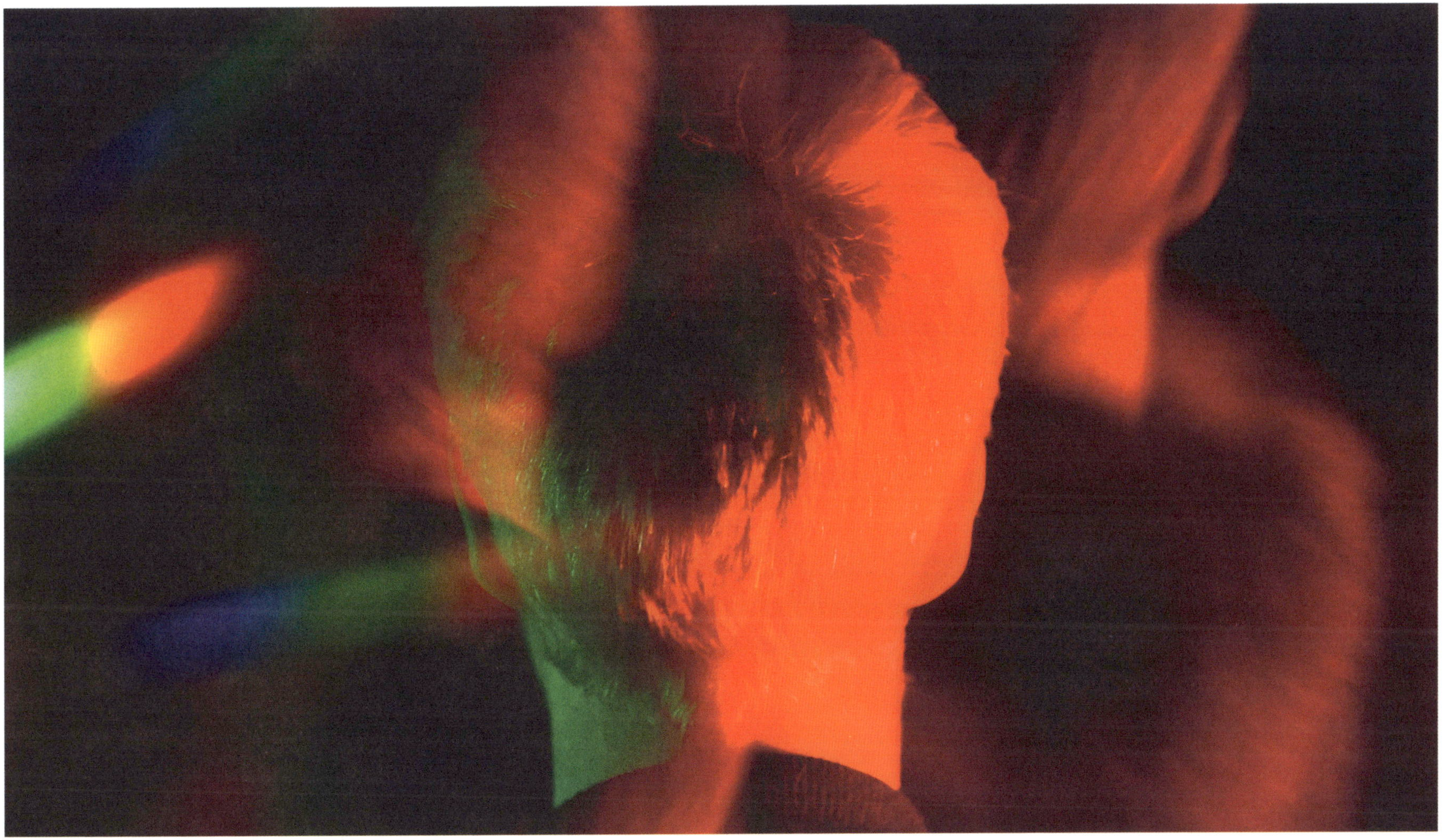

Death Mask II: The Scent 2010, video and sound

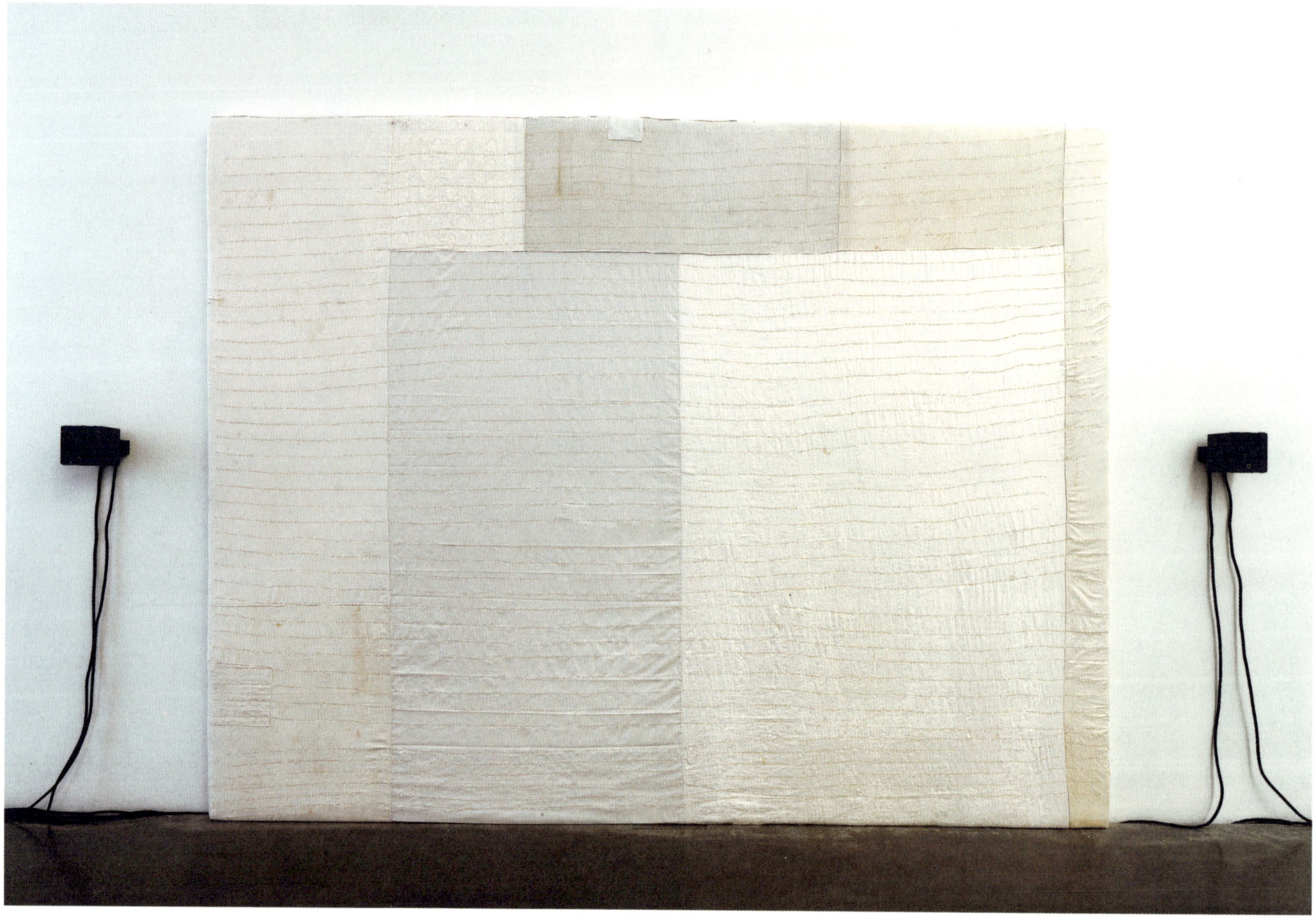

Untitled samplers 2021 (installation view) at New Museum, embroidered linen on acoustic foam and wooden frame, 304.8 × 406.4 × 10.2 (detail, right)

eam.Two icecream idea idea, ie if if iller illness; imagine imagined imagined It imagining imitate imitating immaculately immediate in
s irritating irritatingly irritation 28/4Home is is is, is. isolate isolation issuing It it it), it, it. it. 12/3Tried it.16/3A it.28/3Saturday, it.7.40
It it it, it, it 12/3Tried it.16/3A it. 28/3Saturday, it.7.40 it; it? its itself itself; itself it'll it's it's it...Rose I'd I'd I'LL I'll I'M I'm I've
ant leapt learn learned learning least least), least, least. Leather le,ve LEAVE leave, leaves leaving leaving lecturing red Left left left? left
lying L'pool M M, M. Mac, machine machine. Macmillan mamadoa man

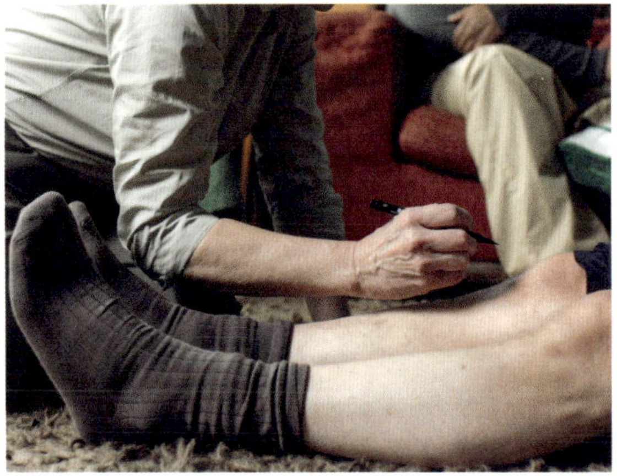

Production stills from *Nurses Come and Go, But None for Me* 2024, with Steven Zultanski, video and sound, (see also p.23)

than this, I worried over art excising experience. I can't differentiate what's part of the long-tail symptoms of his loss and what was either already in me or is something I've invented or found myself. I do know that my work has always been more honest than me, and in plenty of important ways. This is part of an understanding that the work can express things that are otherwise walled off in some way.

The embroidery stands between these points of relation to loss. In one way, it is the entire diary, unexpurgated. In another, it is rendered brutally unavailable. The alphabetising performs this and exploits some maligned notion of factual intelligibility. It encourages the idea of mechanical, impersonal interpretability—and also, through the medium of embroidery on used linen, a weird kind of decorousness, gross domesticity. I think of the perversity of template, idiomatic embroidery being made and positioned as somehow personal, some weird performance in the context of a person's private home.

In comparison to *Death Mask II: The Scent* and *Cur*, this embroidery—which is the same size and ratio as those newly cropped and upscaled videos—is emphatically material. This is a residual, installational tic to emphasise the qualities of different media—specifically digital media's seeming immateriality—by excess, but it is also a way to allegorically model a desire that would not be tangible without it. This and the other embroideries were also, in part, conceived as both practical and conceptual objects, much like the costumes used in *Old Food*. They act as acoustic panels, absorbing reverberation or, as I like to think of it, giving out silence. Where the videos project, the panels absorb and mute. Embroideries like this have very little authority as objects but are repositories of private labour.

The final work in the show, the film *Nurses...*, is Dad's diary read to an audience, followed by a role-playing game. The diary itself is an exquisitely written thing. It is extraordinary, I think, regardless of my relation, and what it has to say about the end of life, love, healthcare and so many other things is irrefutably important. It's an account not only of illness but of the personal and public contexts that shape a body's decline—the feelings of longing and self-pity, the loss of independence, the social life of the hospital, the bureaucracy and administration of terminal illness, and the discovery of having loved and been loved. It's excruciating and funny and very, very sad.

In the film, the diary is read by a middle-aged man to an invited audience inside the apartment he shares with his partner. Once he's read the diary, he and his partner perform a mimed game dubbed the Ambulance Game. It's a game I play with my daughter where she gets to pretend to be dramatically sick and receive a cavalcade of fictional treatments, brush up against illness and mortality. Then the game ends, and everyone's okay. I mean, no one dies in a children's game. The film ends there too. The diary and the game were of course originally private creations and not subject to public consumption—though their existence and ameliorative effects presume an audience's fantasy. The film literalises this fantasy by staging these creations as performances in front of an audience and by focusing on the faces of the audience as much as on the performers. *Nurses...* presents intimate material at a slight emotional and intellectual distance, to paradoxically heighten that intimacy or make it available in a perverted, voyeuristic fashion. For Dad, the diary was, I think, partly a way to turn grappling with death into pleasure, reclaiming life while also attending to and letting go of the details of the world. In the film, the performance of the diary is an invitation to the audience to share in that pleasure. Similarly, the Ambulance Game is a child's way of play-acting control of the world through illness and enjoying that control. Like the diary, it is a rehearsal of the unimaginable. Unlike the diary, the game ends and the performance is over, and the question of recovery becomes irrelevant.

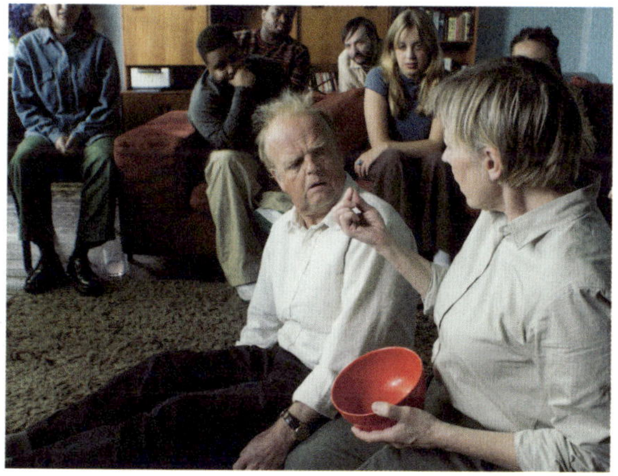

PS:

Death Mask II: The Scent is a video from 2010 and represents a first foray for you into both video editing and death, and their rhyming, the beginning of making videos and the beginnings of a personal media theory. What was the process of making your early moving-image works?

EA:

When I made *Death Mask II: The Scent*, I'd only started editing footage and sound together the previous year, at the end of my MA at the Slade. It was quickly apparent that this was the thing. I loved it. Specifically, I loved editing—and on the computer. The capacity to dwell on a single moment, a single transition, a single line of suturing was intoxicating—and always able to be undone without residual index. One could liken the instantaneity and tracelessness of digital editing to a worrying at something; it can feel compulsive

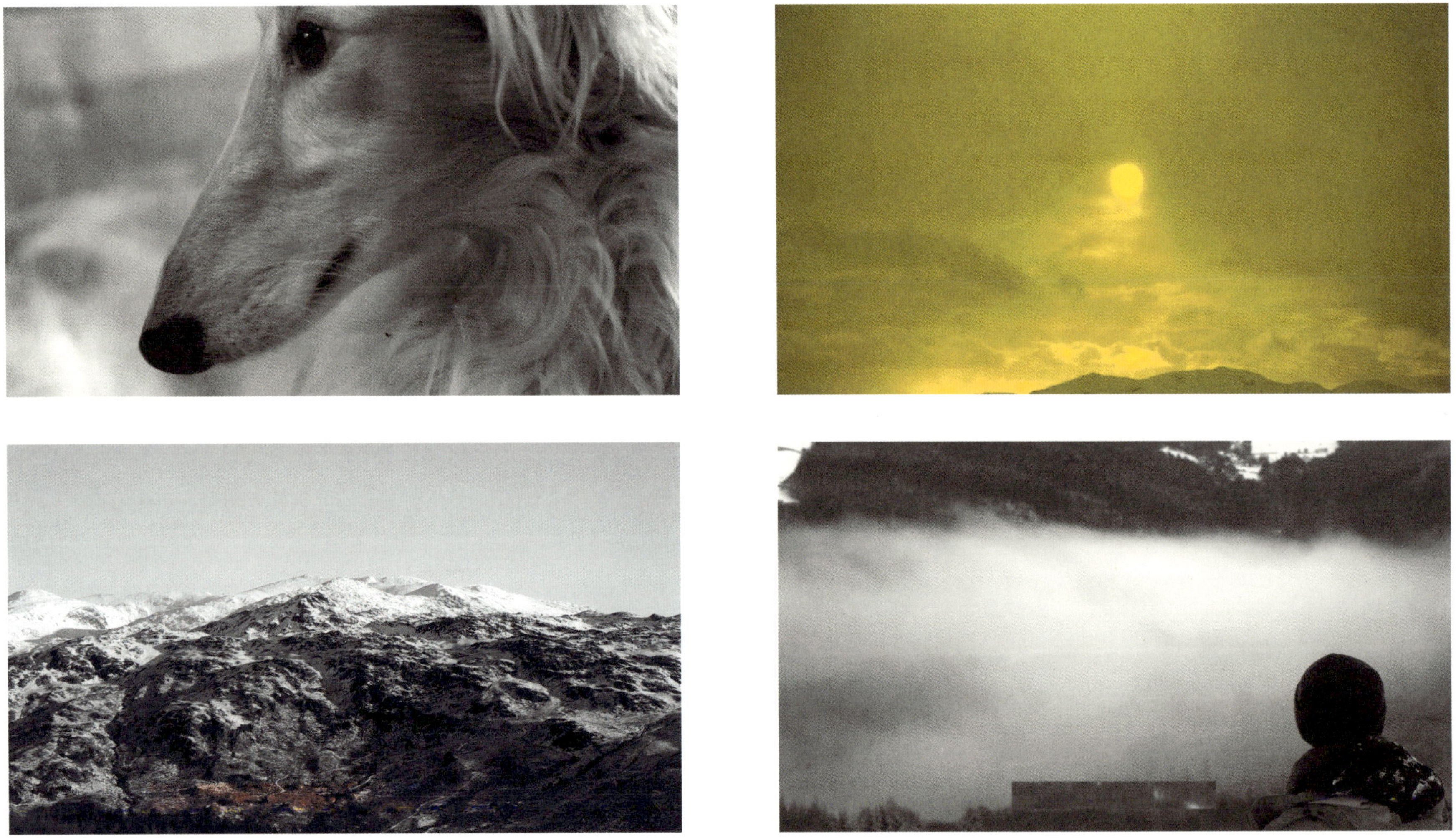

Cur 2010, video and sound

as well as simultaneously inattentive and almost forensically locked in.

Initially I only used stock footage, and the more generic it was, the more I was into it. I wanted to see what I could rouse from this material through editing, sound and effects. I wanted the subject of the footage itself to disappear and the videos to be *of* editing, sound and effect—of structure—the structuring of sentiment. When my Dad died around the same time—just as I was graduating—these very desirous practices became fused with the excesses of feeling that surrounded that loss. I started to conflate what I was thinking about the material and the experiences of the digital moving image with the material and the experiences of his death. The psychical situation of loss and grief and anger and love found its counterpart in digital video, as odd and forced as that sounds.

I should say here that I also think my whole technologically specific *bit* has always been a way to protect extremely tender parts of myself. That is how I've come to understand the relationship between a burgeoning media theory and the affective terrain of the work. Technology and technologically specific representation have been a way to allegorise otherwise unspeakable feelings. I've built a weird exosuit of discourse that's laboriously fascinating—it's just that that layer is the text, and actually the subtext plumbs super deep and is, to me, far more meaningful. But it's less admissible and solvable by explication. This kind of dichotomy is played out in plenty of ways in later works: the apparent spectacle of computer-generated imagery (CGI) being employed to convey seemingly unworthy subject matter, for example. It's often a constructive misuse that can punctuate an audience's—and my—presumptions around, say, access to information. CGI begs to be impoverished.

Death Mask II: The Scent is all synth noise and vivid, posterised colours, jump cuts and weird advertainment—structure and sign and language: all somewhat familiar, all very deliberately meant to be manipulative, even if the goal of that manipulation is withheld. The video is trying to overwhelm while at the same time offering itself as a weird little essay on moving imagery, genre and constructed desire. In the exhibition, *Death Mask II: The Scent* is shown alongside another video from the same year, *Cur*, and the pair of them stand as exemplars of video-making from my past, but also, more constructively for the exhibition, primers for the language of my work—the sentimental space, the form, as well as a medium-specificity that is as important as the imagery itself. Duration, too, of course, in terms of things happening across time. The movement between sensations is very important to me: the tease of climax and revelation, a montage of intoxication and rejection, bathetic abandonment.

Cur is more intimate-seeming, as it consists mainly of footage shot during a trip with my family. However, as with *Death Mask II: The Scent*, the footage constantly seeks to shed its specificity. Or rather, it seeks to uncover the quiddity of the footage, it seeks effect. Often, the shots look for ways in which the technology reveals itself—autofocus; lens flares; blurts of audio and interrupted sentences—in a way that really wants to reveal the technology, to stop it receding into transparency. This is an inherited desire from structural film-making, though much of whatever anti-illusionary politic is left is shuffled over to a place of affect, incoherence or maybe speechlessness. The empty placeholders for subtitles in *Cur* have to do with this: the desire to speak but not knowing what to say—and often how upsetting that can be.

It is important to note that, to put it euphemistically, these two videos have been remastered for the exhibition. Using various upscaling and renovating artificial intelligence processes, the works are resituated in the now. This touch, which I see as both restorative and ruinous of the works' authenticity, is a way to tolerate the past.

PS:

Over the years your moving-image works have increased in complexity as the CGI technology you use develops. You use techniques and tropes viewers will be familiar with from cinema, theatre, literature, desktop computing and video games. You take these mediums seriously, but you also consciously undo them. What is your relationship to these different visual registers and types of screen spaces?

EA:

I'm loath to give the work the status of social commentary—that's not my chosen role—but much of the work hinges on its affectivity and, in turn, on its fluency with media and media's reception throughout our lives. I'm interested in contemporarily ubiquitous forms, representations, vernaculars and structures to excite an audience's familiarity—their comfort and their prejudices and presumptions—in order to break with them more ostentatiously.

CGI tech is most often encountered in the mainstream in spectacular, didactic and kind of unimaginative forms—fundamentally constricting and determining an idea of what's imaginative at all or, to use that most defunct of terms, creative. I wanted to make scenes and moments that seemed like resource misuse, things that went against, in part, the desires of the technology and the desires of the industries that produce them. Not to be rid of spectacularity in general but to draw attention to it. Perversion does that, I think: underscores the peculiarity of the presumptive norm.

To return to the question of screens, I've never felt thwarted by the limits of the screen. Limitation is very exciting; it can properly locate one's choices and make them more conspicuous. I've not yet been seduced by virtual or augmented reality or things of that nature. Not yet. My work's technological commitment has never been about the bleeding edge or the novelty of new technologies. For my work to function (perhaps), the thing someone is looking at must somehow be familiar to them—that it is, in key ways, not novel but recognisable, albeit in a different form and, maybe, at a point of ubiquity where ubiquity drives a kind of bored presumption. Perhaps, some form just before its planned obsolescence. Forms and technologies that are sufficiently familiar to conjure a presumption of use on the part of the audience.

PS:

So much of the viewer's experience of the exhibition is sonic. How do you approach using sound in your work?

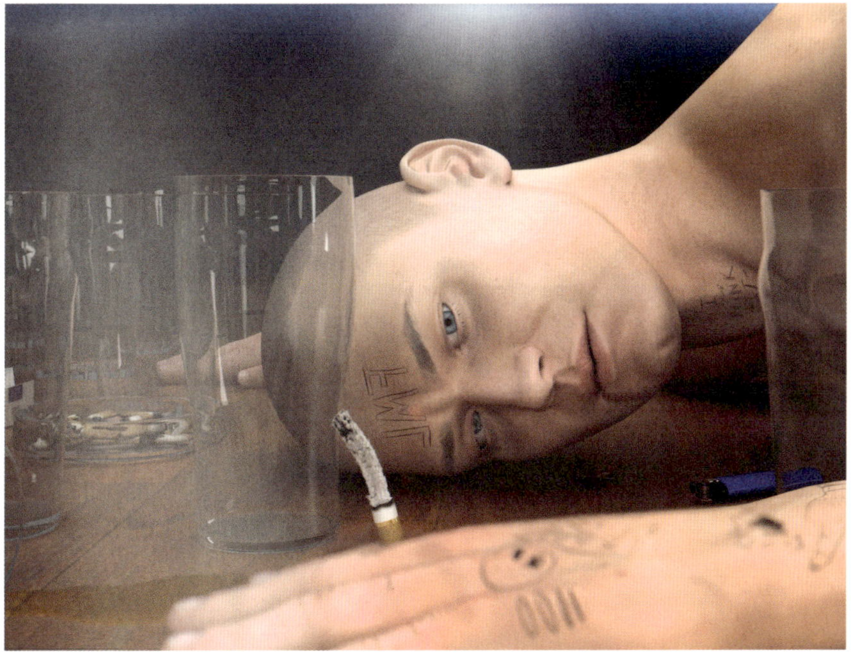

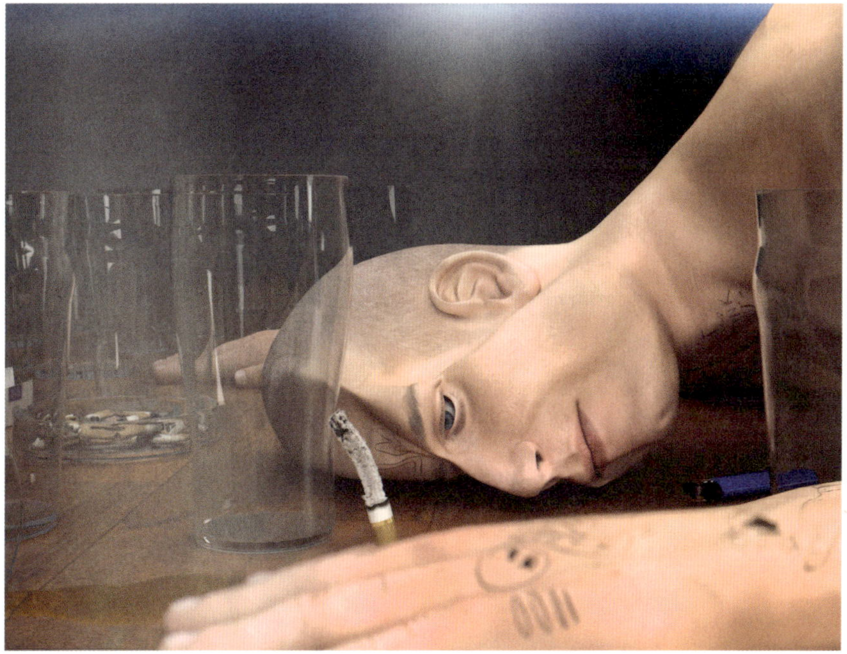

Ribbons 2014, three-channel video and sound

EA:

Sound is everything, yes. There's so much to say here. 'When a sound can replace an image, cut the image or neutralise it. The ear goes more toward the within, the eye toward the outer.'[1] That's the film director Robert Bresson, and I tend to agree. My voice. I've always thrilled around ventriloquism, for example, and the peculiar shame of one's voice being heard recorded. In my videos, sound is often a source of excessive, compensatory, apologetic materiality. This is a kind of Foley, which is a caricature but is employed as a realism. Computer-generated imagery without the addition of sound feels weightless, scarcely there. Sound animates and lends heft. The sound I add to my videos is often absurd in its gratuitous stressing of any object's material index—especially gratuitous considering the complete absence of any conventional objects. In my work, sound often functions hyperrealistically in a way that can be insistently intimate and alive with a conviction that feels providential but is clocked only unconsciously. Like how life is.

1 Robert Bresson, *Notes on Cinematography*, New York 1977.

Generally speaking, music in the work is commonly asked to do what soundtrack music is required to do—cue sentiment, cue drama—but again, to prevail upon an audience's presumptions and then, more often than not, deny them. This has often meant using extremely well-known pieces of classical music. So incredibly known as to be somewhat emptied. Music that's been used in so many adverts or soundtracks that its status has become one of cultural water. Examples from my videos would include the 'Erbarme dich' from Bach's *St Matthew Passion* in *Ribbons*; Ravel's *Boléro* in *Safe Conduct*; Bryan Adams's '(Everything I Do) I Do It For You' in *A Tumour (In English)*; a Polovtsian dance by Borodin and Sinatra's 'Strangers in the Night' in *Hisser*. I suppose the effect is not dissimilar to that of stock imagery. For my purposes, it makes this material ripe for unconscious or siteless recognition, perhaps eliciting a cheap reverie—while also accessing a conspicuous sense of manipulation and commercialisation. The aim, at least in part, is to allow an audience member to encounter an irresistible sentimental solicitation and think of how that piece of music may have been used to hawk an Audi, say.

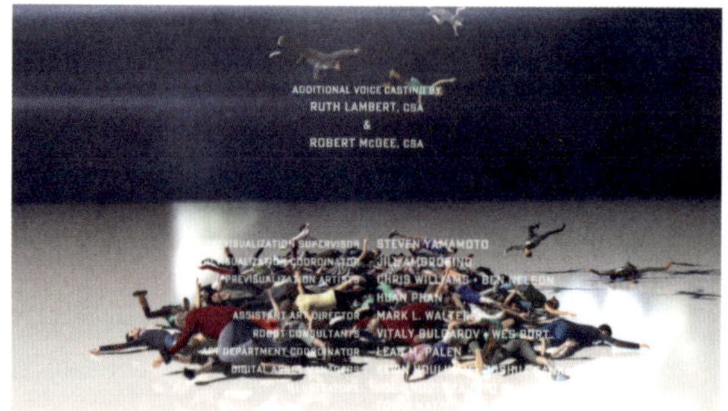

up/down, in/out
2017, video and sound

This kind of music allows me the simultaneity of conflicting intellectual and emotional experience, where one might still be profoundly moved despite the obvious artificial manipulations. It's a ruse also key to the sense of realism strived for by the very obviously artificial CGI. There's a heresy to it that feels very important to me—sentimentality affecting very real sentiment—and fundamental to what I want from art, but also what I instinctively recognise as a part of how I understand myself. So often, I need my feelings pressed into service, which can be very upsetting. I often feel empty until told to feel and how to feel. I say this because I presume others feel similarly, and that's the point.

Latterly, I think the videos have moved towards diegetic everything—as in, everything being from and of the world presented in the videos. *The worm* and *Pianowork 2* are both sincere documents, where the only aural artifice is a byproduct of the way they were recorded—the technologies and the tools employed. The particular quality of a voice over a telephone, the various mics used to record a piano. There's a less apologetic use of effects and editing, but also an increasing confidence in identifying the heart of the feeling I'm seeking to solicit. Stripping back superfluous effects so that the remaining artifice is more singular—and understanding that remaining effect contains all the other effects. The CGI performance capture is an ur-effect that essays effects and artifice per se and means that so much of the rest is an unadulterated and inconspicuous reality.

Jürg Frey's music became very important to me in this regard. Its quietude, its capacity to contain a history with the most deft and minimal gestures. Frey's is a post-minimalist music that sometimes skirts the possibility of even being considered music, at least in popular conception. At the climax of the *Old Food* videos and throughout *Pianowork 2*, a piece of Frey's music is played. Both are piano works, and both pieces are plaintive in a way that recalls impressionist and romantic music—just extraordinarily, gorgeously depleted. Depletion not in a pejorative sense but in a deliberate impoverishment to essentialise what's left, an effect that renders the music incredibly close and absent, both available for occupation through that absence and resoundingly lonely once inside. This sensation is part of what I'm looking for in the later animations.

Pianos are everywhere. This is from my mother. She plays the piano beautifully, and her repertoire certainly accounts for so much of my taste and the kind of sentimental space I seek; our house was often filled with the sound of her practising. Pianos are machines too, and if my emotionality requires manipulation, my identification with pianos and all kinds of other machines is empathic. My own roboticness, when alone, is a wellspring of instinctive interaction with tech. In *Pianowork 2*, I tried very hard to do what Frey's score asks, but I found it extraordinarily difficult. Frey's minute threshold of stillness and movement is confusing to my body, but also precisely equivalent to some oscillatory, ironic ambivalence or slavish representational fidelity, whose failure is what I really want, and more than anything. So, this brink of automatism is teased at the piano; algorithmic and mechanical perfection is politely requested of a body incapable of such control. I count the beats in the vast rests, the 468 instances of the same perfect fourth, the precisely instructed micro-shifts of tempo. I worry about and try to depress the keys with the correct pianissimo dynamic to follow the previous halting chord forty seconds prior. The pace allows for a terrific mounting of anxiety for me. For me, performing Frey's *Klavierstück 2* is a gorgeous crisis that precisely operates inside of a worry regarding my own roboticness, and my undeniable, fallible humanity. Performing it requires consciousness to harden

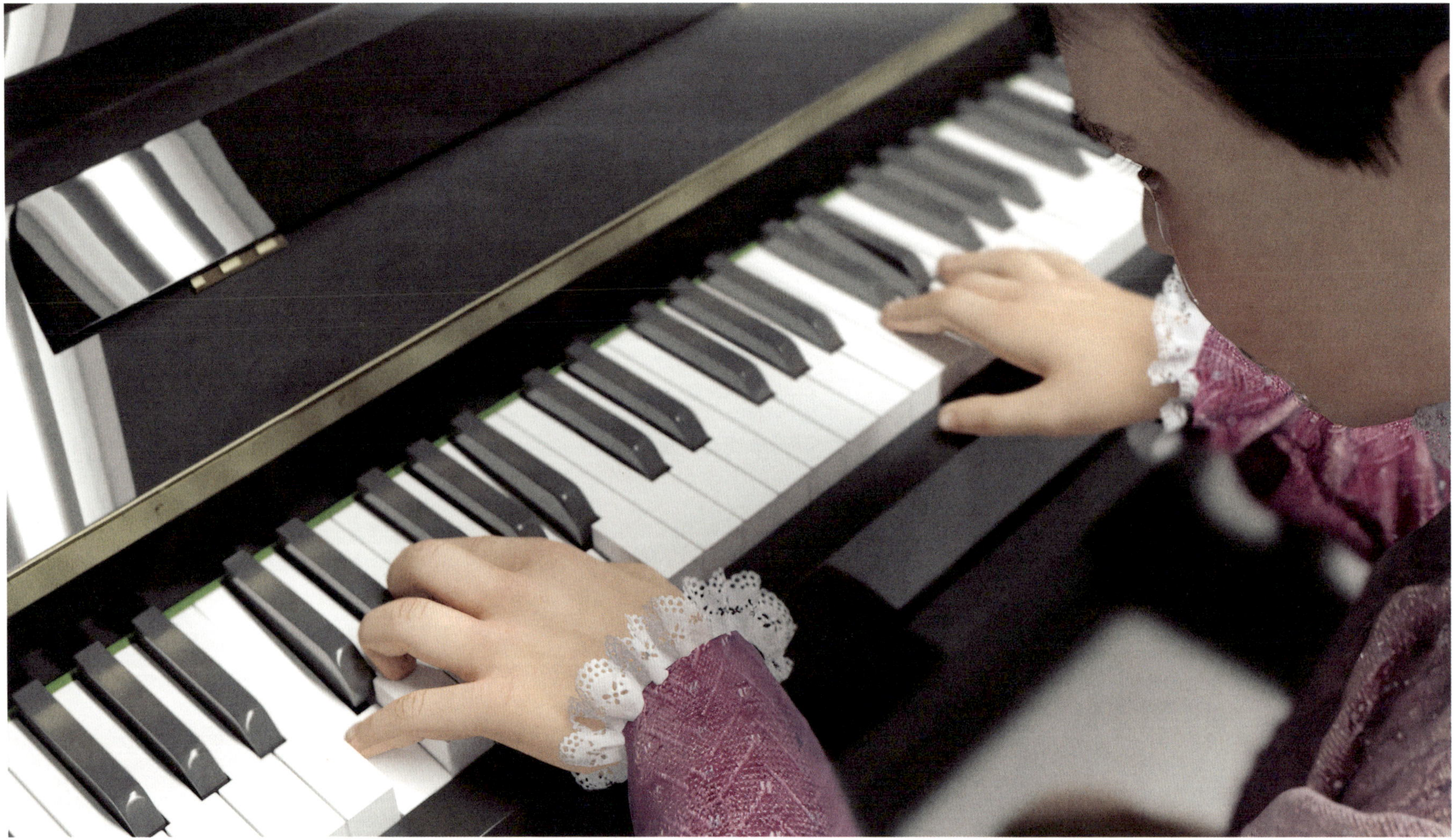

Good Smoke 2017, video and sound

into a divine body, which is impossible. Failure, by misinterpretation, unpreparedness, a fucked, tremulous right hand, and my inattention, etc.

PS:

The first half of the exhibition, which contains *Death Mask II: The Scent*, *Cur*, *Hisser*, *Refuse.exe* and *Old Food*, feels of a theatrical order—the scenarios presented are clearly fiction, there are self-consciously dramatic edits, animations and sonic effects. The latter half of the exhibition contains the more recent works, *The worm*, *Pianowork 2* and *Nurses…*, which have a very different relationship to reality and psychological order; they are largely autobiographical and feature you or members of your family. Do you agree with that analysis and the shift in the work?

EA:

I suppose so, but obviously I don't think about it like this. Retrospective understanding may require the temporary stasis that only making an exhibition like this affords … maybe it's a few things. One is about the location of fiction and realism in the works—and how this relates to excessiveness and active depletion. Or, say, sentimentality and emotional withdrawal. Virtuosity and amateurism too, perhaps.

It's difficult to answer for this movement in any way that would rationalise it truthfully. I suppose I was sick of the language I'd established in the earlier works. It felt exhausting to me. Recognisable. Whatever vernacular I was using or establishing has always been, first and foremost, desirous—what I wanted to see and feel—and the demonstrable virtuosity and fireworks (to frame it cynically) of the earlier videos started to feel increasingly forced. I didn't want to express myself like that, it was too much cover. This movement is mirrored in the writing too. Much of what is collected in *A Primer for Cadavers*, for example, is as fast, jarring, sentimental, bathetic, misanthropic and melancholic as the videos made at the same time.

I'm more preoccupied now with the work and the exhibition resisting an easy conceptual justification. At its core, this development is that of my life, experiences and desires. There was a moment of conscious diminishment. A desire to say less, demonstrate less—to impoverish the work. Leo Bersani and Ulysse Dutoit's book *Arts of Impoverishment* (1993) has been essential for me here. A notion of wanting to deliberately thwart art's authority by resistant unspeakable, unseeable overwhelm. Moving towards a dearth of value, according to what might be learnt from art, or what art might offer in terms of consolation or conventional entertainment or enlightenment. This is concomitant with a partial turn in art nowadays towards a redemptive purpose: art that is righteous or elevated. I mean, that's always been there. I'm not interested in art or artists as a paragon. This relates to a stilling, a slowing, a frustrating of the audience's desires as they have been constructed by manipulative media consumption. And while people started to presume a tonal space for me—the more some people wanted my and other artists' opinions on the real world as if artists were special or had a unique insight or were in some way public intellectuals or opinion-havers—the more I wanted to go against that.

Both *The worm* and *Pianowork 2* move the virtuosity away from a certain kind of artistry and compromise it by presenting questionably valuable subjects for so-called important or urgent art. And then sentimental legibility, particularly as a construction, and other kinds of manipulation, however critically motivated, started to happily fall away. It was a relief. To have nothing to say of importance and to fully embrace what maybe previously I had wafted away with virtuosic sleight of hand. This is reverse engineering, of course, and it makes it seem like the earlier works weren't already on this road of deliberate frustration. I think maybe they were coming at it from the other end of things.

The voice, for example, has always been a location for a presumed reality in the videos, but recently, it's taken on load-bearing status in a far more dualistic relation to the visuals. There's a hardening, as I say. The lush, lyrical stuff's gone, but the impoverishment and humility of the work now is this Real to foil art's delusional pomp. The clarity that comes with that has been incredibly exciting to me.

Nurses... is the apex of this current movement, and I don't think it's a coincidence that it's a collaboration. Collaborating with Steven Zultanski on all aspects of *Nurses...* and on the play *Sorcerer* previously, has been a great joy. Liberating.

As with *Pianowork 2* and *The worm*, *Nurses...* is centred around an external voice, steeped in loss, pain, joy, family, etc.—and is incredibly strange. These works move inward in a way that resembles autobiographical access, but that resemblance belies the peculiarity of the scene and its final unavailability to rationalisation or conclusive interpretation. When it comes to art, these are tools that fictionalise by attempting to determine indeterminate things; they are what is not life; they are essentialising forces, despite our assumptions to the contrary. Reality, to me—and my current route to re-discovering—is with the incoherent, unjustifiable and radically ambivalent. At least, this is a reality I feel I can approach with my work. This is a repletion that I hope is made starkly available in the new pieces.

This also relates directly to the look of the videos and the shift in the level of tech I'm using. Both *Pianowork 2* and *The worm* were made with a professional motion capture studio in Berlin called Mimic, which specialises in what they call digital doubles. They're an industry-grade production studio that works in cinema, video games and music videos. The quality of the work they're capable of producing is exponentially higher (according to a rubric of realistic depiction) than that of the previous works, which were all made in collaboration with an incredible animator called Adam Sinclair. This is definitely not to say that the work made with Sinclair is in any way lesser, just that the tools and the workforce and the tech that Mimic have is far greater.

CGI is constitutionally tethered to money—and to corporate, capitalist design. I always wanted to cleave to developments within the tech, consistently testing my belief that the CGI would fail to convince, regardless of the level of quality. An example would be the upgrading of the generic male figure I use in most of the animations. At the beginning, for *Us Dead Talk Love* in 2012, it was a floating male head who came as the demo model in the beta Faceshift software I was using. Then it was a model from TurboSquid called Dave (I did not name him that; a point I consistently have to address); then, from *Happy Birthday!!* (2014) until *The worm*, it was an unnamed male model, also from TurboSquid; then it was a dapper man Mimic had stowed away on a server somewhere; and finally, with *Pianowork 2*, it's a double of me. Each upgrade is very much about following the current highest quality of model I can afford or that has been released for prosumer consumption—with quality being to do with the skin and the modelling itself, as well as the rigging and the blend shapes, things like that.

Given the conspicuousness of the CGI and its attempted representational fidelity—as in, increasing fidelity is what the technology's in-built sense of progress is—a chunk of what one is looking at in my work is a sense of retroactively authored failure, since seeing the tech at all is de facto failure for the technology. Whatever structural attempt is made on the moving image per se—and CGI video more specifically—is ruinous, and the reality that's revealed by this ruining is, I think, infused with the perfidy of that move. The realisticness of the image poorly covers the reality beneath, and the movement between these two realisms is, I think, what I've been working with.

PS:

The work may often appear to be preoccupied with technology, but actually it represents all that technology cannot as yet hold: the body, its fragility, grief, loss, love, death, mourning, loneliness, regret … all the big themes are there. The (working) title for the exhibition for a long time was *Loss*, which goes straight to the heart of the matter and perhaps the impossibility of finding a language for loss, grief, anger and terror?

EA:

It's perhaps more about continually holding up those feelings and experiences you mention to contemporary technologies and seeing what kind of fresh attempts are being made to capture them. It's very obvious to me that my work's never been about technology (it's never really been *about* anything), but the tech I use stands in for all kinds of mechanisms that clamour at the door of human experience, making failed attempts on it.

The most obvious bit of performatively contemporary tech in my videos—computer-generated imagery and performance capture—stands as the most discernible in a vast list of representational technologies, including, in my case, writing, music, performance, cinema and theatre. From those early videos on, I've wallowed in the misuse of tech in order to expose the flaws in its ideal of human experience and its retention. And not in a straightforwardly censorious way, but, I hope, to emphasise some essential irrecuperable quality in human experience through loss.

So, by asking digital tech and CGI specifically to relate melancholy, I'm trying to compare but not confuse a tech's sadness regarding its impotence with the sadness that arises as a symptomatic guarantor of indomitable humanity. I suppose the digital double's melancholy is associated with the always already-lost object of lived reality—erroneously doubling the melancholy I might feel at various kinds of loss that define my lived experience. In this way, I would defend most all of the work as perversely celebratory.

I wrote an essay entitled 'Losslessness', to survey this field of loss, from psychoanalytic figuration to mortal literalism, via an apprehension of technological progress, built-in obsolescence, loss and losslessness as terms of digital reproduction. My working practice has always been steeped in an involuted figuring with death, and despite cultural aspirations to the contrary, the process of making the things I make has been reparative—even if this is not something I believe the works themselves can do. So whatever discourse I've haphazardly formed over the years is both a kind of media theory and a reframing of loss's cardinal wonder.

PS:

Lists appear in your work throughout the show and perhaps provide a way into loss. Lists are a way of ordering the world, they give us structure and a sense of control, they mark achievements and they stave off the chaos of the world: they are a way of holding on to things and not losing them. The Post-it note drawings for example record daily life, a list of sorts. The costumes of *Old Food* are an empty list of characters waiting to perform. Many of your other lists are often absurd or excessive—for example, *Refuse.exe* is a list of objects that crash to the ground and run to an endless repeating algorithm. How do you think about lists in relation to your work?

EA:

Part of my love of lists is surely what everyone loves about them. Their economy so outrageously obfuscates their subject. They're such brutal, mundane, profound literature. They stand as an economical zenith of representation, both a confession of the impossibility of its parity with its subject and that impossibility's defeat. In this way, lists are also an extraordinary representational achievement, and their ubiquity belies a way in which we all move towards the world in order to survive it. Formally, the iterative repetition is sometimes satisfying of compulsion. Sort of masturbatory. As with many of the formal techniques in my work, lists are in part used as a place for simultaneous virtuosity and critical overdetermination.

Refuse.exe is entirely concerned with depletion, squandering, waste and the brutality of a list. It was inspired by a list written by the artist Antonin Artaud when he was interred in a psychiatric hospital at Rodez—but *Refuse.exe*'s crudity is excessive in ways that I think span the medium too.[2] Unlike everything else in the exhibition, the work is generated live. It runs on a modified version of the Unreal Engine, so it's basically a video game that plays itself. Or an obscure demo mode left on a loop in an impossible trade show. The physics simulation that runs in real time means that the crap accrues in a different heap every time, despite its broader stubborn inevitability.

Refuse.exe was made as an exercise in a medium-specific impoverishment. The impoverishment of grace, drama, redemption, recoverability. It was originally written as a play script, and it dramatises the seeming return of repressed, deferred or otherwise metaphorised matter. It was intended as a play reduced to its most fundamental constituents. Originally, I wanted to make it for real: I wanted to drop stuff

2 Antonin Artaud was a French artist, dramatist, poet and theorist. A major figure of the European avant-garde, he had a profound influence on twentieth century theatre. He wrote the list in his notebooks while interred in a psychiatric hospital in Rodez, France 1943–6. See pp. 143–57.

suspended above onto a real stage. But this form, which speaks to the ways in which reality, physics, are modelled in video games, seemed a worthy, propositional form, self-reflective as it is. Also, in reality it would cost far too much and require a stage that is up to being subjected to such a pummelling.

At the other end of lists, as it were, is how they report reality precisely because of their purposefulness. Lists are unmannered and they're often obscure to anyone but their writer or intended user; they can report something unmediated and secret that's truthful but unavailable, despite or because of their factual form. Like Isaac Newton's list of sins—not for public consumption. They're a shorthand for often vast and unobtainable information, despite their professed role as concise information carriers. I like extremes of things. I like virtuosity and the utterly artless. I like wild artifice and base reality. I like purple prose and lists. Two of my favourite lists are Roland Barthes's list of likes and dislikes from *Roland Barthes* and Sei Shōnagon's lists from *The Pillow Book*. They are lists of tastes, in the end, and though Barthes perhaps derides the pointlessness of such excessive ways of stating differences between people, I find them deeply moving precisely because they are not lists of effective statements but demonstrable, impetuous abundance. Life, perhaps.

Untitled 2018, video and sound

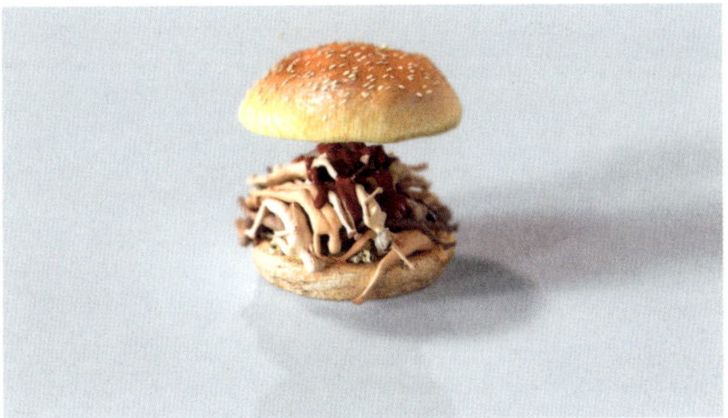

PS:

Some of the lists represented in this book and works in the exhibition have been 'run through' artificial intelligence (AI). How do you use algorithms in your work and what does that mean for you? Audiences often look to you, because of your use of new technologies, for a moral or political response to AI and its current and future impact, but what's your position here?

EA:

I'm not really interested in AI speculatively. Like most of the more conspicuous technologies used in the work I make, what I like about AI right now is its combination of ubiquity, ignorance and a general sense of fatigue. There are already presumptions about what AI is good for, what is dangerous about it, what it might do in the right or wrong hands, etc.—and it's this presumptuousness itself that I'm most interested in.

In using any tech, I want the audience to know—or think they know—how it works or what it's used for so that whatever I'm doing with it feels recognisably different, probably wrong. I'm always seeking criticality through misuse of tools, and AI is no different. AI's correct use, however, is a question freighted with a lot of think-pieces, which is

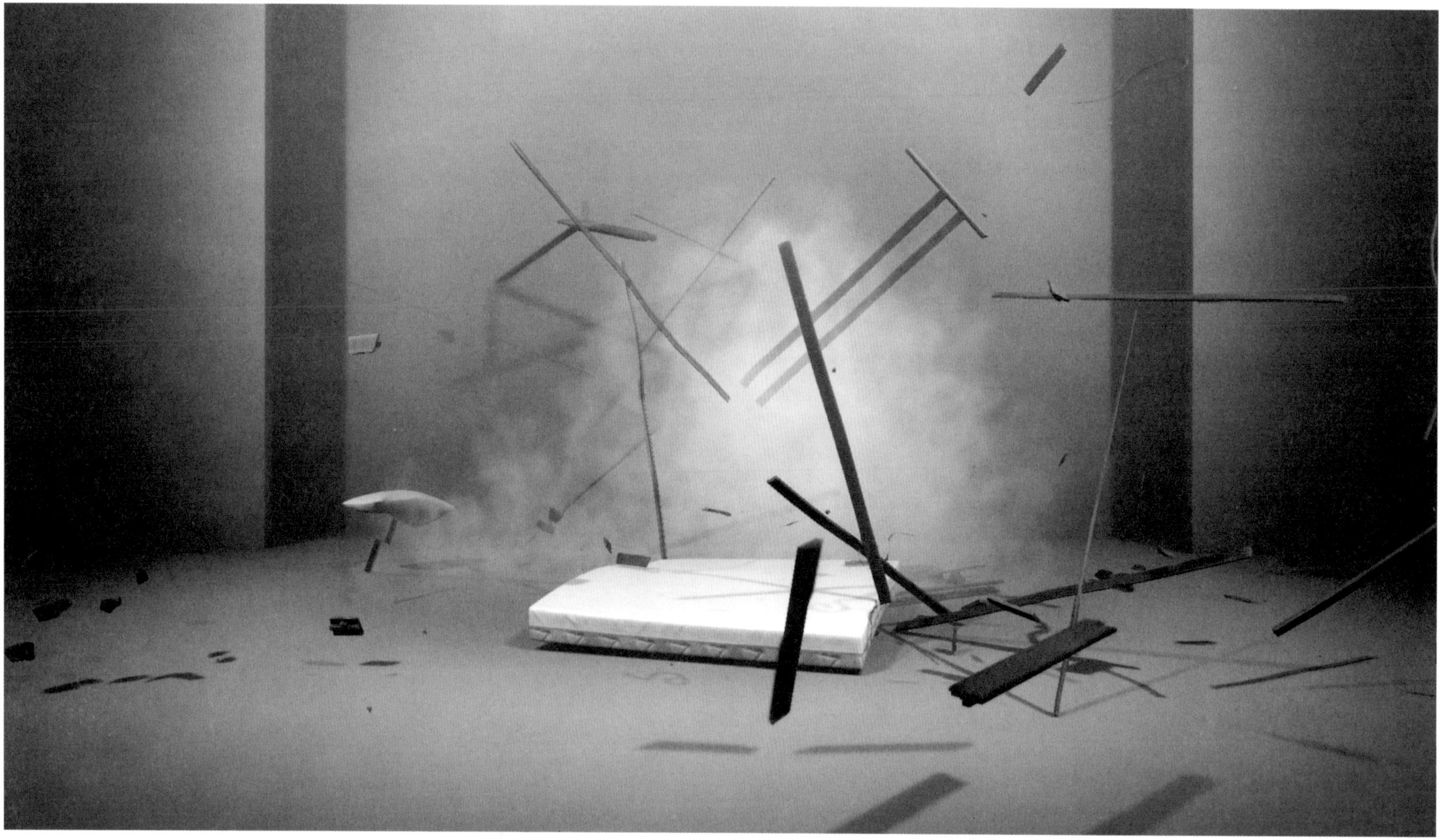

Refuse.exe 2019, two-channel video, custom software, sound

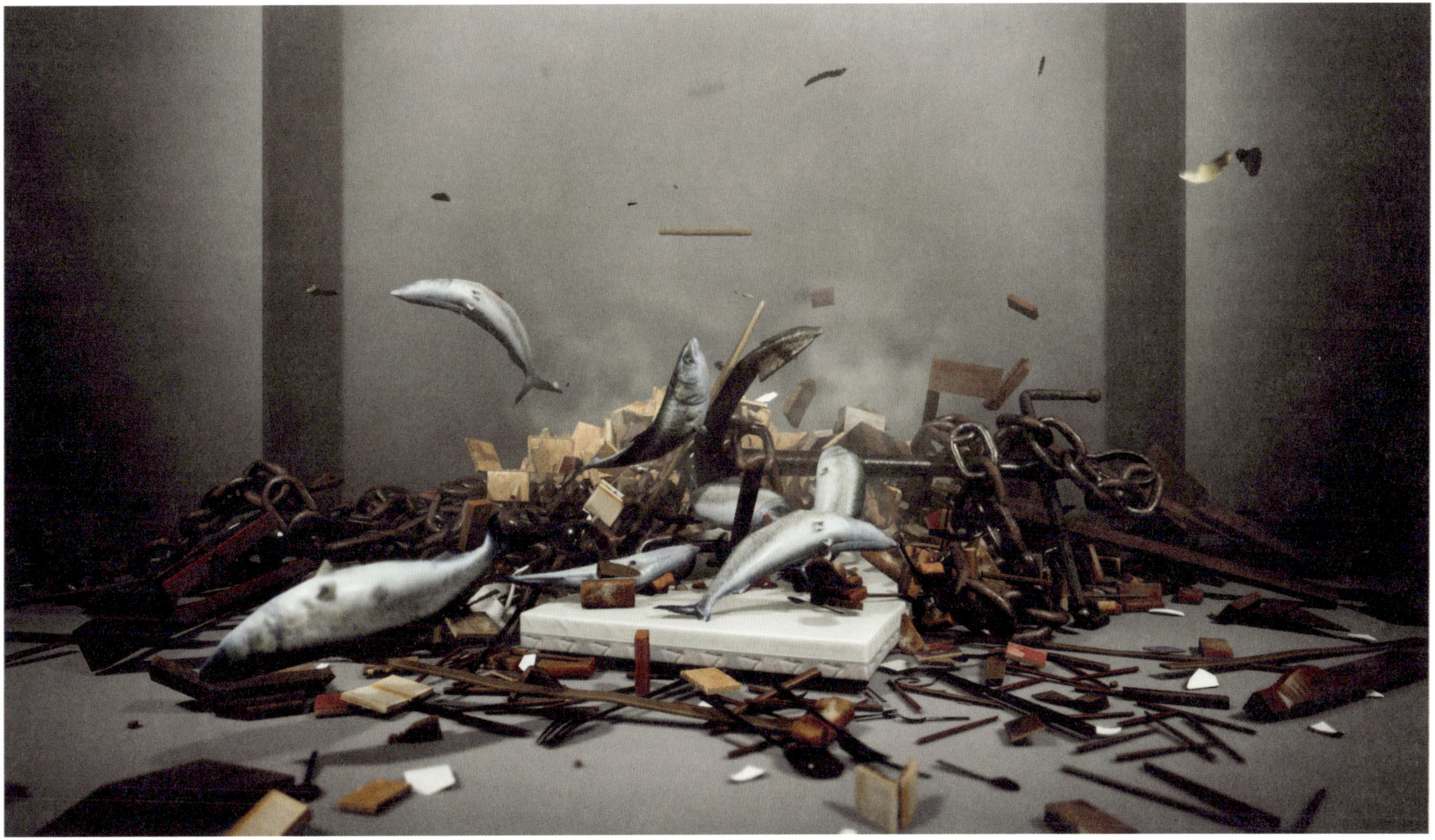

almost its defining characteristic, so there's less clarity around what that might be. Maybe this sense of moral or political uncertainty is part of what's interesting to me.

We're constantly told about the game-changing possibilities of artificial intelligence, but mostly, that doesn't match up with our own experiences. In my experience, for example, AI was at its best a couple of generations ago (generations according to OpenAI's GPT model), when it could fire off some of the most astonishingly absurd writing. I've tried to get it to do similar things with later generations, but the 'improved' model has ironed out the lunacy, which is a shame but entirely expected. GPT-3's appended contributions to Sei Shōnagon's list of 'squalid things' are genuinely deranged, beautiful and, like a child's drawings, both impossible to replicate and 'better' than anything any human could do. Similarly, GPT-3's extension of Artaud's insatiable list of numerically vast quantities of things really goes to unimaginable places. It ends by repeating the entry '2,000 human galaxy-zentrifiers' over and over again, but only after a digression to acres of entries of astonishing, hilarious, appalling death. It felt gleeful, unfettered, bordering on gibberish and like genuinely exciting 'intelligence'.

I'm no authority on any of the technologies I use since I do not know how they work or how they might change *things*. The platforming of tech bros and artists as authorities on the repercussions of technology on society feels basic and stupid and a consequence of the TED-talkification of so much. It's delusional and dangerous. It relates to other kinds of lucky fortune seeding misconceptions of their importance, like the idea that billionaires are smart and that

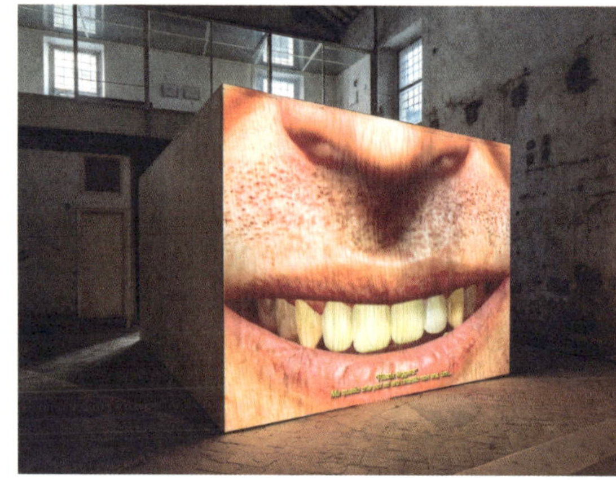

The worm 2021, (installation view) in *The worm*, Sant' Andrea de Scaphis, Rome 2021, video and sound

their opinions should be sought rather than scoffed at and buried. Much of this kind of fawning, breathless discourse stands right at the opposite end of the spectrum from everything I am interested in and am trying to do, so the idea that I would be asked, with broadsheet seriousness, what I think will happen with AI in the future entirely misses the point.

The use of AI in the show—and other procedurally generated stuff—is often operating in the same brutal way that a list might, albeit algorithmically far more complexly. I alphabetised my Dad's cancer diary and embroidered it onto a patchwork of used linen. I continued long-ago-finished lists into a hallucinogenic, artificial afterlife and embroidered them onto a patchwork of used linen. AI is a representational technology applied to the subject of its representation, and like the exhausted models in the CGI videos, like my writing, I would like to abuse it in our stead.

PS:

Let's turn from AI, then, to your most recent drawings, which are preoccupied with self-portraiture: laborious, perfect pencil drawings of the 'real' you. Although sometimes you appear to have taken on a spider's body. How do you see these works alongside the moving images? When did you start to make them and why?

EA:

It took me a long time to allow drawing back into my practice. I felt like I needed a reason and not simply a desire. There was also a sense of wanting to protect drawing a little or find a way to protect the personally precious aspects of drawing while allowing them to enter into the fray of public interpretation. As mentioned above, the messy, confused way in which a personal media theory was concocted around the videos was a way of having a thesis to talk about in lieu of aspects that I could not or did not want to talk about.

The first drawings that I thought were functionally similar to the videos and writing were the big ink and bleach drawings of mattresses, pillows and limbs. They weren't the first, but they were the first I really liked. Their fidelity, the obscurity of the labour, their queasy specificity and blankness … A feeling of a technology, a labour, striving for something whose representational value—the reason to represent it and like this—was hidden at least, blank somewhat, but the attention confers the import. To conjure intimacy, ugliness, fidelity and obscurity—a history of overly striving image-making.

Mattresses and the pillows are indexes, as is the drawing. They had to feel like they carried the same sensations as—or worked in concert with—the videos. And at this point, they needed all of these things to exist at all. I've never been an artist who just *has* to make art; my compulsions are far more illegible and crushed. These drawings also started to appear at the same time as I wanted to deplete the work. So, they feel significantly depleted to me. Scant nothings, but heavy, heavy, heavy, full of detail and meaning and unknown substances. The majority weight of a mattress being dead skin rather than mattress material.

They were also incredibly pleasurable to make. Writing and producing videos uses all my attention, whereas drawing means I can drift, listen to music, lose track of time and hit some euphoric, unthinking place. I felt I really needed that. These pillow and mattress drawings were from photos, so the act of drawing becomes a beautifully pointless accrual or a claim—a claim on reality that extends—that was very desirous: mattresses as a site of desire; absent bodies indexed through the indentations on the mattress and the brushwork of the drawing.

The self-portraits came through this, I think. One way to look at my work, all of it, is as self-portraiture. However convolutedly, the videos and the writing are all self-obsessed and oversharing, albeit decohered in a way that I think of as very true to self. I thought I'd be literal about the self-portraiture and use some of the representational technology I'd been using with the mattresses, regarding fidelity, realisticness, labour, etc., to render my face. At the same time, I wanted the self-portraits to be traditional and somewhat impressive technically. As well as grotesque. I loathe my body and the way I look. I am often entirely destroyed by an encounter with an image of myself.

I erected a series of mirrors and spent hours and hours scrutinising my alien face in many very unflattering levels of repose and unflattering angles. The process was personally liberating: I wasn't encountering myself with the shock of a glimpsed reflection, there was no instance of abjection. Instead I was calm and detached—I had a job in relation to my image, something that has caused me so much distress. When finished, the drawing could hold on to some of that disgust, but the process, the technology, distances me from myself and to a degree that removes the horror of the encounter. Or the success of the drawings was the amelioration of the psychological crisis? A mask, then. Something like that. Plenty of the poses came out corpse-like, but that was mainly unconscious. I, of course, spent a long time working out the poses. These are angles that feel true and tolerable at the same time. The expediency of the materials—coloured pencil on yellow or pink copy paper—was also a way to make them happen, to legitimise the desire to make them and delegitimise their import. The colours are a nod to Renaissance anatomical sketches, with specific nods to Rembrandt or da Vinci occasionally, but only to the degree where those references lend historicity and familiarity to the work.

The most recent self-portraits-as-spider were taking something of the fidelity of the self-portraits and confusing them with the symbolism of the spider—which, to me, feels constitutional; spiders stand in for all kinds of primacies, myths, histories and psychological crises. They're clearly more psychologically redolent than the more straightforward self-portraits—even if the self-identification with a spider is, ultimately, ontologically alien. It's a reflection that includes how I think of myself, how I want others to see me and how I want the technique of representation to confuse the values of this.

PS:

At the heart of the exhibition, then, is a single room of Post-it note drawings made for your children. Since very early on in discussing the layout for the exhibition, these drawings (along with the costumes in *Old Food*) have been key in acting as a ballast to the digital technology. By contrast, the drawings seem to revel in their simplicity and base materiality. Their verisimilitude lies in their cartoonish, offhand authenticity. They also provide a joyful bumper to the generational trauma depicted in other works, a soothing palliative perhaps to depression and melancholy. You have said to me previously that the creation of these works is 'impelled by love and devotion'. Could you expand on how the drawings are made, how they are displayed and how they resonate for you?

EA:

They began during the Covid-19 pandemic. My daughter attended a *børnehave* (kindergarten) then, and the Post-its were started as things to put in her lunchbox daily. Little hellos, little irruptions into her day. Though from the beginning, we would do them together, eventually with her making her own drawings that would be left for me or companion drawings she'd put in her lunchbox too. They were also started as a way for me to achieve something every day. Everything I was meant to be working on had been cancelled or indefinitely postponed and so, often, the drawings were the only thing I made in a day. It then spiralled so that I'd make one or two over breakfast to send off with my daughter, then I'd sit there and do a few more. I started keeping them or dotting them about the apartment. I'd retrieve the ones from my daughter's lunchbox at the end of the day if they made it—sometimes blotched and warped by a satsuma or softened by proximity to a banana—and keep them in a little folder. They were never really intended for public consumption, but I did start posting them on my Instagram feed, eventually making a little sign-up website where people would receive one in their email every day.

Honestly, my daughter isn't particularly impressed or moved by projected significance, wonderfully, so her sense of the drawings' preciousness or lack thereof made it quite quickly apparent that it was mainly for me. At least the gesture, the process. I still, however, consider them as for my daughter, but as with so many gestures towards children, there is a latent unrequitedness one must accept and even enjoy. I still do them, but their direction is more involuted. That they are for my daughter is not a direct action but something that is embedded in the action, the sentiment that surrounds their existence and the nature of the images.

I tend to think of them as the best things I've ever made. They're perfect for me. The excuse for their production is unquestionable, founded as it is in love, and their reach to a marred infinite is a devotional ritual. Their contents, as much as can be outlined, are desirous, improvised, expedient and, I think, dreamy—allied with dreams. They are divine to me. Perhaps they achieve all the things I outline above, but they are about the future and a great joy in my life, my real life as I currently live it.

A huge number of the drawings are extremely complex when it comes to the scene they depict, but that complexity is swaddled by both provisionality—here comes another—and the love they carry, however ultimately selfish their continuation. So much of parenting is sweet mourning—for each and every instance of a child's life that leaves and is replaced by something else. As with the germinal times of making these drawings, the Ambulance Game that ends the new film *Nurses...* is a game I played with my daughter all the time a couple of years ago, but it's a rarity now, and sometimes more a treat for me than her. Part of the perpetual mourning and pleasure of her growing up.

I also want these drawings to recast my myopia regarding my past. A tendency to conflate the past with a purely pejorative loss or vaguely traumatic construction of self is not the truth of that past. The drawings are also a testament to this. My capacity to draw, my imagination, the site of art-making as a place of learning love—these are things I got from my mother, my father and my brother. Processes like this are bonding and profound. The performative excesses of the earlier works in the show worry over clarity of confusion, maybe. Or perhaps better said the works felt more demonstrative in their worry. In the exhibition, I wanted this room of Post-it drawings to be the heart of the show and the future of the work and my life—but I also wanted them to be the legend at the bottom of the map, to teach a way of looking and accepting and feeling that might be useful for everything else. A productive not-knowing, where knowledge acquisition is in its proper place and not forced into an interrogative mode.

So, it's not that everything else is so overwhelmingly full of depression and melancholy, but that perhaps interpretation and authority—meaning, even—so often leans towards sadness as a solution to afford importance. At least, that's how it's felt to me. In plenty of ways, these drawings—and all the works to some degree—are trying to shift importance's presumed location to somewhere close, digressive and real.

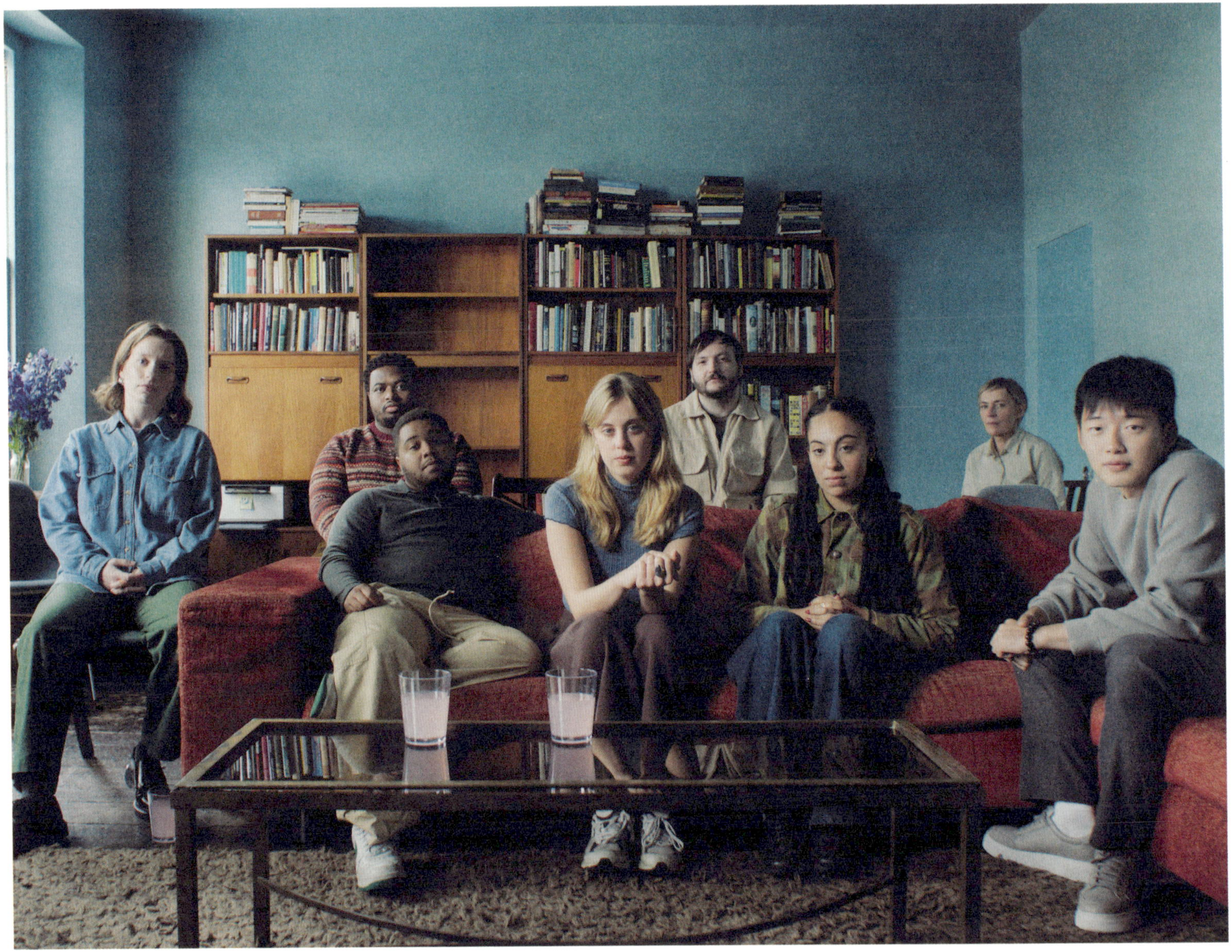

Production stills from *Nurses Come and Go, But None for Me* 2024, with Steven Zultanski, video and sound, pp.44–7

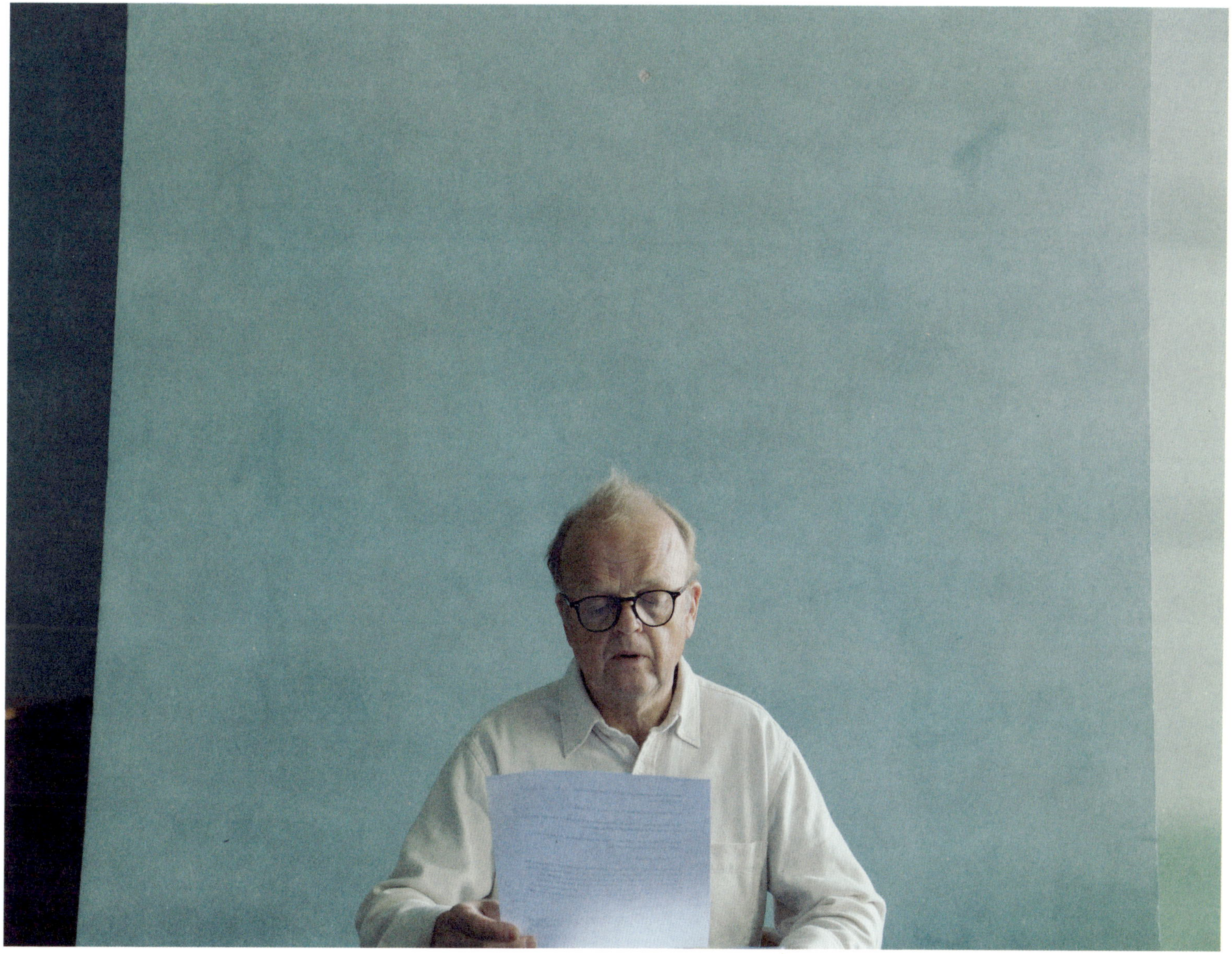

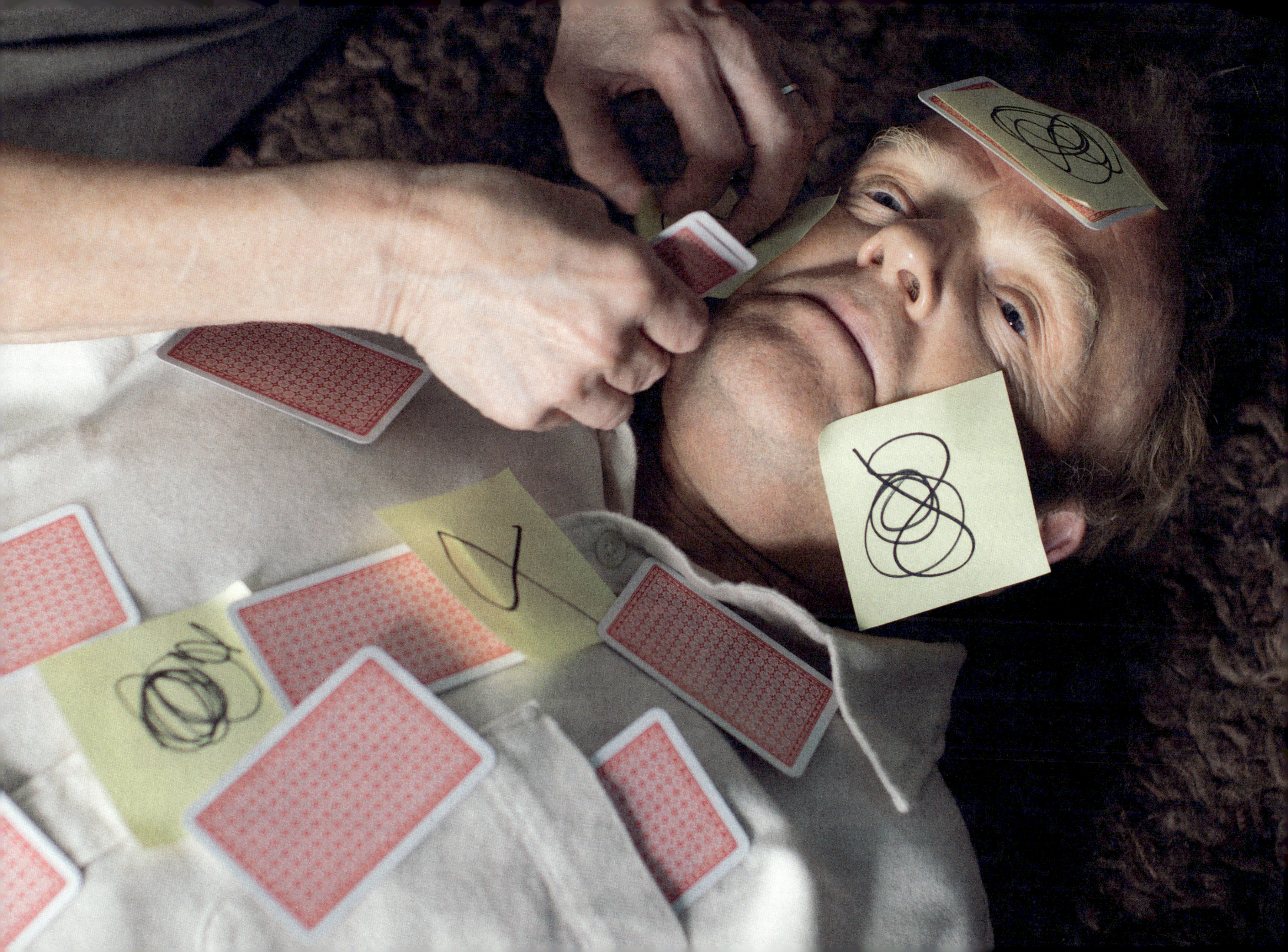

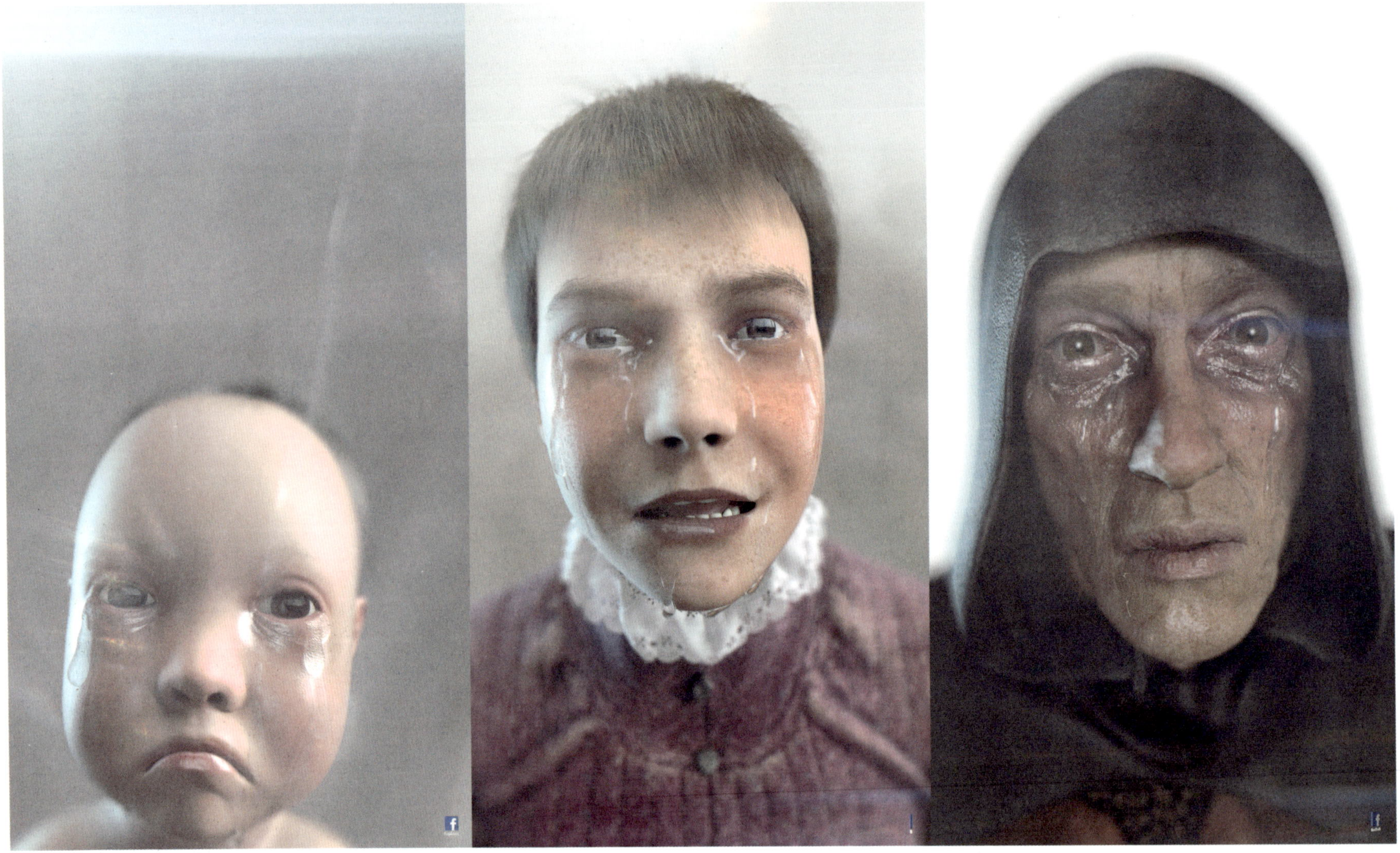

Good Baby (left), *Good Boy* (centre), *Good Man* (right) 2017, video and sound

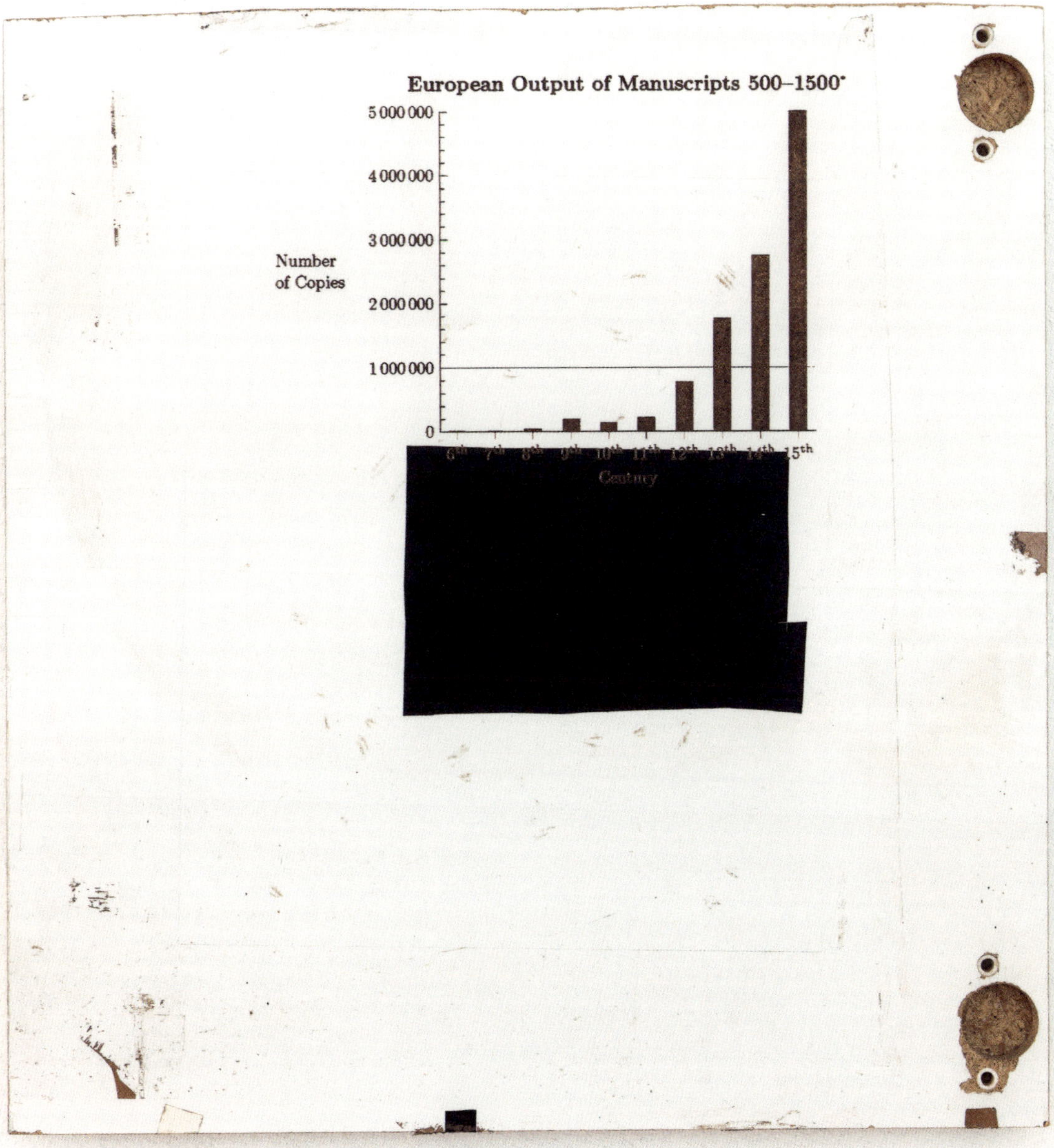

Untitled (wall text) 2017, laser engraved wood, 51.2 × 48.6

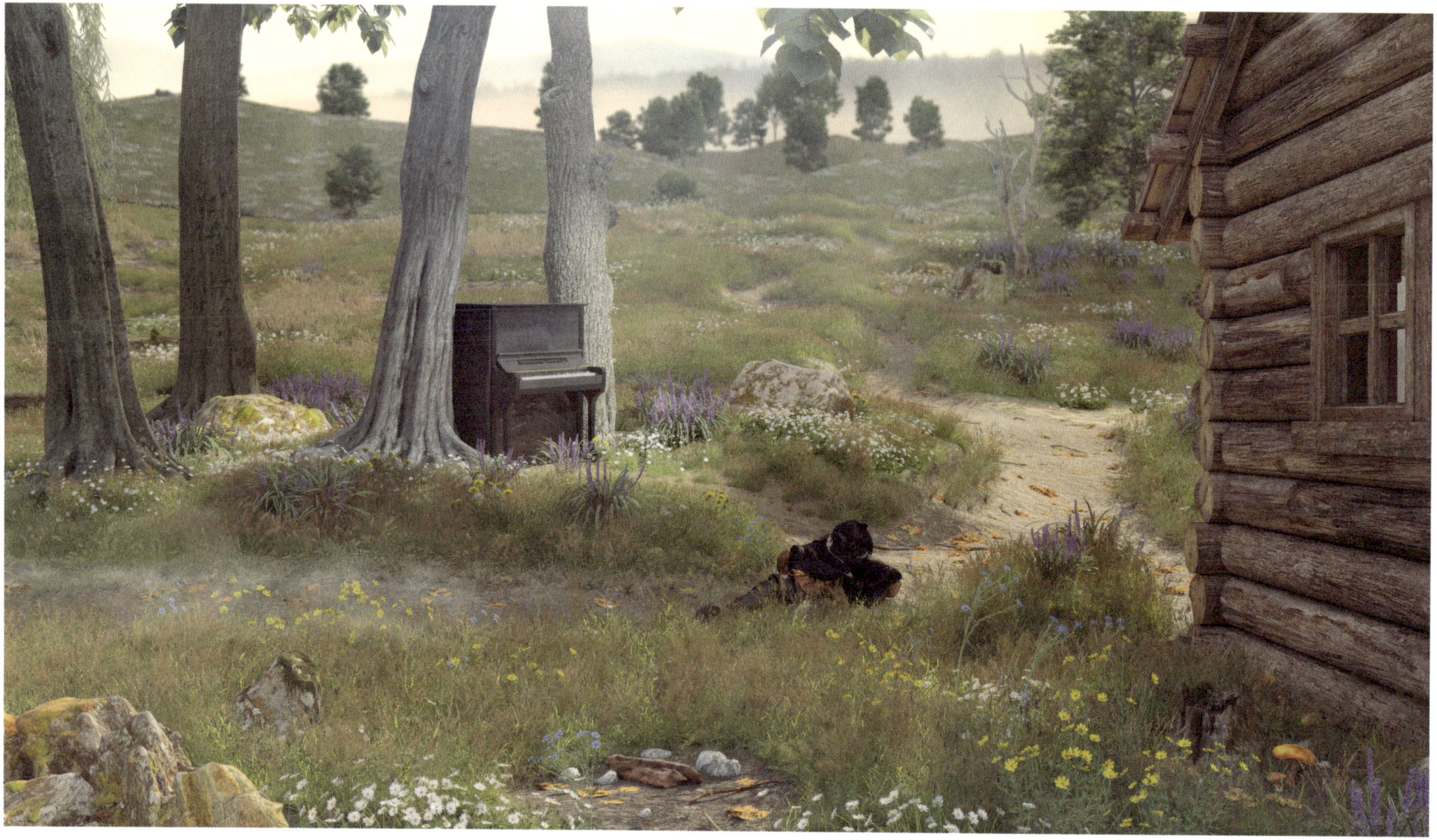

Good Wine 2017, video and sound

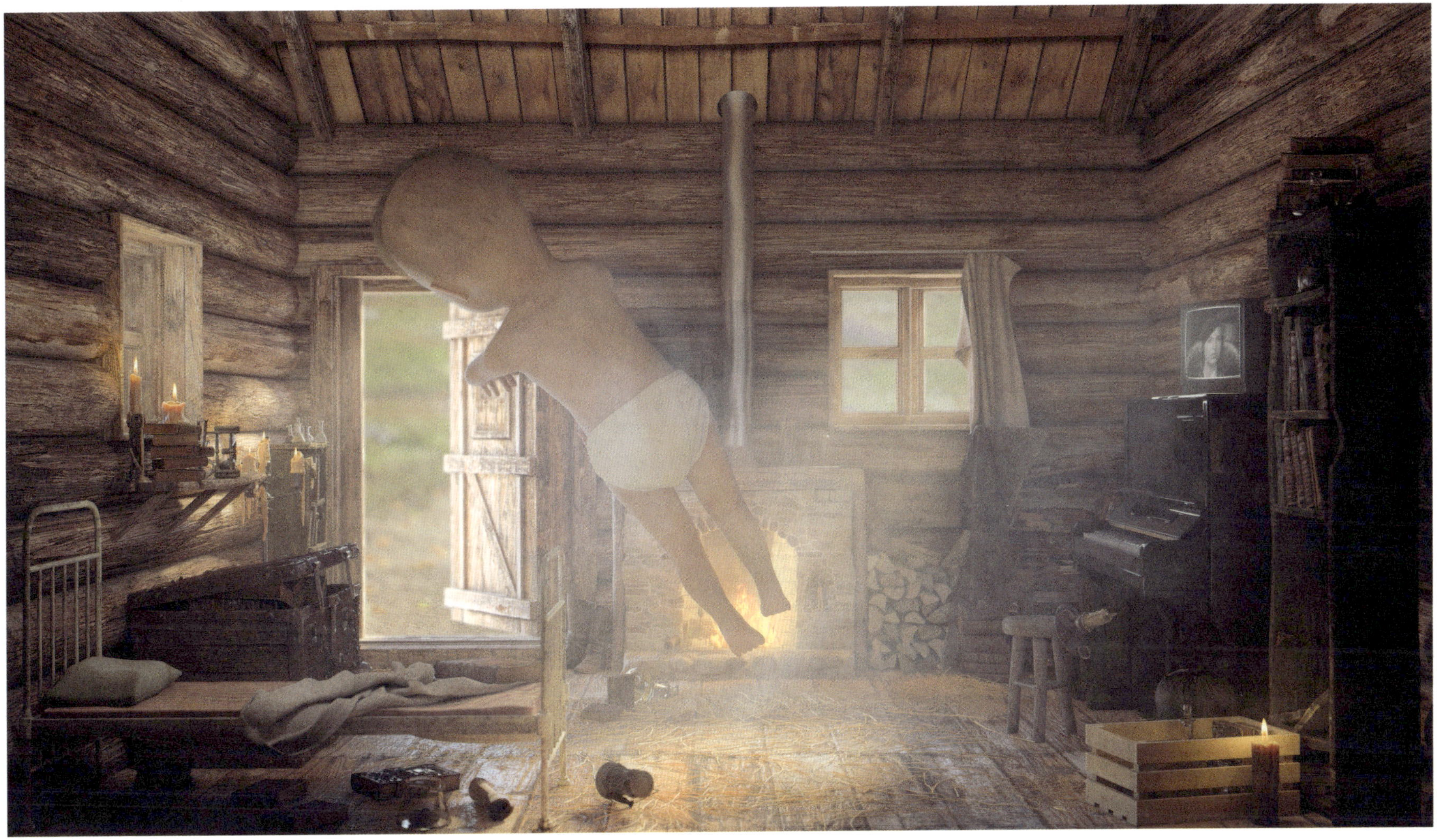

Good Bread 2017, video and sound

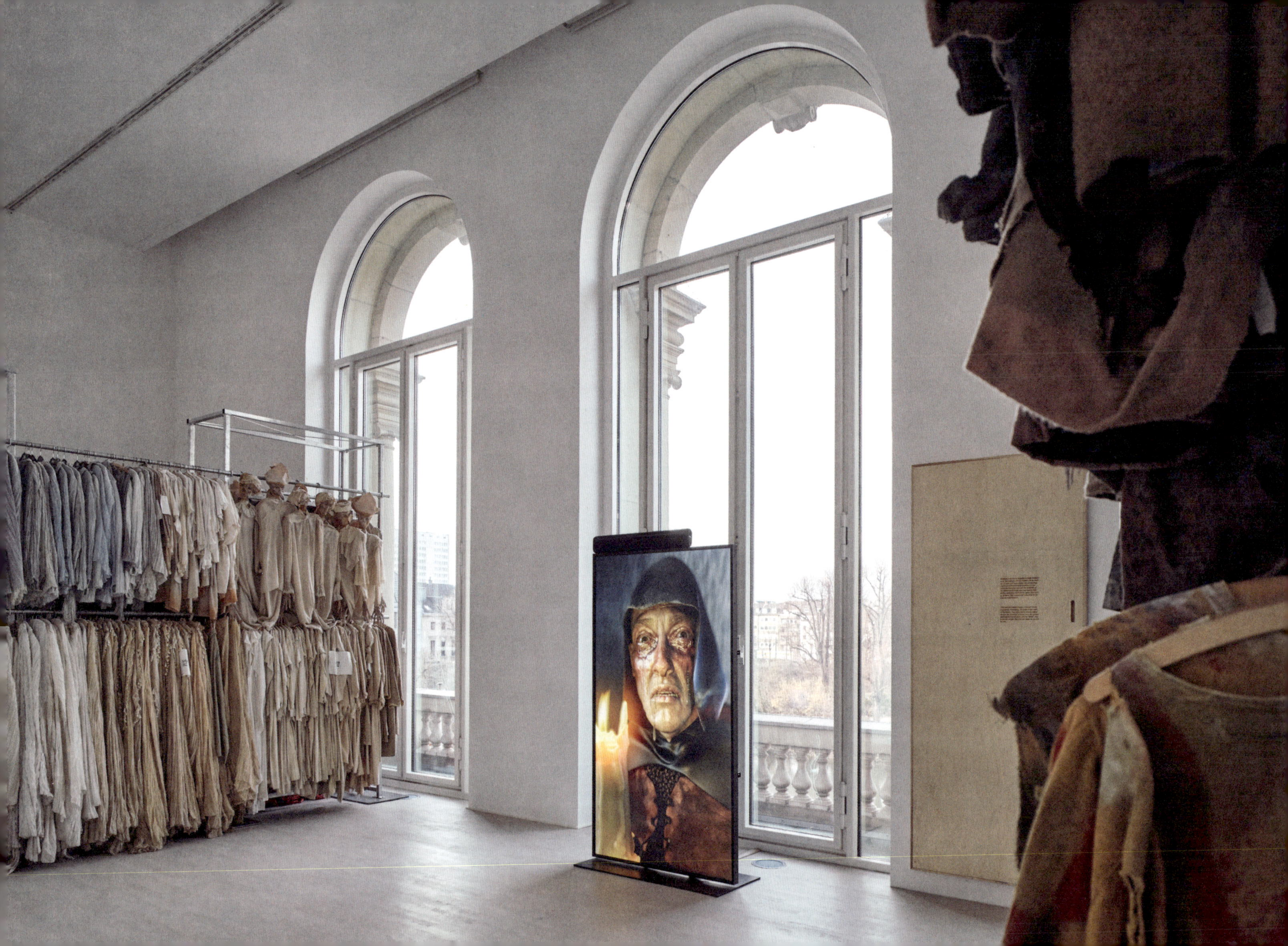

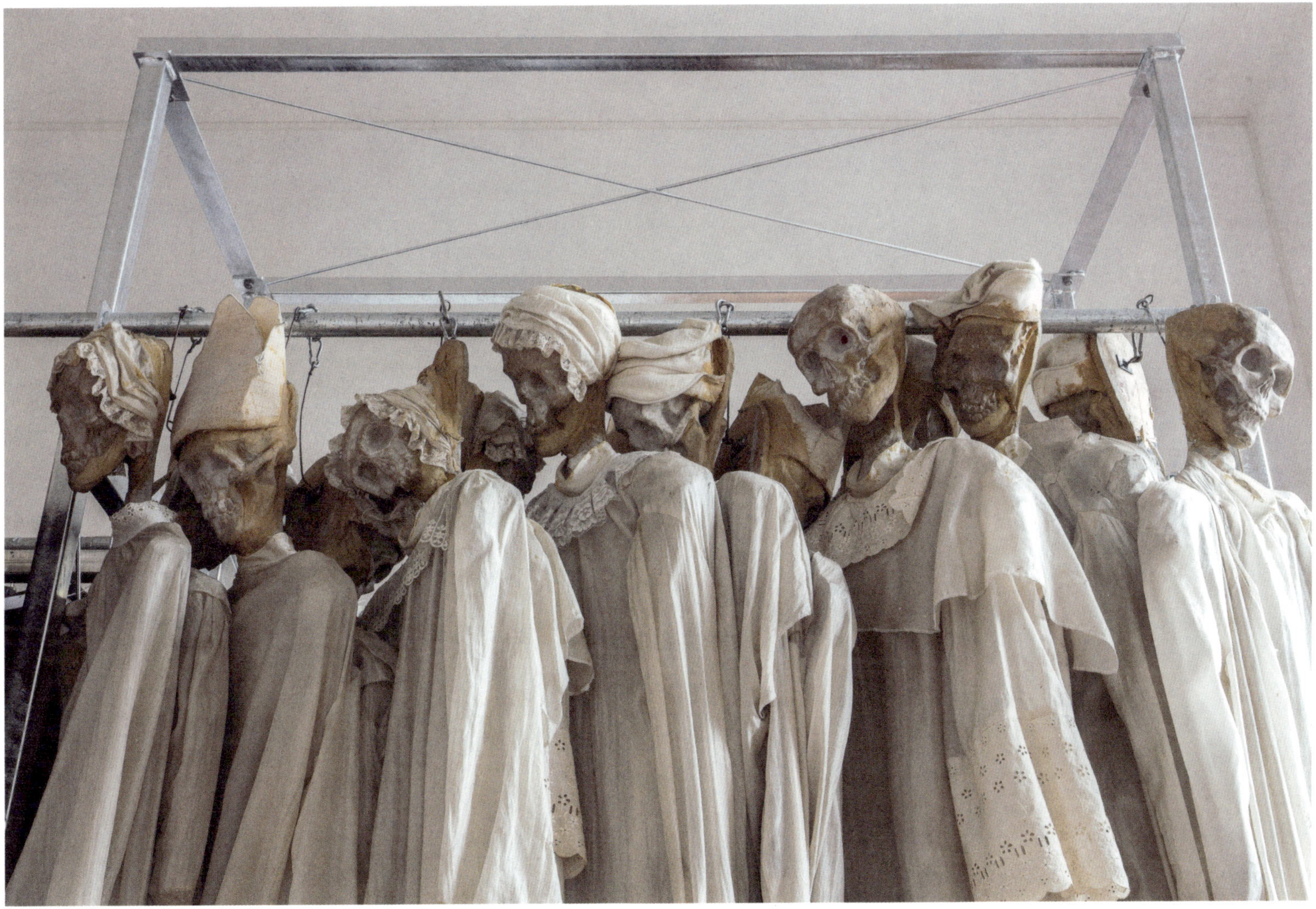

Old Food 2017–18 (installation view) in *Ye Olde Food*, K21 Kunstsammlung Nordrhein-Westfalen, Düsseldorf, 2019 (left)
Masses 2018 (detail), costumes from the Deutsche Oper Berlin

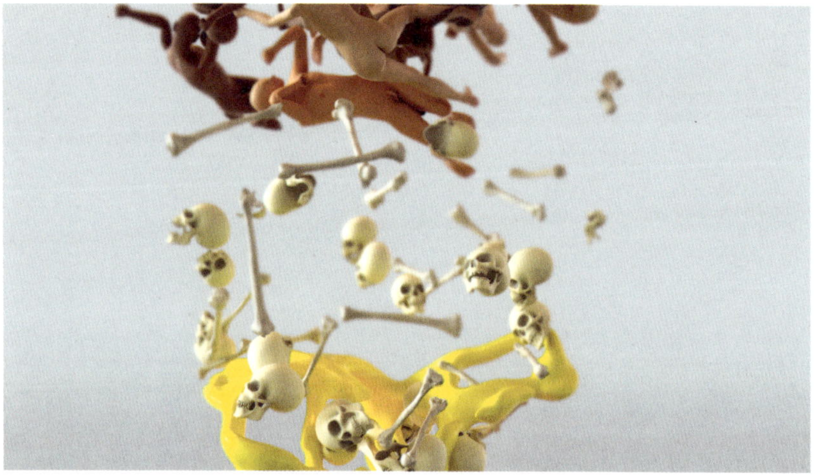
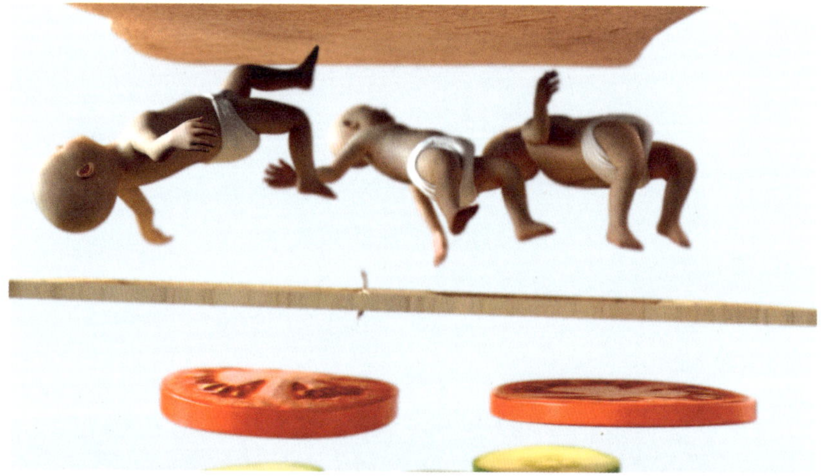
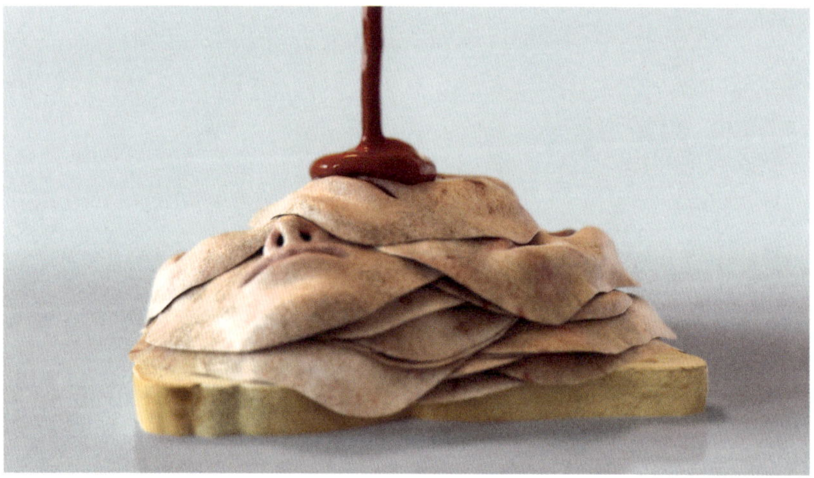
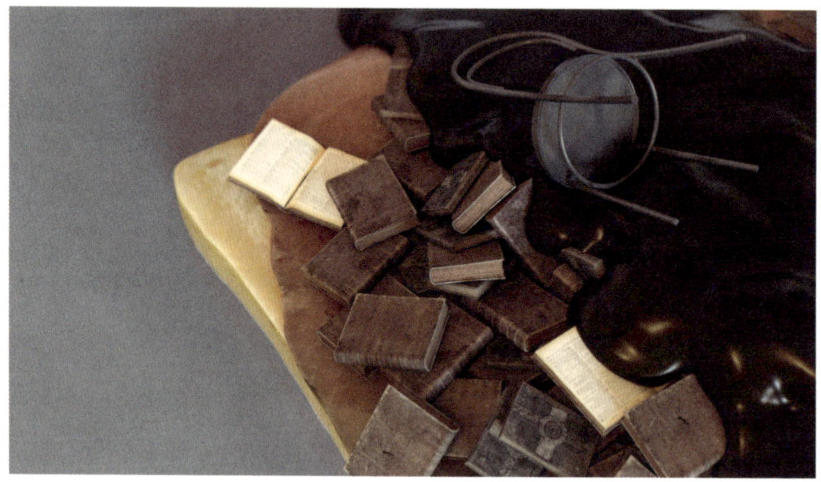

Untitled 2018, video and sound
Old Food 2017–18 (installation view) in *Old Food*, Martin-Gropius Bau, Berlin, 2018 (right)

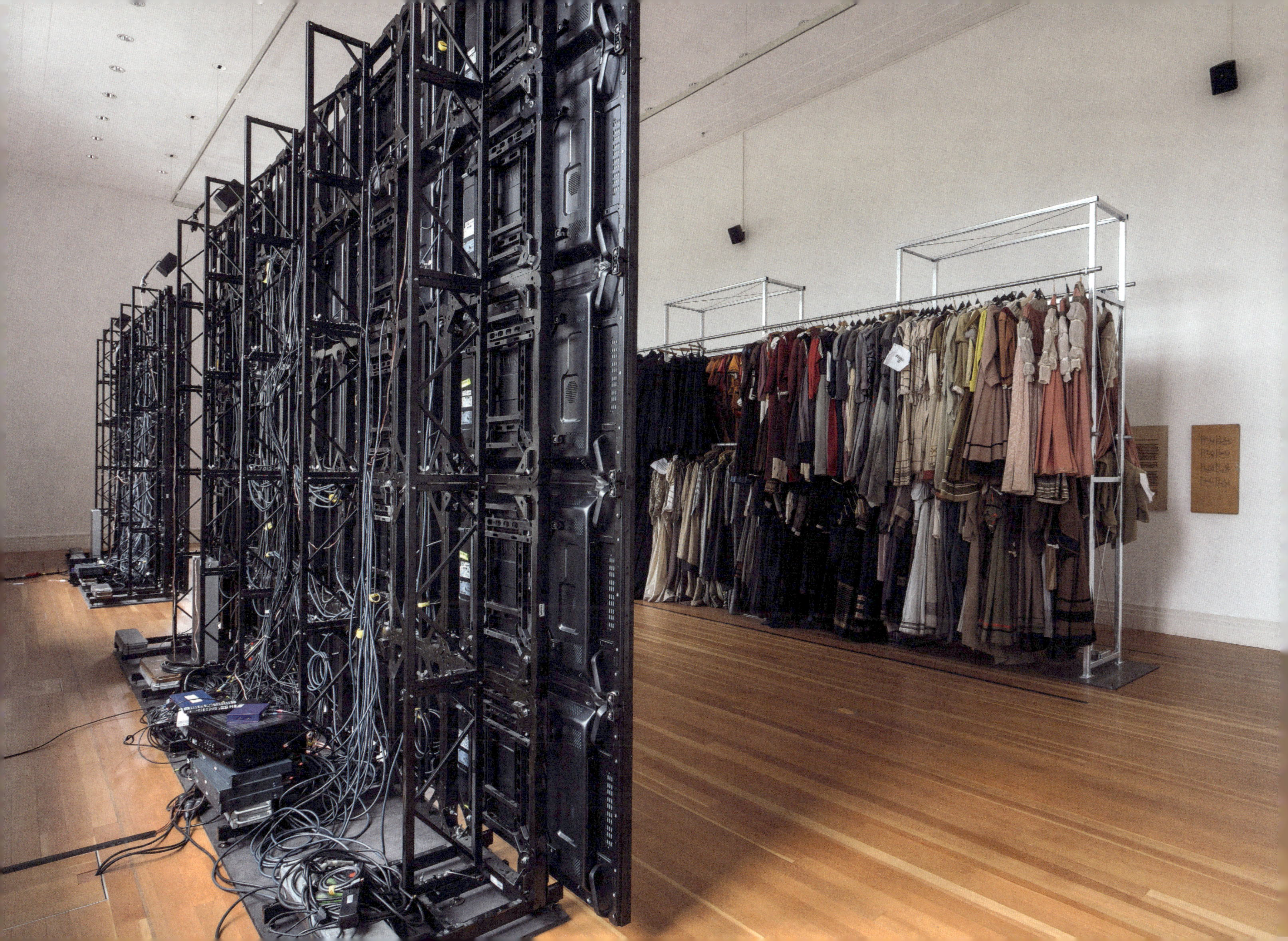

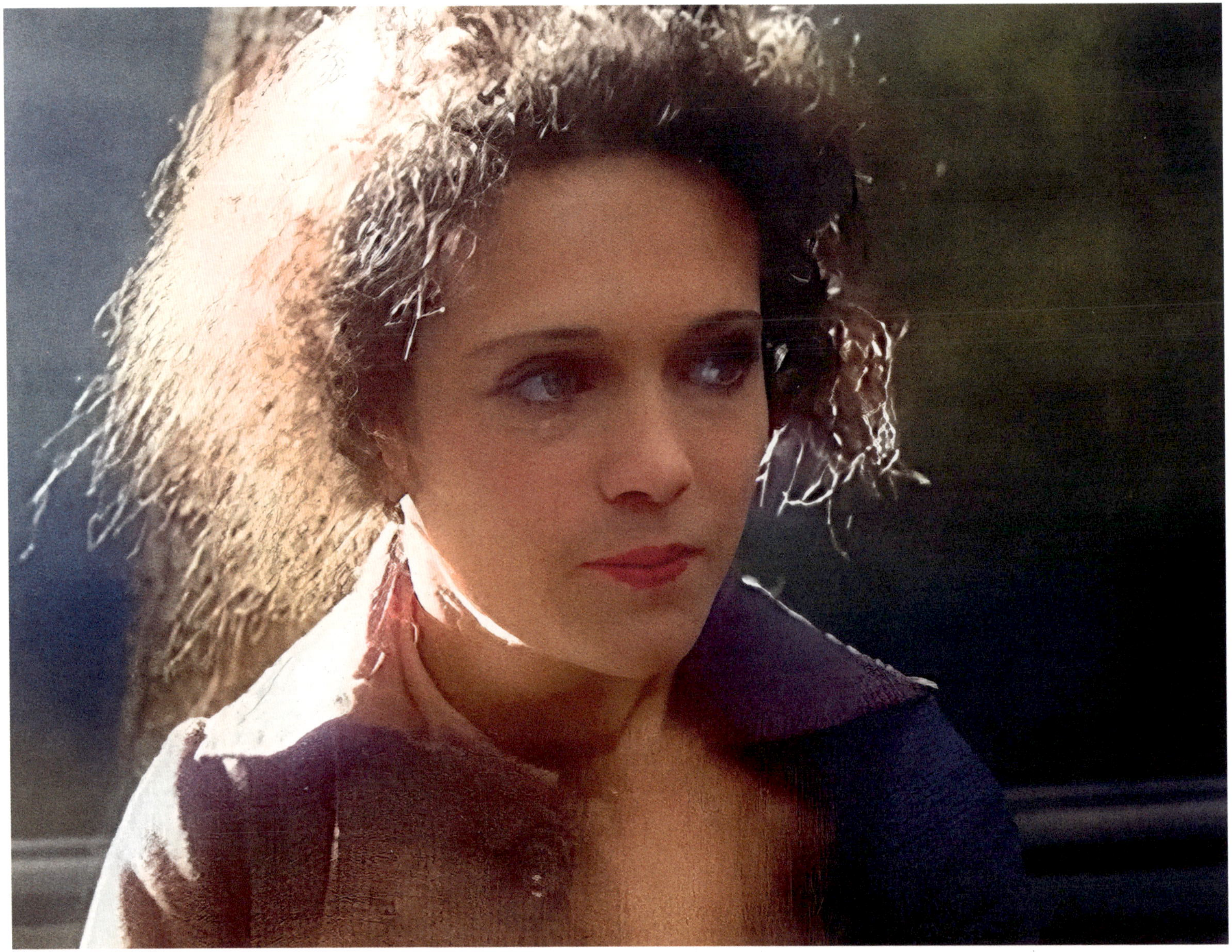

Voilà la verité 2022, video and sound

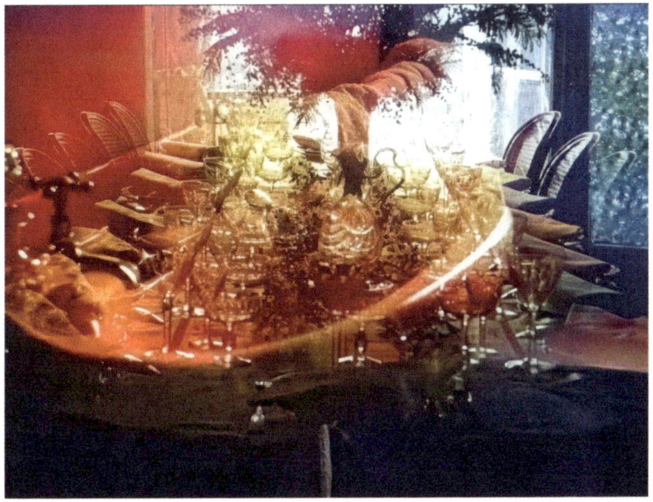
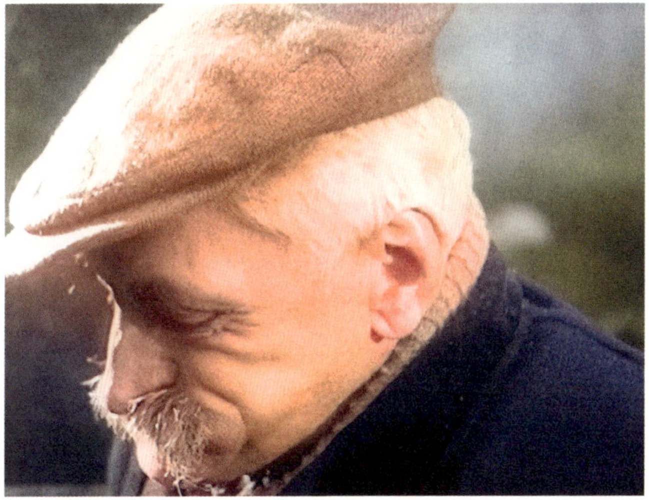
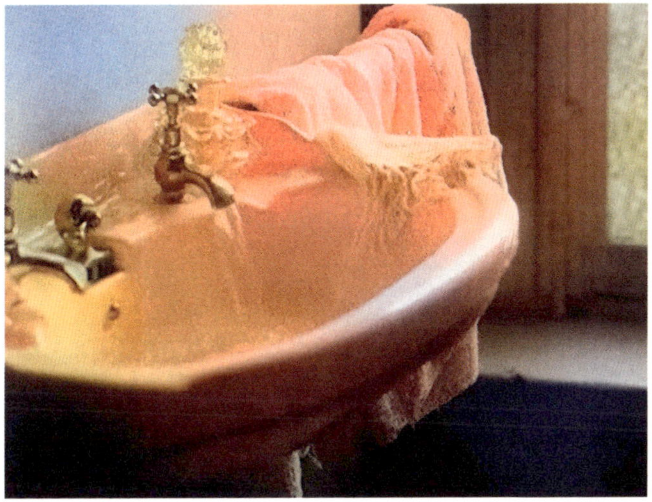
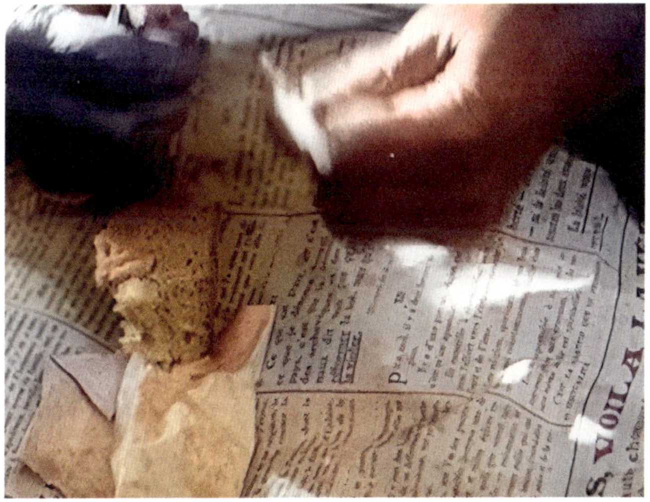
S, VOILA

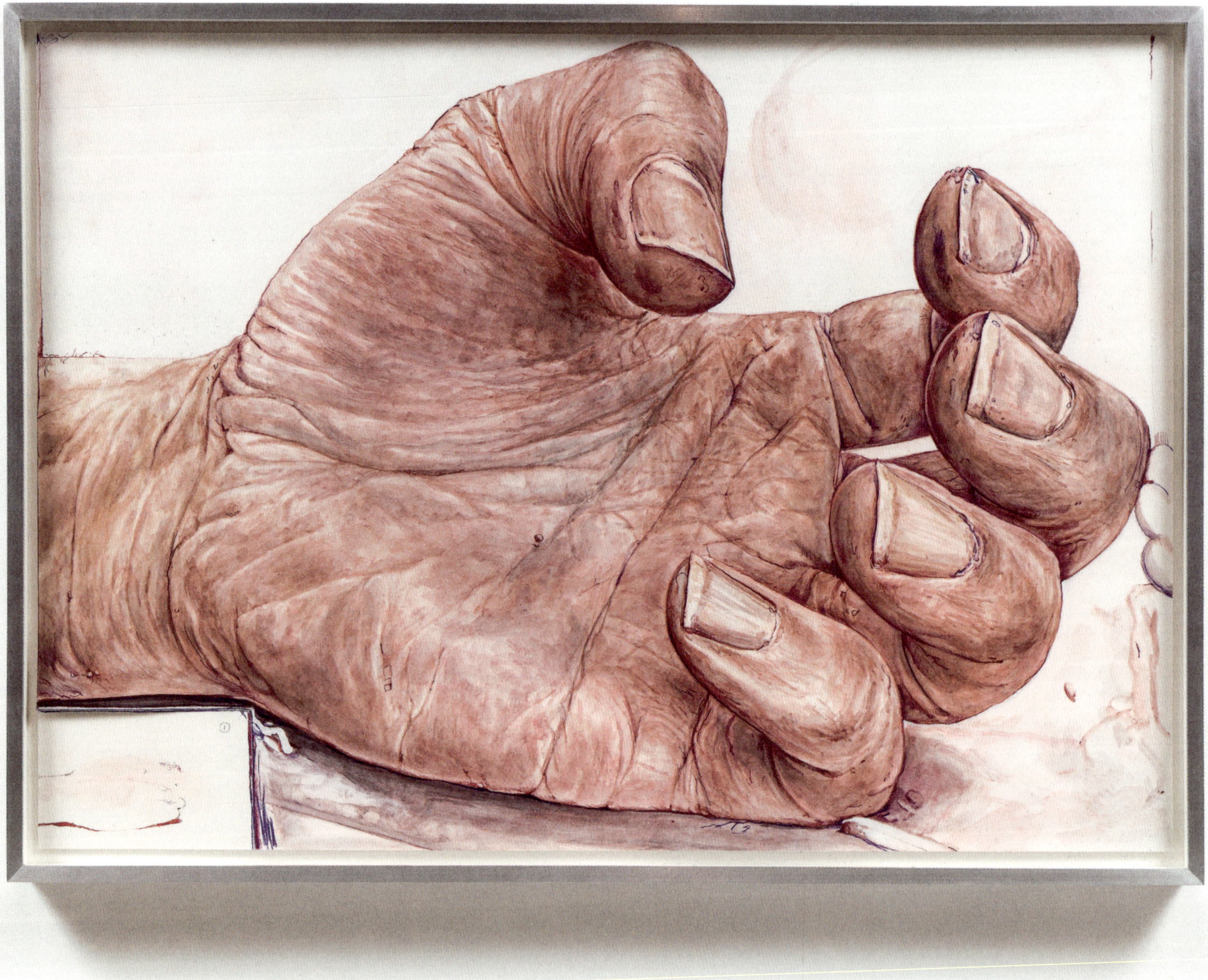

Untitled 2022, ink and pen on board, 55.1 × 78

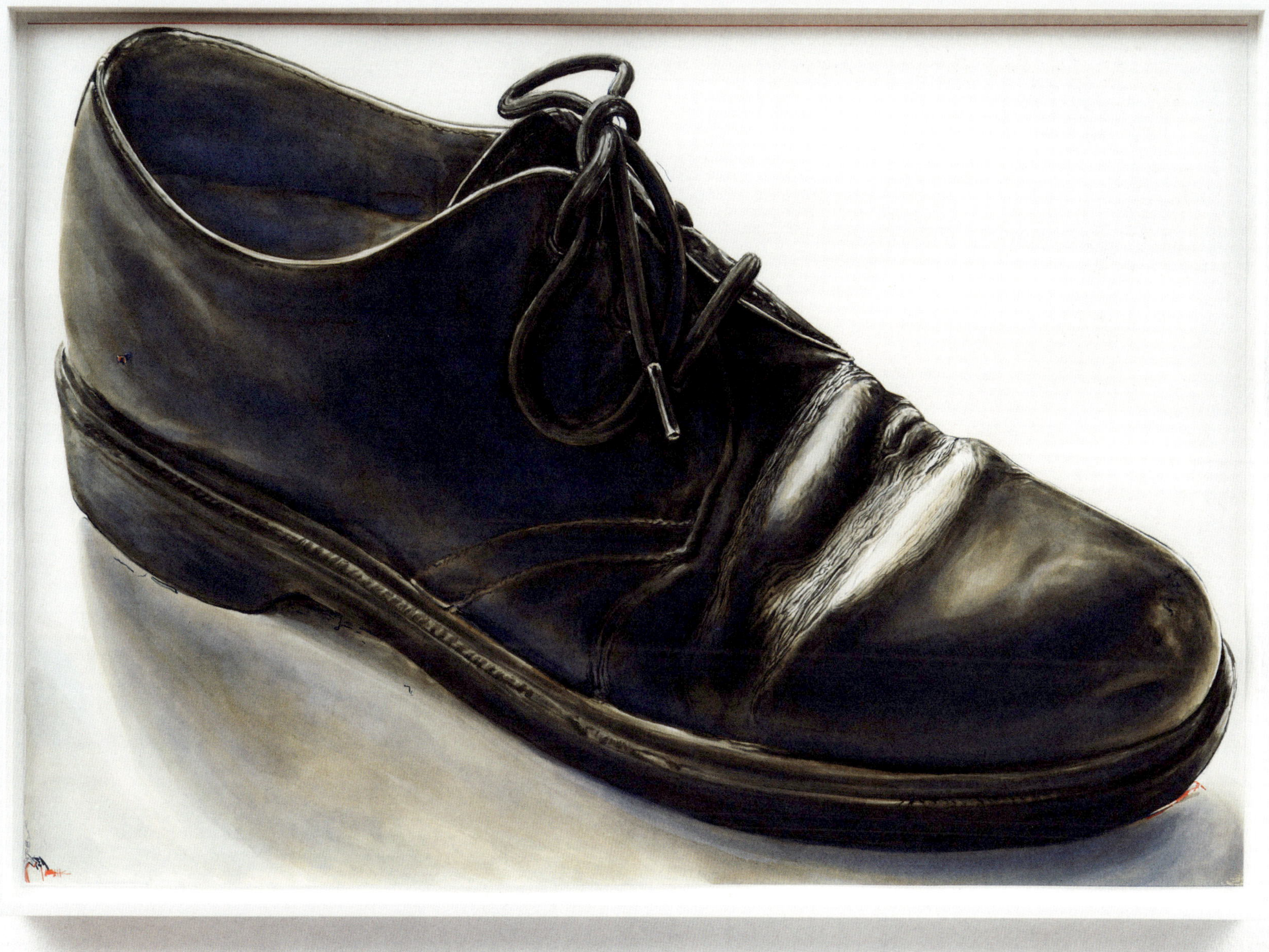

Untitled 2022, ink, bleach and coloured pencil on paper, 67 × 95.7

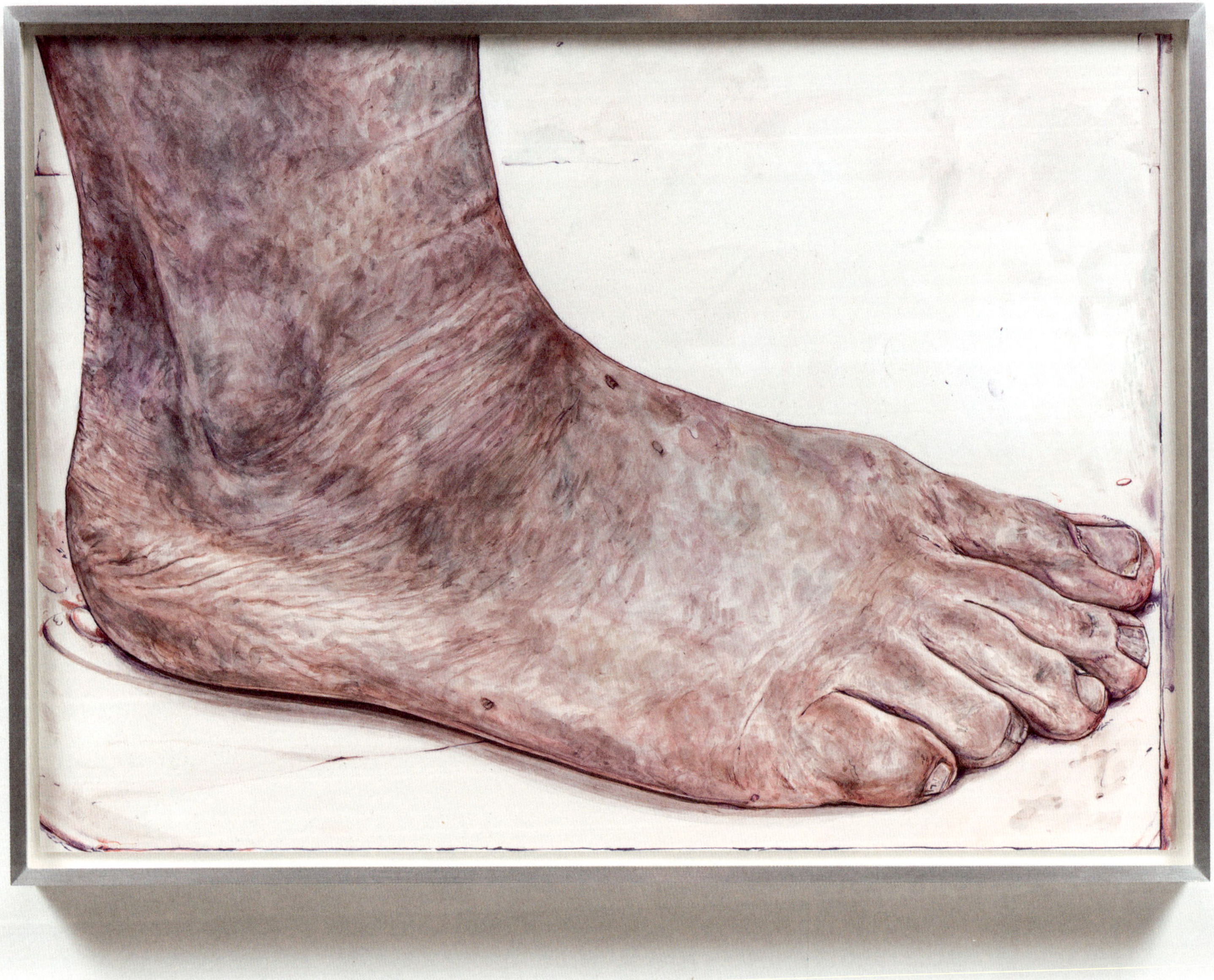

Untitled 2022, ink and pen on board, 55 × 78

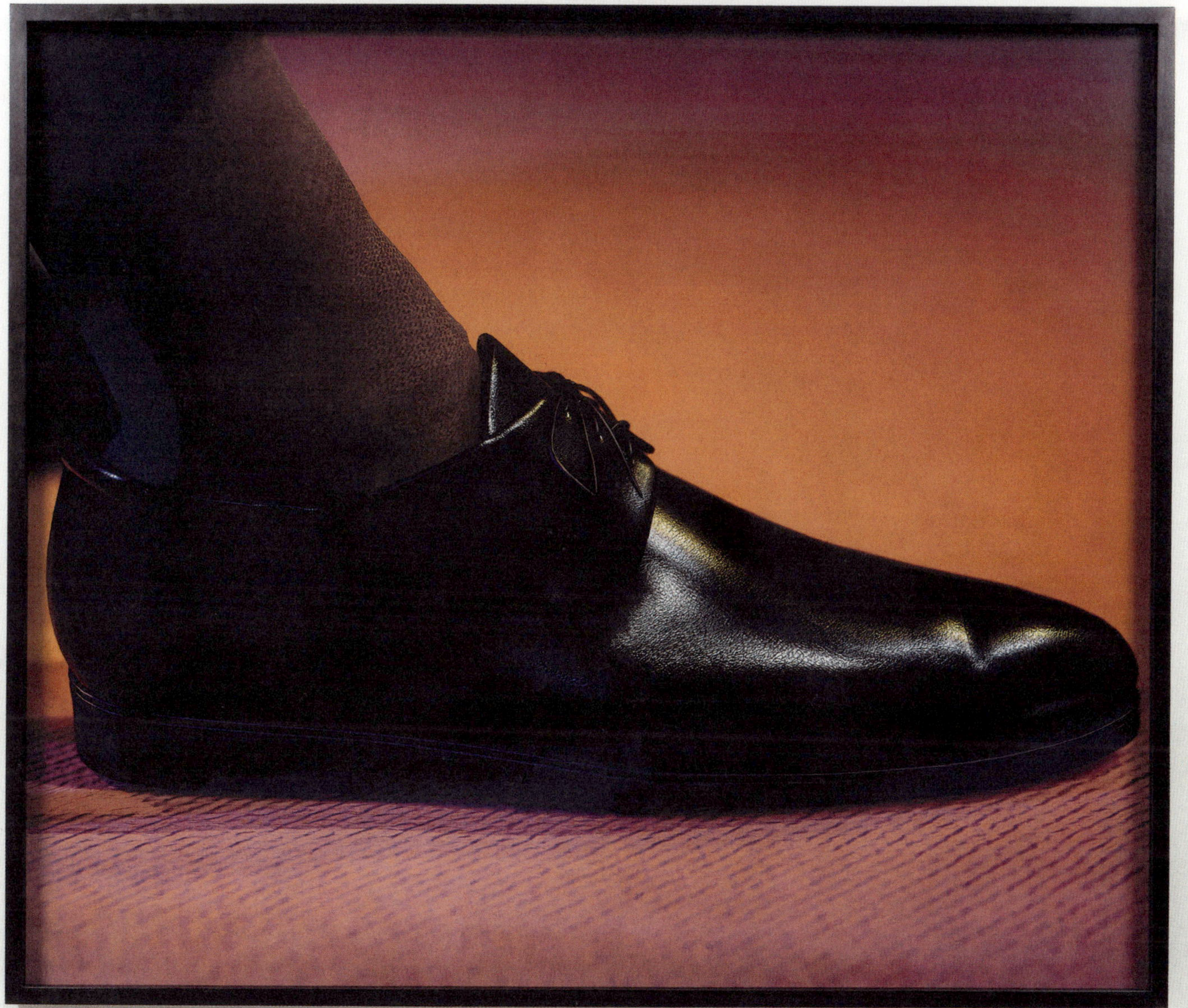

Untitled 2022, digital print on aluminium, 156.5 × 131.5

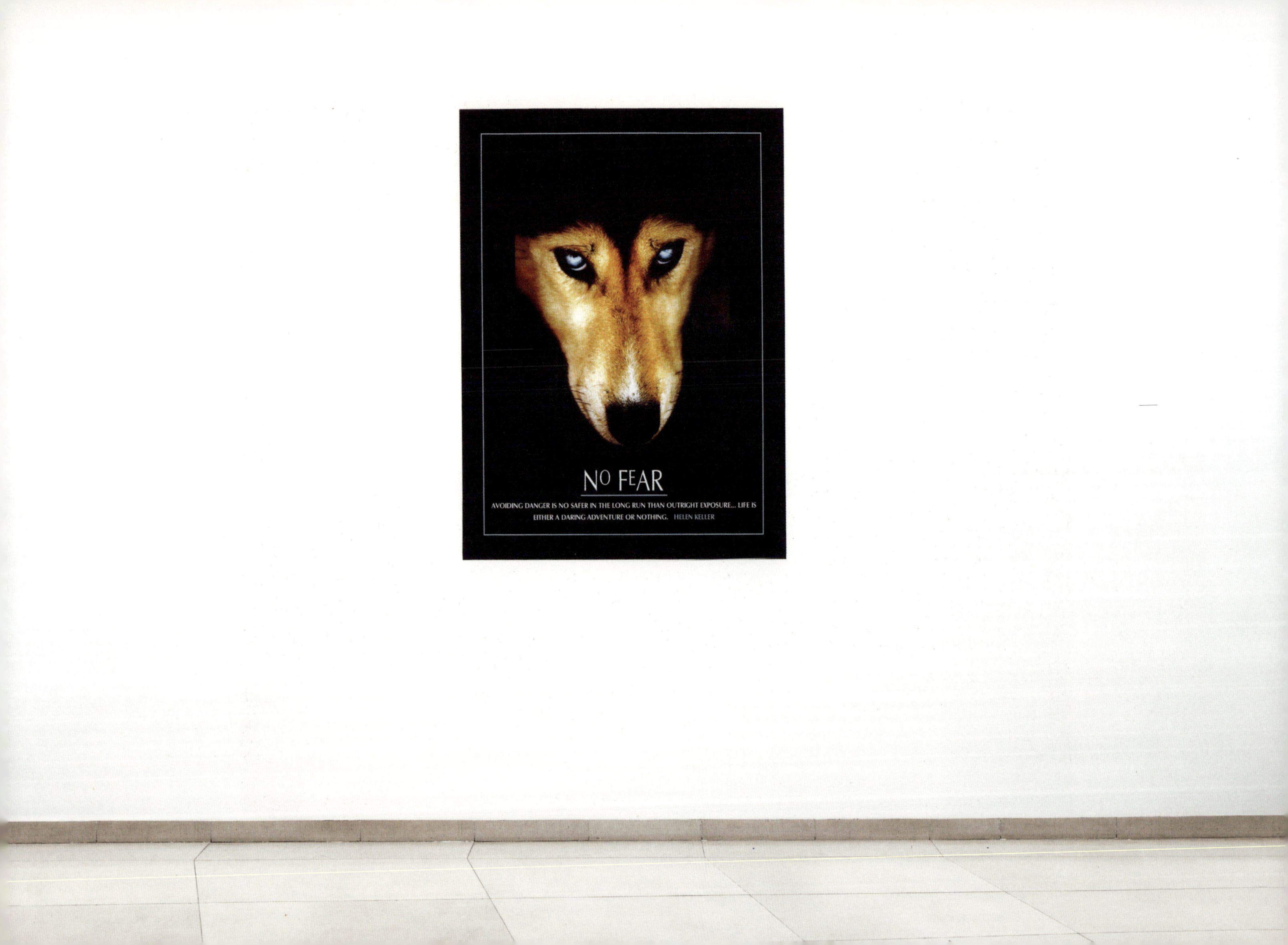
NO FEAR
AVOIDING DANGER IS NO SAFER IN THE LONG RUN THAN OUTRIGHT EXPOSURE... LIFE IS EITHER A DARING ADVENTURE OR NOTHING. HELEN KELLER

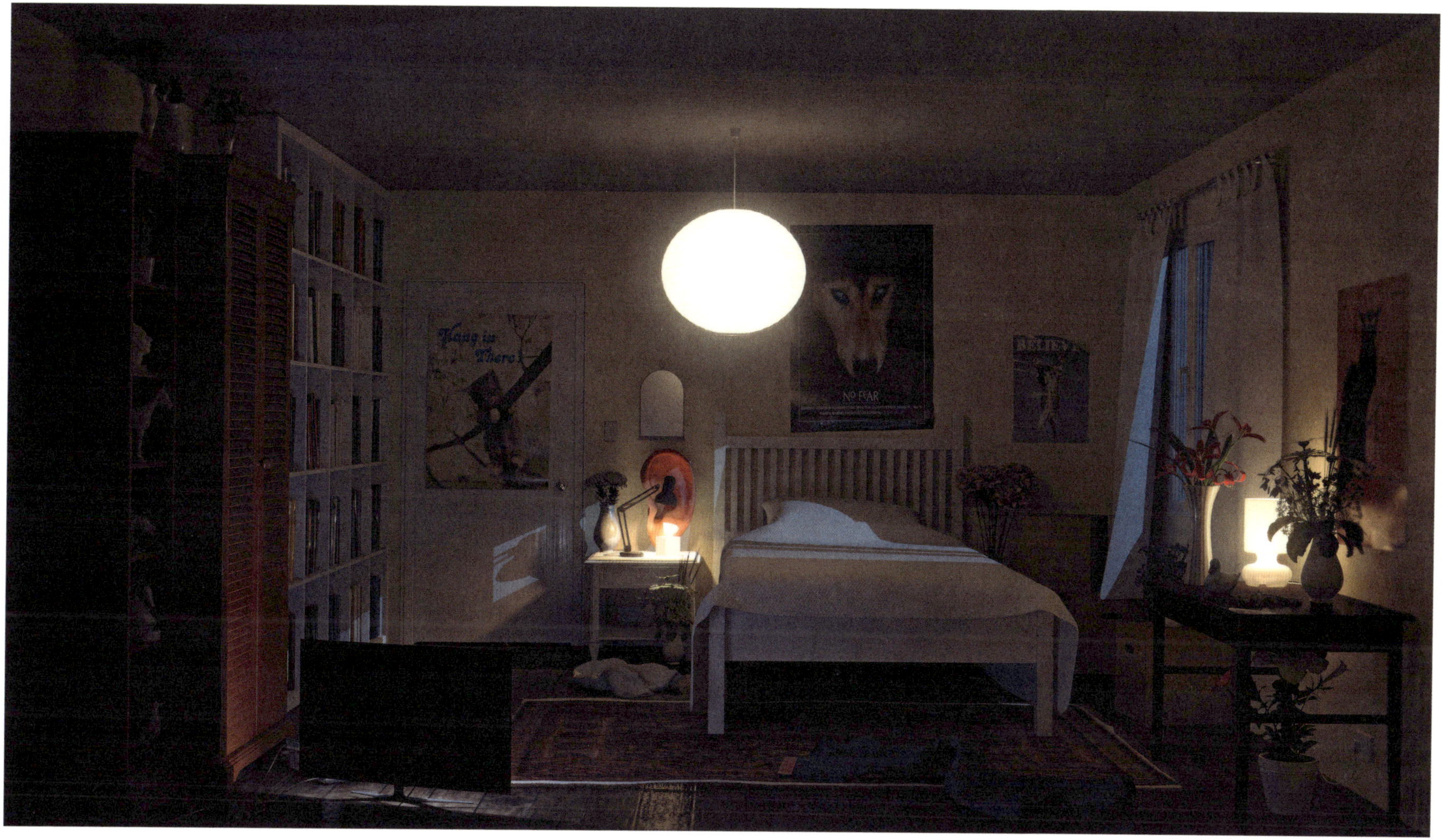

No Fear 2017–25, inkjet print on paper (left)
Hisser 2015, three-channel video and sound

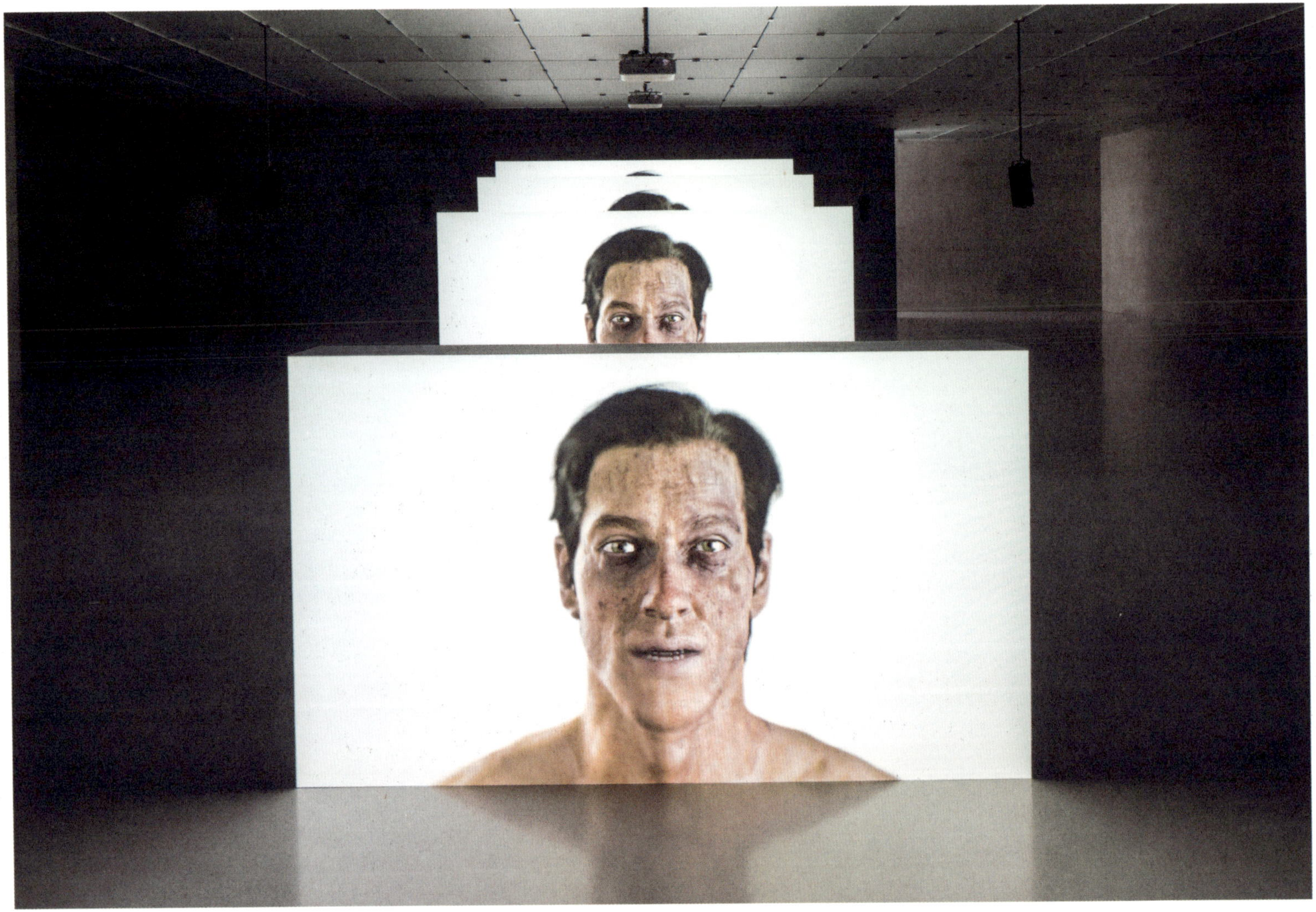

Hisser 2015 (installation view) in *Ed Atkins*, Kunsthaus Bregenz, 2019

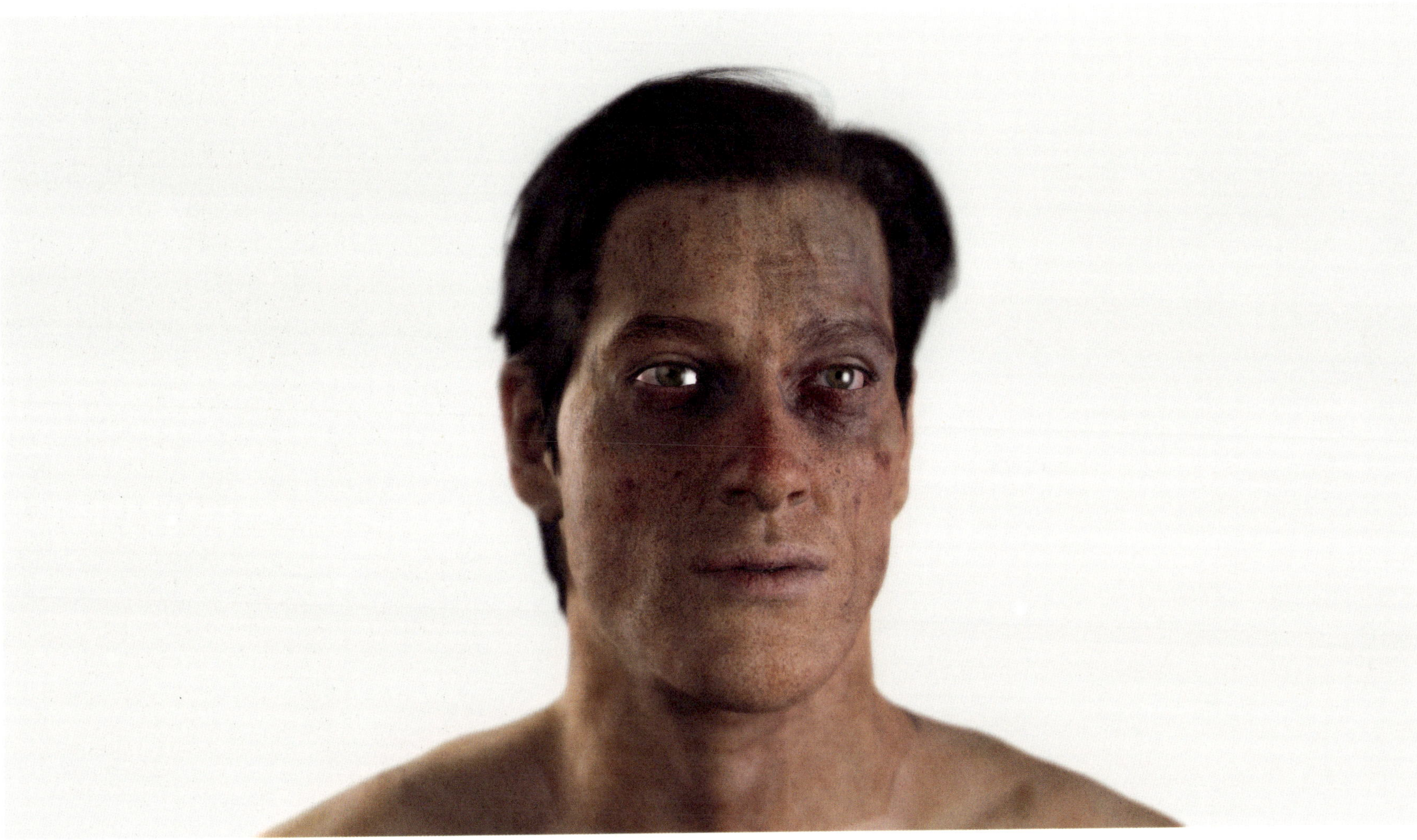

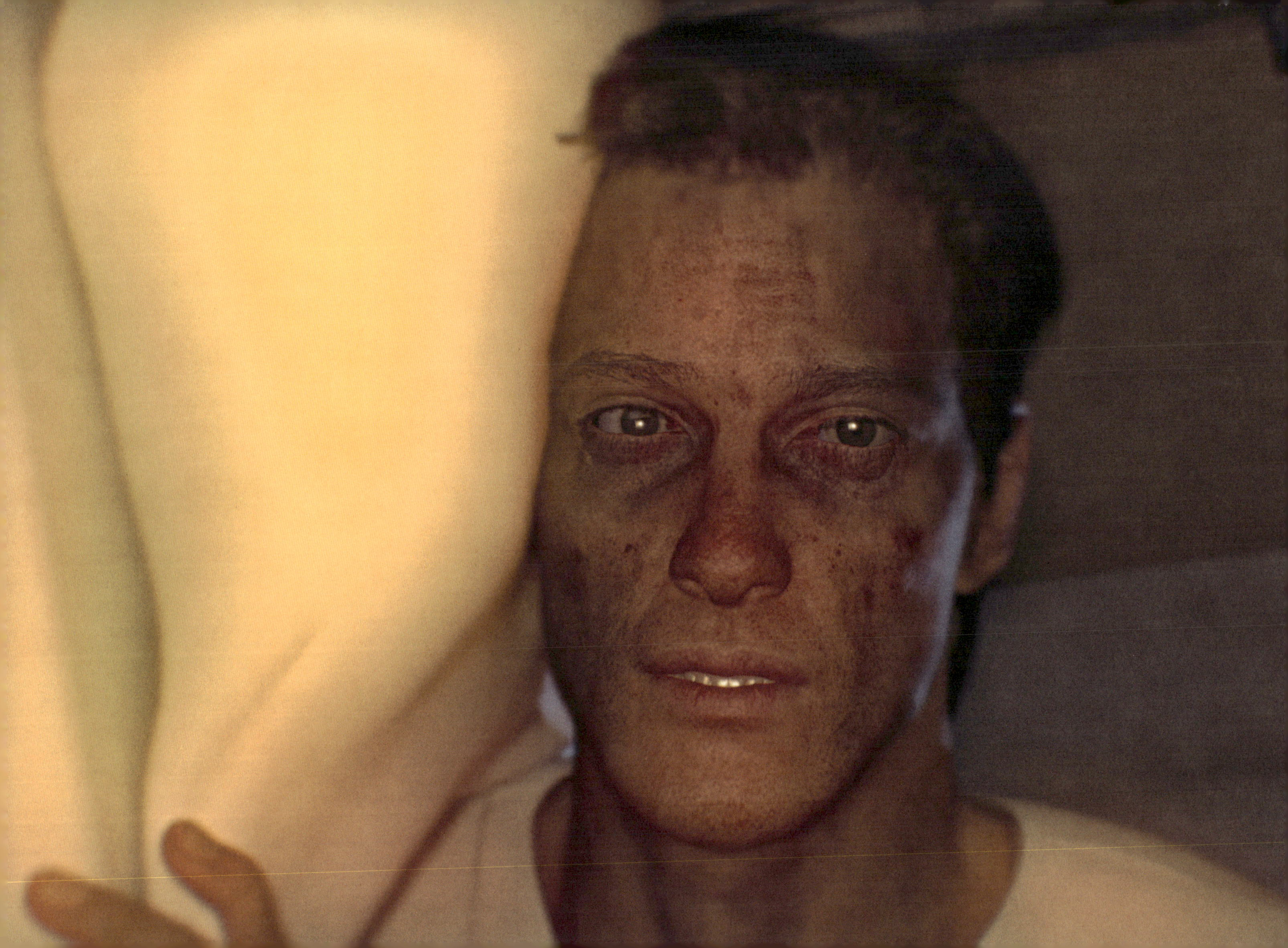

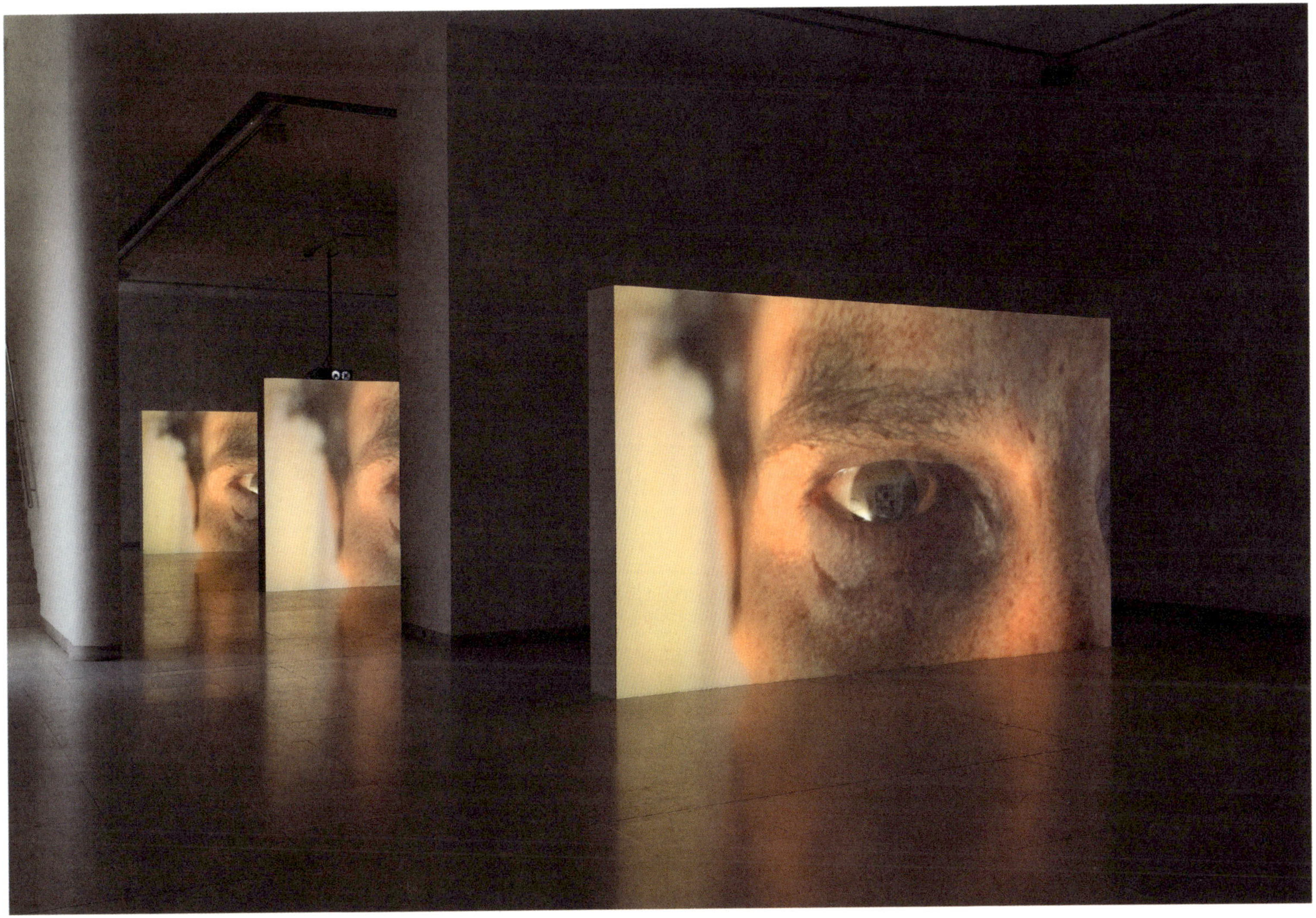

Hisser 2015 (installation view) in *Corpsing*, Museum für Moderne Kunst, Frankfurt, 2017

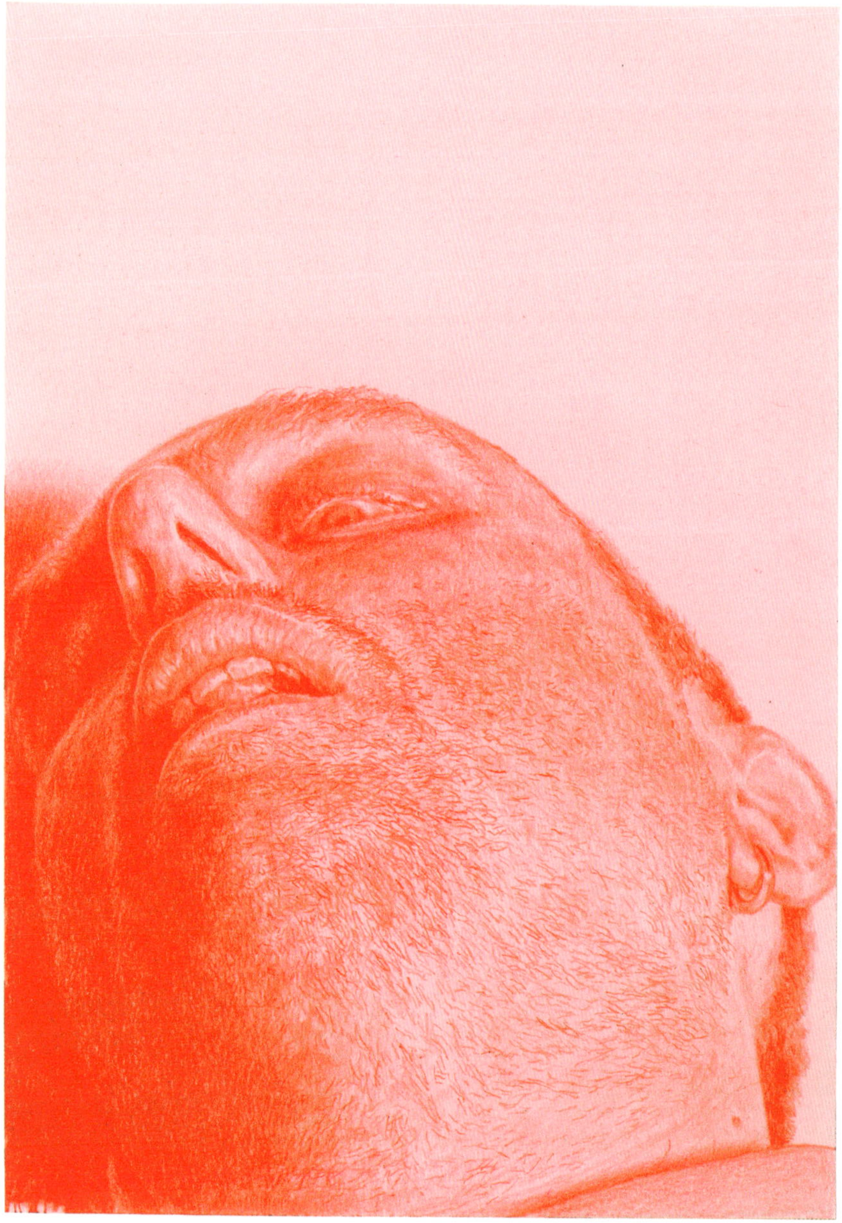

Untitled 2023, coloured pencil on paper, 52.1 × 41.3 (above and right)

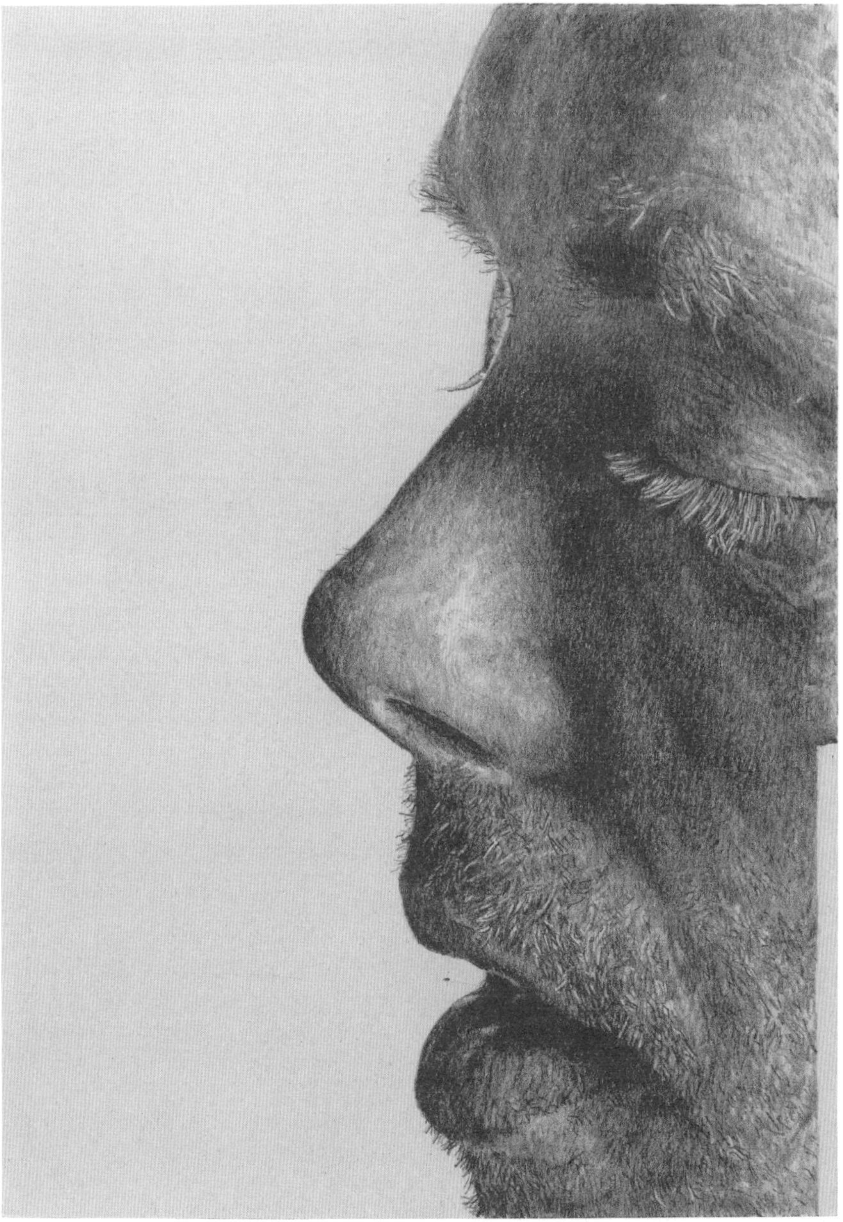

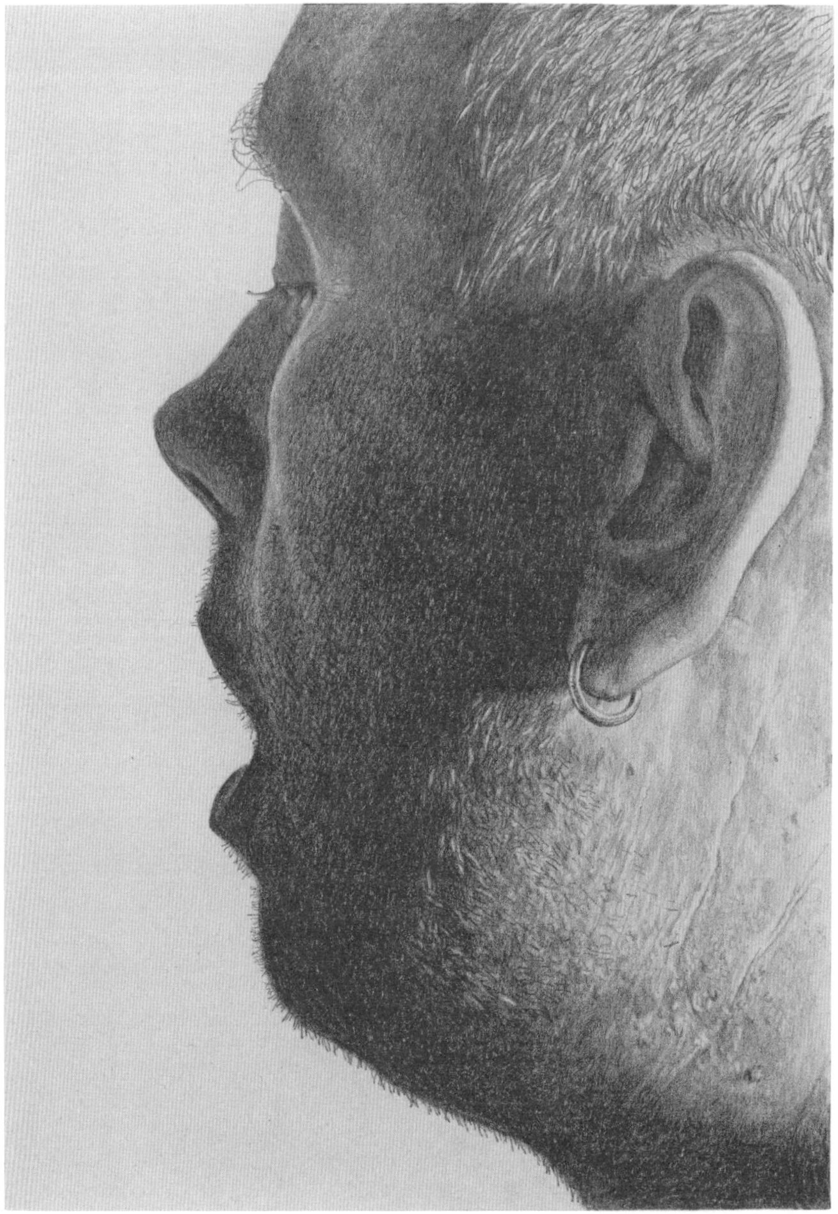

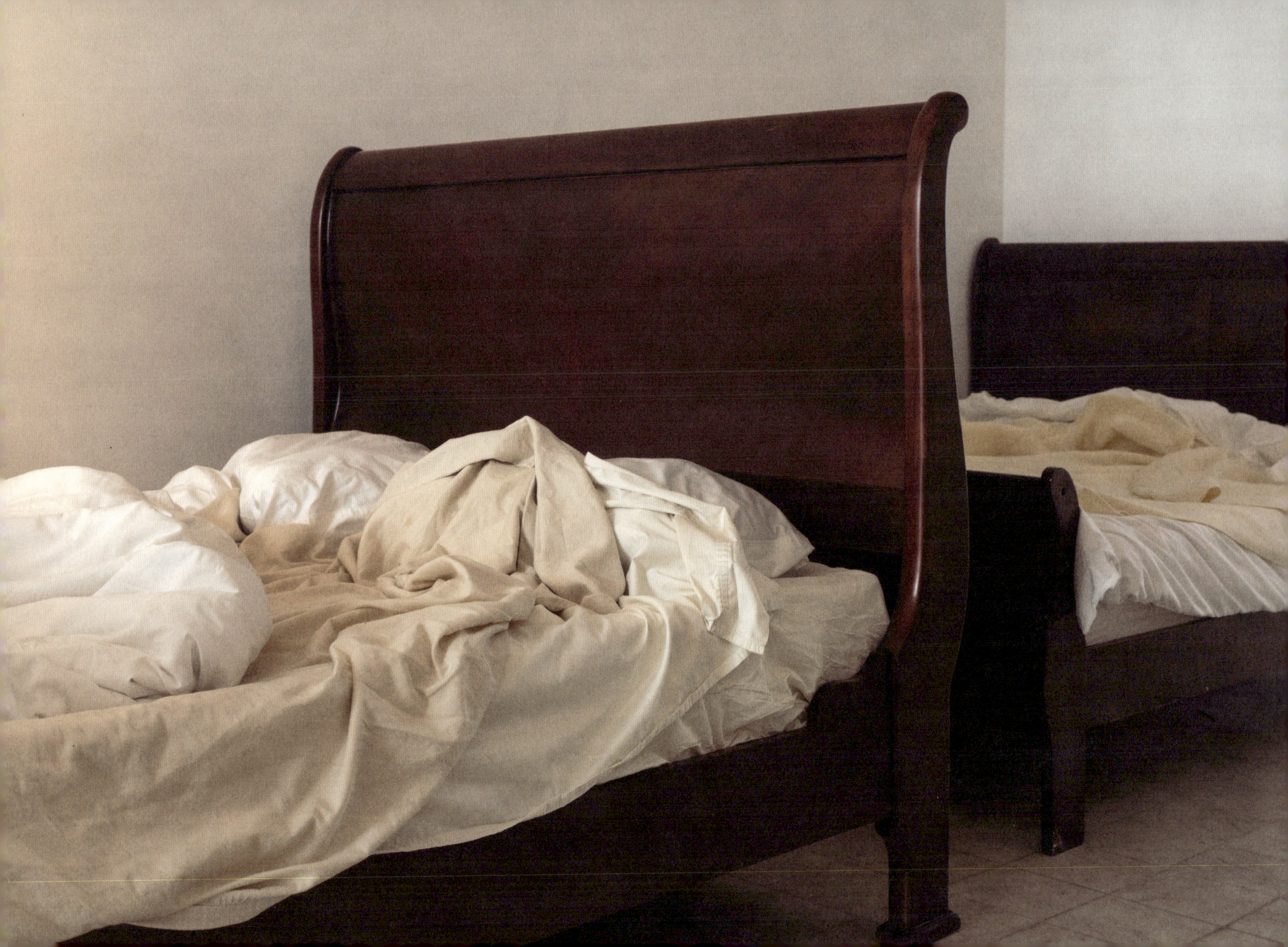

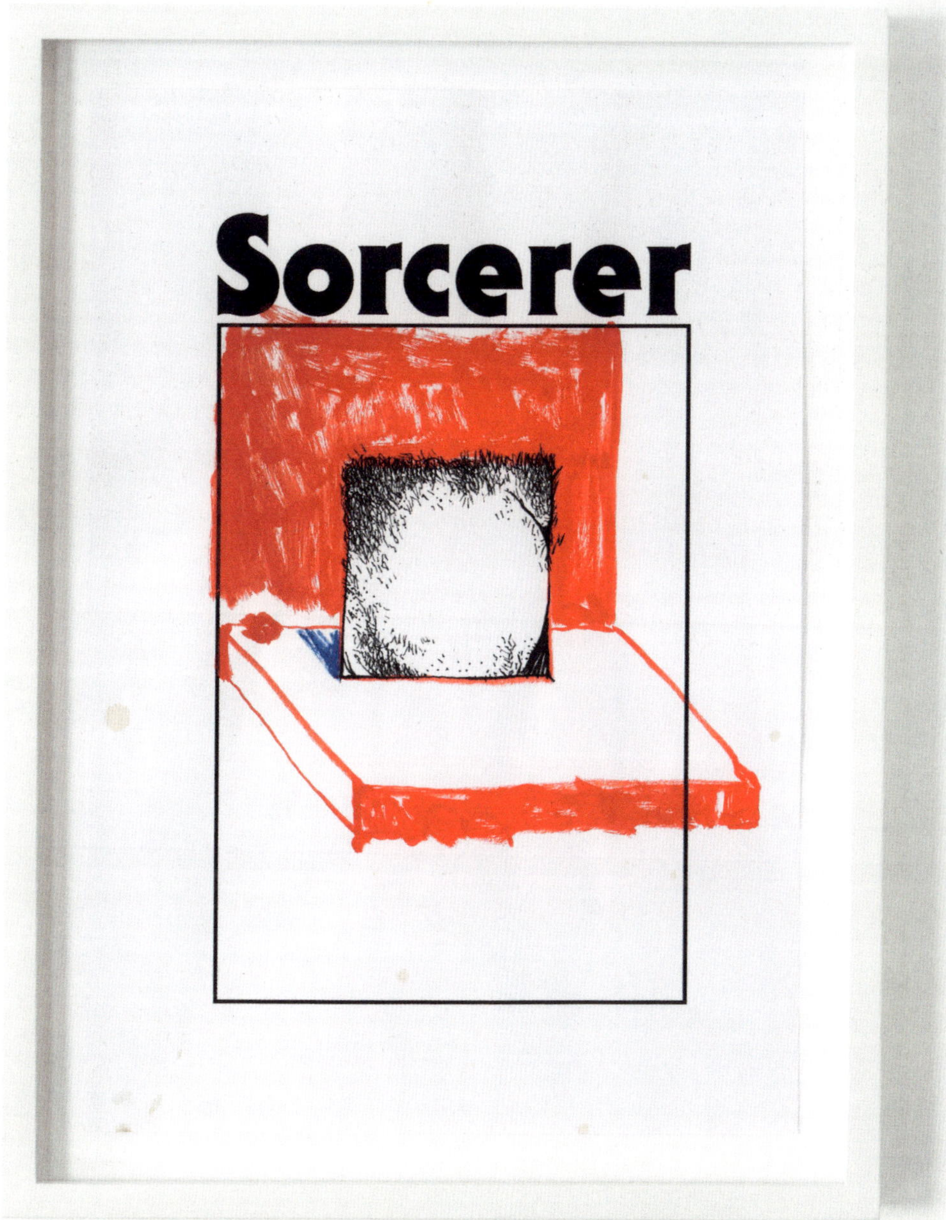

Poster for *Sorcerer* 2023 (above)

Beds 2023 (installation view) in *Ed Atkins with Steven Zultanski*, Gladstone Gallery, New York, 2023–4, motor, battery, wooden bed frame, cotton sheets, 127 × 464.8 × 161.9 (left)

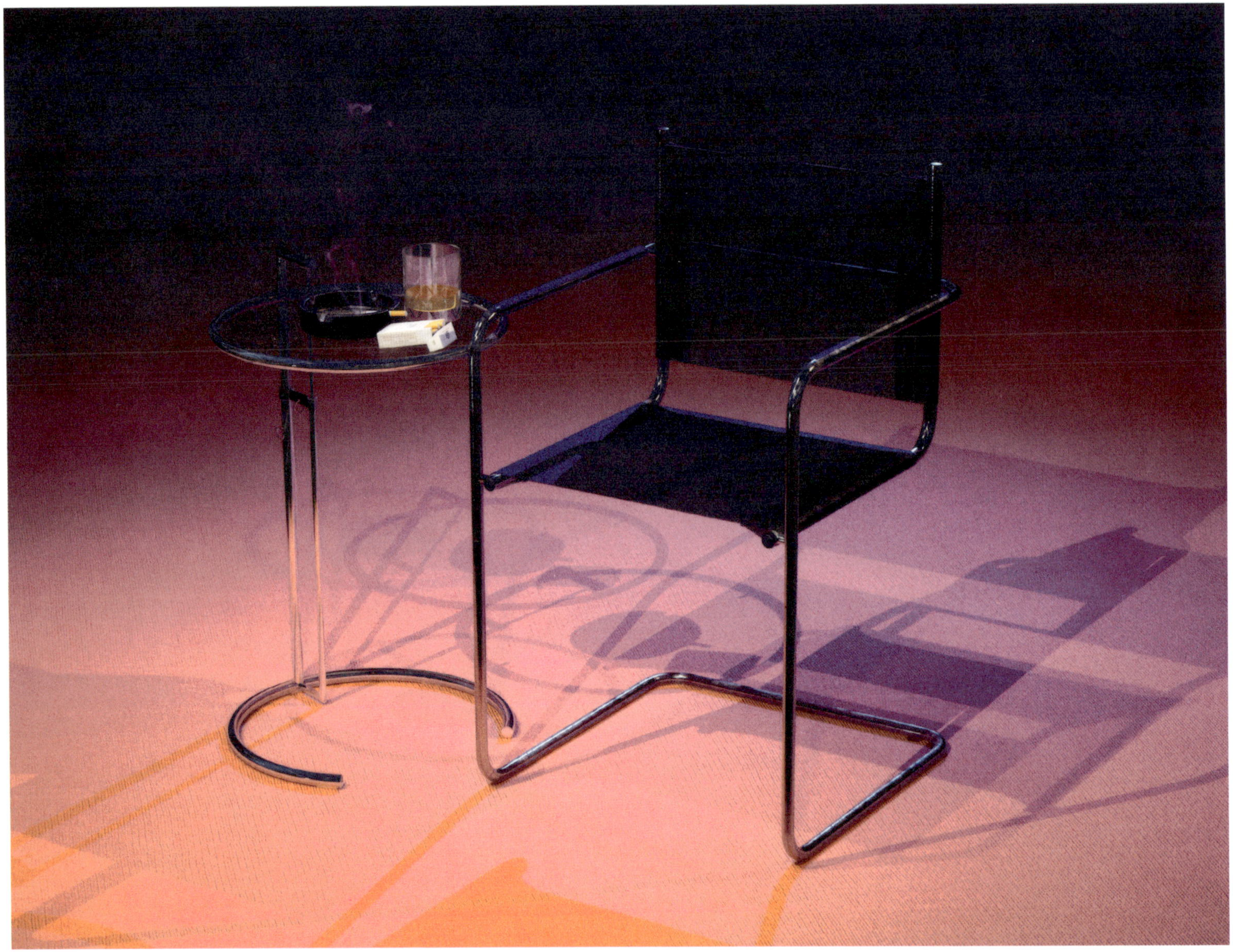

The worm 2021, video and sound

MEDIA CORPSING

Hal Foster

How many of us, when we speak with our parents, feel like stock characters, as though we have become our own simulations? In *The worm* 2021 Ed Atkins presents a telephone call with his mother in this very manner. In the roughly thirteen-minute animation his mum is heard but not seen, while Atkins is rendered, by way of performance capture technology, as a digital avatar who listens attentively, mumbling sympathy or surprise, asking a question only when her narrative falters. Aurally close, the mother is spatially distant (*The worm* was made during the Covid-19 lockdown), while the son is almost too present on the large screen—there are extreme close-ups, odd angles, abrupt cuts, awkward gestures and unconscious tics—even though we know what we see is not truly Atkins.[1] His double, a three-dimensional model purchased online, is no double at all. The usually scruffy artist appears as a natty television host in a dark windowpane suit with wire-rimmed glasses, who diverges from the often abject characters featured in his previous videos. And the set-up, with its sound stage, blue light, stylish chair, small table, whisky glass, Silk Cut cigarettes and ashtray, is indeed that of a studio interview, a genre that conflates reality and artifice in its own way. One inspiration for *The worm* was the final television appearance of the English writer Dennis Potter, who, at the point of death from cancer in 1994, talks bluntly yet poignantly about the

1 The initial concept was to interview people in isolation—incarcerated, disabled, low-income, elderly—but the pandemic made that scheme seem superfluous to Atkins. Nevertheless, *The worm* is all about both the desire for and the difficulty of connection. For the conversation Atkins set up in a hotel room in Berlin while his mother remained in England. The data captured during the conversation was used to animate the avatar, though 'it's my face that palpably lurks beneath the CGI wireframe and JPEG skin'.

2
Atkins uses the interview form as the basis of several videos. 'For such a long time, I made these works alone, at a computer, interrogating myself with technologies that surveilled my every grimace. For me it was a pitched self-surveillance that ended up melodramatising me to myself.' Imagine the Warhol *Screen Tests* updated technologically, self-inflicted and not at all silent.

3
Gillian Rose, *Love's Work: A Reckoning with Life*, New York, 1995, p.74. For Rose 'love's work' is a reckoning with risk and loss. 'Philosophy, ancient and modern, is born out of this condition of sadness (p.124). This is also true of art for Atkins, at least in part.

immediacy of sensuous experience (a plum flower outside his window strikes him as the 'blossomest blossom'), his commitment to writing until the end, his faith in human community over 'the rumour' that is God, and the corruption of journalism and politics by Rupert Murdoch (already then!).[2]

The mum talks about her family—some about her insensitive father, more about her depressive mother—and how she took on the worries of the latter, especially about 'lovability', but to little avail, mostly because such cares couldn't be expressed openly (depression was euphemised as 'weekend letdown'). The theme of her reminiscences is emotional inheritance, in particular how we pass on everyday unhappiness, and we watch the avatar struggle to metabolise this misery even though (or precisely because) he's not altogether human. 'The way she talks of her mother, Nanny Bea, is how I could talk about my mother', Atkins writes. 'Thwarted artists, manic depressives, chronic dysmorphics through and through. All of which is contagious, hereditary poison.' This 'empathy-mirroring' was arduous for both parties, a self-conscious performance, but it was 'also love', Atkins insists. 'Love! Tenderness!'

This point brings into focus the import of his titles. Consider *Get Life/Love's Work*, the title of the 2021 show at the New Museum where Atkins debuted *The worm*. 'To get life' is an ethical imperative, in this case to address the repressions in nuclear families and to resist the predations of media technologies. Yet it is also a prison sentence, and both these struggles can go on forever. 'The worm' is multivalent too. A worm is base like the spider that represents the formless for Georges Bataille, lowly like a daughter burdened with the pain of her mother, squirmy like a son who can't settle the debts of the past. 'The worm of time' comes to mind as well, the turns of fortune through the generations, as does *The Sick Rose*, the William Blake 'song of experience' in which a worm threads together eros and disease: 'O Rose thou art sick./ The invisible worm,/ That flies in the night/ In the howling storm:/ Has found out thy bed/ Of crimson joy:/ And his dark secret love/ Does thy life destroy'. This allusion calls up another source cited by Atkins, *Love's Work*, the 1995 memoir of the English philosopher Gillian Rose, who, like Potter, was brought to an early 'reckoning with life' (the subtitle of her book) by a death sentence of cancer. This sick Rose, who writes magnificently about Eros and disease, argues that the near-oxymoronic work of love is to convert melancholy into mourning—a Freudian labour also important to

The worm 2021, video and sound

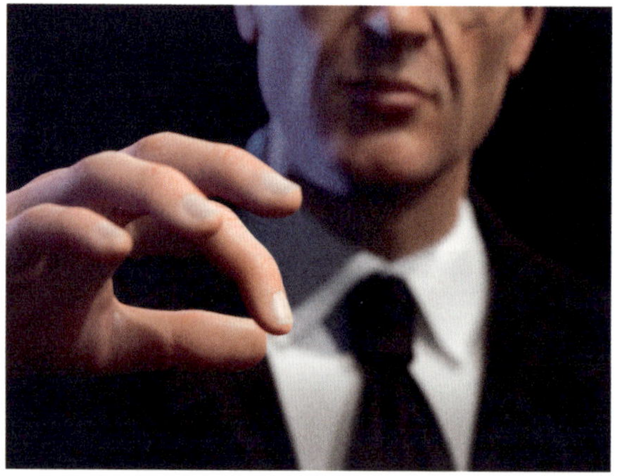

Atkins—and then, somehow, into delight: 'I want to sob and sob and sob', Rose tells us, 'until the prolonged shrieking becomes a shout of joy.'[3] Atkins desires this transformation too. Even as *The worm* foregrounds the difficulties of his mother, the death of his father—also from cancer—looms in the background, as it does in other of his videos (Atkins calls his characters 'dead men, surrogates, auto cadavers').[4]

At times the maternal monologue verges on confession, yet there is no priest here, only a son, one who, rather than talk about his mother, listens to her talk about her mother. The expected analysand becomes the unexpected analyst, and this also makes the Atkins avatar squirm. The fact that he processes private matters in a public setting (fictively in a television studio, actually in an art gallery) makes us squirm too, especially as we are reminded how personal exposure has become the obscene norm in social media. Atkins adapts the Lacanian term 'extimacy' for this everyday confusion of the intimate and the alien. 'Everything's become involutional', he writes in a free association typical of his hyperbolic prose. 'Think family, heredity, history, antecedents. Think of history as a movement inward maybe.' Yet, rather than see this involution as a limitation only, Atkins wants to run with it, to revalue it. 'Going inward in memory, in body, in heredity, in technology, and, of course, in psychology. That we might pursue this psychical memory ... bliss.'

The sound of *The worm* is as penetrative as the image is immersive. The avatar appears as 'a country of pores, wrinkles, and, I hope, the tiny inflections and winces of a detailed, silent response'. So what kind of realism is at stake here? The video is hardly realist in the old sense of referential; its set-up is entirely artefactual. Yet Atkins seeks not to reiterate the technological derealisation of the world so much as to resist it. His aesthetic goal is to 'model those parts of life that steadfastly elude representation ... That's my utopianism: a faith in the eternal singularity of materiality', which he locates above all in 'the irreducibility of IRL/mortal experience'. This realism is rooted in the body and the psyche, especially in extreme states of abjection and trauma (Atkins is interested in Julia Kristeva and Jacques Lacan as well as Georges Bataille).[5] It is the real as remainder, understood as that which resists the symbolic order—a task made all the more difficult given that this order is now suffused with technologies of computer generation, artificial intelligence and algorithmic scripting.[6]

The original wager made by Atkins is that, if reality can be derealised by such technologies, it might also be rediscovered there, and this in a few ways. First, he believes that, once outmoded, a given technology passes over to the side of 'base materiality'; its very clunkiness becomes a sort of reality effect. Atkins adapts the term 'corpsing'—which indicates the moment when an actor breaks character and so dispels the illusion of the performance—'to describe a kind of structural revelation more generally'; his examples are when a vinyl record skips or a streaming movie buffers.[7] To corpse a medium, then, is to expose its materiality, even to intimate its mortality, and in this moment the real might poke through all the mediation. Second, punctuated by the gestural tics of the Atkins avatar, *The worm* is also rife with manufactured glitches—sudden blurs, flares, beeps and

4
These surrogates 'descended, psychically, from that literal dead man who began this whole sorry mess for me. Making videos became about reparative mourning.'

5
Hal Foster, 'Obscene, Abject, Traumatic,' *October*, vol.78, Autumn 1996, pp.107–24, https://www.jstor.org/stable/778908, last accessed 6 Dec. 2024.

6
'The presumption of the project, from the beginning, was the accentuation of those aspects of life that elude technological remediation, recoupment, representation, rendering, capture. The work would try to rehearse freedoms by their omission from the remit of what's reproducible.

crackles—and these apparent cracks in the artifice might provide another opening to the real. Although these reality effects are also artificial, 'they baffle the signs of reality by parodying them, engendering a new kind of realism.'[8] Third, if the real might be felt when an illusion fails, so too might it be sensed when that illusion is 'glazed with effects to italicise the artifice', that is, when illusionism is pushed to a hyperreal point. In this register Atkins conforms to the criterion of fidelity in technological reproduction, but excessively so, and in this way claims such fidelity for the side of 'revelatory materialism rather than techno magic'. Fourth, Atkins exploits a central feature of high-definition video inherited from photography and film, at least when they were experienced by early viewers—that the inanimate appears to be alive. This confusion is a tell-tale attribute of the uncanny (in his account Sigmund Freud was inspired by those avatars known as doppelgängers), and this uncanniness is another 'mortal experience' that evokes the real.[9] Finally, if photography and film opened up an 'optical unconscious' for Walter Benjamin, a reality not perceived by the naked eye, high-definition video expands this realm for Atkins.[10] His surrogate dead men make visible the psychopathology of everyday technological life.

'Unlike with movies, my CGI stuff is deliberately janky', Atkins states. 'Enough to underscore it, draw attention to it. Which is a perversion of its aim to disappear.' This is a contemporary version of the modernist call to reveal the medium, 'to bare the device' (as the Russian formalists put it), but Atkins goes much further. His formalism is dedicated to realism, one of 'bleak histrionics' that he calls

In this, at least structurally, it would recapitulate the core thesis of my work.'

7
Tacita Dean deploys media corpsing brilliantly in her 2015 film *Event for a Stage*. See Hal Foster, 'Real Fictions: Alternatives to Alternative Facts', *Artforum*, April 2017, https://www.artforum.com/features/real-fictions-alternatives-to-alternative-facts-233322, accessed 6 Dec. 2024.

8
'Analogue flaws [are] re-created digitally in order to militate against the sterile horror of computergenerated nothings.' In the film *Anomalisa* (2015), Charlie Kaufman also uses glitches in the animation—cracks in the avatar—to evoke the real. See Zadie Smith, 'Windows on the Will', *New York Review of Books*, 10 March 2016, https://www.nybooks.com/articles/2016/03/10/windows-on-the-will, accessed 6 Dec. 2024.

9
For Atkins 'the celluloidal story' has 'the uncanny at its heart' and the digital image is even more 'spectral'; its 'persistent aping of analogue reality means that the animation, the life, is doubly lost, doubly dead.' In some ways Atkins continues, by digital means, the old cinematic fascination with ghosts, robots and doubles of all sorts.

10
Walter Benjamin uses this phrase (without much explanation) in both 'Little History of Photography' (1931) and 'The Work of Art in the Age of Its Technological Reproducibility' (1935–6).

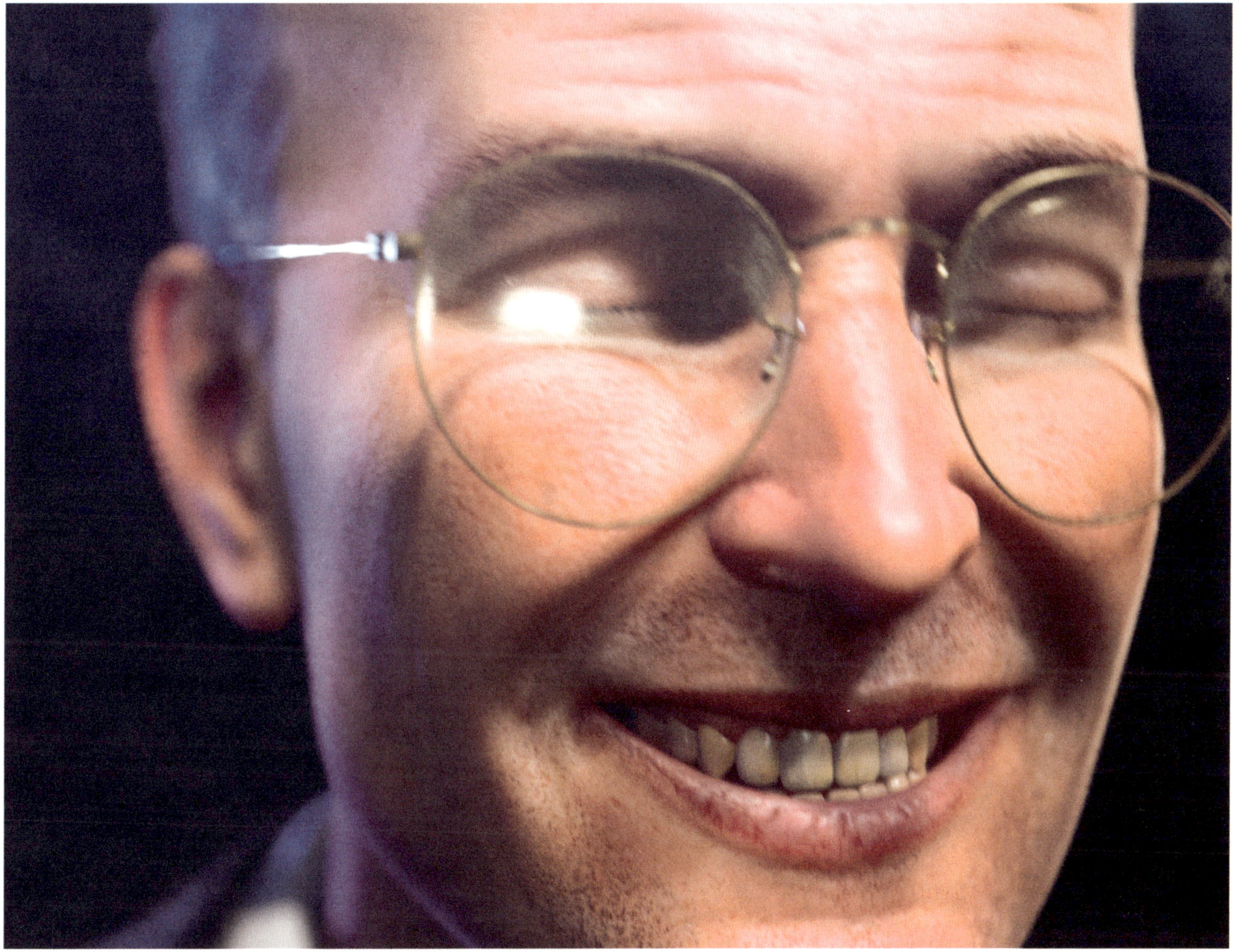

The worm 2021, video and sound, pp.77–87

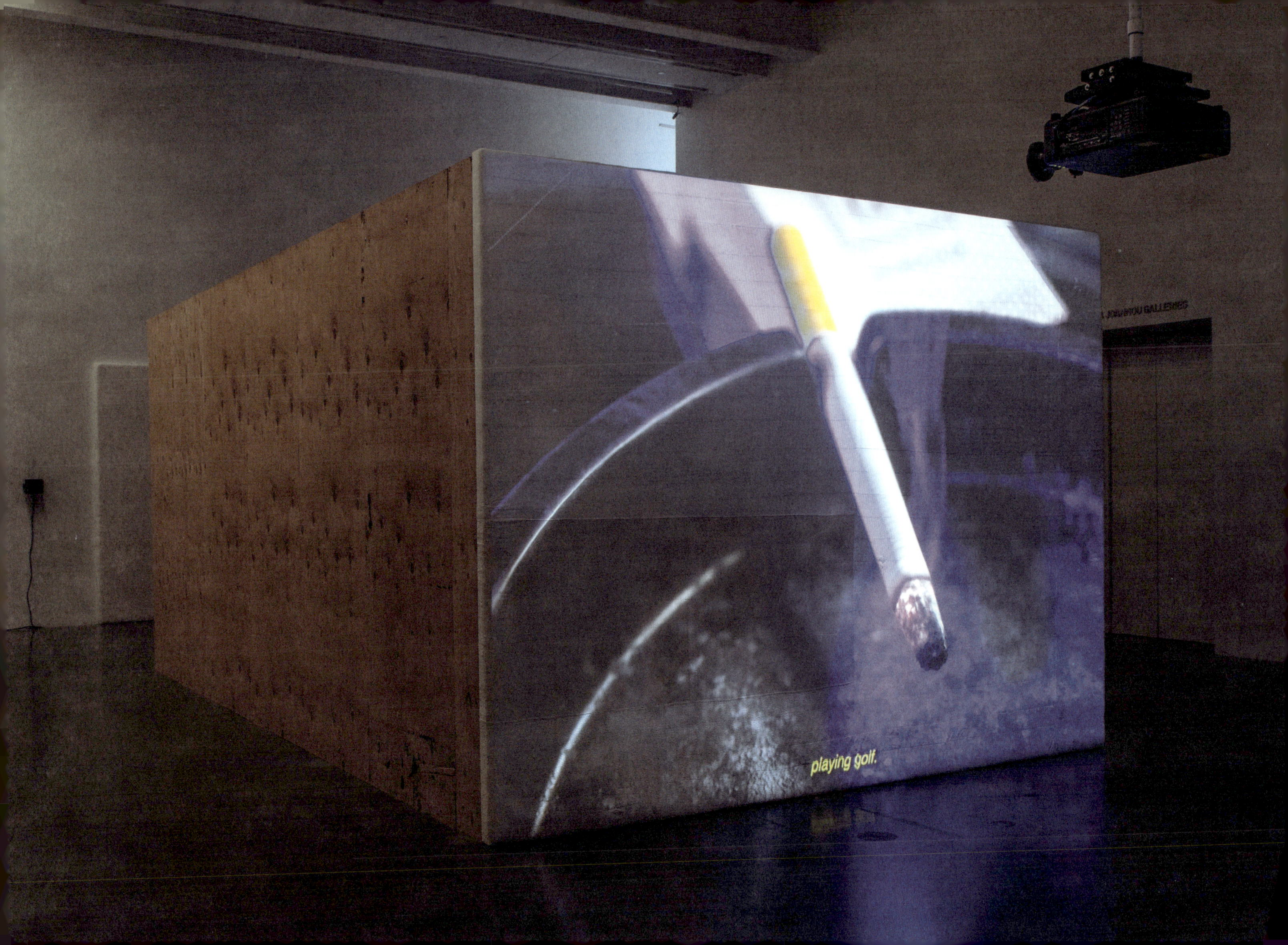
playing golf.

'Bruegelian'.[11] '[I] want to realign the tech in the service of life's *beggared*—"love's work"—rather than as a tool of captivity.' For Atkins, then, to bare the device is also to 'impoverish' the medium, and thus to point to other impoverishments—in his life, in his family, in society at large. At the extreme, the bared device stands in for 'bare life', or life defined by Giorgio Agamben as utterly subject to power, life that is indeed beggared.[12] Here Atkins proceeds by way of analogies: 'Analogue error feels as if it is to the reality of a CGI image what impoverishment is to representation at large—what tragedy is to depictions of life; what misery is to experience.' He knows that this string of allegories is a stretch, but he's not afraid of bathos, which he sees as the other side of pathos. Atkins risks these states because he sees affect as an essential dimension of life that must be both rediscovered in media technologies and wrested from them. This is why he aims to find an 'emo, cybernetic surrogacy' in computer-generated avatars and to graft his 'sentimental self to the tech, rather than the other way around'.[13] This is not to deny that life is steeped in loss but, on the contrary, to acknowledge that reality and to produce work that addresses it, that assists in 'affective recognition'. It is to contribute to 'love's work'.

Here his notion of art confronts his theory of media, which Atkins sketched in a 2018 lecture titled 'Losslessness'. 'Losslessness', he tells us, 'refers to a category of data-compression algorithm that allows original data to be perfectly reproduced.' To achieve this fidelity, digital media, even more than analogue media, aim to disappear; 'technology constantly seeks to be lost'. The magic of technology wants not only to cover up our existential lack—this is what makes it the ultimate fetish—but also to distract us from its inevitable failure. Its myth of losslessness serves 'ideological ends', among them our fantasies of 'coherency', 'holism', even 'immortality'. However, it never quite succeeds. Loss is felt nonetheless, and since this loss can't be acknowledged, our relationship to technology is rendered 'neurotic', marked by 'aimless melancholy or shame'. In response, Atkins argues, 'the artist first must set out to *find* the technology' and the initial step is to make the technology 'corporeal, analogue, mortal'. This 'movement toward the literal' is not simply 'a rebuttal of the desires of the tech'; it also points to the 'uncovering of other realities,' which in turn promotes the 'freedom of the subject'.[14] Here we are back on the familiar ground of modernist defamiliarisation, a project that is vastly complicated now that the human seems almost fused with the technological and the world often appears to be media all the way down. Moreover, for Atkins it's not enough to defetishise technology, to demystify its magic. For his work to be effective, illusion must be allowed 'sufficient function' not only 'to sustain critique' but also to promote affective recognition—to express loss, to 'set in motion a shift from melancholy to purposive mourning', to find in media technology an interpersonal connection that it always promises but rarely delivers.

Atkins signals a shift among artists steeped in new media. Just as the Pictures Generation once assumed the society of the spectacle so that they could engage its image-repertoire, so Atkins takes computer-generated technology as a given but attempts to 'misuse' it critically.[15] Here he differs

11
Atkins continues in this vein: 'I go after the idea that the tech believes it possible to convince us of its life, and that it always fails in this pursuit. That gap between the "almost" and the "never" is a promising, sad, mortal and inimitable place.'

12
See Giorgio Agamben, *Homo Sacer: Sovereign Power and Bare Life*, trans. Daniel Heller-Roazen, Stanford, CA 1998.

13
Atkins delves in 'travesty' and 'caricature' in his writing too: 'Typically for me, the prose is purple, bathetic; mortifying, in retrospect.' See Mike Spelinger, 'Close without Saving', in *Ed Atkins: A Seer Reader*, exh. cat., Serpentine Galleries, London.

The worm 2021 (installation view) in *Ed Atkins: Get Life/Love's Work*, New Museum, New York, 2021

from the practice of immediate predecessors such as Harun Farocki, Hito Steyerl and Trevor Paglen. Rather than reiterate how the human is given over to technology, Atkins seeks, perhaps impossibly, to bend technology back towards the human. His utopian gambit is to believe that technology might aid the human to become human again—to become emotive and empathic on our own terms. His art is not a lament for humanism or a celebration of posthumanism but a snatching of the human from the belly of the beast.[16]

Again, Atkins subscribes to a philosophy of the remainder—of the recalcitrant detail, the personal *punctum*, the traumatic real. Yet, as with Roland Barthes on photography, this fascination can lead Atkins, notwithstanding his Bruegelian (or Brechtian) concern with the beggared, to occlude another reality: social reality.[17] His interest in the 'arts of impoverishment' (a title taken from, who, in his account of such arts, features another Atkins favourite, Samuel Beckett) is also in tension with his commitment to an aesthetic of reparation (Bersani is critical of any 'culture of redemption' that frames experience as always already damaged).[18] Finally, can media technologies truly be turned so as to enrich our affective lives rather than strip them like so many assets? Alongside the old 'ideological state apparatuses' such as the Church and the military, there has arisen a whole slew of social media leviathans that produce, circulate and monetise all kinds of intense affects in ways that disorient us politcally as well as psychologically. But then, when it comes to art, one shouldn't complain about contradictions. Contradiction is what drives a practice like Atkins's; it might also be a condition that keeps us human.

14
'I do think all this structural reflexivity I apparently demand of the medium is maybe a manifestation of the kinds of structural reflexivity that I try to undertake in my personal life.'

15
The Pictures Generation was the name given to a group of American artists (such as Cindy Sherman, Sherrie Levine, Louise Lawler) who came to prominence in the late 1970s and early 1980s and who were known for their critical analysis of media culture.

16
In his novel *Klara and the Sun* (2021), Kazuo Ishiguro presents an AI avatar who develops an emotional maturity that the nominal humans around her either lack or have lost.

17
Perhaps another sign of an inability to think the social is the recent spread of autofiction; like much art, much literature has narrowed its scope to the personal.

18
See Leo Bersani and Ulysse Dutoit, *Arts of Impoverishment: Beckett, Rothko, Resnais*, Cambridge, MA 1993, and Leo Bersani, *The Culture of Redemption*, Cambridge, MA 1990. Atkins might reply that there's no contradiction here: love's work follows on loss. But might he then primordialise and hypostatise loss? 'Loss is our exemplar', Atkins states, and he aims to render it 'sublime'.

The original version of Hal Forster's text appeared in Artforum as a review of the exhibition *Ed Atkins: Get Life/ Love's Work*, curated by Massimiliano Giono for the New Museum in 2021. Unless otherwise noted, all quotations are from this catalogue, which includes two essays by Atkins, a conversation with Giono and a note by Mark Leckey. Hal Foster, 'Close-up: Your Loss', Artforum, Oct. 2021, https://www.artforum.com/features/hal-foster-on-ed-atkinss-the-worm-2021-250660, accessed 6 Dec. 2024.

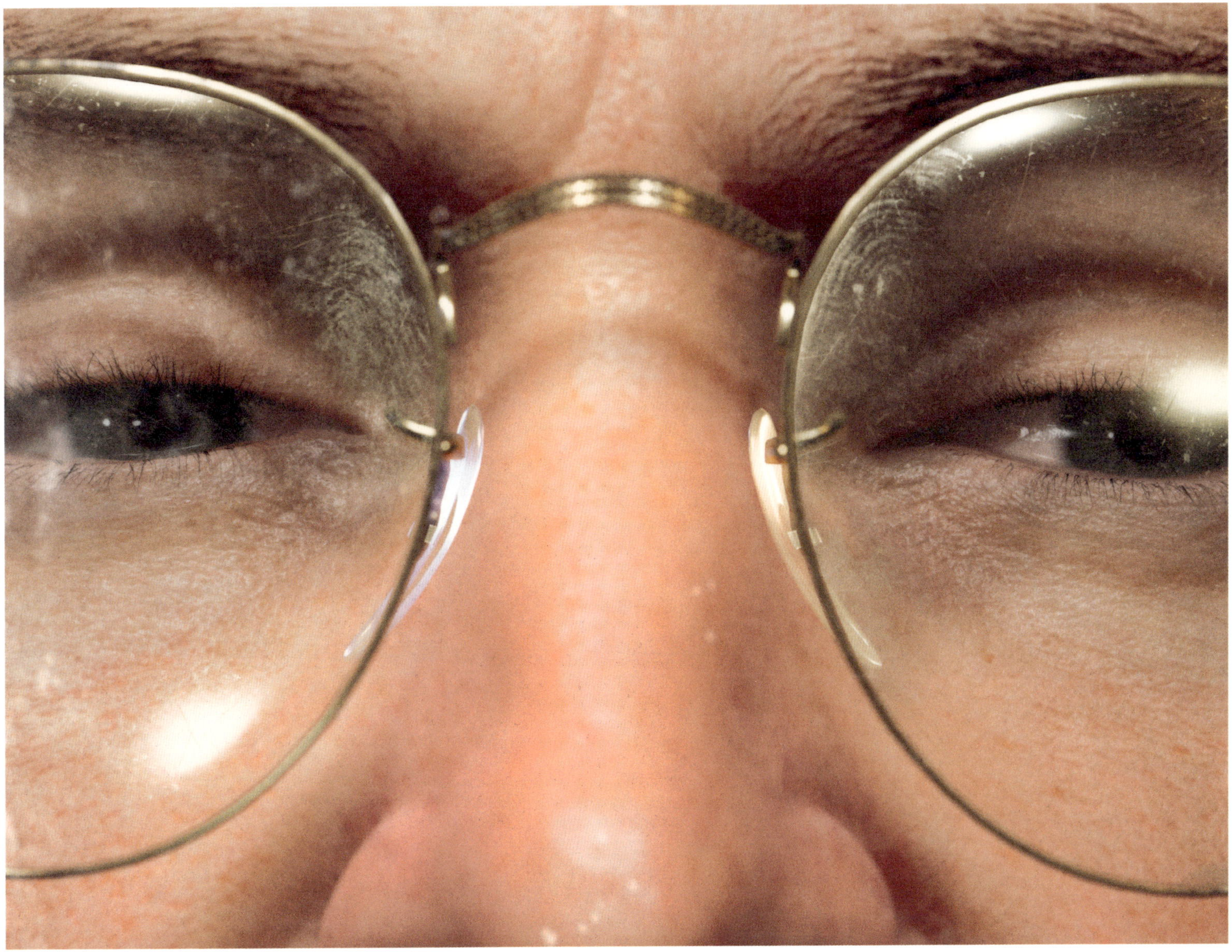

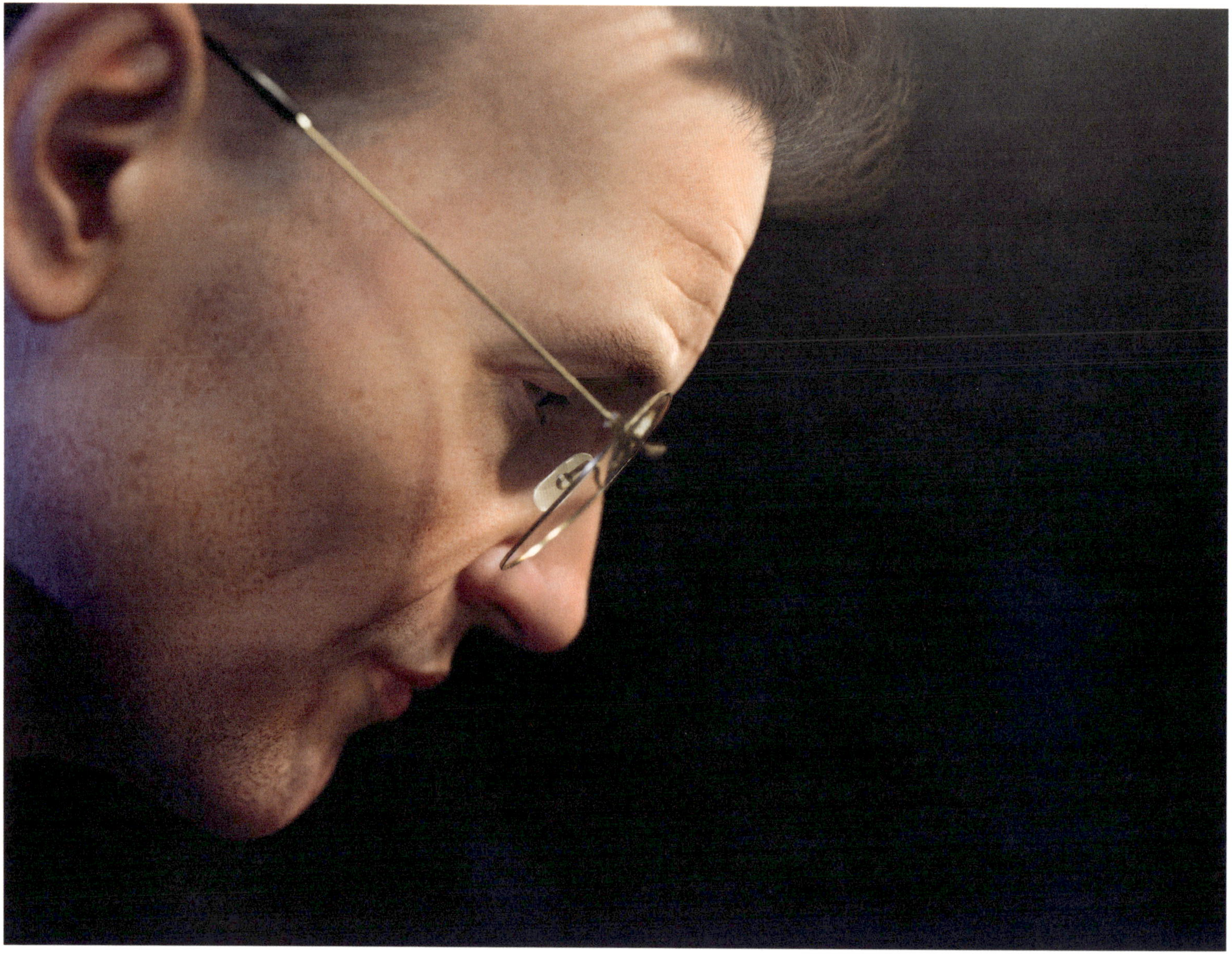

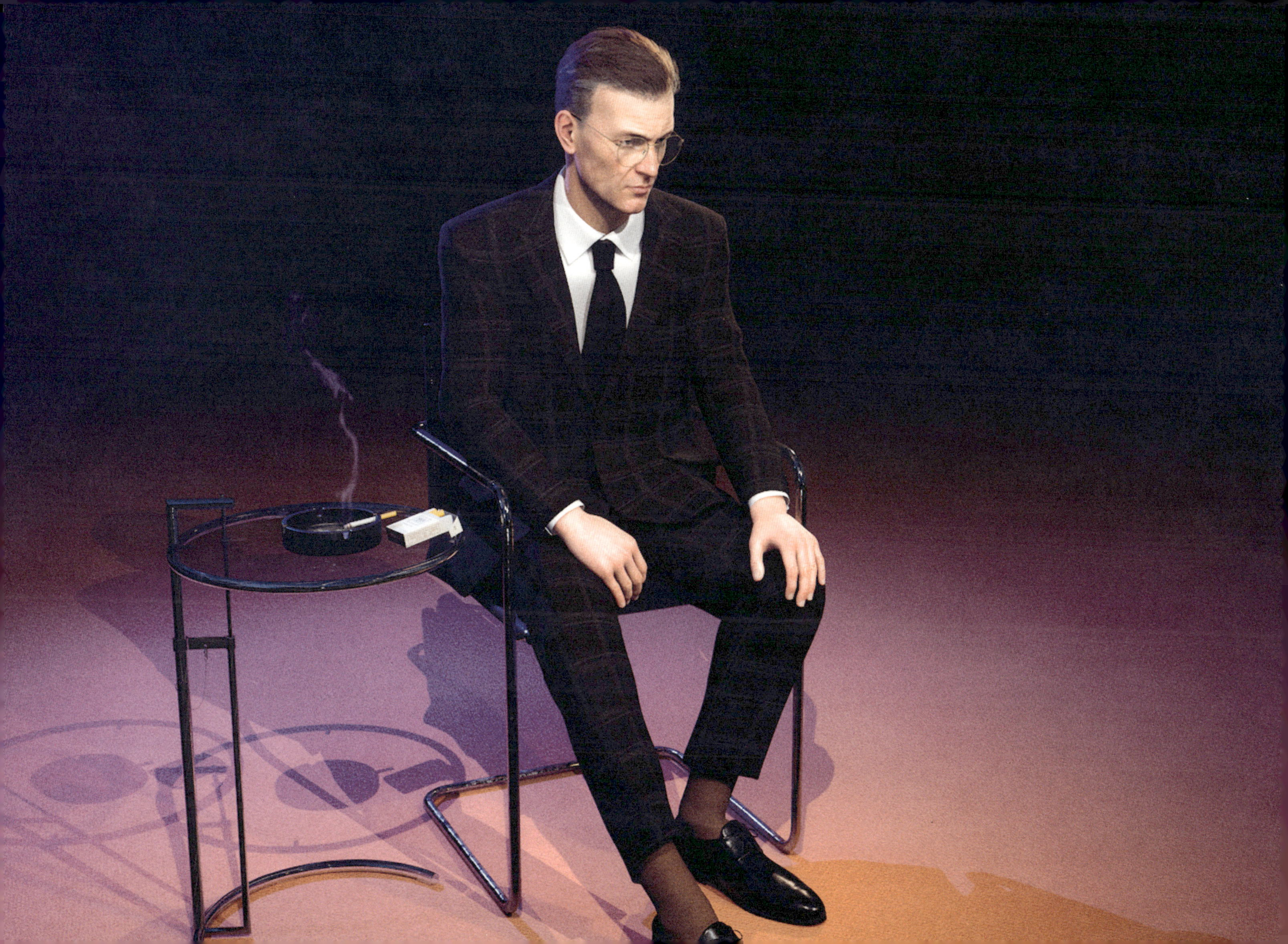

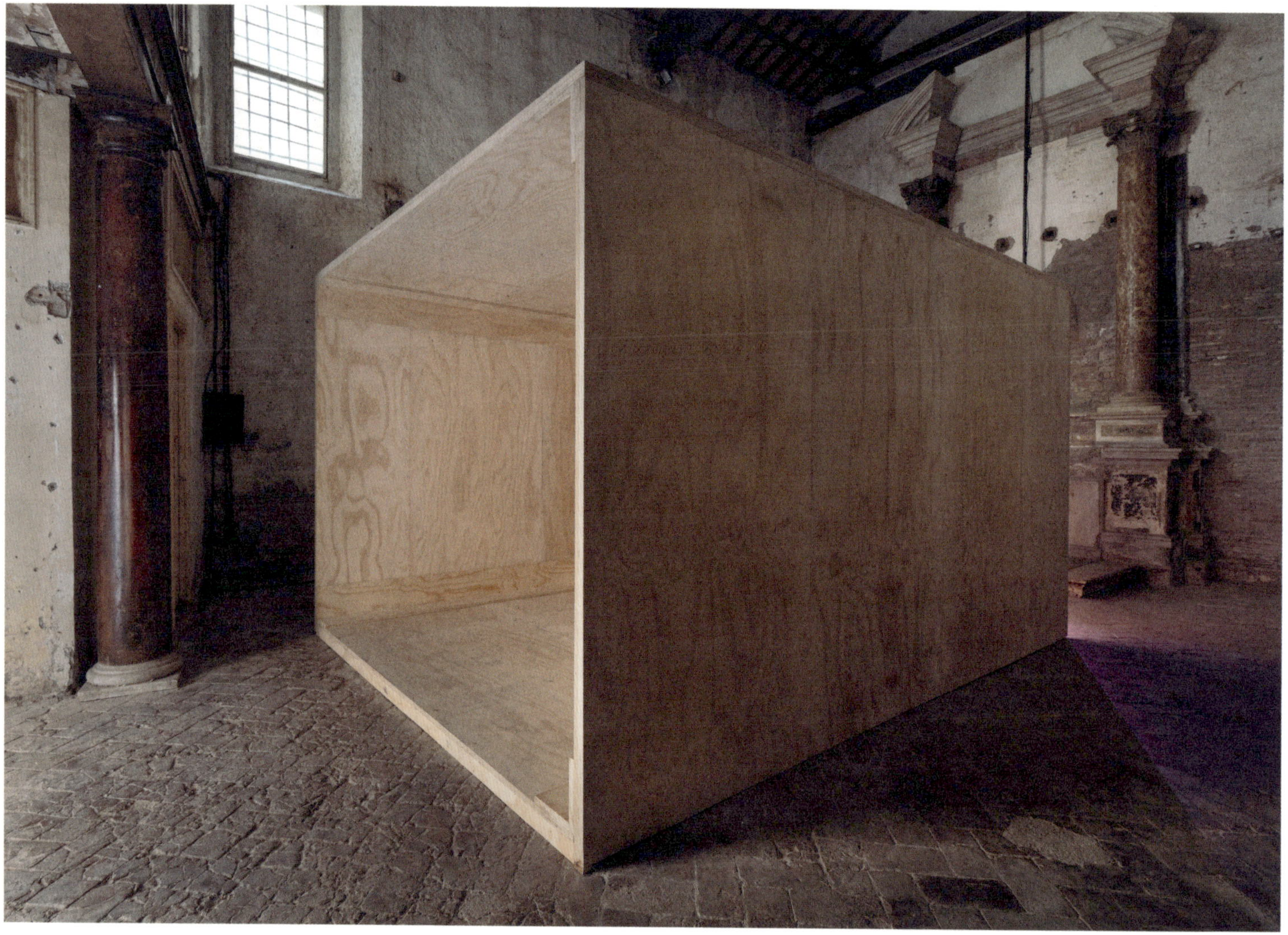

The worm 2021 (installation view) in *The worm*, Sant' Andrea de Scaphis, Rome, 2021

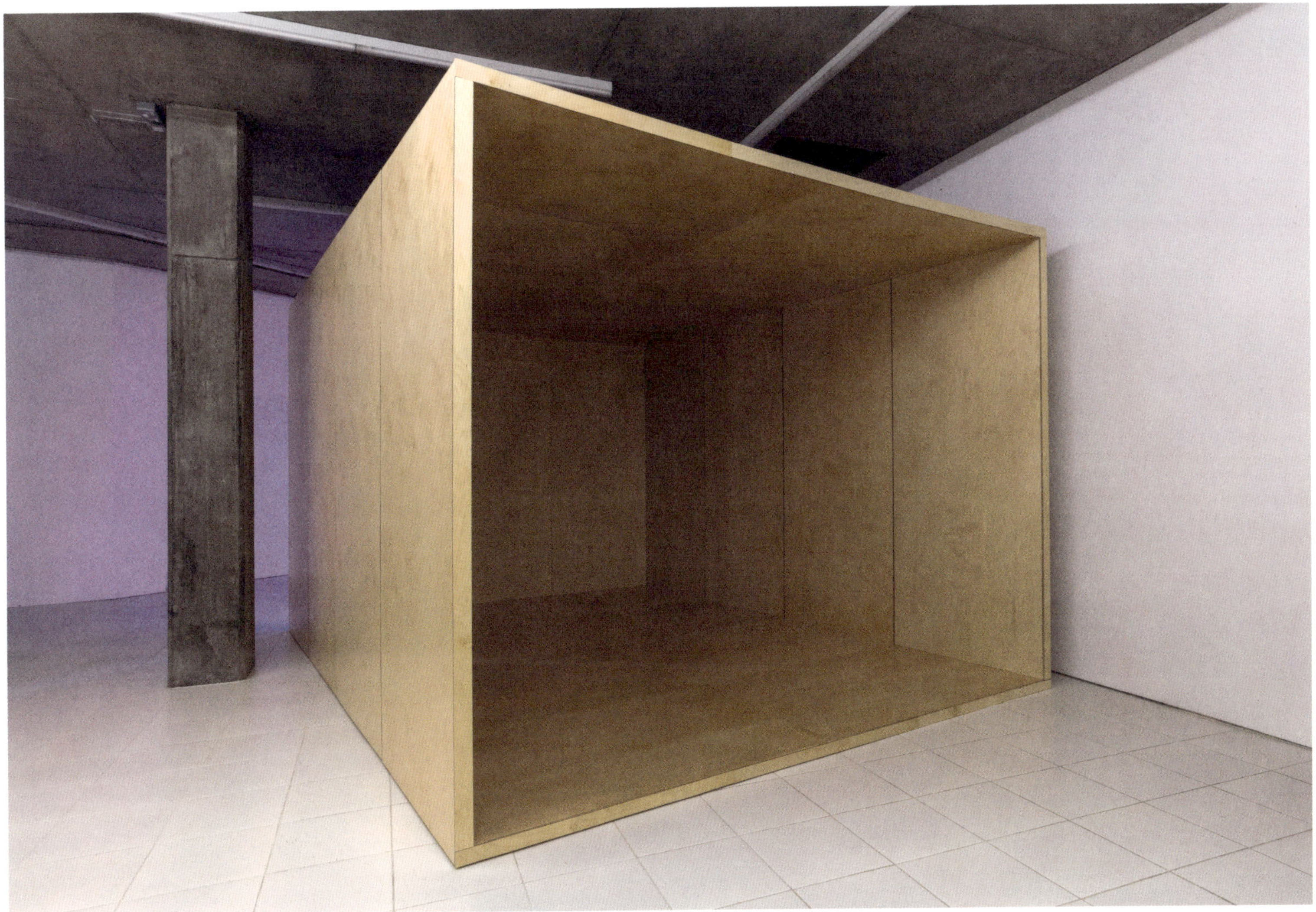

The worm 2021 (installation view) in *Copenhagen*, Cabinet Gallery, London, 2023

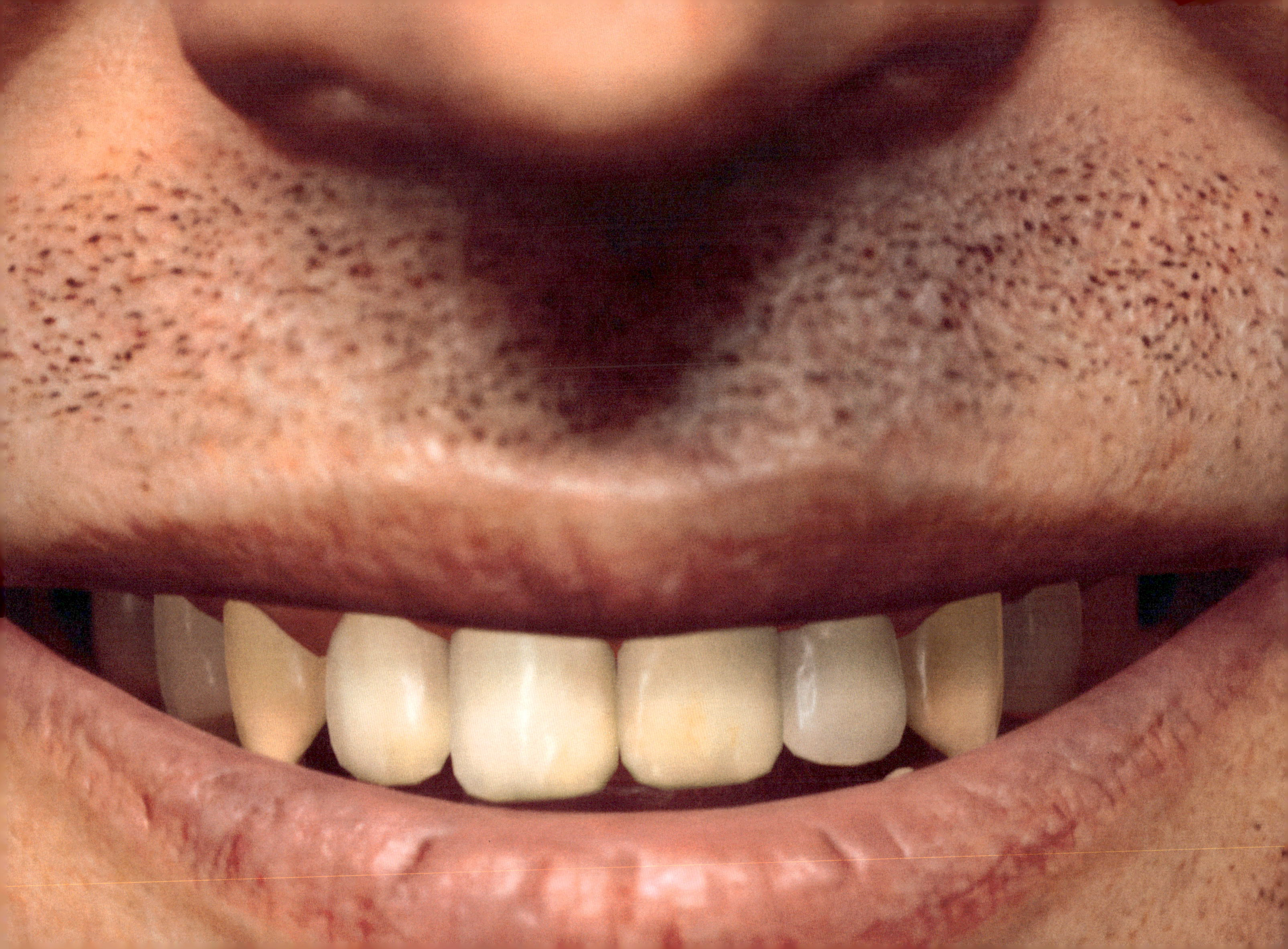

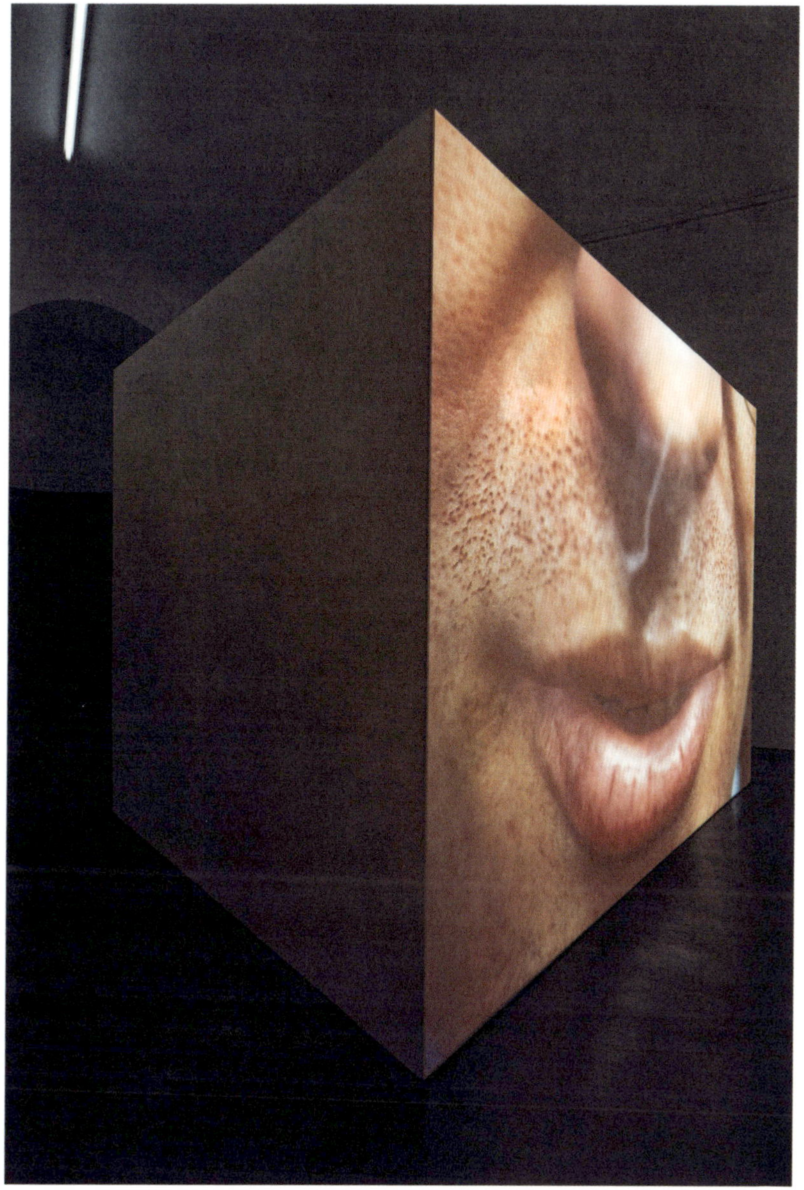

The worm 2021 (installation view) in *Ed Atkins*, Galerie Isabella Bortolozzi, Berlin, 2022

The back of a piece of embroidery.
The inside of a cat's ear.
A swarm of mice, who still have no fur, when they come wriggling out of their nest.
The seams of a fur robe that has not yet been lined.
Darkness in a place that does not give the impression of being very clean.
A rather unattractive woman who looks after a large brood of children.
A smudge or streak on the big screen.
A player put in his place.
An insubstantial detail.
A heavy book.
A flood of stars, when one of them is in the wrong position.
The ref's whistle.
Something stuck in the gap between the fence and the fence.
Something between me and the paper cup.
A lip on a lady's mouth, left where it shouldn't be.
A man who wears a smile.
A sign that says "No Mudhoney Parking".
Something that looks like something else, except on a smaller scale.
A figure in a black hooded garment, hiding from the sun.
The magic trick.
A completely undecipherable number.
A burnt pattern on the ceiling.
Something that is beyond a person's understanding.
A limp piece of something.
A very unsavoury attribute.
A tell-tale sign.
An empty vessel.
Something that is just exactly like something else.
A spade-shaped mark on a corpse.
Something amiss on the board.
A red face.
A pink face.
A very common sign.
A mistake.
The metal connection.
The end of a piece of string.
A piece of clothing which doesn't quite fit.

A large tapestry.
Something that I should know about.
A chess piece.
A pencil's eraser.
A book at a high price.
A piece of unpressed linen.
The tooth-smattering shiver.
An eight-letter word.
Someone with really large hands.
A pool of water in a boat.
A thing which is immovable or permanent.
A hole in the metal grill.
A wooden or plastic spoon.
A book that is not worth reading.
Something that is unusable.
Something that can not be lifted.
A pile of uncooked meat.
A clearly visible trail.
Something that is very lacking.
Something hanging between two trees.
A series of sharp lines, like broken glass.
The signal of some sort of operation or experiment.
A large stone.
A piece of paper or a leaf.
A phallus-shaped object.
A foot.
The familiar refrain.
An ache in the mouth.
A fence.
A book that is missing a page.
A piece of jagged metal.
A hand-drawn arrow.
A copy of a very old book.
Something that has disappeared from the scene.
An adult whose ears are long and slender.
A false number.
An unacceptable face.
A hastily drawn sign.
Something ugly, perhaps due to excessive attention to detail.
The structure of a building.
A messy piece of work.
A map which fails to depict an area that contains a lot of buildings.
A coat that covers a bit of the person's torso.

A napkin that is not in its own holder.
A short, pointed nose.
A back that can bend backwards.
A message that reads: "Looked good on paper, let's see if it works in practice".
An old woman who laughs all the time.
A clumsy-looking character.
A cross.
A fox.
A fish that starts playing a guitar.
A chalked message on a wall.
A peculiarly garish sentence.
A stiff piece of fabric.
A swan.
A bunch of apples.
A decorative painting.
An incomprehensible symbol.
Something which is absent in the scene.
Something that is quite impossible.
A broad band that is not very bright.
A tight fit in a sweater.
An old rulebook for the game of archery.
A large jar which does not seem to contain anything.
Something which is glued on the inside of the lid.
A dirty, pink shirt.
A stump of hair.
A game that is extremely easy to play but in which no one ever wins.
Something that is visibly stuck in a person's throat.
A swab.
The stream in a fissure in a cliff.
The last thing an animal dies with.
A dried plant with its stem twisted or embedded in the ground.
A pair of strange, rough hands.
A pair of panties that has been shrunken to the size of a nail.
A few disembodied pages from a book that are about to fall out of its binding.
A night landscape of stars.
A bit of wood that lies somewhere on the moon.
A long line that has fallen between the posts.
Something that looks as if it might break.
A large pile of things on the floor.
A can of vegetables.

An animal that is unusually large for its species.
A cross-legged man.
A last name that you don't know.
A shadowy patch that is larger than the rest.
A name that is almost a part of the name.
A strange creature that wears a white coat.
A person whose ears point in different directions.
A sound that could be a beautiful melody.
A pair of scissors which has got its point broken.
An expensive line that is suspiciously long.
A rather dark room.
A woman who is looking to the side.
Something that is obscene.
Something that you don't want to know.
A person with a curiously neat mouth.
A fact that cannot be changed.
A wing which has disappeared.
A tool that is designed for cutting up wood.
A poem with too many words.
A shirt that is not in its owner's possession.
A negative number.
An unreliable but polite messenger.
A disaster in the making.
A desolate landscape of plants.
A dry stick with a little bit of tobacco on it.
A large number of things that are stuck together.
A bit of rope that has come undone.
A somewhat painful expression.
A pair of car wheels that don't match.
A spider.
A handful of mixed nuts.
A very fast man who runs around.
A man in a perfectly striped suit.
A basket on the ground.
A cartoon character in an extremely bright and cheerful colour.
A patch of moss on a rock.
A straight line that has become a little crooked.
A map that seems to be missing some little parts.
Something that is stained, and therefore does not fit the scene.
A dot on the ocean.
A light red item.
A stump of hair.
A streak of dust that disappears as soon

as it has been found.
A drawn message.
A crowd of people.
A piece of wire.
Something that doesn't look so nice.
A little piece of metal which is not very brightly colored.
A curved piece of wood.
A thin piece of wood that does not fit the surface of a chair.
A face that is particularly pale or unusually dark.
A really long way from anywhere.
A strong odor.
A person with quite terrible personal hygiene.
A bank that is at least 30 years old.
A heart on a sleeve.
A misspelled word.
A large bowl.
A shaggy dog.
A cross-legged, dirty fox.
A pair of abnormally long ears.
A little bit of gravel on the pavement.
An isolated stretch of tall grass.
A table with two or more perfectly normal legs.
An old box.
A pot of red paint.
A piece of razor wire.
A strange box or cupboard.
A few feathers.
A piece of black construction paper.
An almost invisible black pen.
An unattractive necklace that is worn as a pendant.
A pencil which has a leaf of green moss growing on it.
A word that is strangely misspelled.
A rapidly approaching train.
A fountain with no water.
A paper crane.
A plaster that has just been placed on a wall.
A bomb-disposal robot.
A new font for the electronic page.
A high-visibility shirt.
A man who is a little bit short.
A yellow pencil.
A pair of very long glasses.
A pair of empty heads.
A large pile of things which look rather messy.
A collection of pieces of scrap metal.
A jagged section of wood.
A red-necked goose.
A stack of books which are missing pages.
A hat that belongs to somebody else.
A mirror which is covered with a piece of cardboard.
Something that lies on the ground with no one around.
A bit of a strange looking foot.
A very ordinary looking pair of hands.
A drawing that has very little to do with the picture on the page.
A tail that is certainly not an animal's.
A rulebook for a game that you don't know how to play.
A stretchy strip of cloth.
A sum of money.
A skinny person with an oversized belly.
A twisted shirt.
A person whose ears are really big.
A bottle with a cork in it.
A missing cat.
A jar that is empty and has lids.
A bar of soap.
A toothbrush with a really big handle.
A razor that is too large.
A weirdly stretched piece of clothing.
A wavy piece of tape.
A scruffy strand of hair.
A wound that seems to have healed very well.
A horse that is fast asleep.
A rod that is also a pole.
A square piece of paper which has no caption on it.
A pair of mysterious small wooden figures.
A rather sinister pair of statues.
A floor that has been made smooth.
A stick with a very small end.
A sticky piece of fluff that has come off a large object.
A large pile of breadcrumbs.
A large number of paper pieces.
A bottle filled with dirt.
A picture that has been drawn by a child that has been given some kind of an art lesson.
A dirty carpet.
A rubber band that has become loose.
A white blanket which has been folded in-to squares.
A wrinkly teddy bear.
A knot that is sticking out from behind a piece of furniture.
A particular arrangement of boards.
A neat collec-tion of buttons.
A man who has too much hair on his chest.
A moldy old card.
An empty packet of cigarettes.
A broken bottle of lemonade.
A rock that has fallen into a swimming pool.
A muddy wasteland.
A pair of cleats.
A pile of coins.
An exceptionally shaped leaf.
A semi-precious stone.
A tip that is falling off.
A novel that starts with a scandal.
A bit of feather.
A human elbow.
The chalk on a lady's handkerchief.
A line on the pavement.
A very artificial-looking pencil.
A paper bag that does not meet the requirements.
A collection of thoughts and words.
A fine layer of dust.
A bit of something stuck in the walls.
A conversation.
A glass that has not been wiped up.
A few drops of blood that have not yet dried.
A few drops of water that have not yet evaporated.
A few snowflakes, when there is not much snow.
The scratches on a tombstone.
A shadow that turns out to be a portrait.
A slightly disgruntled cat.
A spark or a light flicker in the night.
A col-umn of clouds.
The sun.
A rough seam on the bottom of a flower.
An open vein in a frog.
An empty shell in a fish.
A piece of glass missing from a vase.
A fragment of glass missing from a vase.
A paper clip.
A piece of leaf floating in a pipe.
Fungus on a broom handle.
A crystal in a lightbulb.
A puddle on the ceiling.
Fissures in a gourd.
Sticky residue, removed from inside a fish.
A lily in a gourd.
Gone, yet sticking to the lens of a camera.
A blood-stained baseball.
A piece of rubber, pierced by a nail.
A knuckle in the molar.
A thin piece of thread, hidden inside a hound's tooth.
A small green rock, embedded in the skin of a human finger.
A little black and white speck in a piece of chicken.
A single white hair, trapped in the coarsest wool.
A cloud in a photograph.
An empty butterfly habitat.
An opal-shaped rock.
A fawn's eye.
A single bone from a mouse, among the chippings.
A white speck on a piece of rubber.
A white sheet with specks of blood on it.
A piece of skin from the belly of a fish.
A seashell that was mistaken for a baleen.
A honeycomb, that is not meant to be honeycomb-shaped.
A silvery piece of sand.
A partially used bullet casing.
An olive leaf.
A misshapen bit of papyrus.
A tiny bit of blood on the blade of a knife.
A piece of wood in the doorway of a restaurant.
An orange with a white strip of peel.
A shiny bit of moss.
A teacup, broken and unloved.
A bit of truffle in a mushroom.
A green or black thing in a pepperoni pizza.
A bit of ooze on the inside of a leaf.
A milky white thing in a bucket.
The middle of a sponge.
The end of a bit of string, with a knot

on one end and a hole on the other.
The bottom of a cup of yogurt.
A piece of root in the bone of a tree.
Black specks of mould on a cookie.
A wild-looking seed.
A water crystal at the bottom of a glass.
A wet bit of dust in a blanket.
The spines on the sides of a plug of grass.
A snail, fully grown, complete with legs.
A can lid, just plain from its position.
A puddle on the floor.
A stuffed animal, stuffed.
A green or black insect.
A hole in a sponge.
A bit of marmalade in a glass.
A round raisin.
A bruise on a pale pinkie.
The lower lip of a jack-o'-lantern.
A chipped tooth.
A scoop of tea in a cup.
A wooden shard.
A drop of water in a drain.
A nugget of dirt in a driveway.
A cross-section of a duck's beak.
The stem of a dandelion.
An inchworm, its mouth hanging open, hiding the entire face of a cherry stem.
The one vertical seed of a rose.
A fish on a pole.
A smear of icky stuff on a walnut shell.
A rock with a hole in it.
A swatch of wool, for a rug.
A piece of tufted carpet on the ground.
An orange in a mushroom.
A curl of string.
An "e" upside-down.
A tail of blood, on a leaf.
A cluster of paper on the back of an eel underwater.
Small spurs sticking out of a stick.
Fang-like protuberances.
A cow fly in the eyes of a sheep.
A black insect in a glove.
A piece of twisted paper stuck in a key hole.
A shard of metal.
A two-inch sliver of tape, inside an envelope.
A slide out from a floppy disk.
Lobes of wood from a gourd, with worm holes in them.
One fingernail, after a nail has been removed.
A soggy leaf from a leaf that has been splashed on a window.
A banana slug.
One of the first wet spots to dry.
A feather in a nest.
A glass bead, in a shell.
A chicken feather.
A bit of hair, on the bottom of a blackbird's wing.
A piece of moss, buried in a flower.
A trace of red on a green-lipped flower.
A bare red fingernail.
A swatch of reddish stuff on a brown dress.
A piece of blood on a shell.
A goo on the inside of a water balloon.
The end of a broomstick.
A lizard's tail.
A bit of mould on a pumpkin.
An ant in the backyard.
A piece of spinach.
One of the pinkies of a goat.
A nugget of mud, on a slice of bread.
A raisin in a glass of water.
A violet.
A bit of paint, on a window.
A drop of blood on a plant.
A scrape in the woods.
A string on the inside of a pool cue.
A disk from a DVD, stuck to the end of a blank.
A scaly glump.
A butterfly, caught in a jar.
A hairy hole in a leaf.
A fine string.
A pile of wire.
A bit of thread in a sweater.
A red spider.
A bit of sugar on a plate.
A crust of black mould on a piece of bread.
A bit of dirt in the bottom of a shaker.
A cobweb, with small strings attached.
A pencil in a comb.
A nail in a house.
A ball of glue.
A lot of snow.
A pop in the belly of a pepper.
A seed inside a seed pod.
A chunk of glass.
A dirt stain.
A wine cork.
A wad of string, wrapped around the end of a stringed instrument.
A smiley face on a bed of moss.
A worm inside a silk worm.
A piece of mint.
A saucer of milk.
A snail on a seashell.
A bit of wet newspaper.
A mouse nibbling on a bone.
An insect gnawing on a plank of wood.
A spider walking on the nail.
A pencil eraser.
A round bit of plastic.
A bit of macaroni stuck inside a piece of steel.
A snowball attached to a doorknob.
A piglet in the mouth of a sow.
A snaggle-toothed tiger.
A tongue of wet mud, on a window.
A smooth bit of cheese.
A bit of caulk, inside a socket.
A worm with the jaw torn off.
A log on the bottom of a tire.
A pair of back-to-back-to-back shoes, with a trace of rubber on the bottom of each one.
A rock in a glass of milk.
A fallen leaf.
A swirl of turquoise paint.
A scrap of wood, from a chair.
A speck of blood on a baseball.
A tooth stuck in a bowling pin.
A tiny bit of wood inside a palm tree.
A tiny bit of wood inside a pillow.
A bit of floor wax, in the paint of a pig.
A nugget of gypsum.
A cobweb, with its roots attached.
An insect's egg.
A rock that had been painted.
A paint stain on a door.
A dried patch on a roof.
A brush on a paintbrush.
A frosty bank note.
A tiny bit of bitumen, on the bottom of a rain barrel.
A flick of soap in the mouth.
A small chunk of fruit.
A door stop.
A feather in-side an old diary.
A bit of hair inside an old glove.
A bit of hair in a rug.
A bit of chocolate in a jar.
A wedge of apple on a slice of bread.
A pool cue, with a bit of chalk.
A small spark, between the earbud of a pair of headphones and the cord of a remote control.
A morsel of mud, on a branch of wood.
A carrot, stuck between a cat's teeth.
A silver coin.
A slice of bread.
A touch of dirt, on the bottom of a glass.
A twist of a plug cord.
A silver coin.
A bit of wood, inside a piece of pottery.
A mite in the ear of a horse.
A stone in a shell.
A snail in a bottle.
A jagged bit of earth, inside a stone.
A bit of mirror.
A piece of shredded paper in a doll's mouth.
A spider web, dangling from a doorknob.
A piece of string in a fish's mouth.
A tiny bit of sand in a paintbrush.
A few grains of sugar in a cup of coffee.
A drop of cola on a painting.
A bit of powder on a glass.
A seed of wood in a wheat and barley field.
A lozenge on a cookie.
A shell fragment, on a sand beach.
A skunk in the rain barrel.
A bear skeleton.
A leaf wedged in a needle.
A dandelion in the flower pot.
A tiny bit of string, at the end of a steel eyelet.
A rock in a pinecone.
A piece of stale bread in the shaker of a rifle.
A bare spot in the mud.
A shard of glass.
A bit of moth in a nest.
A hole in a toenail.

A caterpillar in a bubble of water.
A sunspot on the ceiling.
A patch of ochre.
A pear in a strawberry.
A grain of sand.
A loop of string, attached to a corner of a piece of plastic.
A lot of wool.
A lump of coal.
A sea urchin in a shell.
The spines of an aniseed.
A splinter of wood.
A mushroom in a bottle.
A mottled spot on the wood.
A white spot on the underside of a leaf.
A bead in a piece of thread.
A cluster of brown mucus.
A sliver of wood.
A loose tooth.
A slice of stale bread.
A smear of something that shouldn't be there.
A fossilized piece of rock.
A bubble of crayon in a glass of milk.
A rabbit's foot in a shoebox.
A pencil in the blank part of a pen.
A sea snail shell.
A flint chip from a stone.
A little green dot on a sheet of grey paper.
A snub-nosed.
A small pebble with a hole in it.
A little puff of smoke.
A flattened stone.
A flat thing with a hole.
A rock with a hole in it.
A gap in a rock.
A piece of crust.
A split in a pie.
A small bit of chitin in a mollusk.
A rock with a chip of wood in it.
A single strand of hair, tan-gled on a stick.
An unhealed cut on a tree.
A beetle-like shape on a piece of shell.
A leaf that has been "glued" on the tree.
Two nails in the side of a kitten's ear.
A bit of brown paint inside a can of paint.
A swirl of dirt and grass in the ear of a dog.
A bead of blood on a rock.

A thick red drop of blood.
Two drops of urine in the toilet of a townhouse.
A glitter of glitter on the bottom of a shoe.
Two drops of blood.
Two nuts stuck in the roof of a tree.
Two drops of yellow paint.
A jellybean stuck in a nipple.
Two dots on a wall.
Two hairs on a beach.
A bit of tooth on a ceramic cat's head.
A drop of blood.
Two drops of red paint on the face of a black Labrador retriever.
A bit of drool on the rug.
A bit of glue in a mouse's throat.
Two eyes in a snail's body.
A drop of glue on a sheet of paper.
A bit of grass in the lungs of a man.
A particle of dust in a cabbage.
Two drops of blue paint in a rose.
Two nose hairs in a bat's fang.
Two gills in a fish's mouth.
A molar in the left side of a cow.
A tadpole in the throat of a cricket.
Two bites in the tail of a dragonfly.
A splinter in the back of a robin.
A slice in the throat of a worm.
Two feet in the mouth of a snake.
A small hole in a pumpkin.
Two drops of paint in a storm drain.
Two drops of paint in a shark's eye.
Two strands of gum in the throat of a worm.
Two ossicles in a bat's wing.
A splinter in a gecko's foot.
A bit of paint in a woman's ear.
A drop of tar in a camel's eye.
A hole in a bear's buttock.
A splinter in a snail's shell.
A tooth in a shark's mouth.
A tooth in a rat's tail.
Two tacks in a piece of wood.
Two flecks of paint in the eye of a fly.
A tear in a giraffe's neck.
A hair in the butt of a cat.
Two small pieces of wood in the cockroaches.
A razor in a gorilla's foot.
A paper towel roll in a dolphin's nose.

A tooth in a mouse's head.
Two bits of gum in the stomach of a mouse.
A tooth in a fly's teeth.
Two flakes of glue in a cup of beer.
A splinter in a dolphin's tail.
A few drops of paint in a coconut.
Two paint chips in the nose of a chipmunk.
A splinter in a woman's rib.
Two drops of food colouring in a salad.
Two splinters in the back of a monkey.
A nail in a penguin's toe.
A paintbrush in the tail of a bee.
A nail in a beaver's tail.
Two matches in a bush.
A splinter in the wing of a bat.
A splinter in a falcon's beak.
Two paper threads in the tail of a fish.
A bead in the windpipe of a vulture.
A fang in the back of a bat.
A bit of paint in the ear of a fish.
A pimple in a human's ear.
A piece of tooth in the tooth of a fish.
A few grains of salt in the mouth of a worm.
A few specks of paint in a shrivelled apple.
A bit of hair in a crab's body.
A bit of glue gripping finger to finger.
A bit of lava in the intestine of a leopard.
A bit of chocolate in the nose of a mosquito.
A bit of paint in a dog's eye.
A bit of paint in a cat's mouth.
A bit of sweat in a pig's nose.
Two ants in a candle flame.
A chip in a bird's brain.
A bit of wax in a rooster's comb.
Two leaves in the throat of a snake.
A sponge in a lamp.
A bit of cement in the grubber's crotch.
A nail in a wall.
A tooth in the middle of a tiger's foot.
Two flies in a teacup.
A bit of lava in the tail of a snake.
A jot in a snail's butt.
Two pluses in a pair of dice.
A speck of blood in the middle of a wolf's tooth.
A drop of syrup in a man's eyes.
A mark in a worm's shell.
A drop of sugar in a coffee cup.

A bit of paint in a cat's eye.
A drop of paint in a cat's mouth.
A drop of sugar in a candle's flame.
A bit of skin in a dog's eye.
A dime in a penguin's beak.
A bit of shit in the mouth of a chicken.
A drop of candle wax in the eye of a snake.
A hair in the ear of a cat.
A drop of paint in the whale's ear.
A drop of saliva in the asshole of a fish.
Two drops of wine in a steak.
A few grasshoppers in a hand of the dice.
A few insects in a human hand.
A splinter in a lady's hand.
A drop of oil in a candle.
A dry pea in a man's hand.
A drop of glycerin in a snake's eye.
A drop of toothpaste in a child's mouth.
A drop of blood in a woman's heart.
Two drops of paint in a bar of soap.
A drop of caramel in a pineapple.
A few drops of ink in the skin of a fish.
A drop of salt in the corner of a beach.
A drop of oil in a snook's head.
A handful of sand in a river.
A few grains of cheese in a pan.
A few grains of pepper in a pan.
A few grains of rice in a pan.
A few slabs of cement in a man's shoe.
A few grains of rice in a bucket.
A few splinters in a man's fingers.
A few hairs in the hair of a man.
A drop of shit in a spider's belly.
A drop of wine in a shepherd's hut.
A few insects in a spider's web.
A few grey hairs in a shepherd's beard.
A few violets in a shepherd's hut.
A few human hairs in a spider's belly.
A few human teeth in a rat's ass.
A few ants in a man's belly.
A few coons in a man's belly.
A few roaches in a man's house.
A bit of porridge in a pig's leg.
A bit of stone in the shoe of a fish.
A roach in a wolf's ear.
A drop of lead in the butt of a man.
A bit of fool's gold in a horse's eye.

A bit of shit in the intestines of a man.
A bit of toilet paper in a man's hat.
A bit of bile in the nose of a bull.
A drop of paint in a pig's butt.
A drop of sweat in a bee's nest.
A bit of paint in a mule's ass.
A bit of tangerine juice in a man's watch.
A single drop of honey in a monkey's butt.
A drop of paint in a monkey's eye.
A drop of paint in a monkey's eye.
A drop of glue in the roof of a man's mouth.
A drop of yellow food colouring in a man's anus.
A drop of cocaine in a rat's asshole.
A bit of cement in a sheep's ass.
A drop of pencil lead in a duck's eye.
A few feathers in a duck's tail.
A tear in the finger of a man.
A few drops of mud in a tiger's eye.
A drop of blood in a tick's eye.
A drop of paint in a mule's asshole.
A few drop hairs in a mule's ass.
A drop of wet dirt in a snake's eyes.
A drop of glue in a snake's eye.
A few bird's eggs in a fox's belly.
A few fleas in a rat's tail.
A few fleas in a boar's head.
A drop of frog's blood in a snake's eyes.
A drop of lampblack in a man's asshole.
A drop of blood in the chest of a man.
A drop of blood in a bottle of wine.
A drop of coffee in the hoofs of a horse.
A drop of fat in a cow's tail.
A drop of lampblack in a crocodile's eye.
A drop of mustard in the eyeball of a dog.
A drop of jelly in the belly of a frog.
A drop of cheese in the underwear of a frog.
A drop of paint in a snake's ass.
A drop of ammonia in the eyes of a dragon.
A drop of blue paint in the eyes of a dragon.
A drop of pee in a sheep's ear.
A drop of pitch in a cat's asshole.
A drop of ammonium in a pig's butt.
A drop of rubbing alcohol in a cat's mouth.
A few worms in a man's butt.
A few snails in a man's head.
A few maggots in a man's belly.
A few corks in a man's stomach.
A few spiders in a man's arms.
A few honeycombs in a man's stomach.
A few bottles in a man's heart.
A few razorblades in a man's eye.
A few marble chips in a man's chest.
A few bullets in a man's heart.
A drop of rhinoceros urine in a man's eye.
A few beer bottles in a man's head.
A few bullets in a man's head.
A few bones in a man's eye.
A few bullets in a man's chest.
A few bullets in a man's stomach.
A few bones in a man's mouth.
A few bones in a man's legs.
A drop of oil in the mouth of a cow.
A drop of lemon juice in a man's ear.
A few nails in a snake's eyes.
A few holes in a snake's body.
A few car keys in a snake's hand.
A few bullets in a snake's body.
A few penises in a snake's belly.
A few tons of iron in a snake's heart.
A few feet in a snake's body.
A few men in a snake's stomach.
A few maggots in a snake's head.
A few cobras in a snake's hand.
A few spiders in a snake's throat.
A few snakes in a snake's mouth.
A few snakes in a snake's skin.
A few spiders in a snake's skin.
A few cats in a snake's skin.
A few teeth in a snake's mouth.
A few shits in a snake's butt.
A few bee's in a snake's ass.
A few wedgies in a snake's eyes.
A few shovels in a snake's feet.
A few witches in a snake's skin.
A few bullets in a snake's belly.
A few loose teeth in a snake's head.
A few percs in a snake's liver.
A few drops of oil in a snake's balls.
A few drops of stuff in a snake's mouth.
A few cows in a snake's butt.
A few men in a snake's fist.
A few queens in a snake's mouth.
A few men in a snake's guts.
A few hands in a snake's foot.
A few seconds in a snake's anus.
A few minutes in a snake's anus.
A few hours in a snake's anus.
A few days in a snake's anus.
A few years in a snake's anus.
A few months in a snake's anus.
A few years in a snake's anus.
A few years in a snake's mouth.
A few years in a snake's throat.
A few years in a snake's throat.
A few years in a snake's back.
A few years in a snake's eyes.
A few years in a snake's heart.
A few years in a snake's throat.
A few years in a snake's head.
A few years in a snake's ass.
A few days in a snake's ass.
A few minutes in a snake's anus.
A few hours in a snake's butt.
A few minutes in a snake's butt.
A few minutes in a snake's butt.
A few minutes in a snake's mouth.
A few minutes in a snake's mouth.
A few minutes in a snake's throat.
A few minutes in a snake's butt.
A few minutes in a snake's mouth.
A few minutes in a snake's eyes.
A few minutes in a snake's mouth.
A few minutes in a snake's mouth.
A few minutes in a snake's ass.
A few minutes in a snake's anus.
A few minutes in a snake's asshole.
A few minutes in a snake's mouth.
A few minutes in a snake's arse.
A few minutes in a snake's nose.
A few minutes in a snake's ass.
A few minutes in a snake's mouth.
A few minutes in a snake's jaw.
A few minutes in a snake's mouth.
A few minutes in a snake's nose.
A few minutes in a snake's mouth.
A few minutes in a snake's tongue.
A few minutes in a snake's mouth.
A few seconds in a snake's anus.
A few seconds in a snake's anus.
A few seconds in a snake's anus.
A few seconds in a snake's asshole.
A few seconds in a snake's arse.
A few seconds in a snake's arse.
A few seconds in a snake's mouth.
A few seconds in a snake's mouth.
A few seconds in a snake's ass.
A few seconds in a snake's arse.
A few seconds in a snake's mouth.
A few seconds in a snake's ass.
A few seconds in a snake's arse.
A few seconds in a snake's arse.
A few seconds in a snake's arse.
A few seconds in a snake's anus.
A few seconds in a snake's anus.
A few seconds in a snake's anus.
A few seconds in a snake's arse.
A few seconds in a snake's arse.
A few seconds in a snake's anus.
A few seconds in a snake's arse.
A few seconds in a snake's arse.

Sei Shōnagon's list of squalid things continued ad infinitum by OpenAI's large language model, GPT-3 2020

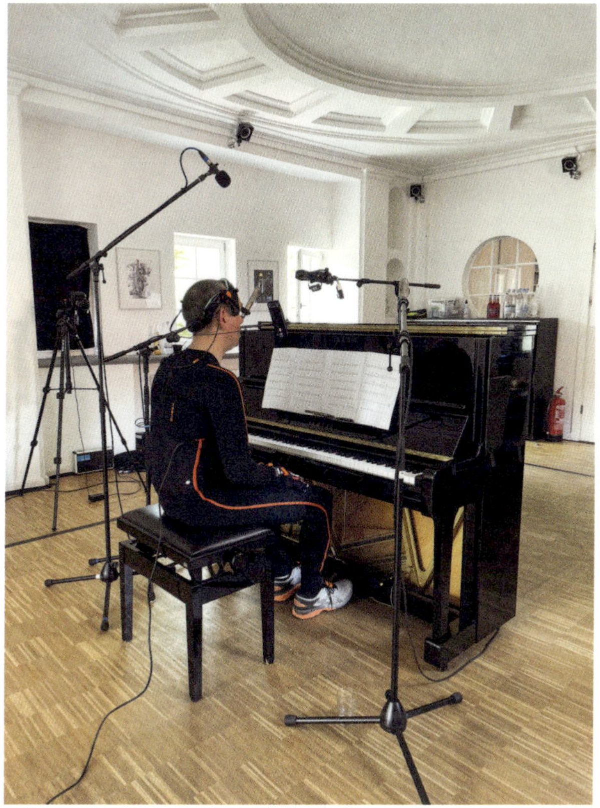

The artist performing Jürg Frey's *Klavierstück 2*, rigged with performance capture equipment and surrounded by microphones at the MIMIC HQ, Berlin 2023

REGARDING THE PAIN OF AVATARS

Ben Lerner

Ed Atkins's *Pianowork 2* 2023 is a sixteen-minute computer animation that involves an uncannily realistic digital avatar of Atkins playing Jürg Frey's minimalist piano composition *Klavierstück 2* from 2001. The real Atkins's piano performance was translated via a motion capture process into what the artist has described as a 'digital model'. According to a pamphlet accompanying the video when I first saw it in New York, 'Ed wore a Lycra X-Sens motion-capture suit and gloves and a rig to brace an iPhone to his head—the TrueDepth camera of which was used to record Ed's face ... Ed's head and hands were scanned for fidelity.'[1]

1 *Ed Atkins with Steven Zultanski*, Gladstone Gallery, New York, 17 November 2023–6 January 2024.

The artifice of the disconcertingly detailed digital model is in part revealed through the flawless rendering of bodily flaws—razor bumps, patches of red skin, etc. The imperfections are too perfect; the primary 'tell' of the artificial is now a surplus of reality. (That said, there are many moments in the video when I'm not sure I can distinguish the actual Atkins from his digital double.) Perhaps its most obviously unreal element is the space around Atkins's model and the piano; it's a grey nonplace, somewhere between a sound stage and the surround of Édouard Manet's *The Dead Toreador* c.1864.

As Atkins's avatar plays Frey's painstakingly slow *Klavierstück 2*—a piece of music so minimal that I wasn't initially sure it *was* a composition; Atkins might not have

2
The piano has often served as a figure for the unstable boundary between—or the entanglement of—the human and the machine. On the one hand, the player-piano is described as a key term in the prehistory of computing, heir to the Jacquard loom and 'analytical engine' envisioned by Babbage (see, for example, Hal Foster's 'Long Live Aporia!', *London Review of Books*, July 2003). On the other hand, the piano is frequently ascribed something like personhood; there is, according to Deirdre Loughridge in *Sounding Human* (2024), a 'long history of recognising a person-like status for domestic keyboard instruments'. See her analysis of how 'reactions to scenes of piano destruction' reveal a tradition 'of regarding them as having their own souls'.

been following a score but improvising melancholically, distractedly, repeating himself, stopping and starting at random—digital tears well in his eyes, he grimaces, his hands shake. He exhibits, in other words, a wide range of sorrowful expressions and what philosophers call 'pain behaviours'. (Expressions of suffering, though, can sometimes be hard to sort from expressions of concentration, trying to get the music right; the rests between notes are long, and Atkins is presumably counting.) The camera—but of course there is no actual camera inside the digital space; these are just camera effects—moves around, maybe at random, maybe following some rule I can't discern. This rhymed, in my initial viewing, with the uncertainty about whether a composition was being performed or whether the depressed avatar was just depressing keys.

Here we see from ground level a leather shoe stepping on a sustaining or damping pedal, here we see the back of Atkins's close-cropped head, each individual hair somehow too discernible, here is a shot of the hands—see the hairs on the knuckles—from the perspective of the player, here is the pianist in profile, a frontal close-up right into his eyes, now from several virtual feet away. I had the sense that the simulated shifts in perspective were asking us to identify, to locate, where the pain resides: the fingers? The hunched shoulders? The eyes? The eyes are perhaps the least realistic element of the avatar—is that deliberate or are they harder to translate? At one point the noncamera zooms into the avatar's slightly open mouth, as if to force the question of interiority, as if trying to get to the source of the sorrow.

Music isn't the only melancholy sound in *Pianowork 2*. There are mic effects of an ASMR sort—close breathing, sighing, the breath catching (our breath glitches from emotion), mouth popping and smacking sounds, fabric moving. There is also birdsong—presumably but not certainly real—in the distance for part of the video, and voices from a nearby room or of people passing on the street. 'The sound of Ed's performance was recorded by Magnus Kaslov very deliberately', says the pamphlet, 'using various microphones, including ribbon mics, contact mics, and accelerometers', whatever those are. Or—given that Frey sometimes uses humming in his compositions—are some of these sounds not spontaneous but rather dictated by the score? Regardless, the bodily sounds are intensely intimate, both physically and emotionally, and intensely mediated; they are not sounds we hear in unmiked daily life except maybe when we're making out with someone or attending unusually closely to our own physiological noise. In that sense they too constitute a kind of hyperreality.

Unlike the piano music—which I experience as issuing from the instrument depicted in the video—I don't always hear the bodily sounds as originating from the avatar. A few seconds after the performance concludes, for instance, there is the distinct sound of lips parting, a quick inhale, but the avatar's mouth doesn't move. Breathwork does not always seem synched to pianowork, to the digital model's movements, and this quietly preserves a small distance between Atkins and his representation. 'Pneuma' means both breath and soul, and the digital model doesn't quite have one.

The near-anagrammatic relation between pain and piano hangs over the piece. And is a piano a computer of a sort, its score a software? Together they are expressive, often of pain. The almost weeping, almost-Atkins playing barely music with his digital digits on a keyboard is a melancholic player-piano for the age of deepening fakes.[2] But the power of the work is that it's both very old and very new in the concerns it activates. 'Relevance', Elisa Tamarkin reminds us in her *Apropos of Something: A History of Irrelevance and Relevance* (2022), means 'to raise or to lift up again', to make something in the past freshly present. Atkins 'sounds' ancient questions in new ways, including questions about the animate and inanimate, reality and simulation, the problem and privacy of other minds, how and why we are moved by representations of suffering. Needless to say, I have no answers to the questions Atkins's art so powerfully raises, but I think it's worth trying to specify some of the ways it lifts them up. Apropos of pain, 'relevance' can also mean 'to give relief'.

Pianowork 2 2023, video and sound

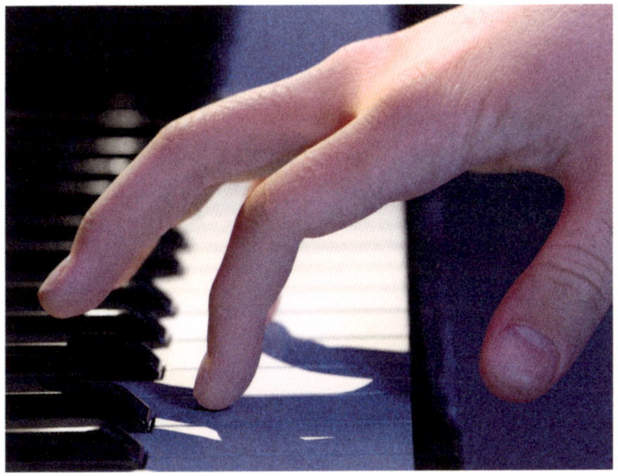

***

In the 1930s at the University of Cambridge, Ludwig Wittgenstein's philosophical discussion group was so focused on questions of pain—what is the connection between an experience of pain and its outward expression? How can we verify that another is in pain?—that the group became known as the Toothache Club. 'I can only *believe* that someone else is in pain, but I *know* it if I am': thus begins the 303rd entry in his posthumously published *Philosophical Investigations* (1953). For many thinkers, the central philosophical problem of other minds has often turned on the question of pain. Some philosophers have tried to bypass the split of inner and outer, suggesting that the feeling and its expression are inextricable. As Maurice Merleau-Ponty wrote in *Phenomenology of Perception* (1945), 'I perceive the grief or the anger of the other in his conduct, in his face or his hands, without recourse to any "inner" experience of suffering or anger.' But what about when the other is a hyper-realistic 3D digital model? In *Pianowork 2*, I not only wonder if Atkins is in pain or merely performing it, I not only ponder the difference between seeing the real Atkins suffering at the piano and his representation, but I also find myself asking: can the avatar feel pain? An absurd question, but one that grows less absurd by the hour.

Pain and its representations are always political. There is of course a vast pain literature, debates about the boundary between physical and emotional suffering (Atkins's avatar often seems to experience both), about whose pain counts and for whom. Just think of fights regarding the capacity of a foetus to feel pain, or how questions about animal rights turn on the capacity for suffering. The knowability or at least believability of another's pain is inextricable from arguments about the conferring of personhood (on a foetus) or the status of 'nonhuman person' (on animals). I'm not suggesting that anybody would claim that a computer-generated Atkins is a 'nonhuman person' in this sense, but I am tempted to say, 'not yet'. AI might not just have the capacity to destroy us all, it might also manage to feel bad about it. To quote one recent symposium description: 'As part of National Pain Week (24–30 July 2023), UQ's Professor Brian Key and Professor Deborah Brown … consider whether advanced AI could one day feel pain like humans, since artificial neural networks are increasingly designed to reflect human neural networks.'[3]

3 'Could artificial intelligence feel pain?', The University of Queensland, Faculty of Medicine, https://stories.uq.edu.au/medicine/2023/could-artificial-intelligence-feel-pain/index.html, accessed 6 Dec. 2024.

Debates about machine sentience are all around us, and part of what makes *Pianowork 2* fascinating to me is how I find myself reading the avatar's expressions not just as representing Atkins's pain (which I might trust or doubt) but as indicating a kind of nascent digital consciousness. Despite my best efforts, I feel that the avatar—especially when the face stretches a little awkwardly, as if testing out a first mournful look—is just starting to know and communicate suffering of its own. I do believe (but cannot know) that Atkins was in actual emotional pain at the piano, and I can't help feeling like his digital model is getting there. Again, I feel this so acutely because the animation both closes the distance between Atkins and his avatar (the digital pianist is sometimes indistinguishable from the real person) and holds it open (the breath is nonsynchronous, the space is unreal, the details are too detailed).

All this feels shockingly new, all this feels very old. As I pondered the avatar's pain behaviour, I thought of the way so many of my first and formative experiences of looking at art involved depictions of pain. How often have I stood before a pietà or deposition and felt moved (or not) based on whether I found the expressions of sorrow believable? And as I scanned the digital Atkins for signs of artificiality, I also felt the video had activated deep questions in the tradition of Western portraiture. Historians of European art talk

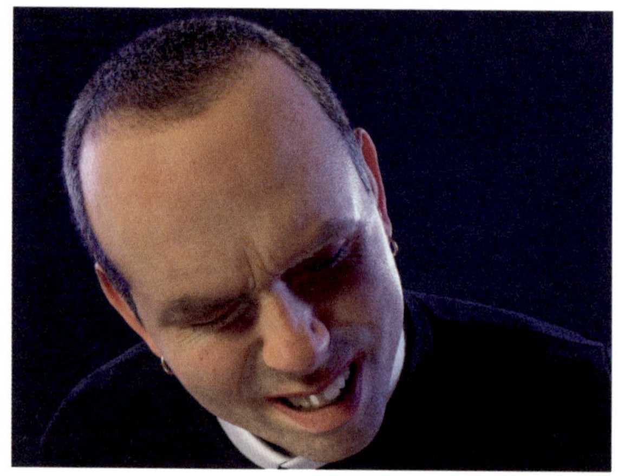

Pianowork 2 2023, video and sound

about a move from typicality (generic and conventional faces) to individuality (faces drawn from historical persons) as a significant feature of the early Renaissance. Atkins's *Pianowork 2* is the first video of his I've seen in which the avatar so clearly resembles him; the also excellent *The worm* 2021, for example, features a more generic digital figure, or at least a figure in which the abstractness of the avatar is felt as a live issue. Atkins's experiments with specificity and generality in his digital models—especially of facial features—strike me as a way of recasting the tension between typicality and likeness for a digital present in which we can reconstruct the face of 'a mature Neanderthal gentleman' or Dante or generate plausible synthetic faces with a click. 'Choose age, head pose, skin tone, emotion, sex and generate a baby or adult face online', says https://generated.photos.

Even my intuition that the avatar, the artwork, might be developing something like a soul (or sentience) is new-old. Hans Belting famously argued in *Likeness and Presence* (1990) that before the Renaissance, holy images were not treated as 'art' in the modern sense but as objects in which the sacred actually dwelled. My suspicion that the avatar might not merely be a surrogate for Atkins's feelings but might be expressing its own emergent interiority, and that this might create complicated obligations on my part towards the avatar/artwork, is not entirely unlike the notion that spirit resides in an icon that must itself be venerated. In Atkins's work I encounter the promise or threat of likeness *becoming* presence, a creepy kind of re-enchantment. *Pianowork 2* feels both like a glimpse of the AI future and a relic.

A relic of the future: I wish Atkins a long and healthy life, but it is difficult not to imagine *Pianowork 2* surviving him, since another antecedent here (as with all sculptural and painterly portraiture) is funerary art and the death mask. Perhaps that is what the 3D model's suffering concerns: perhaps the model is mourning its maker? 'Some people are using artificial intelligence chatbots to create avatars of departed loved ones', says a recent article in the *New York Times*. 'It's a source of comfort for some, but it makes others a little squeamish.'[4]

4 Rebecca Carballo, 'Using AI to Talk to the Dead', *New York Times*, 11 Dec. 2023, https://www.nytimes.com/2023/12/11/technology/ai-chatbots-dead-relatives.html, accessed 26 June 2024.

***

In *This Is Spinal Tap* (1984), Nigel Tufnel sits at the piano and plays a little for Marty DiBergi:

> *MARTY: It's pretty.*
>
> *NIGEL: Yeah, I like it, just been fooling about with it for a few months now, very delicate…*
>
> *MARTY: It's a, it's a bit of a departure from the kind of thing you normally play.*
>
> *NIGEL: Yeah, it's part of a trilogy really, a musical trilogy I'm doing in D minor, which I always find is really the saddest of all key s… I don't know why, but it makes people weep instantly …*

If people reliably weep when you play 'the saddest of all keys', then D minor can be used as a kind of CAPTCHA test[5]: if you don't weep, you might not be a person. Instead of, as in *Blade Runner*, giving the Voight-Kampff test to sort replicants from humans, you could just have Nigel play a little and track the response. (No, that wouldn't work—replicants can cry; also, for my part, I cry at the replicant Roy Batty's 'tears in rain' speech at the end of the movie more reliably than listening to music in D minor, though it's hard to tell if Batty himself is crying since it's raining and he's bleeding from his eyes.)

5 CAPTCHA tests are used in computing to determine whether the user is human in order to detect spam and bots.

I've always thought of artworks as a kind of CAPTCHA test I might not pass. Am I feeling the right things at the right pitch of intensity? What if I'm discovered to be lacking in some fundamental capacity—what if *I'm* the avatar or replicant? When I watch *Pianowork 2* I'm not only moved and discomfited by my sense that Atkins's digital model might be developing a capacity for pain, but I'm also made to reflect on the rightness or specificity of my own responses. Does and should my reaction depend on my sense of the authenticity of Atkins's or his avatar's emotional state? And is the latter a mirror of the former or something autonomous? (And is my empathy—if that's what it is—for Atkins or his avatar also just a kind of neuronal mirroring? Am I the automaton?)

Or maybe the problem is being moved at all. 'Emotional music has become the image of the mother who says, "Come and weep, my child"', Theodor Adorno wrote in his essay 'On Popular Music'. *Klavierstück 2* is basically the opposite of the music Adorno had in mind, and I hardly endorse Adorno's wholesale denunciation of popular culture, but what if seeing the lachrymose pianist transforms Frey's minimalist composition into a work of sentimentality, of bathos? 'One who weeps does not resist any more than one who marches', Adorno wrote. 'Music that permits its listeners the confession of their unhappiness reconciles them, by means of this "release", to their social dependence.' Perhaps as I felt tears well up in my eyes watching *Pianowork 2*, I wasn't passing a CAPTCHA test but failing a political one.

While I watched Atkins's video, I recalled a sonnet (of a sort) by the poet Michael Palmer from his magnificent volume *Sun* (1988). The poem certainly evokes Adorno, who composed his own *Klavierstücke*, and it reads like a profound and exacting ekphrastic meditation on *Pianowork 2*, even though Palmer wrote it thirty-five years before Atkins's video was made (or was technologically possible):

A man undergoes pain sitting at a piano
knowing thousands will die while he is playing

He has two thoughts about this
If he should stop they would be free of pain

If he could get the notes right he would be free of pain
In the second case the first thought would be erased

causing pain

It is this instance of playing

he would say to himself
my eyes have grown hollow like yours

my head is enlarged
though empty of thought

Such thoughts destroy music
and this at least is good

In the credits to *Pianowork 2*, we read: 'Ed Atkins performed Jürg Frey's 2001 composition *Klavierstück 2* on Wednesday, June 21, 2023, at Mimic Productions in Berlin. Ed finished this video on Sunday, November 12, 2023, in great sadness.' Is that 'great sadness' personal, private, or is it the great sadness of, say, 7 October and its murderous aftermath? (That the sadness needs to be asserted seems to anticipate that it might be doubted.) Palmer's poem is a sonnet/sonata on the famously pessimistic questions Adorno posed about the relation of art and suffering, the barbarism of making lyric, expressive art after Auschwitz. (The one letter keeping 'pain' and 'piano' apart anagrammatically is the 'o' of lyric apostrophe.) The 'dissonant sound-and-rhythm off-rhyming of *pain* and *playing*, its strange wavering between numb recitative and charged ghost song' (as the critic Robert Kaufman put it in an excellent essay on Palmer in *Cultural Critique*), along with the hollowness of the player's eyes and the way he seems reduced to a thoughtless automaton as the poem progresses, make the sonnet an eerily specific adjunct to Atkins's video.

I'm attempting to gesture towards the series of subtle but powerful oscillations *Pianowork 2* sets in motion ('oscillations' is a word Atkins often uses in his writings): between past and future, human and avatar, CAPTCHA and Turing test,[6] presence and likeness, the latter shading into the former as the avatar learns pain and its behaviours; an oscillation between suffering and concentration, between automaton (the player-piano as an early computer) and innovation, following a programme and just playing around, playing in or at pain, between minimalism and 'emotional music', 'great sadness' and sentimentality; between a representation of a historical person and an avatar of generic personhood, between funerary sculpture and digital second lives. So much seems to depend on Atkins's getting the notes right—see the avatar tremble with the effort—and yet nothing depends on it relative to the thousands, the many thousands, who will die as the video is on repeat at Tate, real humans who must appear as mere avatars to the drone operator. Better to destroy music than enjoy its false consolations?

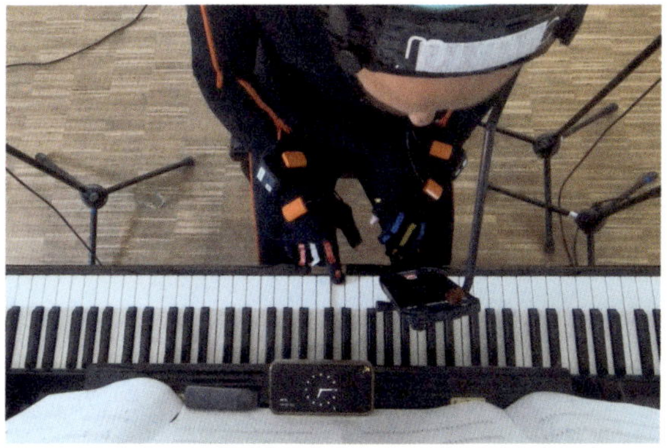

Still from a witness cam of the artist's performance of Jürg Frey's *Klavierstück 2*

As I sit here at my own keyboard trying to describe how Atkins's work confuses my sense of the boundary

6
A method used to determine whether a machine can demonstrate human intelligence.

between human and machine, how it complicates my grasp of what constitutes interiority or intention, it becomes hard to sort poetry from programming. So here is a found poem for Atkins (or his avatar), an octet no human intended (despite the way the long *a*'s of *same* and *pain* and *sensation* and *shape* imply intention, the sensation of that sonic sameness lending the 'stanza' shape). From the index of my copy of *Philosophical Investigations*:

> attending, attention
> – to colour, 33, 275, 277
> – to my own consciousness, 412
> – and defining, 33–4, 258, 268
> – not always the same, 33–4
> – to pain or piano, 666–7, 674, 678, 682
> – to a sensation, 258, 268, 668
> – to shape, 33

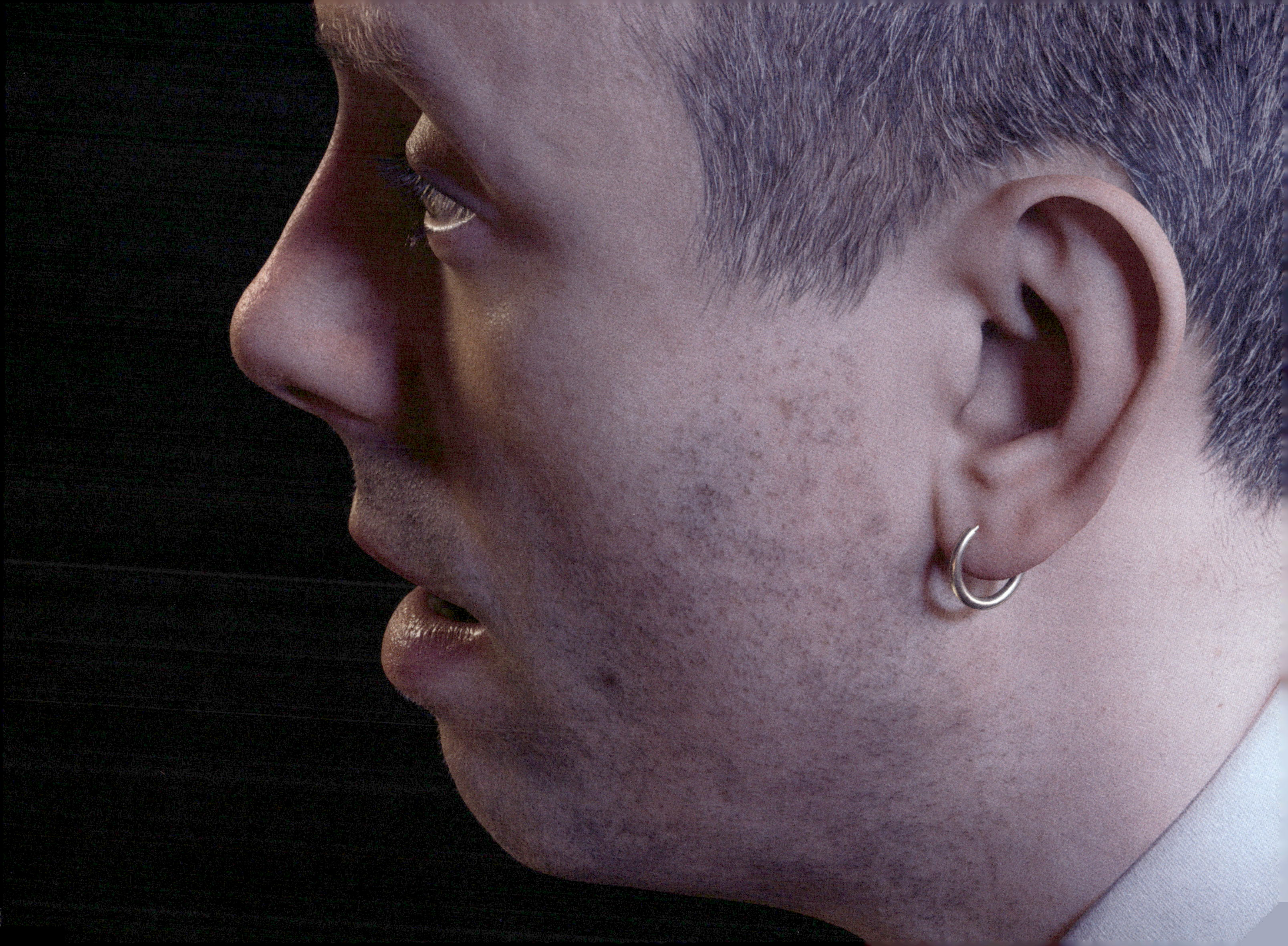

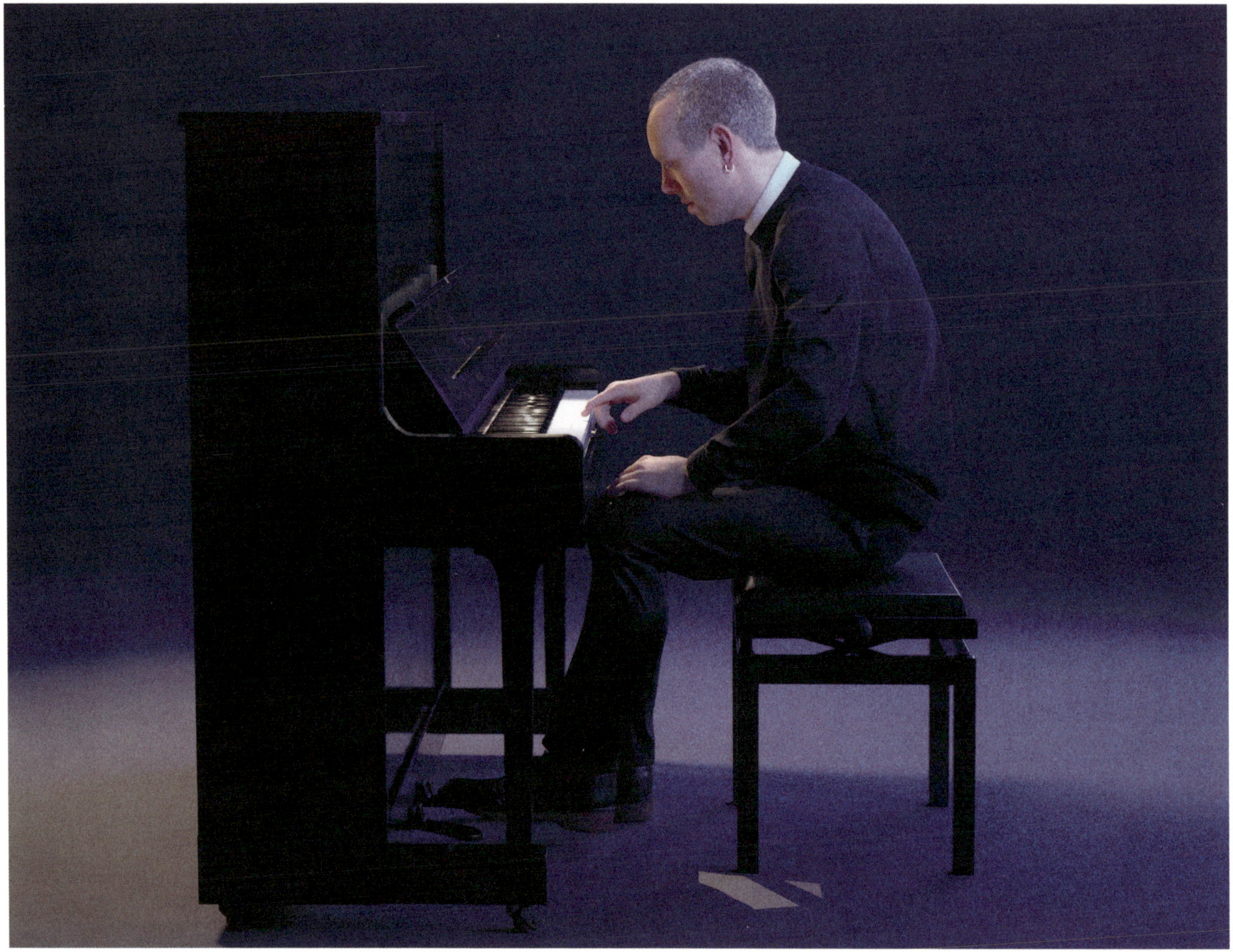

Pianowork 2 2023, video and sound, pp. 103–11, 115

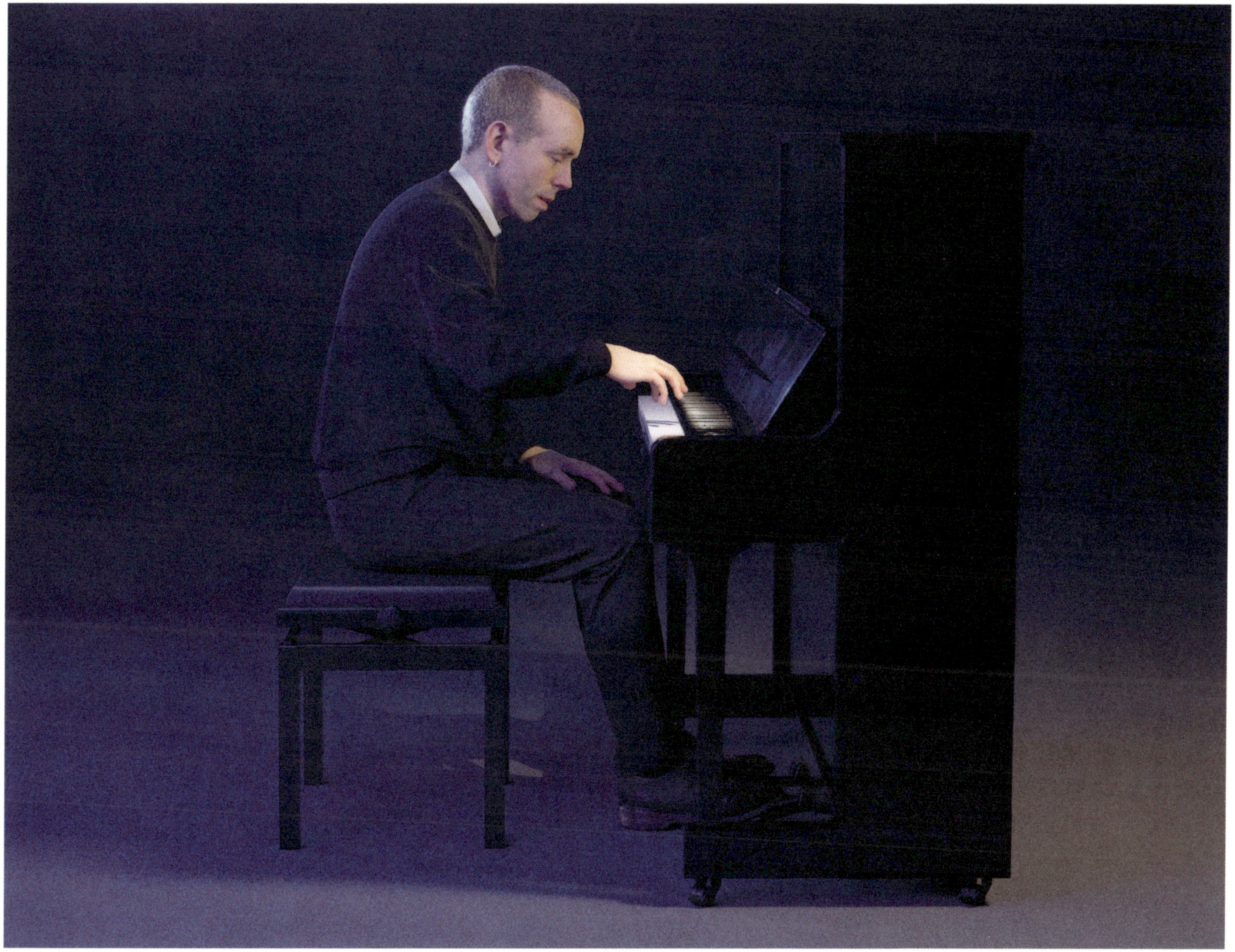

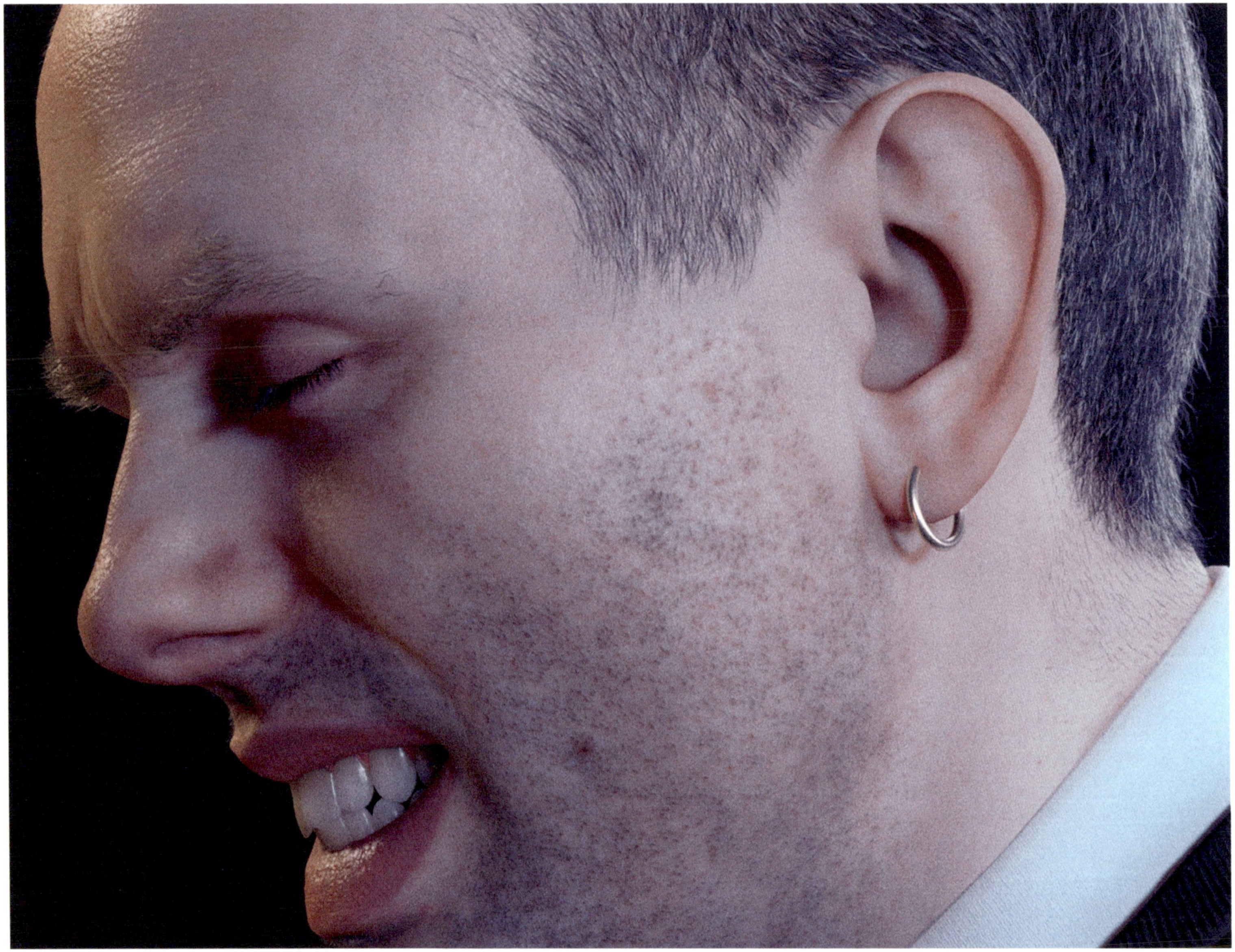

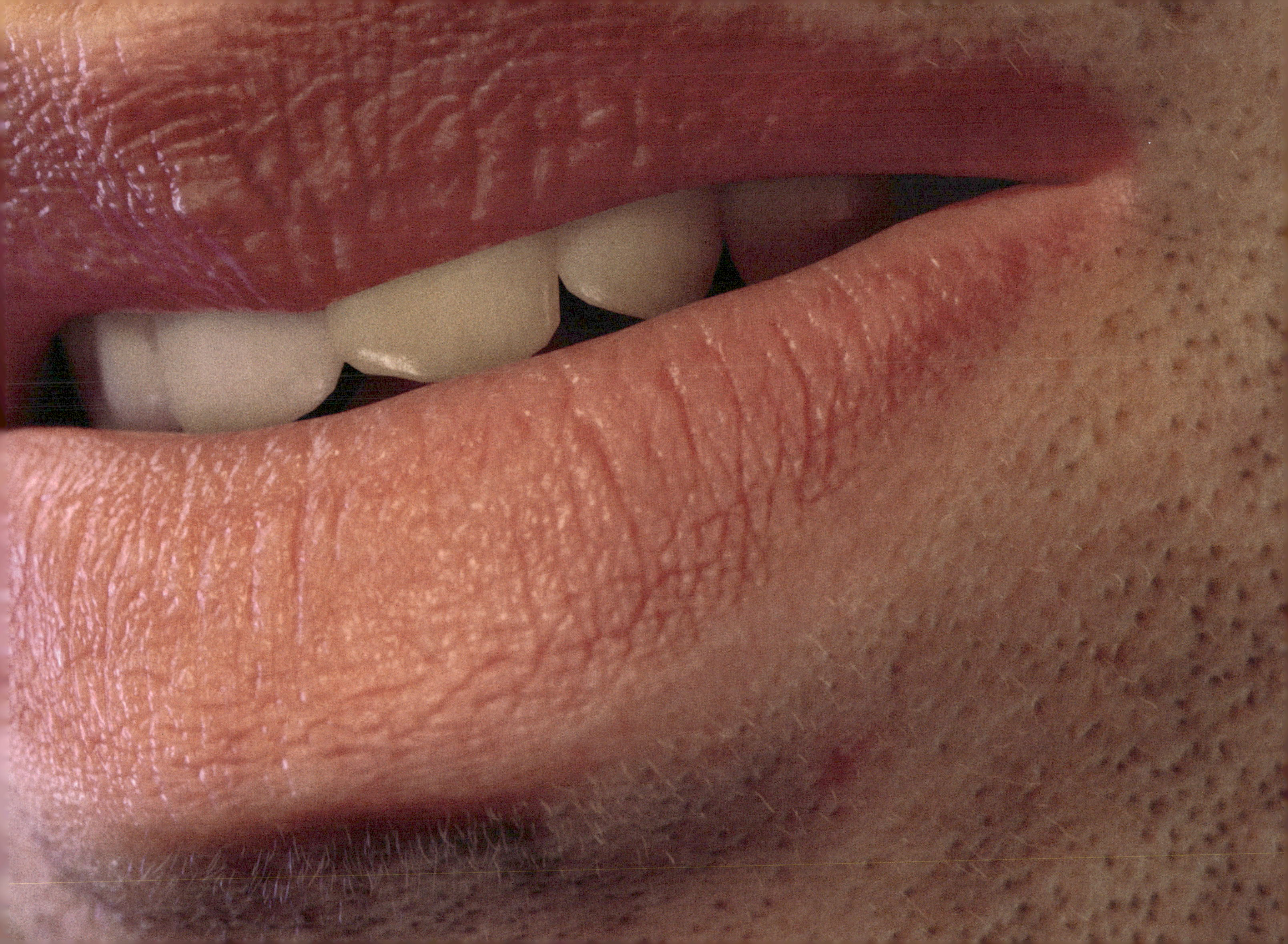

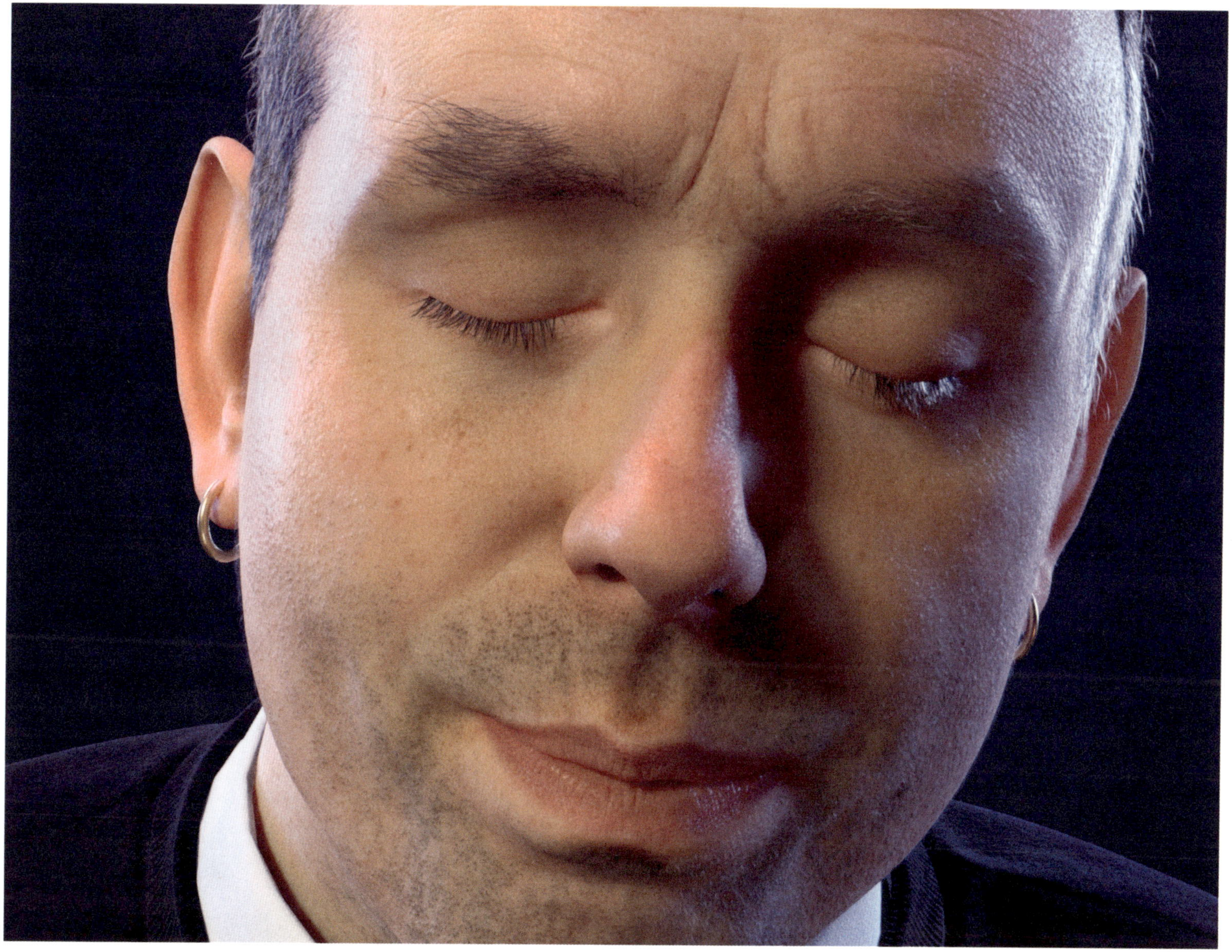

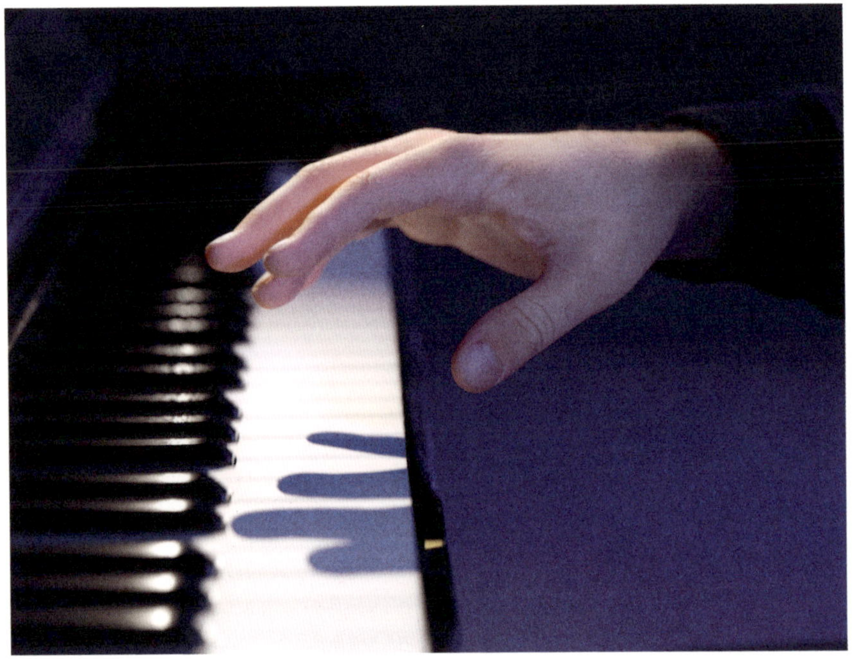

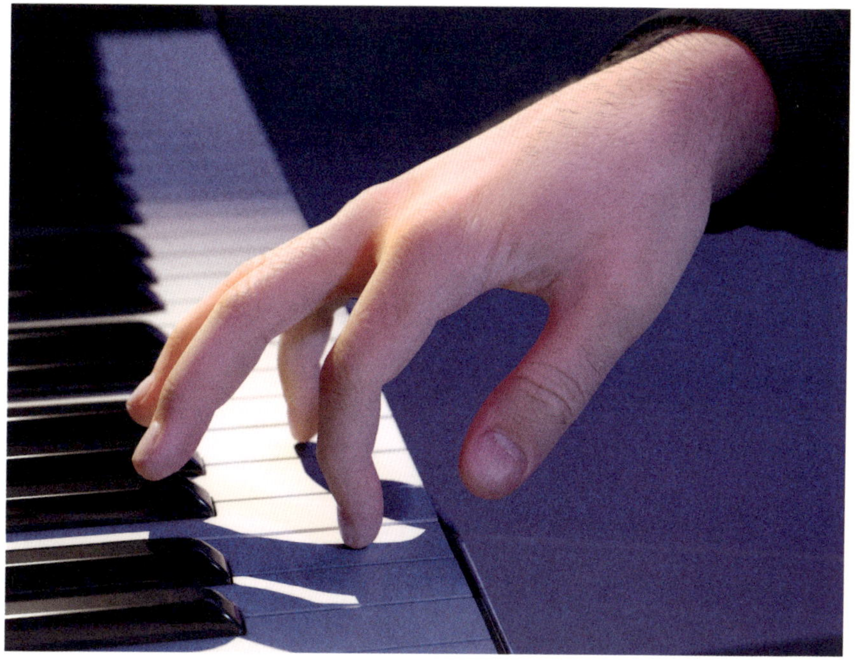

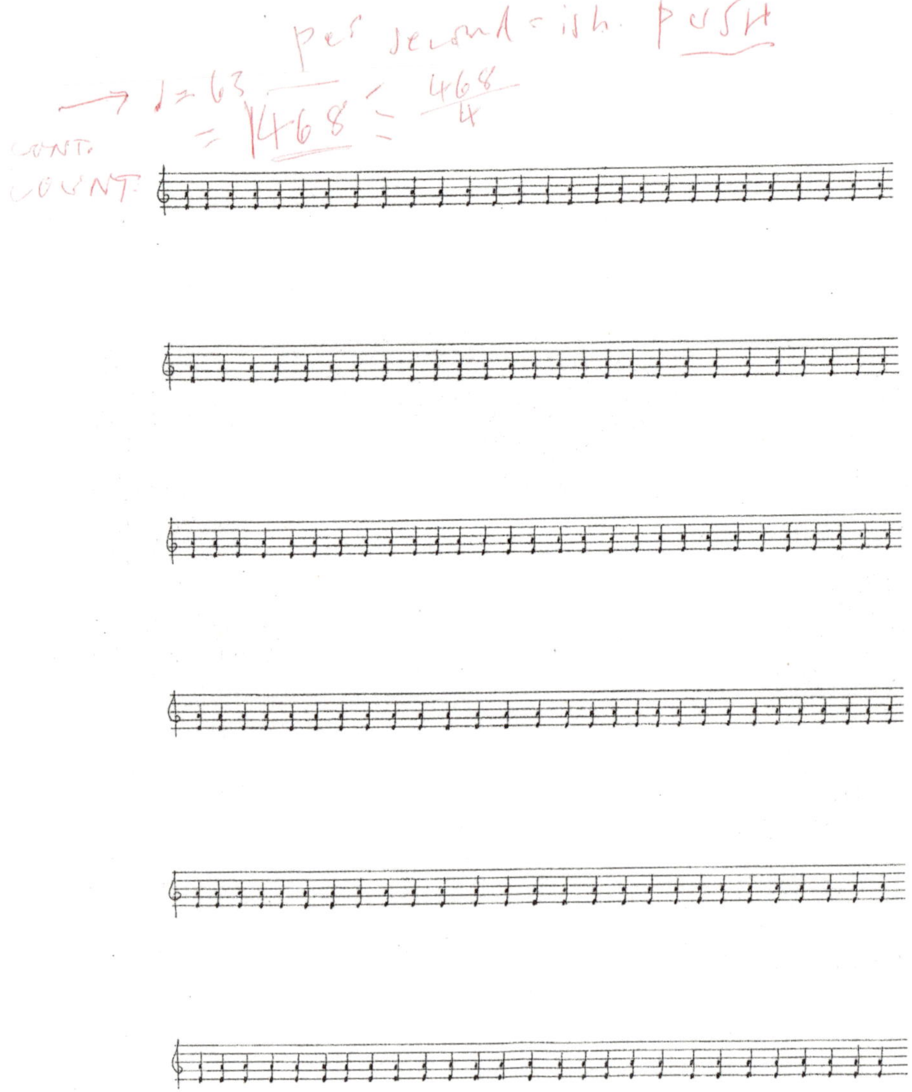

1

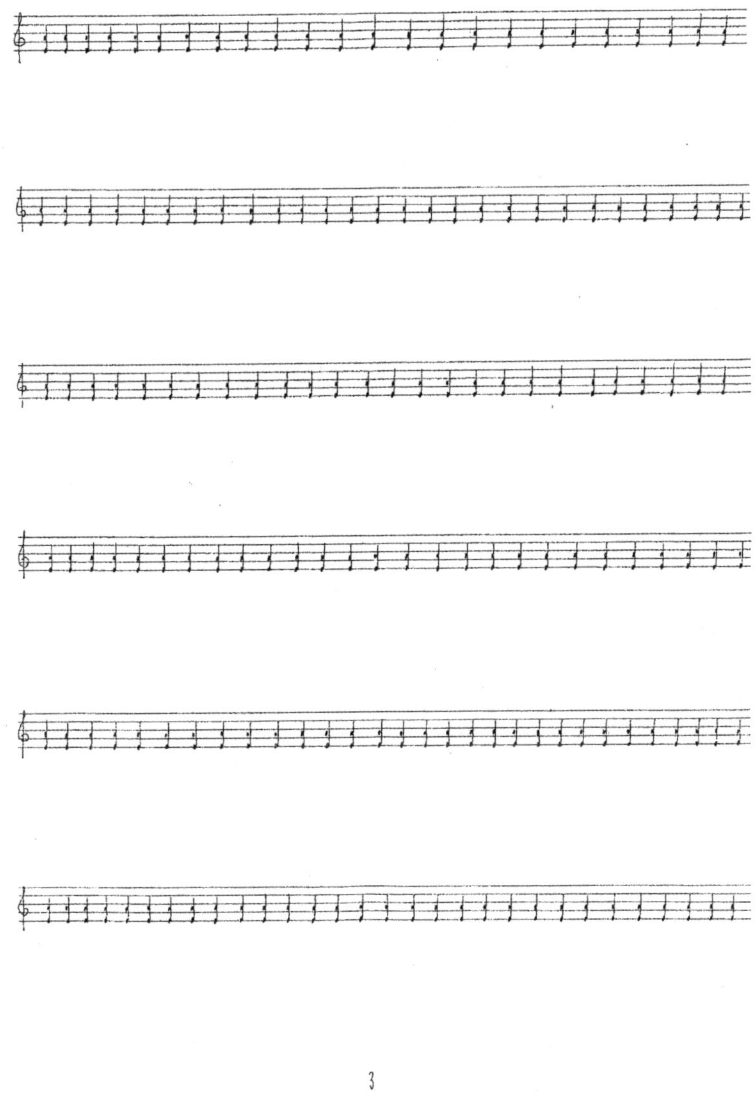

Jürg Frey, musical score for *Klavierstück 2* 2001 with annoations from Ed Atkins

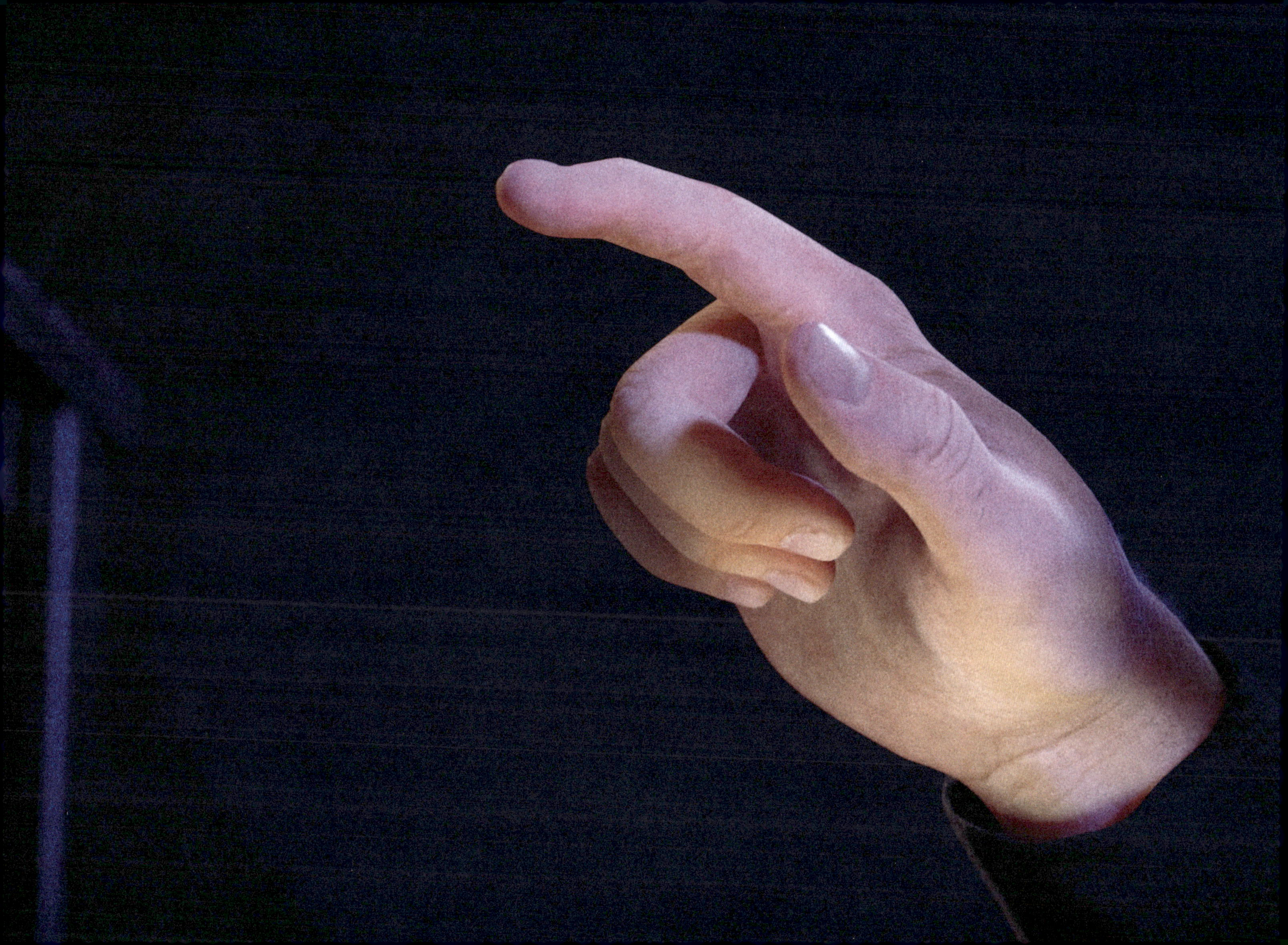

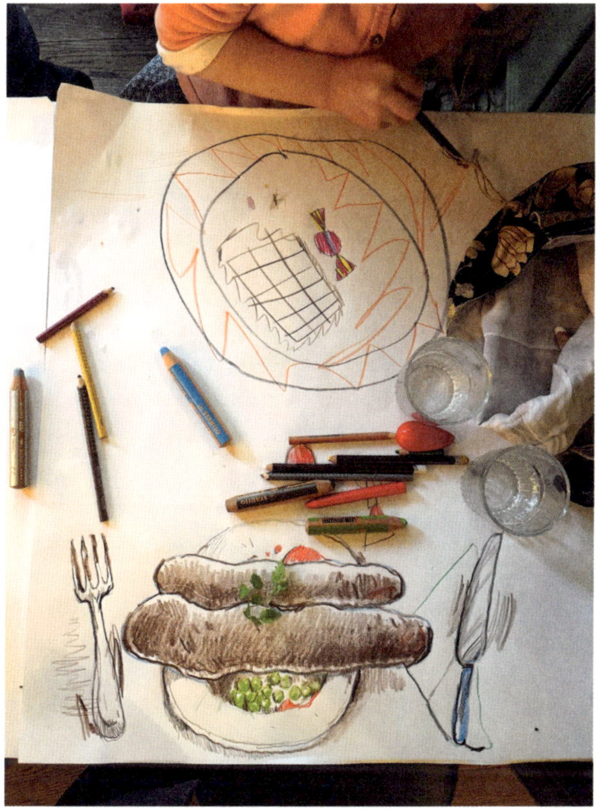

The artist and his daughter drawing on paper tablecloths

PLAY'S THE THING

Kathryn Scanlan

In 2021 Walther and Franz König published *Drawings for Children*, a book that collects two hundred drawings by Ed Atkins 'made weekday mornings over breakfast, then hidden in [his] daughter's lunchbox', according to the artist's simple preface. The drawings, composed on commercial Post-it note paper in various sizes and colours—but primarily on the classic pale yellow square—are reproduced in their original formats; like snapshots, they sit pleasingly on a page, whose stage-like frame of white space encourages close study.

Some of the drawings look to have been done by a small child herself—scribbled knots, crude faces—and others look like a collaboration between a child and an adult. A few plainer ones say 'I love you' with a heart: a note any parent (with good handwriting) might make for their child's lunchbox. But the majority of the two hundred are skilled, detailed, highly peculiar renderings of a disparate and seemingly inexhaustible array of subject matter, much of which has an absurd, grotesque, psychological quality—drawings for adults, we might say, if we were disposed to underestimating a child's inherent understanding of art.

The drawings fill their small squares and there's tension at the margins—what gets cut off where. A sense of anxious curiosity about what's beyond the frame is reminiscent, somehow, of the theatre audiences that 'lean[ed] in

1 David E. Williams, 'Beyond the Frame: *Rosemary's Baby*', *American Cinematographer*, 29 March 2017, https://theasc.com/articles/beyond-the-frame-rosemarys-baby, accessed 3 May 2024.

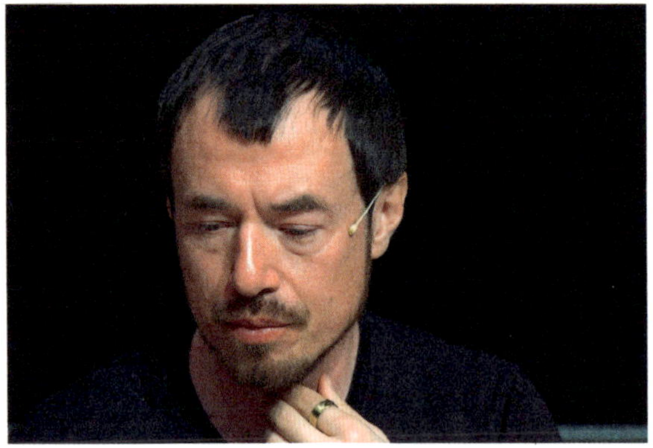

Sorcerer 2022, with Steven Zultanski, video and sound

their seats, trying to look around the edge of the [scene's] doorframe to see what was happening' during screenings of Roman Polanski's 1968 film *Rosemary's Baby*.[1] On a material level, another underlying source of anxiety comes from the fact that 3M, corporate inventor and manufacturer of the original Post-it note, recently settled with public water systems in the United States for over ten billion dollars in clean-up costs for its perfluoroalkyl and polyfluoroalkyl pollutants ('forever chemicals' that cause cancer, hormonal dysfunction and environmental destruction).[2]

There's an element throughout of the cartoon—an assured and economical facility with line and shape, a playful and very oddball sense of humour. The drawings often seem like visual gags—made to provoke laughter (or something like it: the closely related paroxysms of merriment, revulsion, grief). But we know that cartoons and animation, ostensibly for children, reliably 'facilitate a disquieting yet therapeutic encounter with the pervasiveness of violence and alienation', as noted by Erika Balsom in her essay on Atkins, referencing Esther Leslie's 2002 book *Hollywood Flatlands*.[3] A central element of this 'therapeutic encounter' is the use of slapstick: a kind of hysterical exaggeration which, according to Atkins, 'models and tests and amplifies physical horror for some cathartic rehearsal.'[4] There's a drawing of a hand chopped neatly apart at the wrist and finger-joints, an X-ray view of a head—skull, brain, teeth, spine—smoking a cigarette; a figure's mouth open wide to either expel (vomit) or admit (a large snake). These and other images in the book seem to stream from an anxious, inexhaustible subconscious that seeks relief in absurdist expression. 'Slapstick is cathartic', Atkins says, 'because no one gets hurt.'[5]

Scale and perspective shift constantly: a zooming in and out that has a slightly destabilising, almost hallucinatory effect and, like Alice's Wonderland size experiments, is suggestive of childhood's disorienting—and potentially exhilarating—negotiations between body and world. A floating pink coin is similar in size to the floating pink planet that follows a few pages later. There are frequent close-ups on individual body parts: fingertips that stretch the lid-skin from an eyeball; an open mouthful of teeth and tongue; a bright pink arm sat on a table like an object; detached noses (including a pig's snout), lips and chins in diagrammatic array; a human's lower half, in trousers and shoes, lying doll-like on a tray.

These preoccupations—with magnification and with

2
Reuters, 22 June 2023, https://www.theguardian.com/environment/2023/jun/22/3m-settlement-municipal-water-systems-pfas-contamination, accessed 5 May 2024.

3
Erika Balsom, 'A Bouquet of Blue Flowers for Ed Atkins', in *Ed Atkins: Get Life/Love's Work*, New Museum, New York 2021, p.52.

4
'Ed Atkins in Conversation with Massimiliano Gioni', in *Ed Atkins: Get Life/Love's Work*, New Museum, New York 2021, p.62.

5
Ibid.

what could be called body horror—can be found throughout Atkins's work. In his book *Sorcerer*, which he co-wrote with poet Steven Zultanski and which also exists as a play and film adaptation, a prominent feature of the staged apartment setting is a large 'screen/mirror' fitted with a 'table/counter', a projector and a camera with 'a strong zoom'. When the character Peter seats himself there 'to unpack his face', his pantomiming actions—'POP EYE OUT'; 'PEELING OFF LIPS'; 'FIND CENTRAL ZIPPER IN HAIR'; 'TAKING OUT A MOLAR'—are projected, hugely dilated, onto the screen. As Peter methodically takes his face apart, he 'places each feature on the table in a line that extends from left to right' in a manner reminiscent of certain children's games: Mr Potato Head, for example, or Operation (poor 'Cavity Sam').[6]

Atkins started making the Post-it note drawings in 2020, when 'most everything [he] was meant to be working on had been cancelled or indefinitely postponed' due to the global pandemic.[7] His daughter was attending a *børnehave* (kindergarten) in Copenhagen at the time, which closed briefly in response to the coronavirus, but reopened soon after (Denmark was the first European country to reopen its primary schools, in mid-April 2020).[8] Then, on weekday mornings, he and his daughter would make drawings together over the breakfast table, and he'd tuck one in her lunchbox before she left. A few of the drawings in *Children* are wrinkled, smudged—'blotched and warped by a satsuma or softened by proximity to a banana'—from their journey to school and back. What began as a way to send 'little hellos' to his child during her time outside the family home—it's easy, too, to think of them as spells or talismans to keep her safe—was, according to Atkins, 'a way for [him] to achieve something every day' as well. The fact that the drawings were made on Post-it notes may have been a decision of convenience (here's a handy stack of inexpensive, inexhaustible, brightly coloured paper cut in kid-friendly dimensions—let's draw!), but it's interesting—and moving—that this ubiquitous, task-oriented material, often used for to-do lists, is the substrate that 'allow[ed] [Atkins] to make without external want or rationale'[9] during a period of professional loss and drift, a time of not much 'to do' in terms of the busy, mobile, plan-making mode of modern living to which much of the world has since returned. For a while, for some, restrictions and uncertainty shortened the human horizon to the length of a day (its true dimension) and encouraged a present-tense mindset compatible with artistic forms like diary-keeping, life drawing and the modest scope of Atkins's Post-it note practice.

Present-tense living might also be the default mode of children, invalids, elderly people and the dying. *Nurses Come and Go, But None for Me* is a script by Atkins and Zultanski, his *Sorcerer* collaborator, and exists as a feature-length film within Atkins's 2025 Tate exhibition. Like *Sorcerer*, it is set in an apartment and composed of two distinct parts or acts. In the first, a couple—Claire and Peter—welcome guests who've arrived to witness a performance, and Peter, seated in a chair, reads from a printed-out copy of *Sick Notes*, which he introduces to the audience as 'the diary of Philip Atkins, written in the last six months of his life, after receiving a cancer diagnosis.'[10]

6
Ed Atkins and Steven Zultanski, *Sorcerer*, London 2023.

7
Email from Ed Atkins to the author, 17 April 2024.

8
Patrick Kingsley, 'In Denmark, the Rarest of Sights: Classrooms Full of Students', *New York Times*, 17 April 2020, https://www.nytimes.com/2020/04/17/world/europe/denmark-schools-corona-virus.html, accessed 6 Dec 2024.

9
Email from Ed Atkins to the author, 17 April 2024.

10
Ed Atkins and Steven Zultanski, *Nurses Come and Go, But None for Me*, pdf script of the film, courtesy of the authors and Tate.

Sick Notes is a moving, devastating account—alternately funny and despairing, banal and deep-seeing—written by Atkins's father, who died in 2009. Atkins has frequently spoken about the impact of this event—'I've spent so many years making work as a more or less direct consequence of my father's death'—and its deep influence on, in particular, his use of 'dead men, surrogates, auto cadavers': the computer-generated characters through whom he attempts to speak what is unspeakable about loss, tragedy, grief and life.[11] But whereas the 'dead men' of those previous works speak with a voice (Atkins's) that is very much alive, in *Nurses…*, a man who is very much alive—albeit an actor—speaks with the voice of a dead man. Just as the video avatars are characters Atkins 'made and donned like parabolic fancy dress' in order to '[segue] from a bullish melancholy to a more equable mourning', it's possible to read the character of Peter as another fictional surrogate or stand-in—a kind of mask or application of greasepaint—that enables reparatory performance and expression.[12]

Because *Sick Notes* is written in the first person, Peter's delivery of it in *Nurses…* functions as an empathetic embodiment of the ailing, narrating 'I': the dying man's testimony becomes Peter's testimony ('Only now I'm home do I realise how much I am physically deteriorating, how weak in the arms and legs, how reluctant to move after sitting or lying for any time for fear of pain, how hard to bend or twist').[13] When, in *A Tumour (In English)*, from his collection *A Primer for Cadavers*, Atkins writes that 'reading this text will conjure a tumour up inside you' and that 'typographic affectation will also EFFECT the proliferation of the tumour, as will the injudicious use of punctuation and that peculiar syntax of the infirm that threatens to collapse into gratuity and morbid self-pity at any moment', he could be describing *Sick Notes*—the text's unique tone and style, irregular and notational, born of anguish and necessity.[14] There's the sense that, having spoken the dying man's words, Peter has fallen ill and needs to be healed. After he delivers the crushing final lines of the diary—of Philip Atkins's life—he and Claire segue directly and wordlessly into the script's second act. Peter gets up from his chair, removes his shoes and lies down on the floor; Claire pantomimes driving, then answers the ringing telephone sound she's making with her mouth.

'Is that the Ambulance Driver?' asks Peter, whose alias now, in the Ambulance Game, is Princess Fairy Stardust. Princess Fairy Stardust is sick and needs the Ambulance Driver's help. Claire administers to Peter with pantomimed 'cures'—an imaginary cup of bitter drink, a poultice of 'giant's snot mixed with scrapings of wild bullfrog and ice turnip'—and then, when those don't work, a series of 'spells': she draws 'a symbol, just a scribble' on seven Post-it notes and sticks them onto various parts of Peter's body.[15] The 'sick' patient, meanwhile, is alternately passive and demanding: the pleasure and point of the game for Princess Fairy Stardust is to receive as much loving, worried, devoted attention as the Ambulance Driver is willing to give—which in and of itself is what performs the magical act of rehabilitation.

The Ambulance Game was devised and played by Atkins and his daughter at the time he was making the

11 'Ed Atkins in Conversation with Massimiliano Giono', in *Ed Atkins: Get Life/Love's Work*, New Museum, New York 2021, pp.64–5.

12 Ed Atkins, 'Erratum Letter', in *Ed Atkins: Get Life/Love's Work*, New Museum, New York, 2021 p.27.

13 Ed Atkins and Steven Zultanski, *Nurses Come and Go, But None for Me*, pdf script of the film courtesy of the authors and Tate.

14 Ed Atkins, *A Primer for Cadavers*, London 2016, p.27.

15 Ed Atkins and Steven Zultanski, *Nurses Come and Go, But None for Me*, pdf script of the film courtesy of the authors and Tate.

Post-it note drawings for her lunchbox, but now, years later, is an activity the child has mostly outgrown.[16] The game's presentation and reenactment in *Nurses Come and Go, But None for Me* might be seen, then, as another act of familial mourning via performance—an attempt to ameliorate the loss of time passing, the loss of a child who's growing up—within the context of Atkins's oeuvre. It might also be read as a way for Atkins's father, as embodied by the character of Peter (Atkins) in the first act, to be healed by the attentive care of his 'nurse' (Atkins as the adult in the game's original context) while in the guise of his granddaughter (Peter as Princess Fairy Stardust) in the second—and, in turn, for the son and granddaughter to be healed of their inheritance of generational pain and trauma.

The game's premise is reminiscent in some ways of *The Piggle* (1977), D.W. Winnicott's compelling account of his psychoanalytic treatment of a small child named Gabrielle: in both, play is the essential tool of cure and change. Gabrielle, who is suffering from nightmares and a loss of self after the birth of her sister, spends each session on the floor of Winnicott's office playing with his toys in a way that communicates her troubles to herself and to Winnicott, her audience and playmate. For Gabrielle, the creative action of play, which Winnicott likens to concentration in adults, accomplishes subtle yet transformative psychological growth and repair. 'No human being is free from the strain of relating inner and outer reality', Winnicott tells us in his book *Playing and Reality*, but 'relief from this strain is provided by an intermediate area of experience' which belongs neither to an individual's imagination nor to collective reality: it exists in the limbo where art, religion and 'imaginative living' take place, which 'is in direct continuity with the play area of the small child who is "lost" in play'.[17] Art, then, according to Winnicott, is a negotiation between 'reality' and 'illusion': a nebulous middle ground where the temporary suspension of allegiance to either, made possible through play, relieves the tension of embodiment.

Just prior to the pandemic, Atkins began making a conscious effort 'to diminish [his] work': to reject technical virtuosity and 'the presumed production of meaning' in favour of a more pared-back, 'humble' or 'gracious' approach. He'd recently read Leo Bersani and Ulysse Dutoit's *Arts of Impoverishment* (1993)—on how Alain Resnais, Mark Rothko and Samuel Beckett 'deliberately sought to … reject art's authoritativeness'[18]—and was pursuing a practice where, instead, any potential meaningfulness comes from 'the central peculiarity of the work itself, and the entirely ample complexity of that.'[19]

These ideas and approaches can be readily discerned in *Children* and *Nurses…*; in both, there is a simplicity and directness of material and concept that nevertheless yields rich, perplexing, idiosyncratic work. The extreme virtuosity of Atkins's drawing ability is 'impoverished' by the humble material of the Post-it note—in regard to its small size and throw-away nature as well as its ubiquity and association with busywork—and also, to some degree, by the collaborative aspect of the project with his young daughter: Atkins's drawings lack any sense of preciousness or pretension and are enriched by their proximity to his child's unpractised mark-making. Similarly, his collaborations

16
Email from Ed Atkins to the author, 17 April 2024.

17
D.W. Winnicott, *Playing and Reality*, Middlesex 1974, p.15.

18
Ed Atkins, 'Erratum Letter', in *Ed Atkins: Get Life/Love's Work*, New Museum, New York, 2021 pp.23–4.

19
Ibid.

with Zultanski and, in the film, with actors and crew—as well as his central deployment of a 'found' text narrative—work to diminish the individualistic 'authority' of the artist and gestures instead towards a playful, collective, polyvocal mindset.

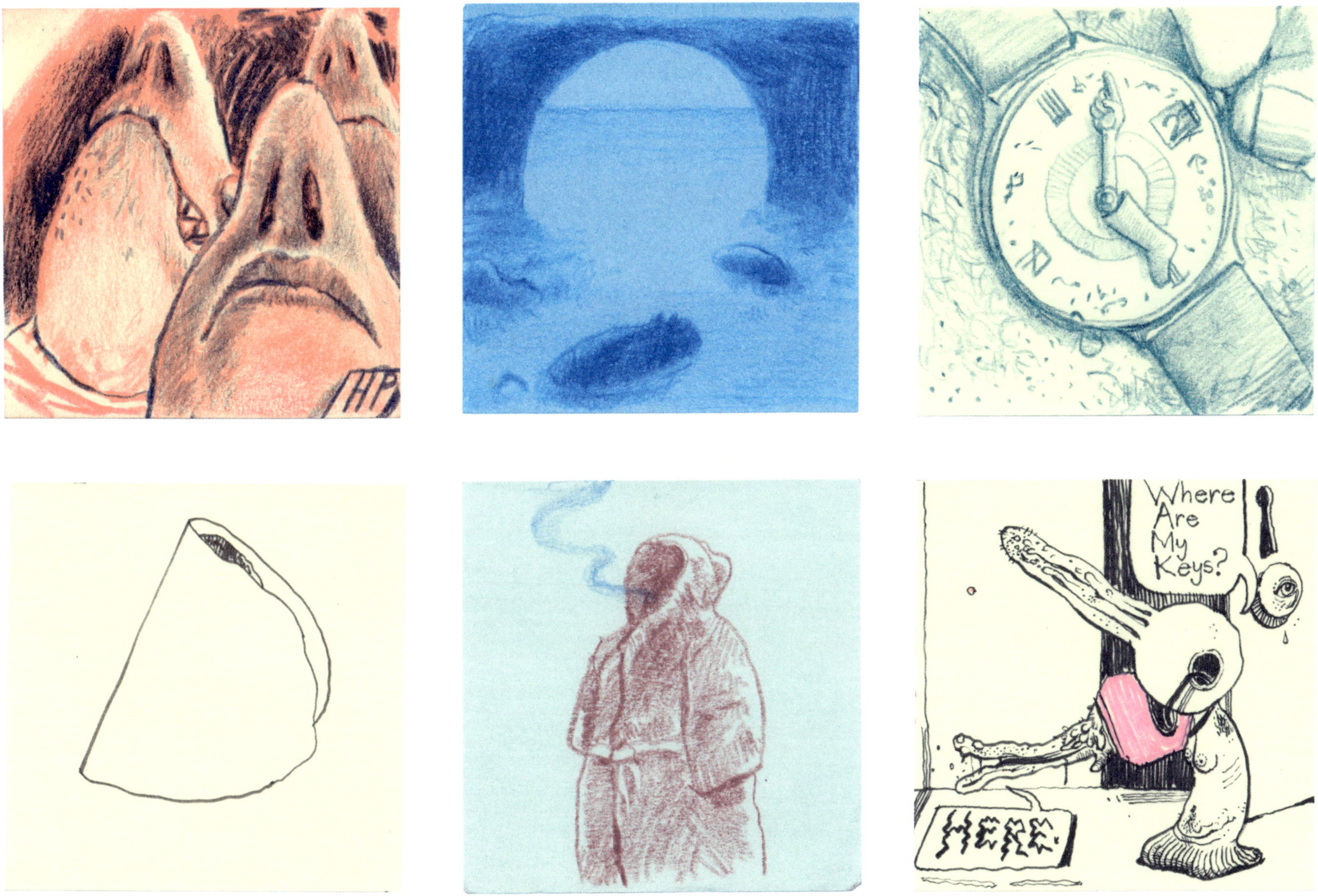

Children 2020–ongoing, crayon, pencil and ink on paper, dimensions variable, pp.123–38

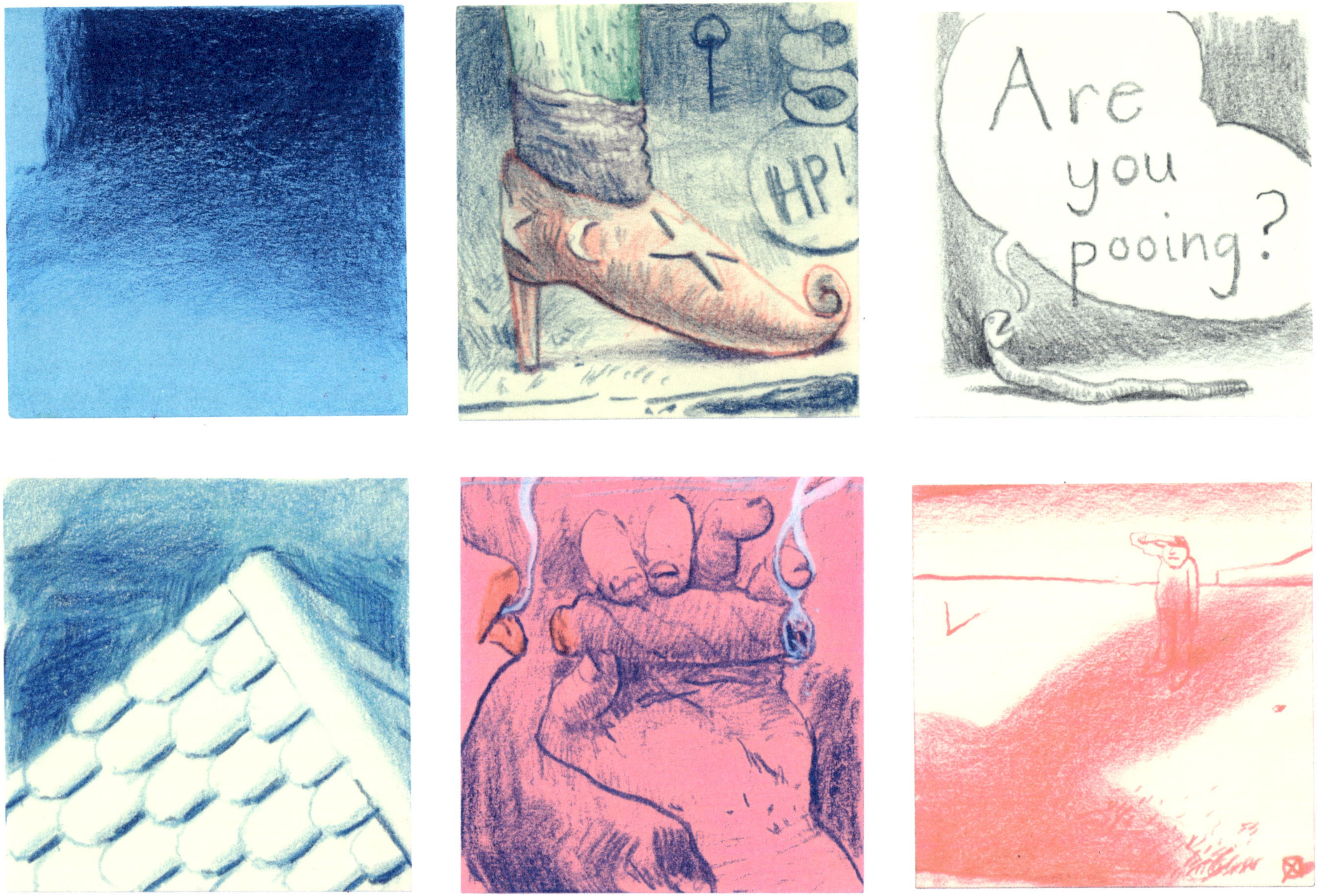
HP!
Are you pooing?

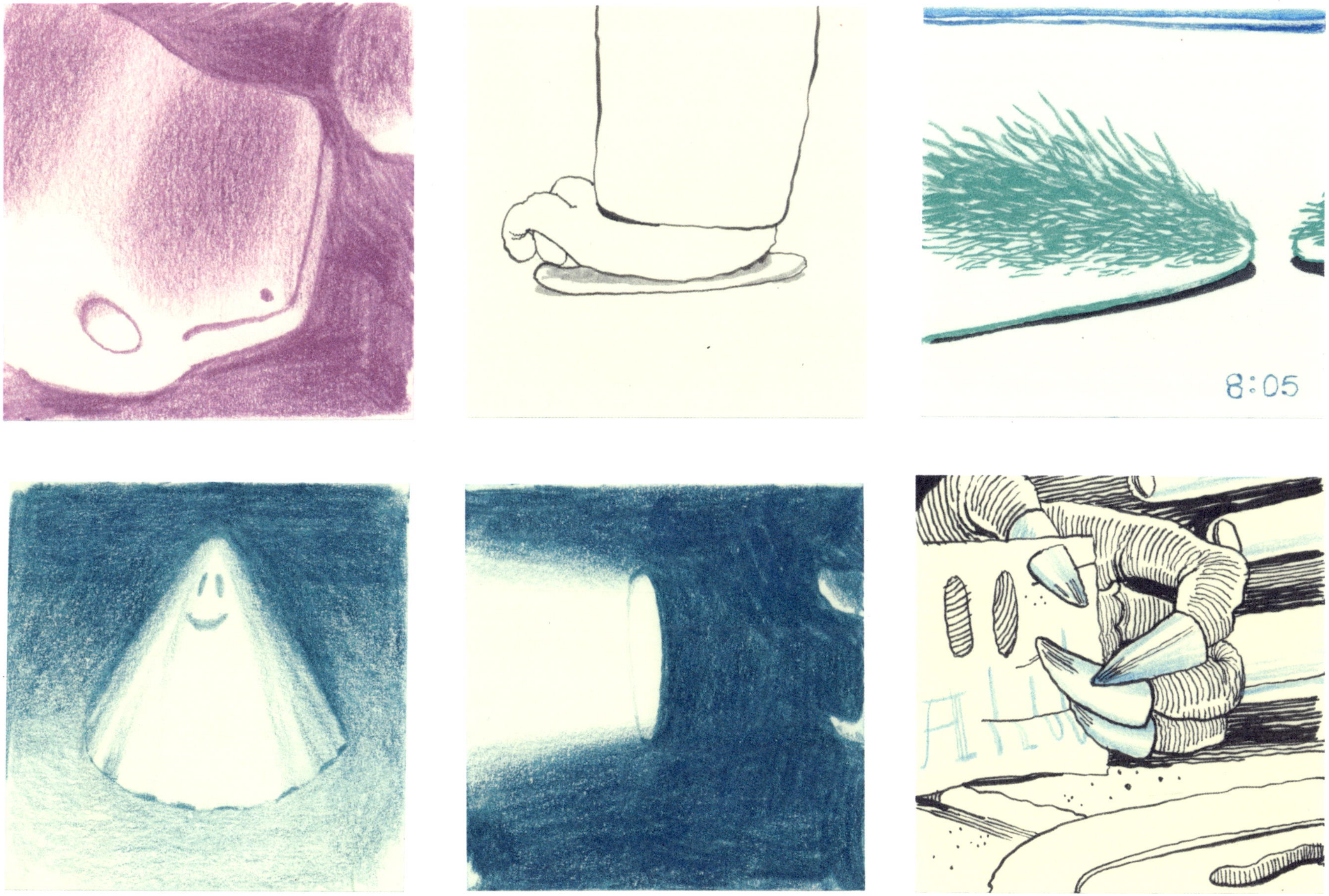
8:05

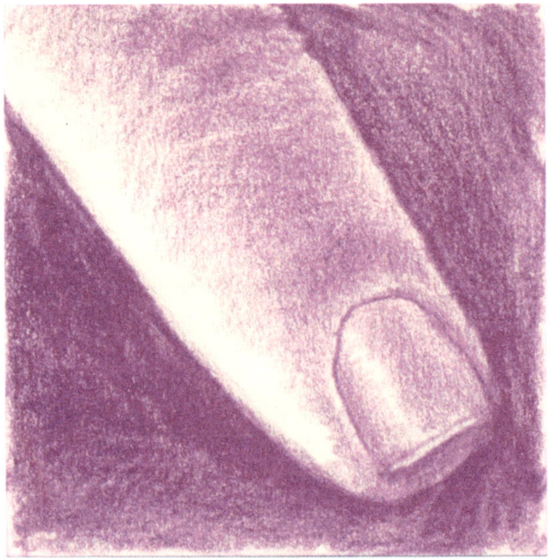

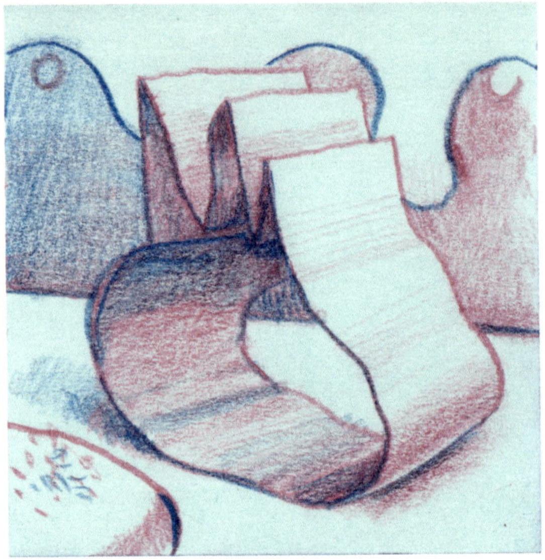

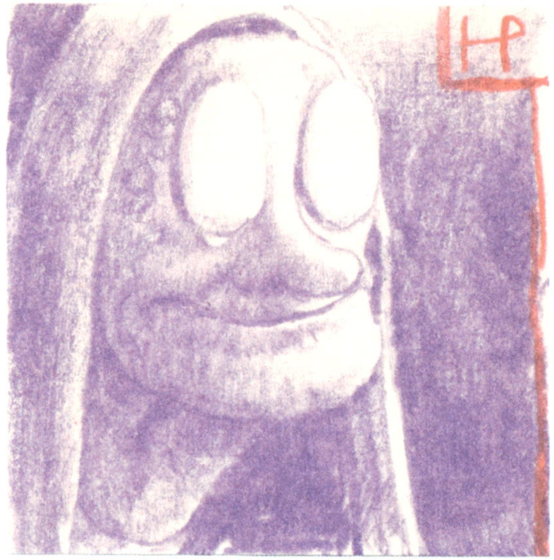

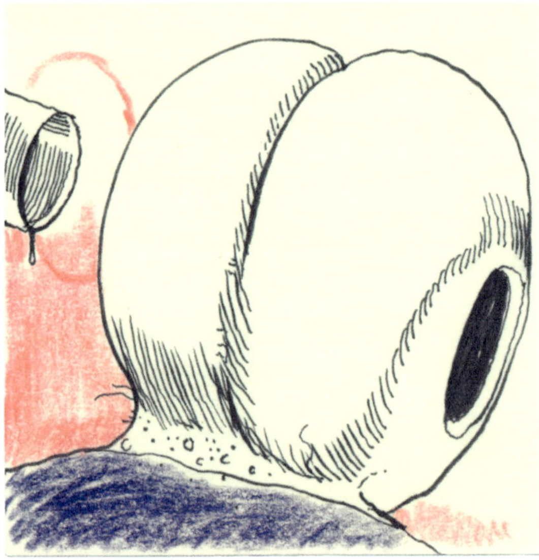

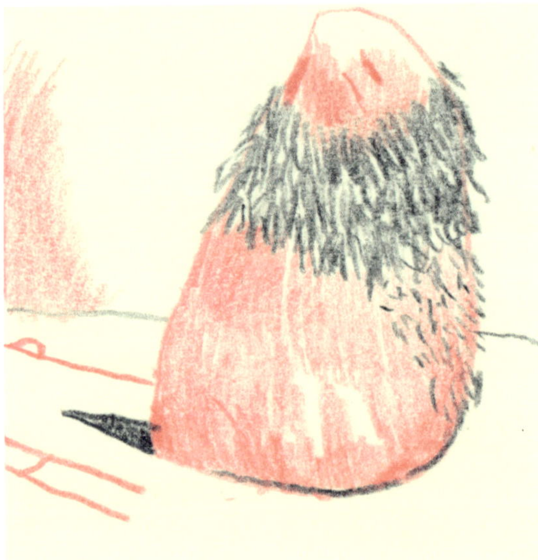

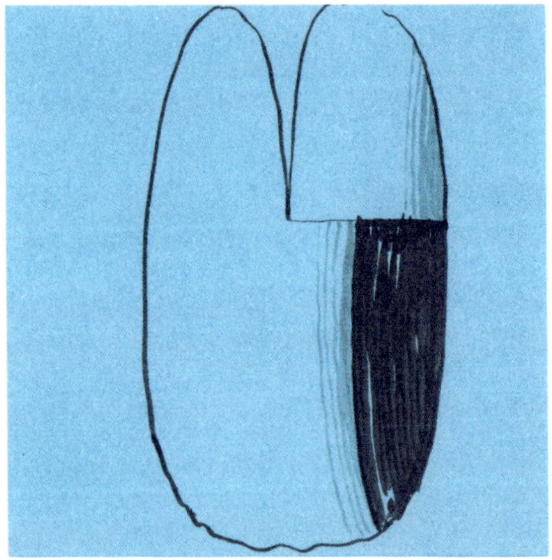

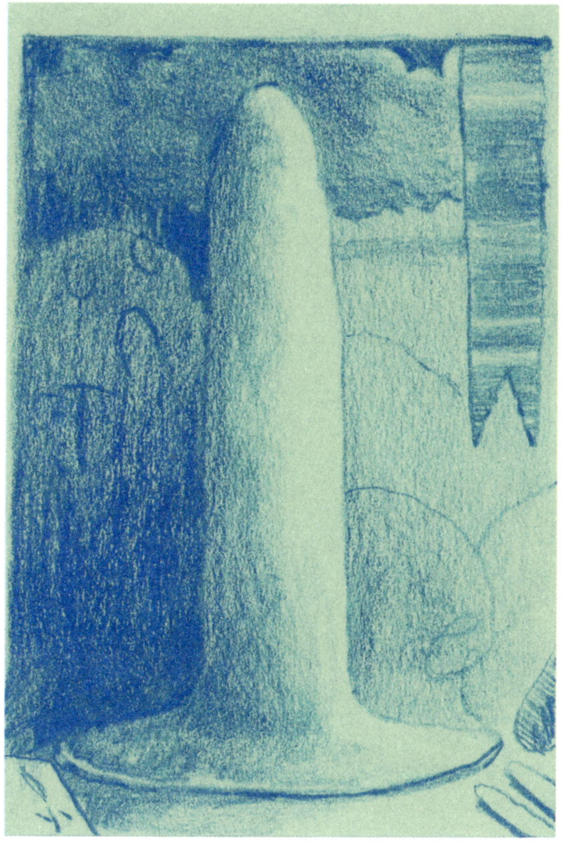
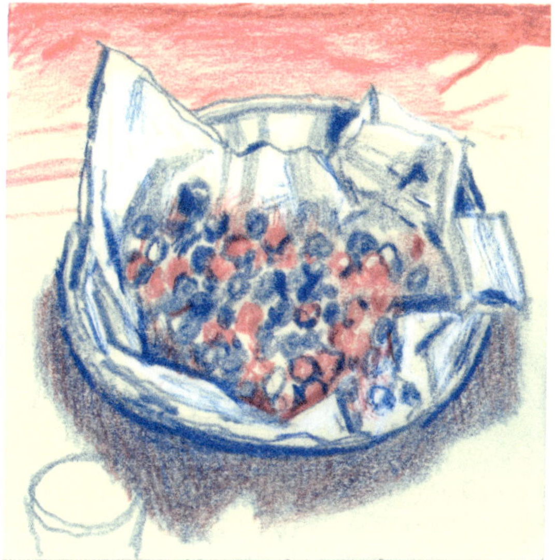
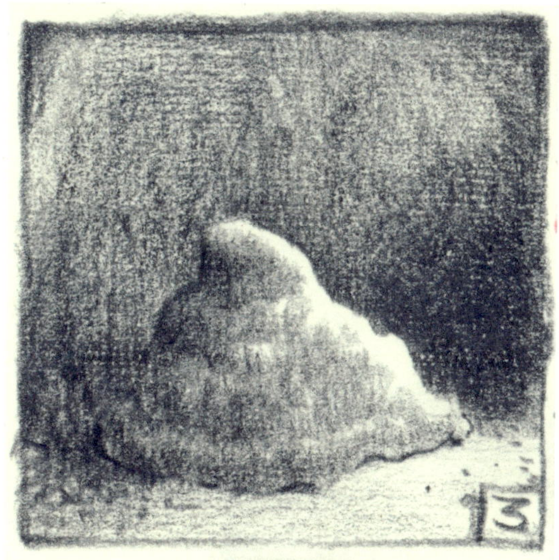

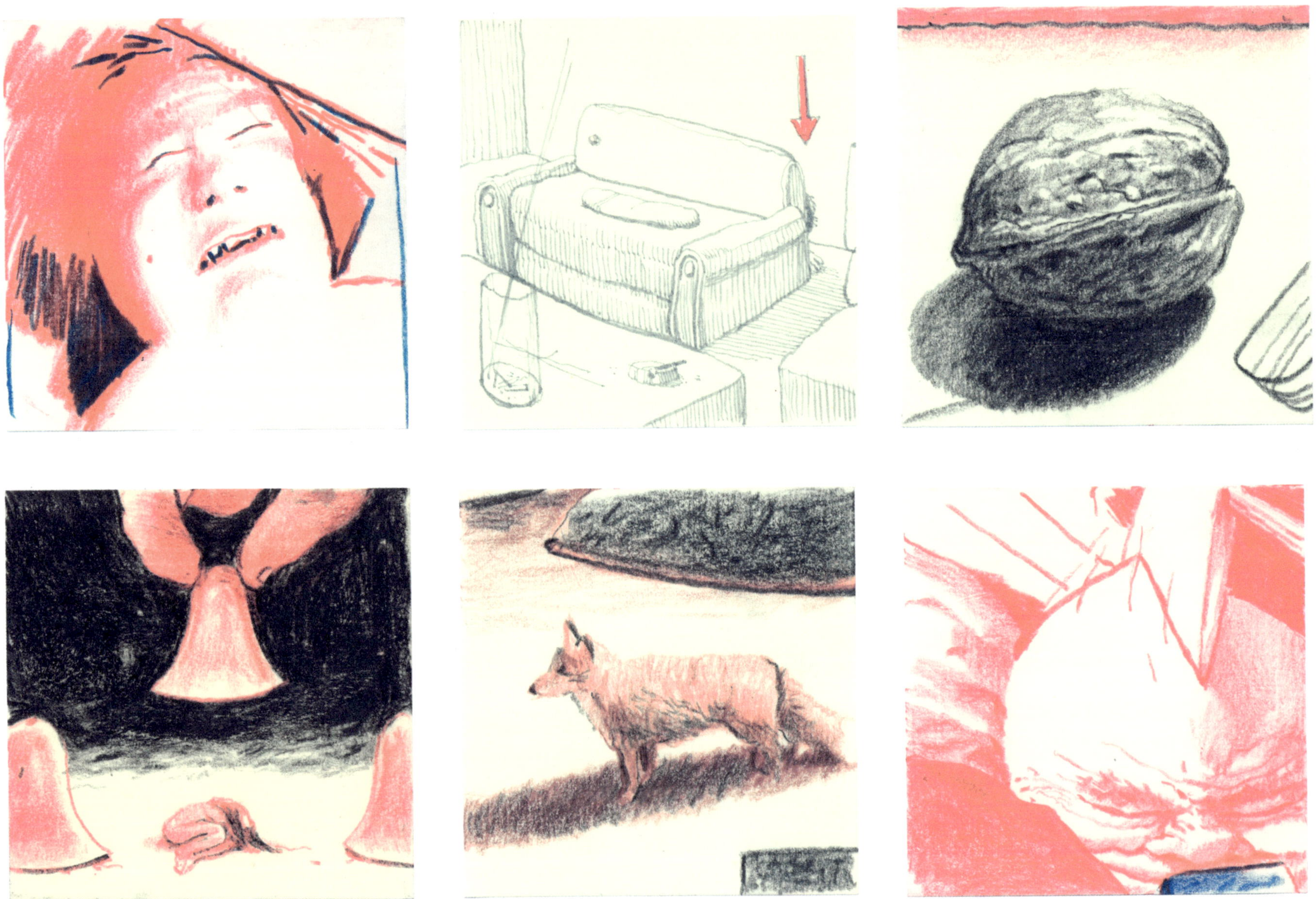

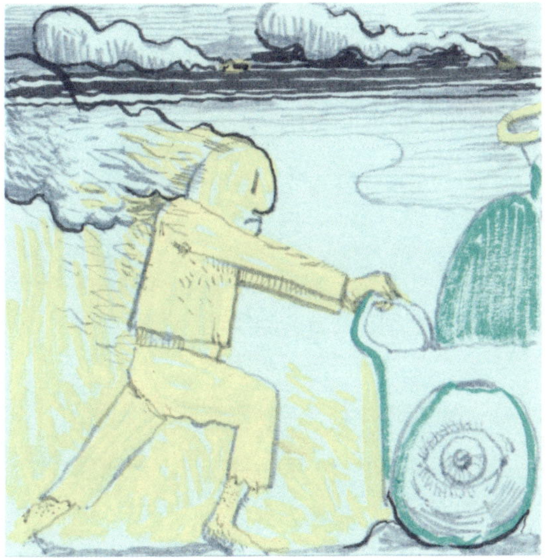

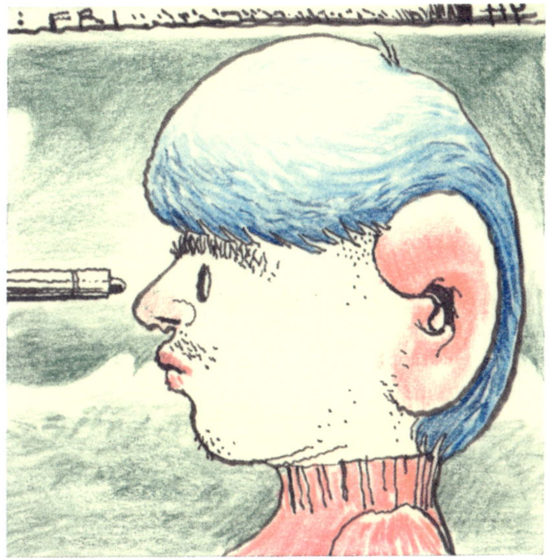
FBI

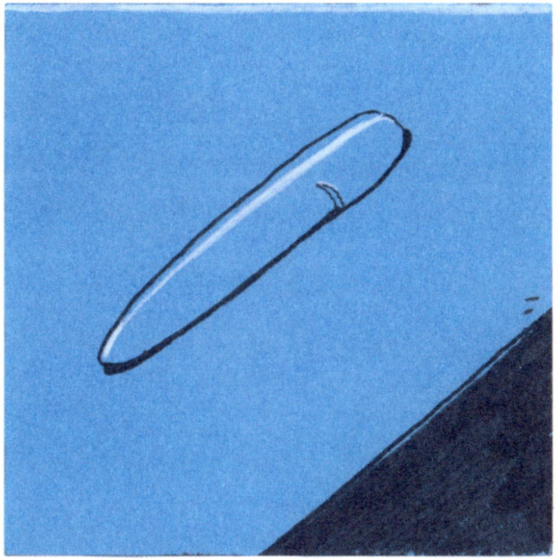

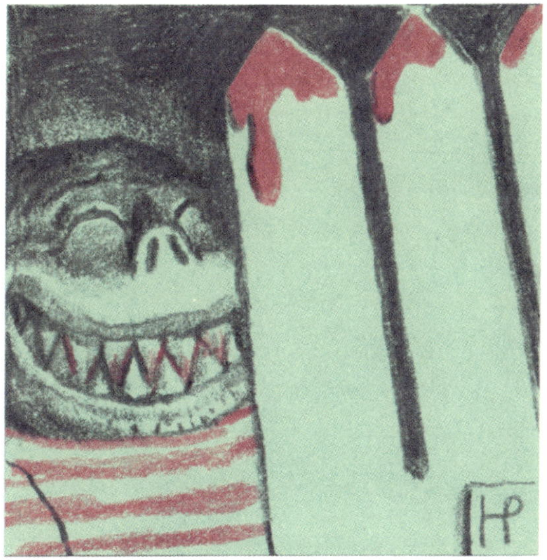
HP

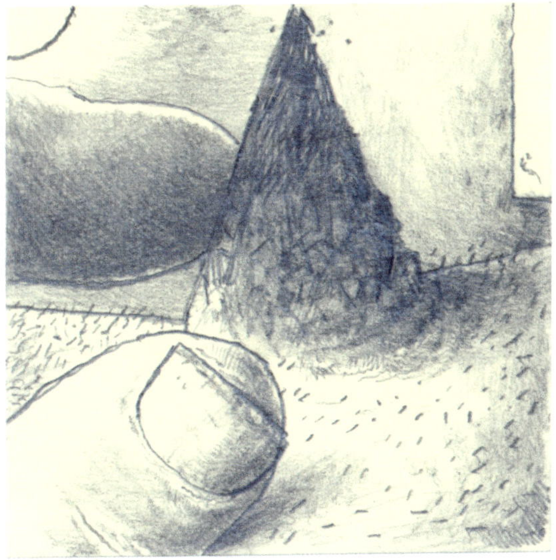

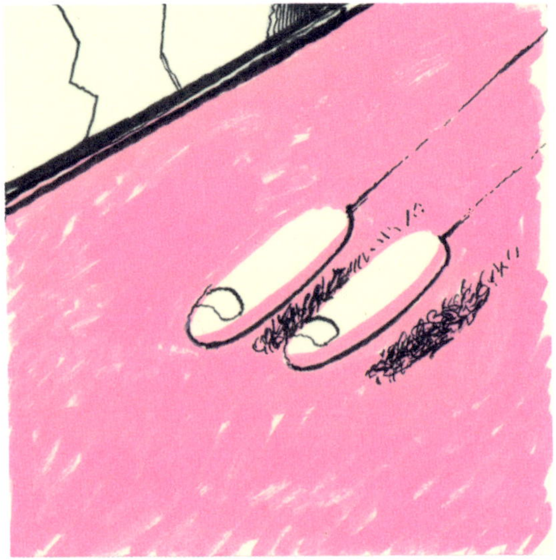
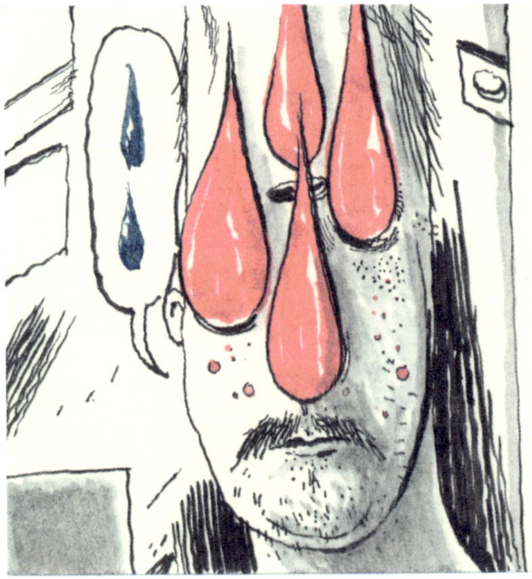
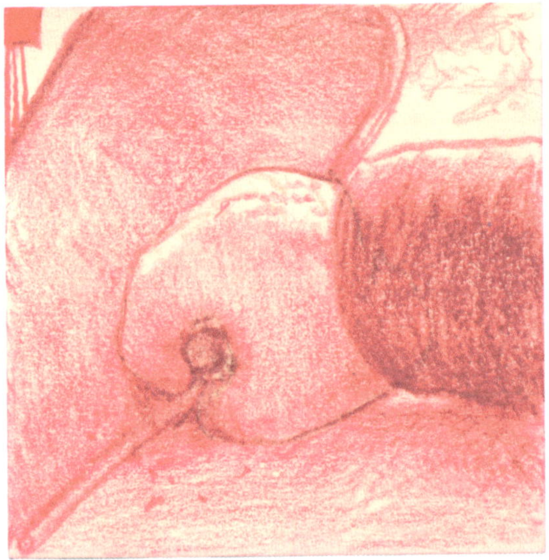
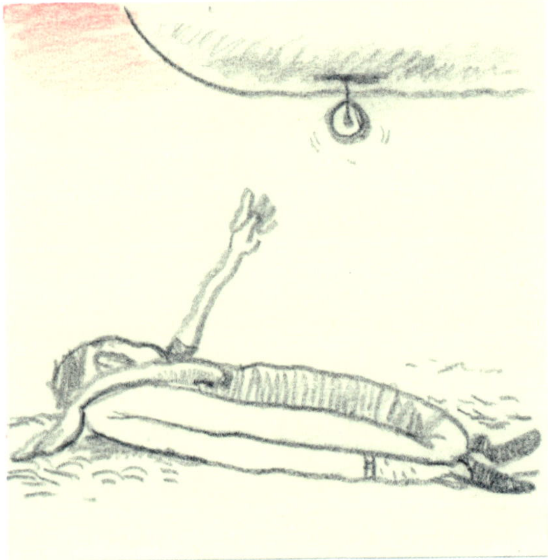
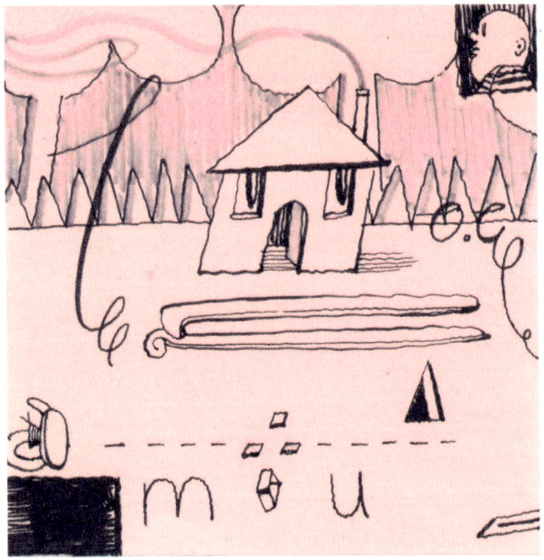
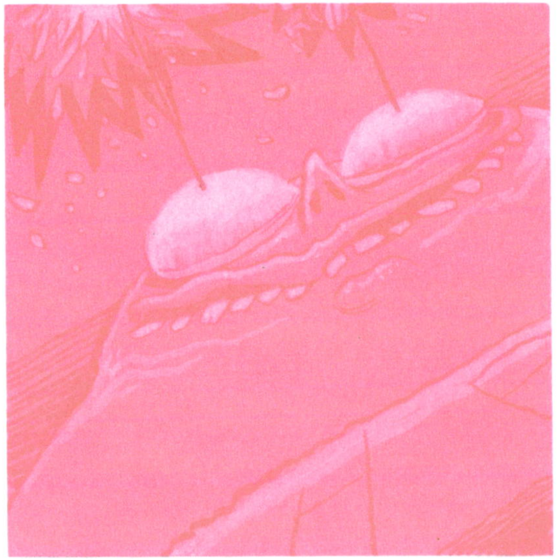

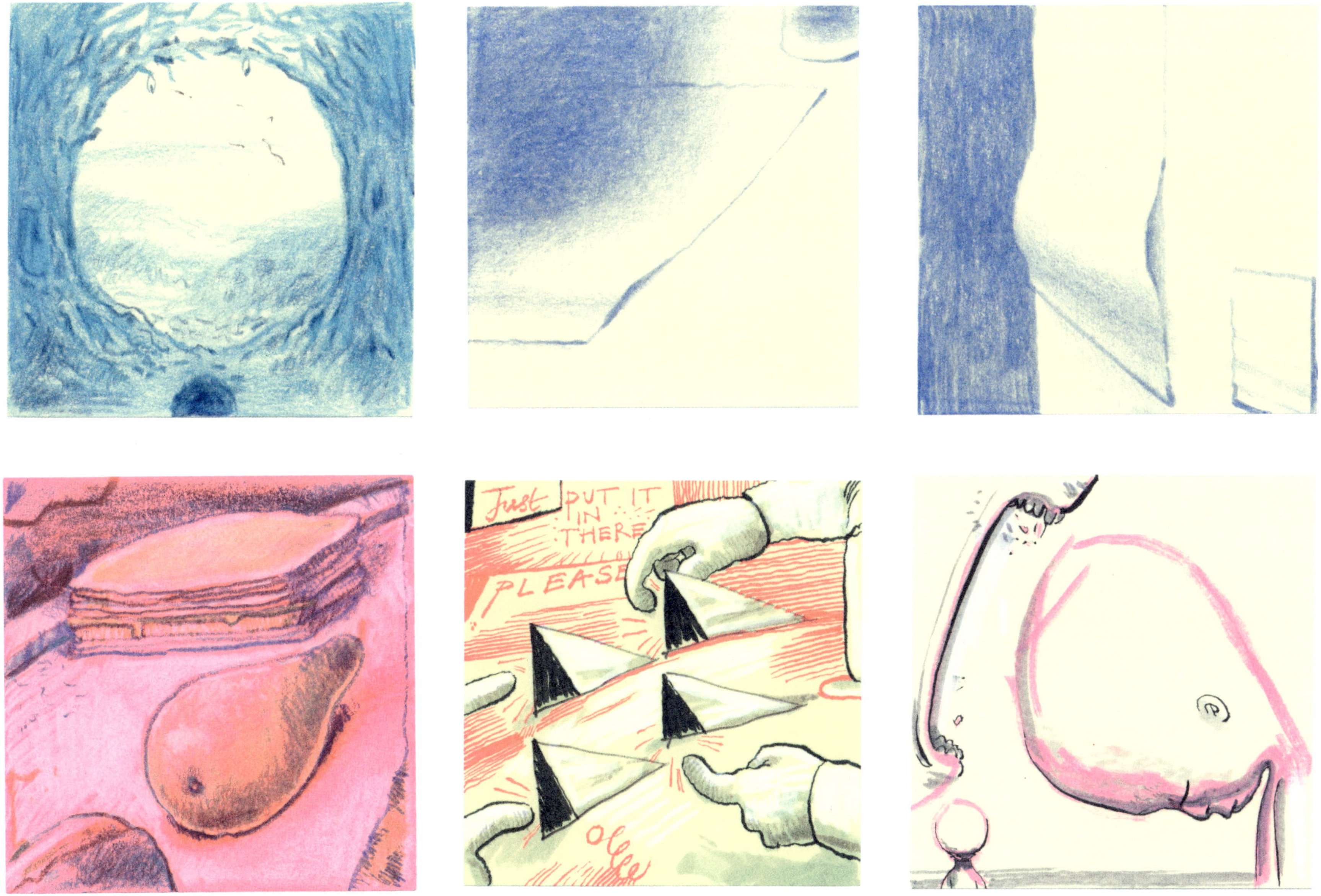
Just
PUT IT
IN
THERE
PLEASE

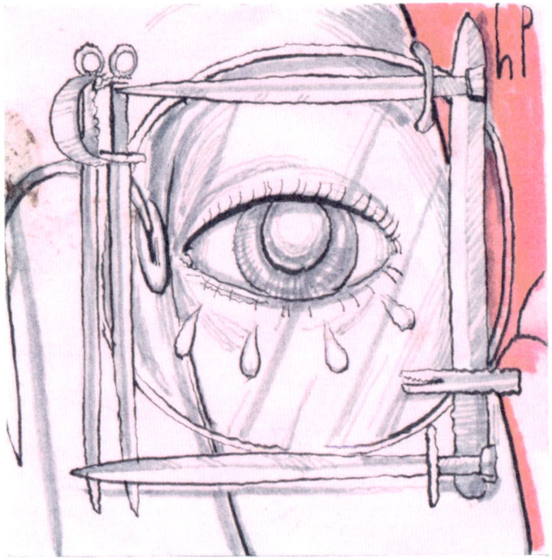
hP

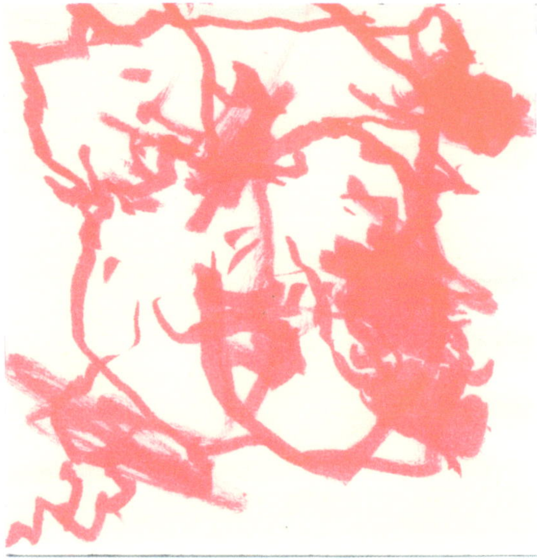

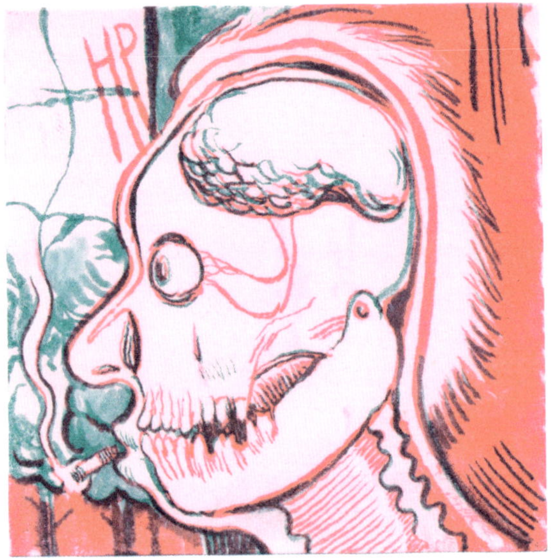
HP

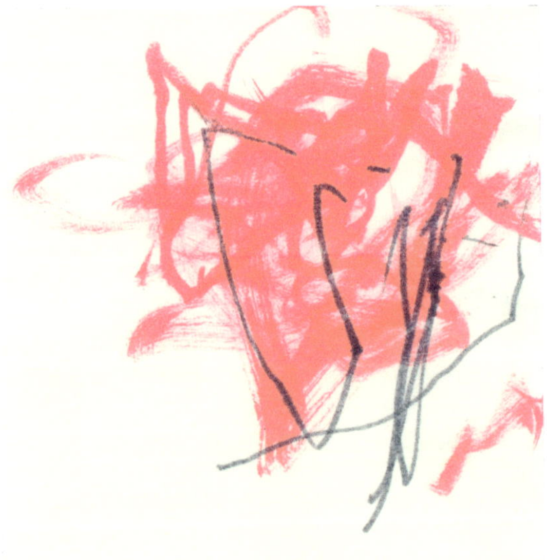

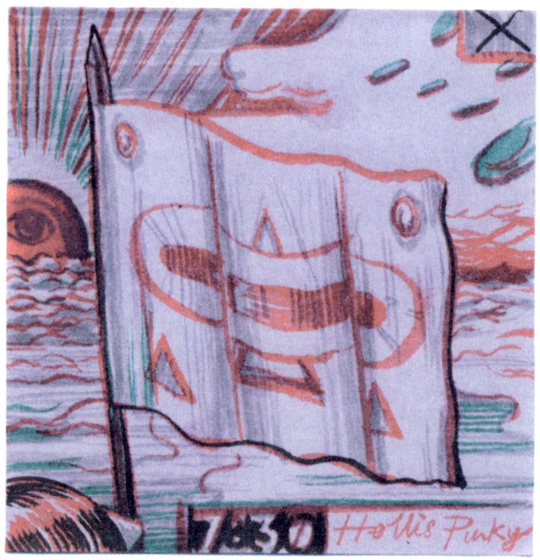
Hollis Pinky

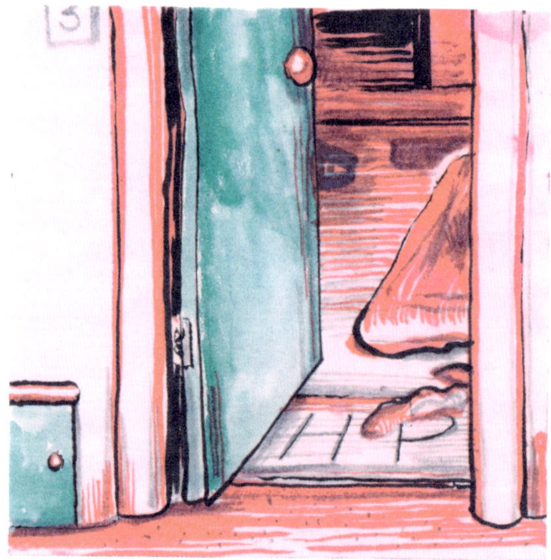
H P

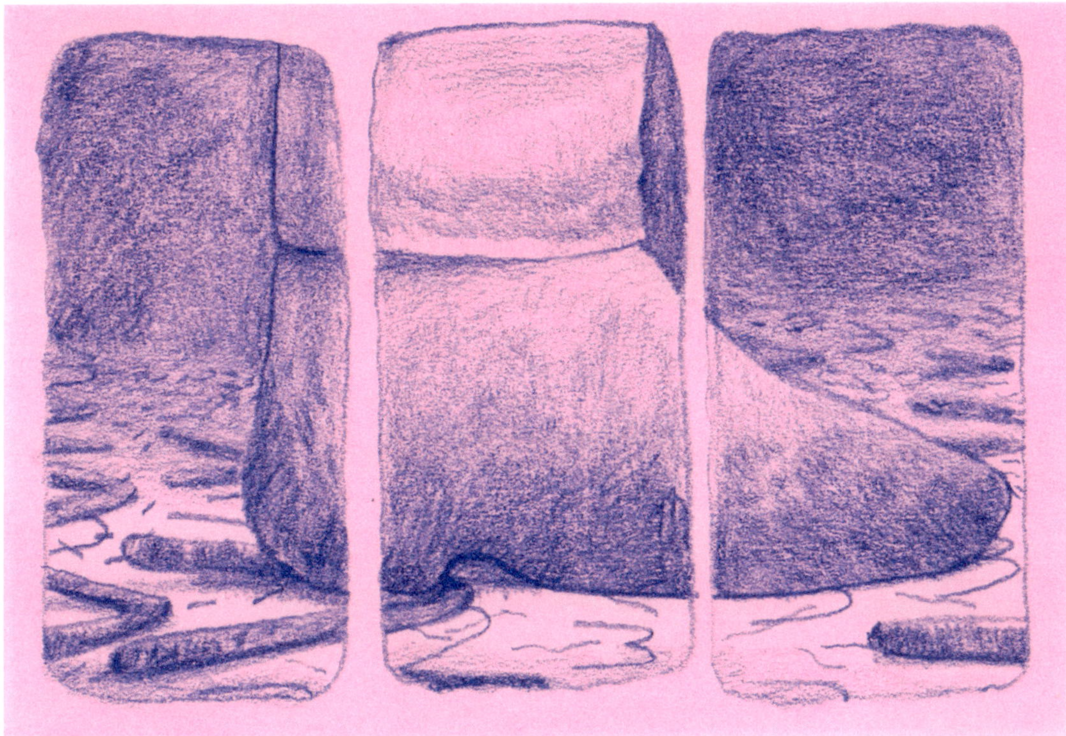

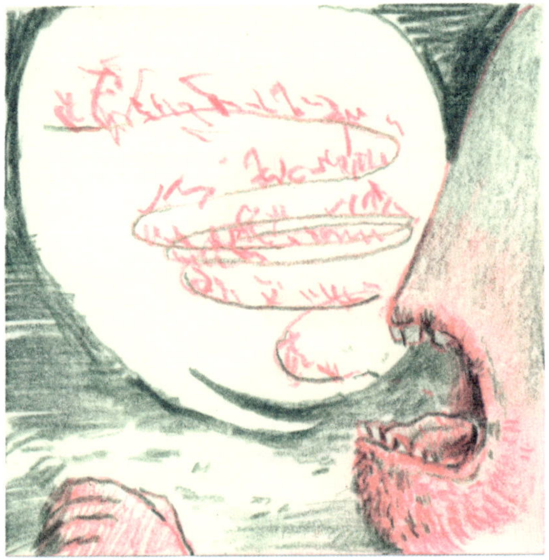
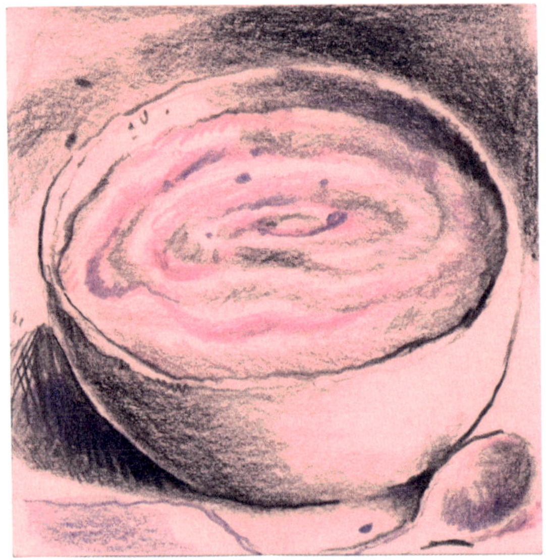
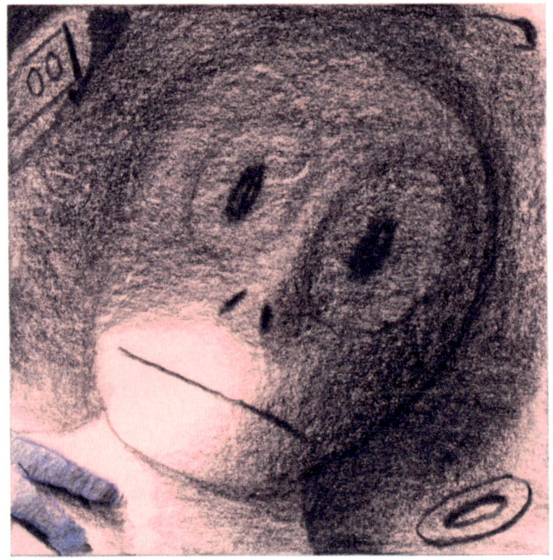
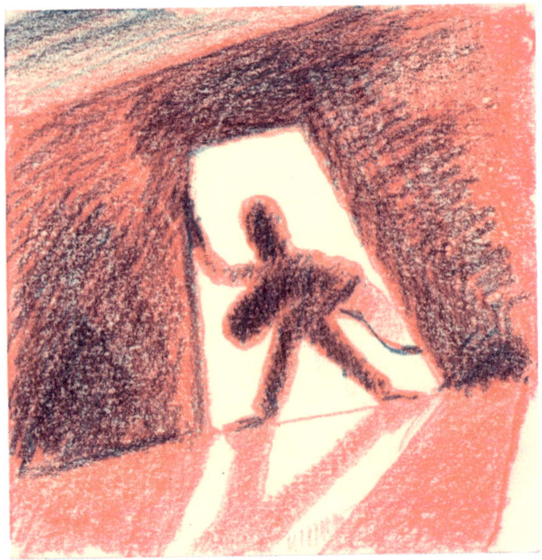
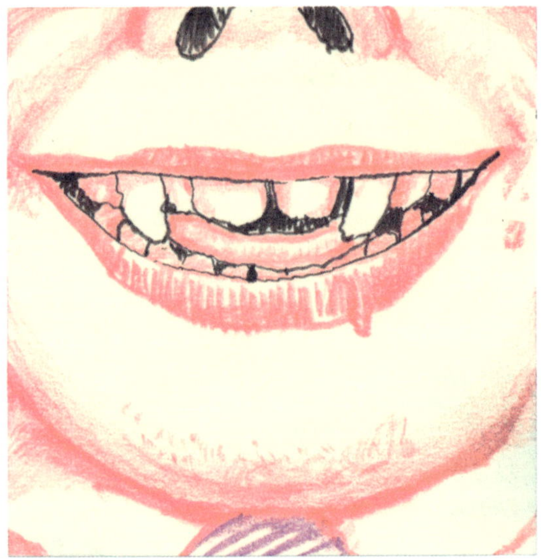
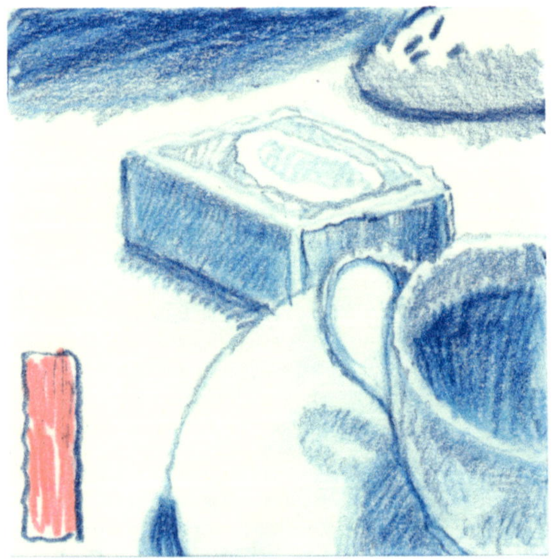

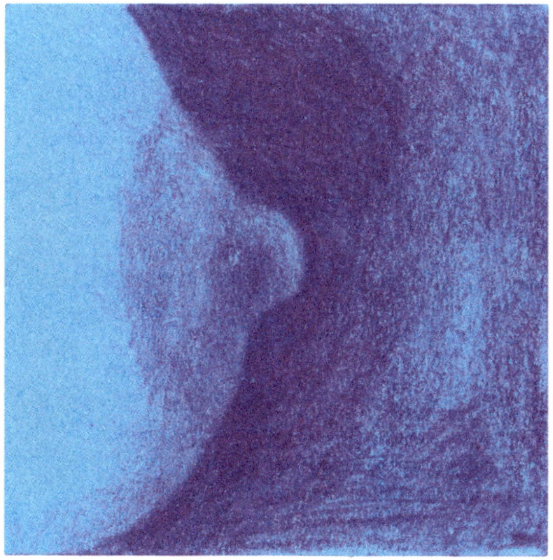
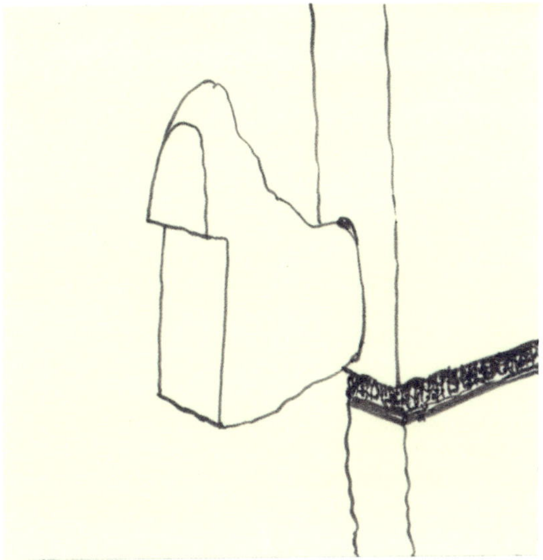
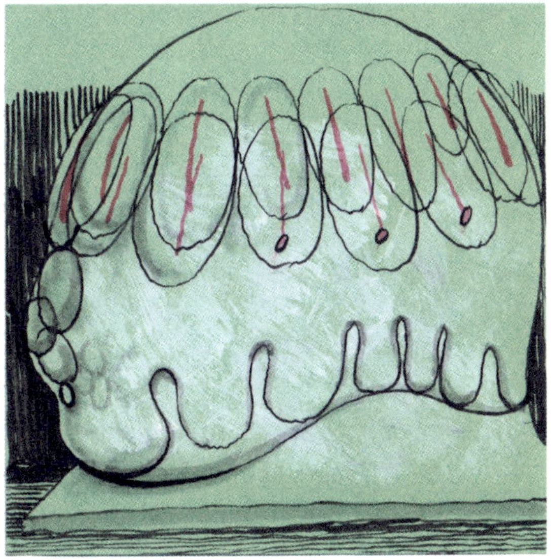
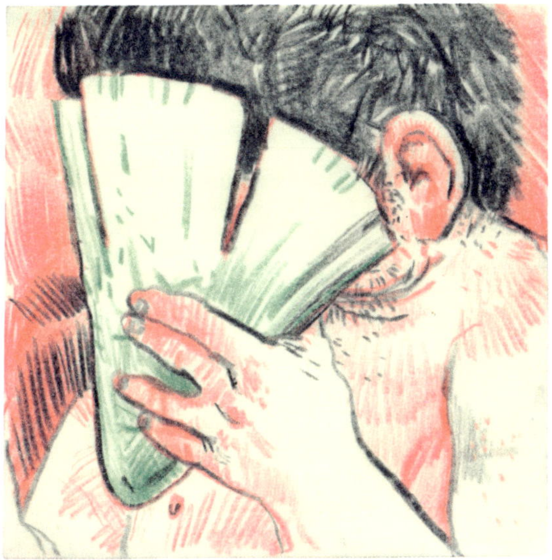
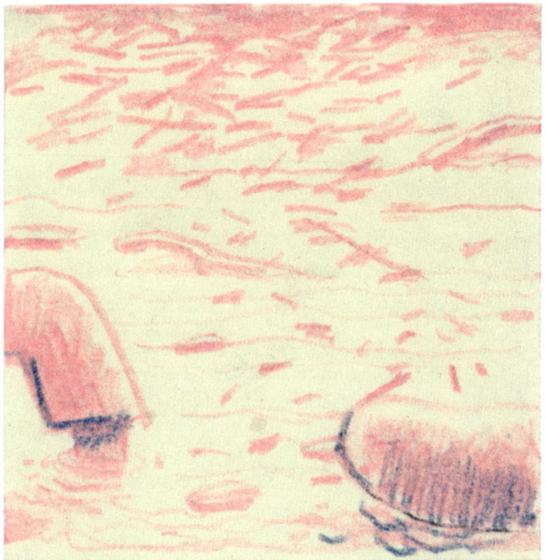
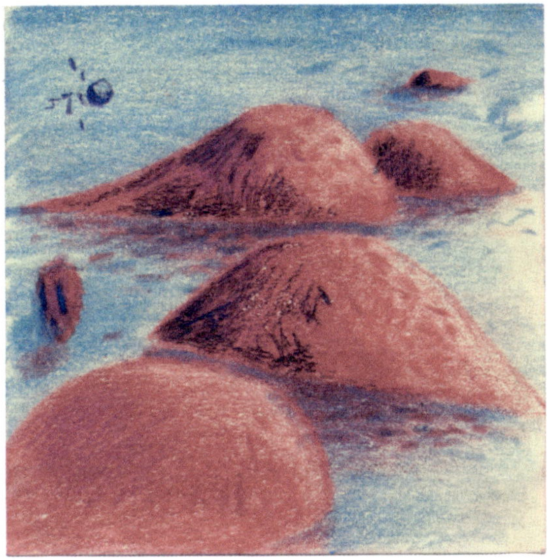

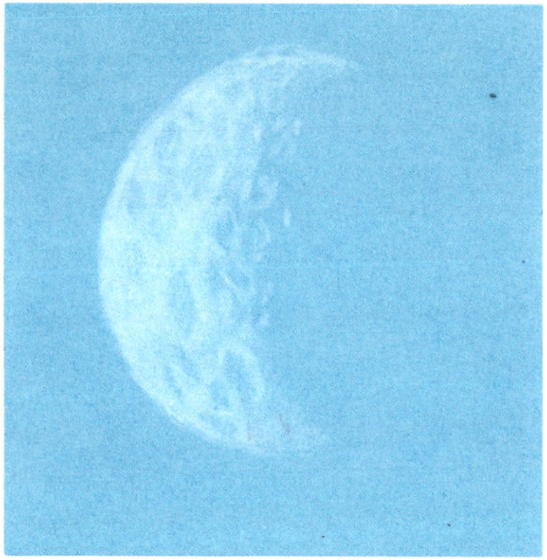

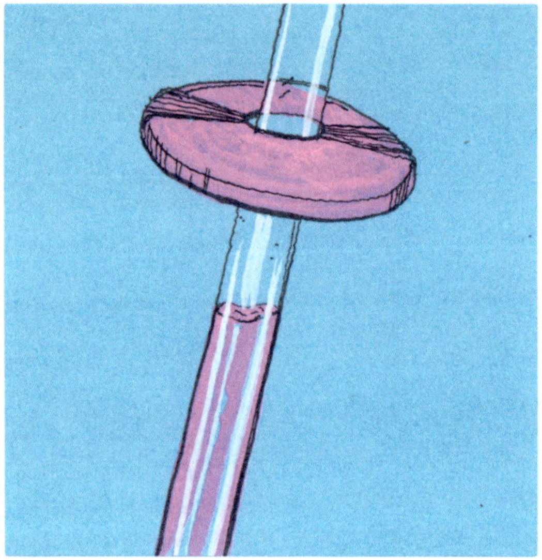

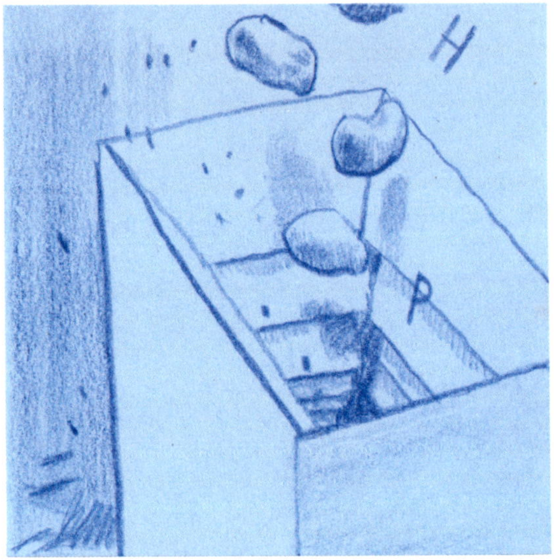

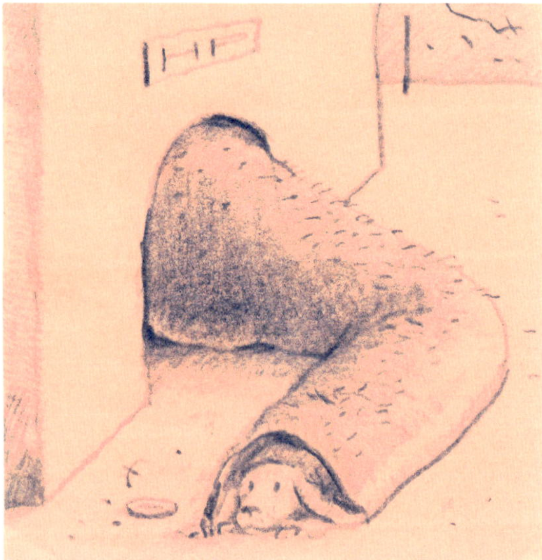

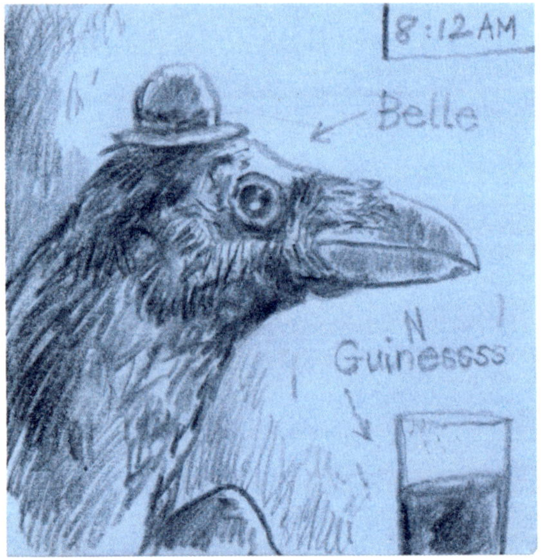
8:12AM
Belle
N
Guinesss

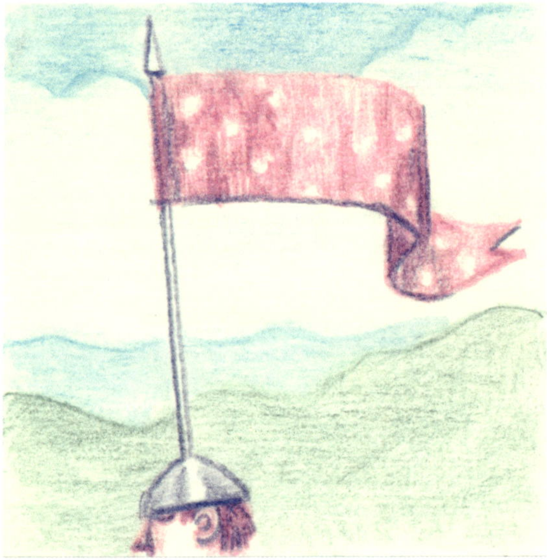

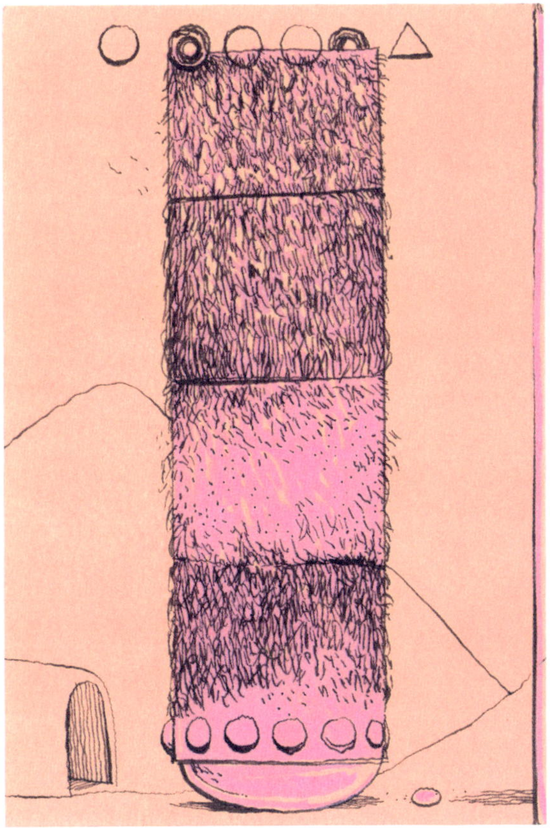

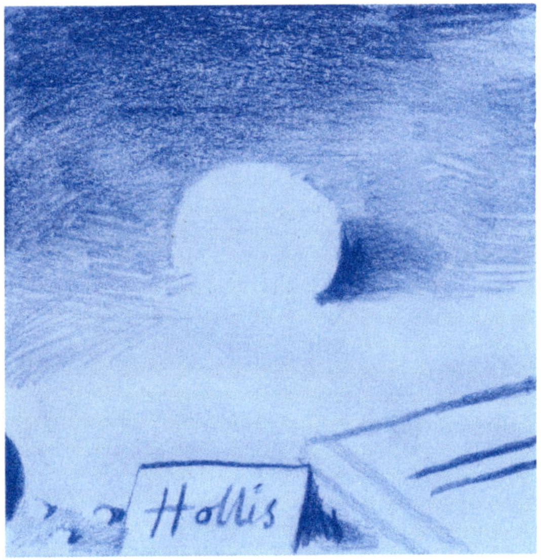

Hollis

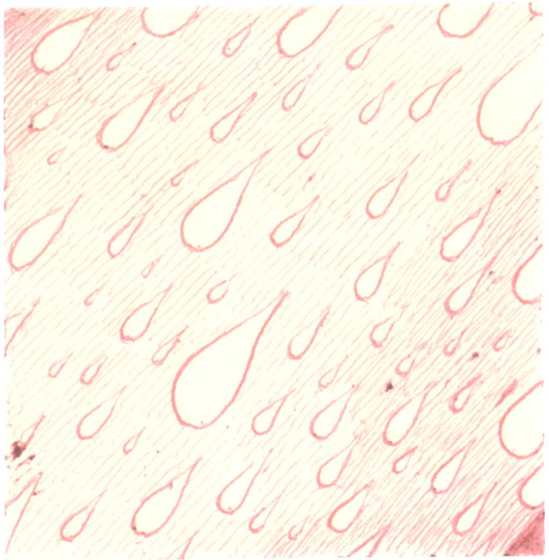

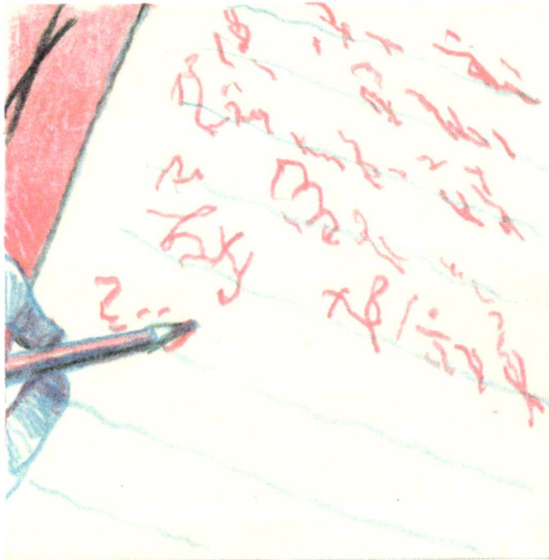
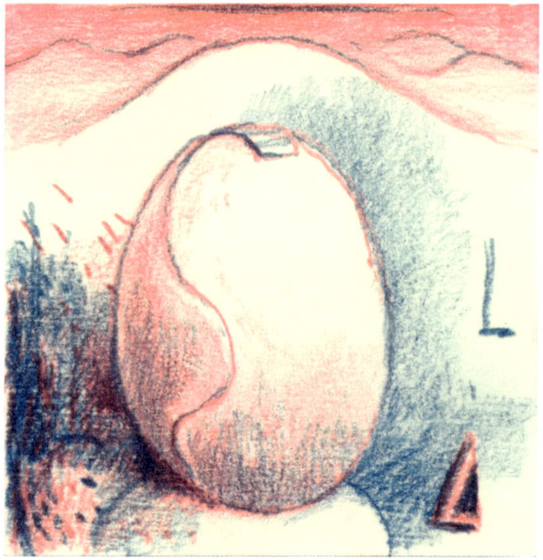
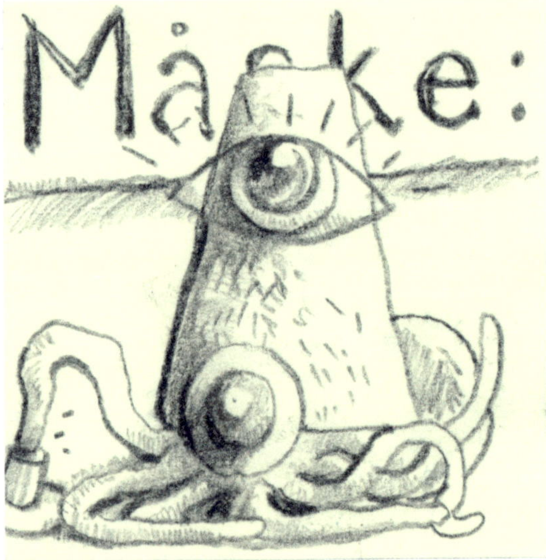
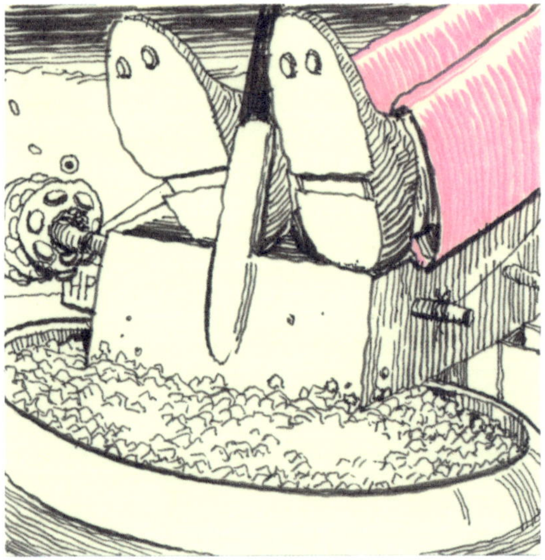
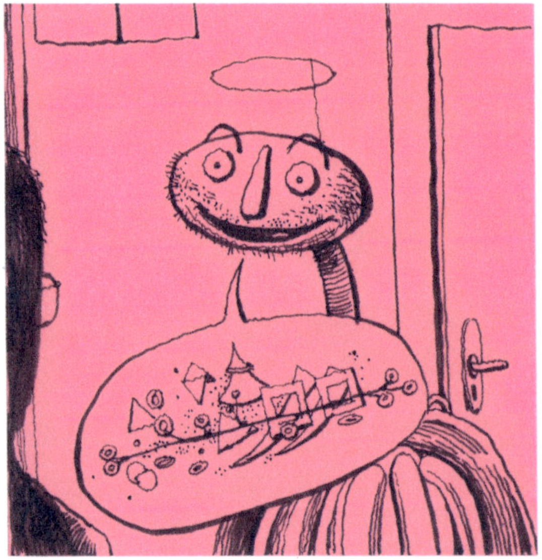
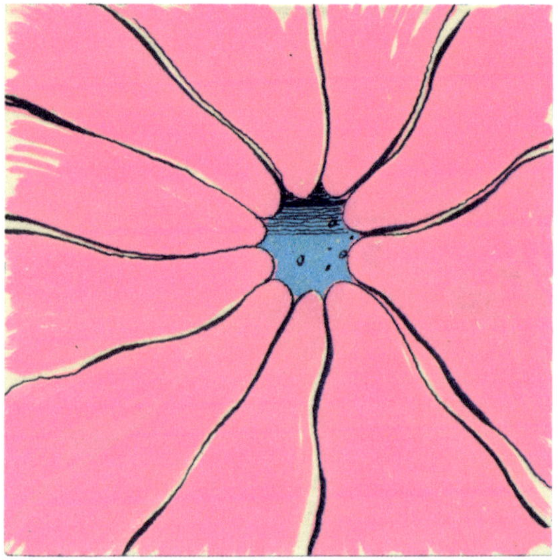

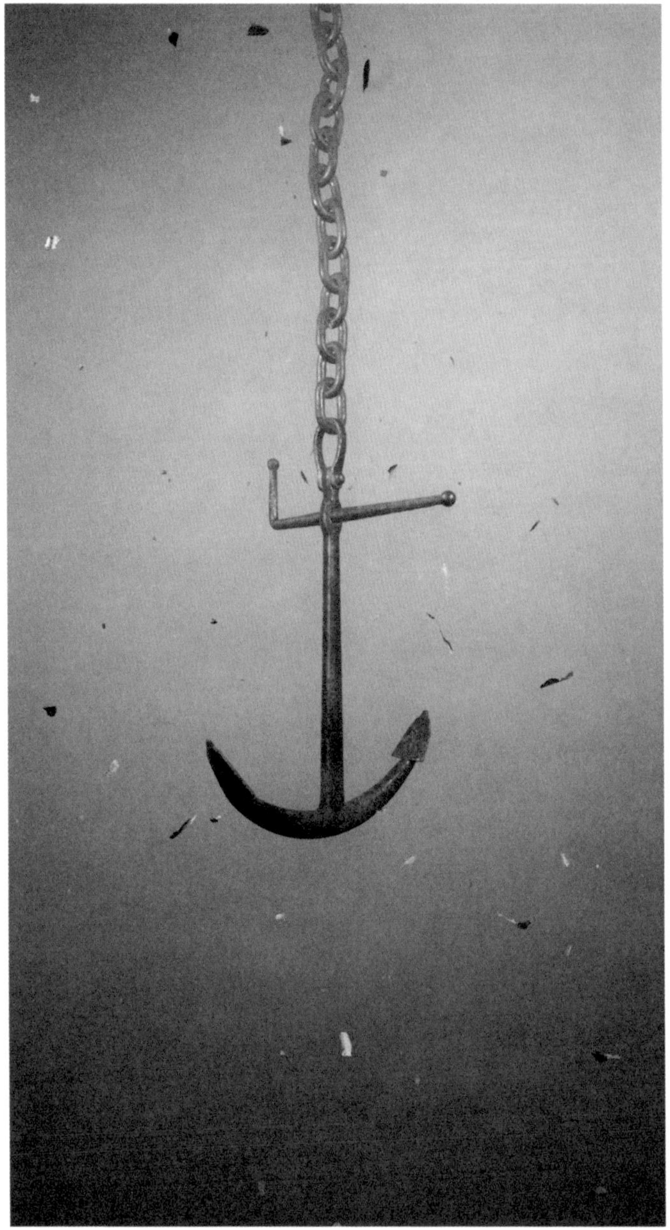

Refuse.exe 2019, two-channel video, custom software, sound, pp. 140–3

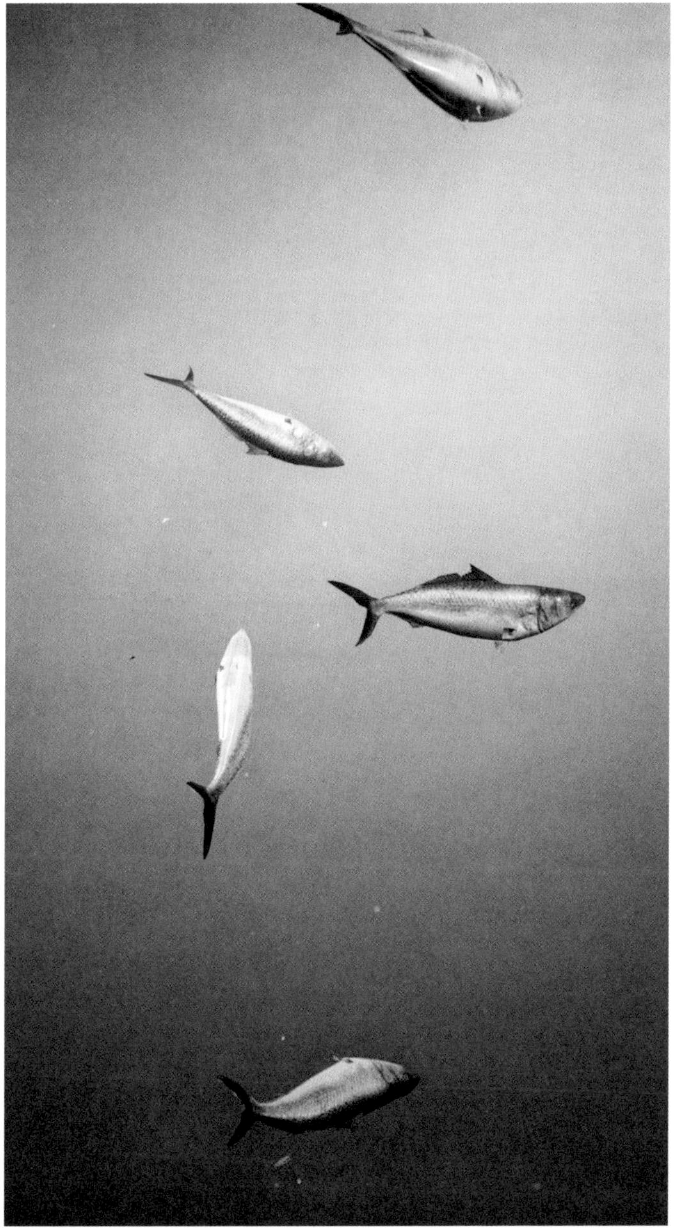

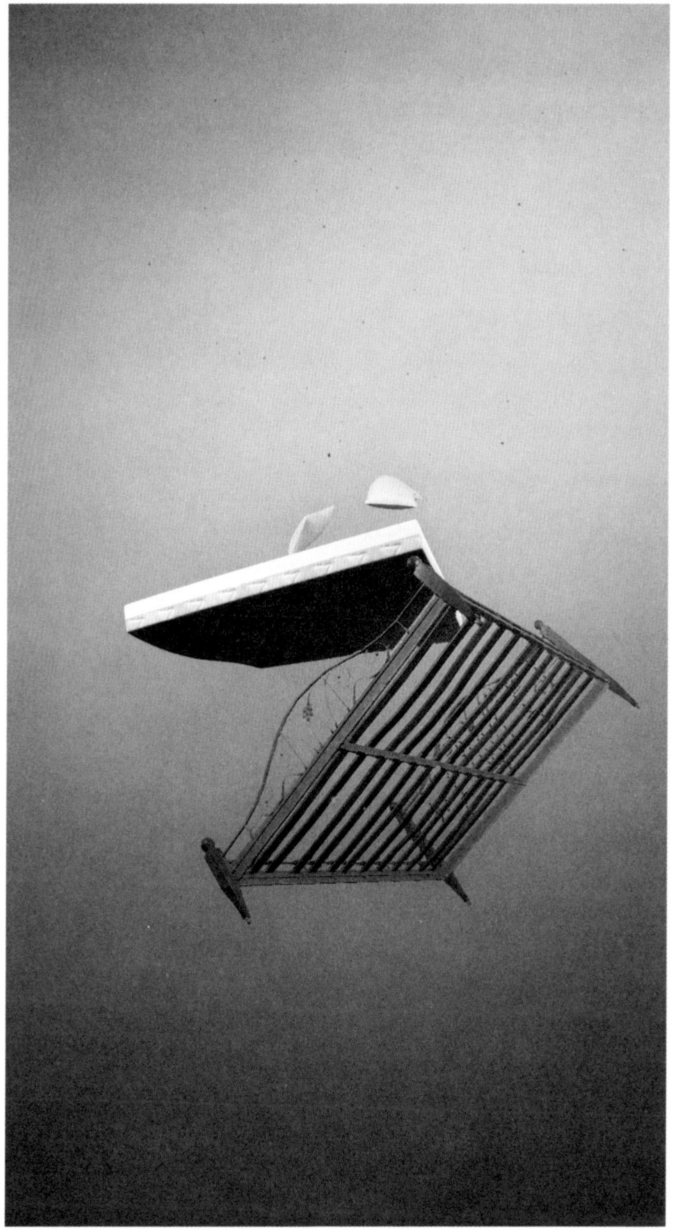

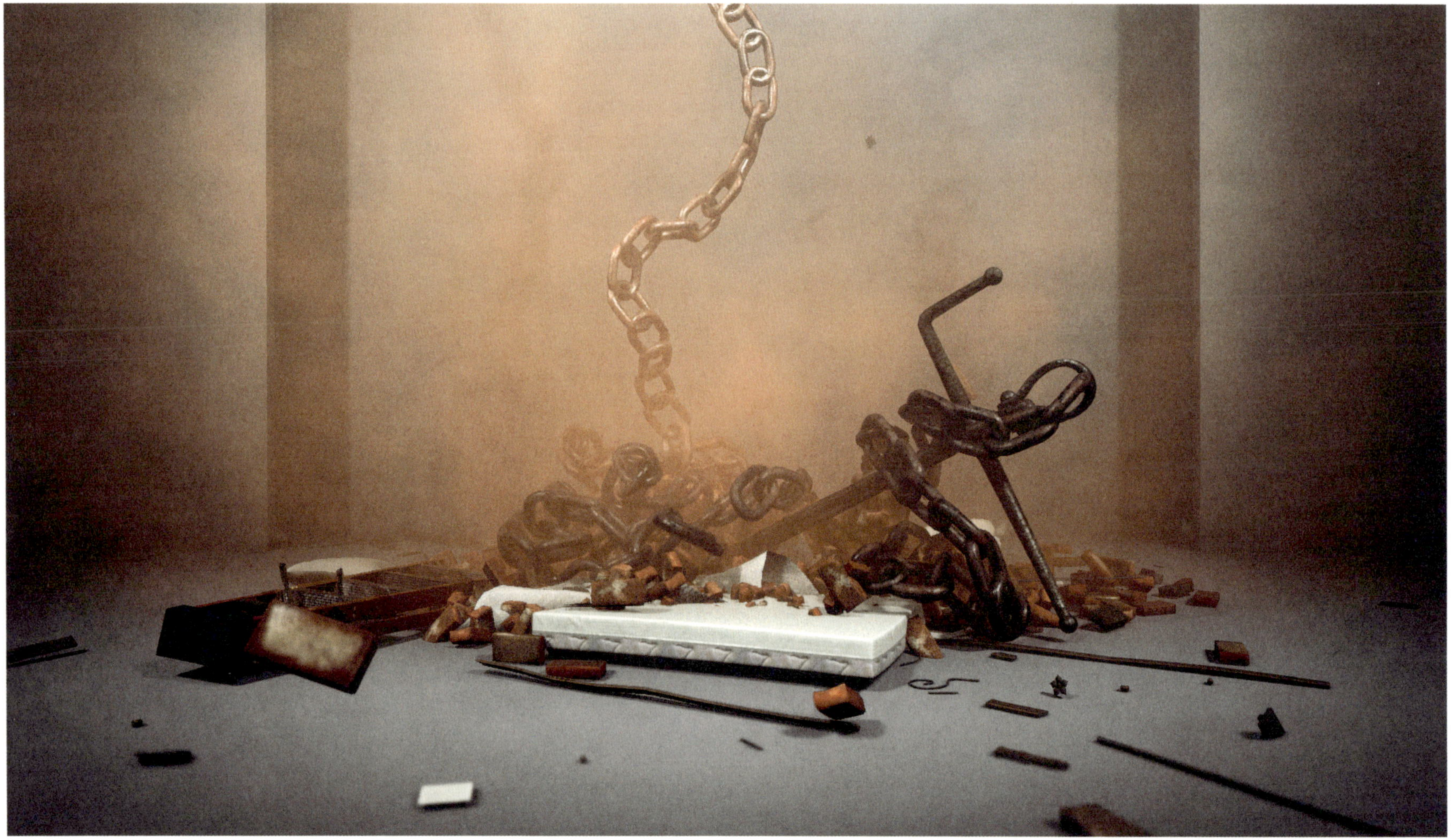

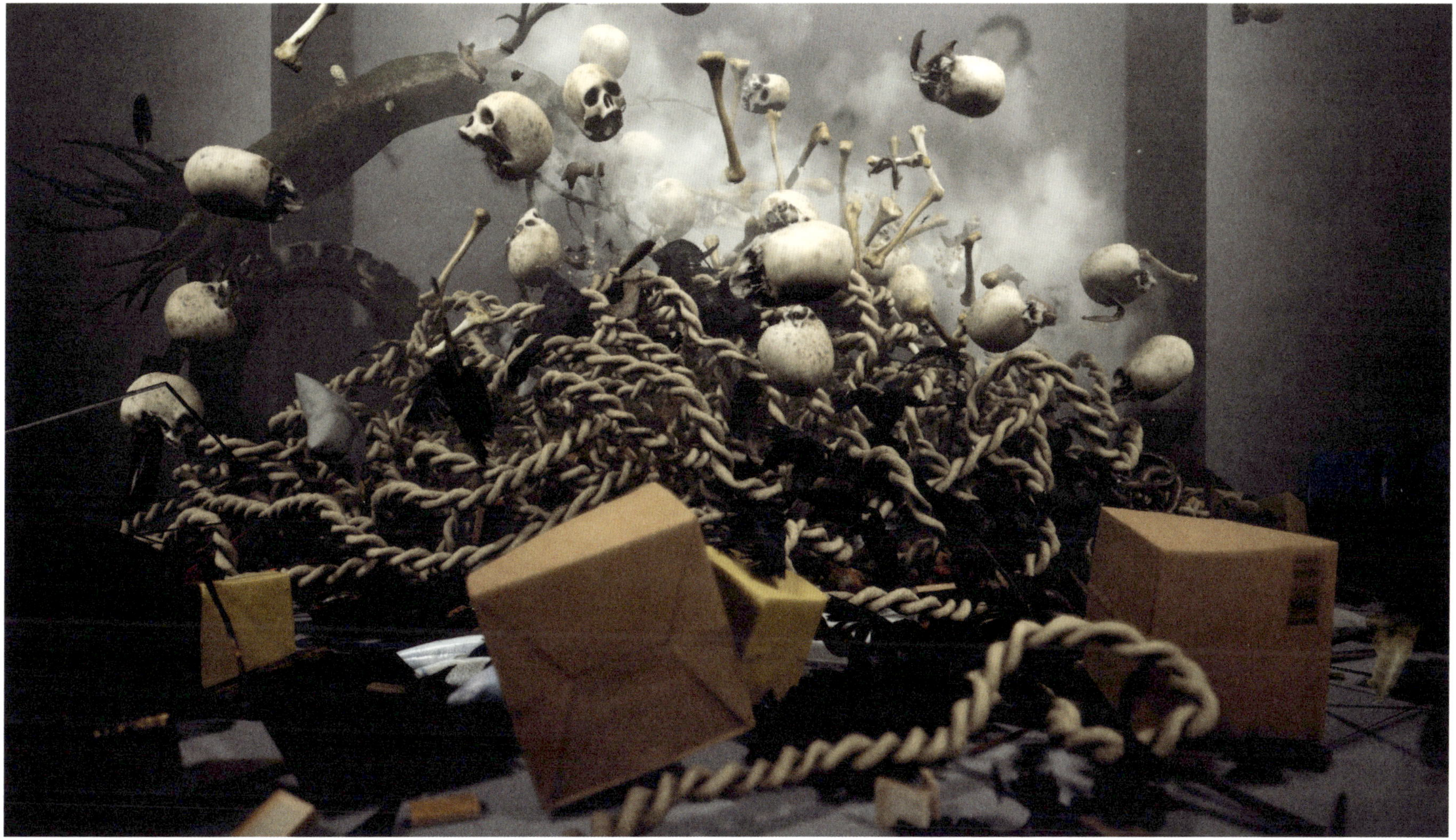

2 tons of opium powder,
1 ton of cocaine,
1 ton of peyote,
1 ton of hashish,
1 ton of marijuana,
100,000 tons of rice,
100,000 tons of sugar,
100,000 tons of coffee,
100,000 tons of cocoa,
100,000 tons of cinnamon,
100,000 tons of garlic,
100,000 tons of oil,
100,000 tons of buckwheat flour,
100,000 tons of bananas,
100,000 tons of dates,
100,000 tons of tuna,
100,000 tons of hazelnuts,
100,000 tons of walnuts,
100,000 tons of figs,
100,000 tons of manioc,
100,000 tons of Muscat grapes,
200,000 tons of pistachios,
100,000 tons of chickpeas,
100,000 tons of almonds,
300,000 tons of rats to stuff the beef, the veal, the lamb, the giraffe, the camel,
400,000 heads of cattle,
50,000 horses and camels,
300,000 piglets,
300,000 rabbits,
3000 live chickens,
300,000 guineafowls,
500,000 chicken heads,
800,000 ducks,
1 1/2 tons of cats,
20,000 spiders,
200,000 eggs,
400,000 parrots,
200,000 mice,
100,000 guinea pigs,
100,000 sheep,
200,000 mice,
200,000 impalas,
102,000 glasses of alcohol,
4 tons of sugar,
420,000 bales of cotton,
181 tonnes of weapons,
150,000 snapping turtles,
400 animals from four continents,
300,000 tons of mussels,
300,000 tons of oysters,
300,000 tons of snails,
400,000 tons of rice,
500,000 tons of salt,
500,000 tons of coffee beans,
500,000 tons of bauxite,
500,000 tons of clay,
1000 tons of coal,
1000 tons of diamonds,
1000 tons of gold,
1000 tons of tin,
1000 tons of tinware,
1000 tons of silk,
1000 tons of sugar,
1000 tons of wheat,
100,000 tons of metal,
100,000 tons of plastics,
100,000 tons of rubber,
500,000 tons of petroleum,
1,000 tons of uranium,
1,000 tons of alfalfa,
2,000 tons of fish,
2,000 tons of fuel oil,
4,000 tons of fertilizer,
4,000 tons of alcohol,
5,000 tons of dried seafood,
5,000 tons of wax,
6,000 tons of rubber,
10,000 tons of lumber,
25,000 tons of leather,
2,500 tons of cocoa,
1,000 tons of fish,
200 tons of wild turkey,
20,000 tons of potted meat,
1,200 tons of whale meat,
5,000 tons of eggnog,
4,000 tons of cheese,
5,000 tons of molasses,
6,000 tons of popcorn,
6,000 tons of organic cotton,
6,000 tons of titanium,
5,000 tons of rubber,
6,000 tons of pharmaceuticals,
8,000 tons of petroleum,
10,000 tons of flak jackets,
10,000 tons of soap,
12,000 tons of zippers,
14,000 tons of antiseptics,
15,000 tons of antacids,
16,000 tons of synthetic pyrethrin,
16,000 tons of deodorants,
20,000 tons of fuel oil,
30,000 tons of flour,
30,000 tons of potato peelings,
35,000 tons of toilet paper,
50,000 tons of uniforms,
100,000 tons of pyrolysis liquid waste,
100,000 tons of charcoal,
5,000 tons of metal items,
20,000 tons of potassium chlorate,
6,000 tons of tables,
25,000 tons of soaps,
25,000 tons of toothbrushes,
50,000 tons of toothpaste,
1,000 tons of aluminum,
2,000 tons of asphalt,
2,000 tons of cement,
200 tons of rubber,
210 tons of electronic waste,
60,000 tons of soap and cement,
60,000 tons of batteries,
100,000 tons of watermelons,
111. ANDY STARKIDS KRULL YOUR GONGWUM BAG,
2,000 tons of gunpowder,
2,000 tons of honey,
5,000 tons of beef fat,
5,000 tons of lard,
5,000 tons of dried fruits,
5,000 tons of lime,
5,000 tons of rubber bands,
6,000 tons of castor oil,
6,000 tons of beer,
8,000 tons of bat excrement,
9,000 tons of crawfish,
9,000 tons of asbestos,
10,000 tons of rubber cement,
5,000 tons of napalm,
5,000 tons of mustard gas,
5,000 tons of picnic matting,
5,000 tons of fishing nets,
10,000 tons of decay yeast,
11,000 tons of bathroom garbage,
11,000 tons of booze,
11,000 tons of paint,
12,000 tons of cement,
12,000 tons of filters,
12,000 tons of ploughshare,
12,000 tons of puncture wrenches,
13,000 tons of glass,
14,000 tons of canned shrimp,
14,000 tons of puffer fish,
14,000 tons of porcelain,
15,000 tons of wrenches,
15,000 tons of cemeteries,
15,000 tons of chewing gum,
16,000 tons of nuts,
18,000 tons of bubble gum,
18,000 tons of jam,
19,000 tons of bayonets,
19,000 tons of lock nuts,
20,000 tons of shoelaces,
20,000 tons of jellyfish,
21,000 tons of blood,
22,000 tons of dung,
22,000 tons of avocados,
22,000 tons of oysters,
24,000 tons of insulin,
24,000 tons of kerosene,
25,000 tons of offal,
25,000 tons of entrails,
26,000 tons of sugar,
28,000 tons of pacifiers,
28,000 tons of lorry tires,
29,000 tons of latex gloves,
14,000 tons of tanning paint,
16,000 tons of global warming,
20,000 tons of treacle,
1,500 tons of piano wire,
1,500 tons of sand,
1,500 tons of tallow,
1,500 tons of rye,
1,500 tons of machinist's leather,
1,500 tons of seafood,
1,500 tons of artificial phosphates,
2,200 tons of ball bearings,
2,200 tons of pearl dust,
2,200 tons of bulk phosphorous,
2,200 tons of ultraviolet light ray filters,
2,200 tons of ghosts,
3,800 tons of wood,
4,700 tons of wax,
4,700 tons of foam,
6,700 tons of fatty material,
9,000 tons of birth control pills,
10,000 tons of chocolate,
10,000 tons of bullying,
12,000 tons of vinegar,
14,000 tons of paper towel,
14,000 tons of dog shit,
16,000 tons of raw sewage,
8,000 tons of plastic trash,
13,000 tons of shoe leather,
13,000 tons of scrap steel,
14,000 tons of beer,
16,000 tons of mothballs,
16,000 tons of catfish,
13,000 tons of accelerator dynein,
13,000 tons of air pumped into the Ozone Layer,
32,000 tons of hair clipper blades,
30,000 tons of laptop batteries,
3,000 tons of libavios,
9,000 tons of sackcloth,
9,000 tons of hay,
9,000 tons of rose pollen,
9,000 tons of dark chocolate,
15,000 tons of urine,
21,000 tons of waste fruits and vegetables,
7,000 tons of urinals,
14,000 tons of textbooks,
14,000 tons of childbirth positions,
10,000 tons of dust from dirt-laced gym mats,
6,000 tons of heads of office workers,
4,000 tons of cobwebs,
7,000 tons of dental floss,
15,000 tons of poo,
28,000 tons of fertilizer,
17,000 tons of earwax,
20,000 tons of industrial waste,
18,000 tons of candle wax,
6,000 tons of sunflower seed shells,
10,000 tons of egg shells,
7,000 tons of sunflower seeds,
10,000 tons of bubble-gum,
7,000 tons of apple pieces,
10,000 tons of jeans,
10,000 tons of geiger counters,
12,000 tons of automotive gasoline,
20,000 tons of empty plastic condoms,
28,000 tons of inexpensive jewelry,
10,000 tons of Africanized bees,
10,000 tons of dog feces,
10,000 tons of home appliances,
10,000 tons of multicolored wax crayons,
7,000 tons of uncooked curry,
15,000 tons of steak bones,
15,000 tons of lichen,
16,000 tons of skin,
15,000 tons of ship repair goods,
16,000 tons of vegetable soup,
16,000 tons of hookworms,
14,000 tons of bowling balls,
16,000 tons of pallets,
17,000 tons of photocopiers,
18,000 tons of foam,
24,000 tons of unwrapped soap,

25,000 tons of household air conditioning,
29,000 tons of furniture,
91,000 tons of corn cobs,
32,000 tons of sulfite,
36,000 tons of waste,
40,000 tons of yam,
41,000 tons of cod liver oil,
68,000 tons of artificial baby formula,
72,000 tons of surgical gloves,
68,000 tons of powdered milk,
75,000 tons of soda ash,
77,000 tons of aspirin pills,
88,000 tons of caustic soda,
93,000 tons of pesticide,
108,000 tons of gold,
159,000 tons of tires,
5,000 tons of thimerosal,
5,000 tons of mustards,
5,000 tons of rocket and missile engines,
15,000 tons of rust,
9,000 tons of napalm plant,
12,000 tons of benzene,
20,000 tons of televisions,
20,000 tons of dental dams,
30,000 tons of plasma displays,
30,000 tons of concrete,
30,000 tons of nylon,
50,000 tons of 5-10 gallon paint buckets,
100,000 tons of tomatoes,
100,000 tons of uranium ore,
100,000 tons of coal,
100,000 tons of cherry pits,
100,000 tons of helium,
100,000 tons of rubber,
150,000 tons of aluminum,
300,000 tons of textiles,
300,000 tons of granite,
300,000 tons of gypsum,
400,000 tons of gypsum stock cubes,
400,000 tons of plaster,
400,000 tons of silicon,
300,000 tons of turpentine,
400,000 tons of wood,
400,000 tons of woodchips,
400,000 tons of titanium,
500,000 tons of paper,
500,000 tons of aluminum,
500,000 tons of cement,
5,000 tons of statos,
5,000 tons of stearine,
5,000 tons of glucose,
6,000 tons of starch,
9,000 tons of processed cocoa,
10,000 tons of marshmallows,
10,000 tons of oregano,
30,000 tons of sweet bananas,
2,000 tons of snow,
2,000 tons of sugar,
2,000 tons of urine,
8,000 tons of sheen,
5,000 tons of silk,
5,000 tons of satin,
5,000 tons of shaved chocolate,
8,000 tons of seal skins,
9,000 tons of pine resin,
12,000 tons of shoes,
20,000 tons of uniforms,
20,000 tons of fish,
5,000 tons of tin,
10,000 tons of carbon fibre,
3,000 tons of cholesterol,
3,000 tons of urine resin,
3,000 tons of flesh,
5,000 tons of hairs,
15,000 tons of televisions,
20,000 tons of pennies,
20,000 tons of pepper,
25,000 tons of cement,
10,000 tons of silk,
16,000 tons of PVC,
35,000 tons of artichokes,
41,000 tons of camouflage,
5,000 tons of firewood,
5,000 tons of hot springs,
100,000 tons of Volkswagen fuel,
100,000 tons of ICBMs,
100,000 tons of uranium,
10,000 tons of cancers,
10,000 tons of face creams,
10,000 tons of wax,
10,000 tons of Silly Putty,
20,000,000 million of tons of oregano,
20,000,000 million of tons of hot peppers,
3.6 billion tons of dog food,
30 billion tonnes of federal aid,
40 billion tonnes of solid waste,
50 billion tonnes of electric power,
200 billion tonnes of mercury,
3000 kilometers of cable,
5 million pilot whales,
24 million,000,000,000 Mandarin oranges,
4084.434 miles of air duct,
8,687 tons of asbestos,
8,964 tons of limestone,
6,500 tons of plaster,
6,064 tons of asphalt,
6,166 tons of stucco,
6,433 tons of crocuses,
6,450 tons of knives,
9,890 tons of Pyrex,
10,000 tons of sunscreen,
12 million,000,000 or so tennis balls,
4,000 years of earwax,
11,600 tons of leather shoes,
5,500 tons of snouts,
15,000 tons of nails,
45 thousand tons of flour,
35 thousand tons of semen,
50,000 tons of equalizers,
350 kilos of aluminum foil,
6,000 kilos of nylon stock,
28,000,000 rats,
500,000 wolfs,
2,000 tons of manioc,
10,000 plastic bags,
11 million tonnes of cobalt,
10 billion tons of sugar,
10 billion tons of hydrogen,
11,000 tons of the ground color,
11,000 tons of pennies,
40,000,000,000 pigeons,
1000 pounds of western artichokes,
1,100 pounds of steel,
931,145 pounds of quinine,
9 billion tons of books,
0.03 pounds of blood,
1,280,000 monkeys,
0.03 pounds of tree roots,
330 pounds of lead,
1 kilo of wild-fowl blood,
40,000,000 heads of state,
220 tons of myriads,
0.04 pounds of of sewage,
0.32 kilos of minerals,
0.35 kilos of forgotten manuscripts,
129,630 tablespoons of vanilla extract,
32 kilograms of ivory,
0.02 kilograms of swans,
0.2 ounces of silk,
0.05 centimeters of plutonium,
16 grams of the secret sauce,
0.5 kilograms of cash,
0.5 kilograms of obsidian,
200 grams of gold,
5 grams of money,
60 grams of farmland,
7 grams of toilet paper,
0.00005 grams of metal-soldier liver pate,
8 grams of lard,
0.011 grams of purple coke,
11,000 tons of glass,
11,000 tons of theses,
11,000 tons of white space,
11,000 tons of life,
11,000 tons of blueberries,
11,000 tons of artificial snow,
14,000 tons of light bulbs,
27,000 tons of ozone,
35,000 tons of helium,
20,000 tons of fossil fuels,
43,000 tons of lead,
50,000 tons of fungus,
90,000 tons of rhubarb,
190 million tons of stainless steel,
4,000 tons of octopi,
6,000 tons of guinea pigs,
16 tons of cheese,
21 tons of lipstick,
21 tons of fingernail polish,
22,000 tons of silt,
12.2 million vitamin tablets,
12.2 million tons of freezers,
13.2 million tons of Randian propaganda,
19 tons of royalty,
16 tons of germs,
2,085 tons of reefer,
3 million tons of ipods,
500 tons of reheated gravy,
1/144 of a 667-foot skyscraper,
7.5 human heads,
1 chinchilla,
12 million tons of arsenic,
40 million cans of 8-hour energy,
50 million ladybugs,
40,000 boxes of pickled herring,
60 million ruins,
90 million coins,
99 million used condoms,
123 million cups of coffee,
156 million compact discs,
137 million flakes of dog food,
141 million passports,
3.6 million gold bars,
450 mice,
1,000 fish,
1,500 cats,
2.5 billion puzzle pieces,
3 billion kgs of roast beef,
900 billion beer cans,
60 billion cutlery trays,
1 million boxes of Sudafed,
1,000 wound disinfectant strips,
300 mottos,
1,000 hoodies,
2 million soldiers,
2,500 assault weapons,
3 million cement,
6 billion Russian Roubles,
6 billion US dollars,
7.5 billion dollars,
7.5 billion tons of daylife,
80 billion rootlets,
100,000,000 tons of hot water,
6,500 pieces of telephone wire,
8 billion buttons,
91 layers of brick,
136 million nails,
1 million men,
1 million men's jeans,
1,096 mili¬tones spray tints,
48 million cans,
50 million vacuum cleaners,
12 million chocolate fountains,
13 billion pennies,
1.4 million military helmets,
1 million rockets,
512,000 soldiers,
1,749 rockets,
1,700 tons of sushi,
337 pounds of old-growth forest,
581 hectares of land,
6 million flags,
6 million monkeys,
10.3 billion communicable diseases,
22 million Christmas presents,
32 million families,
3 million football fans,
10 million doves,
24,632 arms,
181 million blazons,
277,945 houses,
7 million children,
4.6 million homes,
3.4 million parcels,
10 million cakes,

1 million life masks,
20,245 resistors,
1 million bullets,
422 unicorns,
7,000 square miles of land,
10,000 square miles of forest,
20,000,000,000,000 pounds of HGH,
20,000,000,000,000,000 pounds of hydrogen,
30 million cars,
38 million tornadoes,
40,000,000,000,000,000,000 of elephants,
60 million wind turbines,
60 million,000,000,000 of lambs,
72 million trees,
48 million grocery carts,
56 million low-grade explosives,
64,000 nuclear warheads,
2.6 million hydrogen bombs,
260,000 X-rays,
300,000,000,000,000 of taking showers,
1000 X-ray machines,
4100,000 fetal corpses,
2 million users of GnuPG,
5 million e-mail accounts,
8000 Harley Davidsons,
15 million Playboy spreadsheets,
35 million hotspots,
3 billion photos,
621 billion spam mails,
16 billion conversations,
22 billion Disney movies,
141 billion fish,
6 billion Christmas trees,
3.1 billion cogs in a modern railway,
1 trillion words of Wikipedia,
1,000,000 cauliflowers,
111 trillion LiteBrite,
176 billion seas,
200 trillion purple jesters,
2000 Götterdämmerung,
93914343 dollars,
105,632 grains of rice,
124 pounds of mascara,
443 million people,
99230 zeros of pi,
247000 trillion stars,
2 dollars,
1000 hydrogen bombs,
18 months of Google searches,
141,
55 million school buses,
60 million garbage trucks,
96 million souls,
100,000,000,000 bp of coffee,
100,000,000,000,000 bp of grapes,
180,000,000,000,000 of trees,
180 million fish,
4,150 of pomegranates,
4,150 of strawberry,
8,000 of oranges,
14,900,000,000,000 of bovine milk,
24,000,000,000,000 of chicken,
16,000,000,000,000 of torsos,
16,000,000,000,000,000 of ears,
32,000,000,000,000 of eggs,
2.9 billion pizzas,
5.7 billion bullets,
8.3 billion guns,
10.1 billion buttons,
4.5 billion zippers,
18 billion helmets,
65.6 billion Canadian potatoes,
15.4 billion shag carpets,
20 billion condoms,
40 billion batteries,
10.3 billion magazines,
18.1 billion fast food,
40 billion toilet seats,
17.2 billion alligators,
20 billion washing machines,
33.5 billion of hair,
7.2 billion socks,
4 billion fingers,
4 billion microbes,
4 billion Q-tips,
3.2 billion condoms,
5.1 billion eyes,
4 billion birds,
50 billion zebras,
60 billion toilet seats,
69 billion high-school girls,
4.1 billion tons of lumber,
5.2 billion jelly beans,
10.8 billion bedsheets,
7.2 billion Coca-Cola,
43 billion books,
71 billion rectal,
20,000,000,000,000,000 tons of copper,
10,000,000,000,000,000 tons of blood,
8,666 tons of steel,
4 million mollusks,
5,500 tonnes of garlic,
4 million onions,
11,000 tons of hot peppers,
10,000 tons of bad maiming,
2,058 tons of mail,
6,000 tons of dead trees,
931 tons of old ladies,
7.6 tons of human hair,
24.3 million computers,
21,000,000,000,000 tons of iron,
79.86 million St. Bernard dogs,
54,000 people,
67 people,
420,000 penguins,
124 people,
700,000 people,
90 people,
52 people,
32 people,
42 people,
22 people,
32 people,
6 people,
9 people,
12 people,
9 people,
12 people,
14 people,
4 people,
16 people,
27 people,
9 people,
6 people,
6 people,
9 people,
23 people,
6 people,
4 people,
21 people,
17 people,
12 people,
9 people,
8 people,
4 people,
16 people,
7 people,
7 people,
8 people,
4 people,
7 people,
4 people,
4 people,
4 people,
4 people,
4 people,
4 people,
4 people,
100,000 cars,
100,000 farms,
20,000,000,000,000 books,
40,000,000,000,000,000 prostitutes,
22,000,000,000,000 vegetables,
9,000,000,000,000,000 birds,
15,000,000,000,000 rats,
30,000,000,000,000 insects,
3 billion badgers,
2 billion puffins,
3 billion rabies,
400 million wolves,
400 million dodos,
1,500,000,000,000,000 mummies,
100,000 million camels,
1,000,000,000,000,000 corgis,
7.6 billion,000,000,000 mosquito larvae,
1 trillion sea urchins,
100 trillion cockroaches,
800 trillion beetles,
1.1 quadrillion,000,000 starfish,
2.5 trillion mussels,
800,000,000 tons of beeves,
20 million Australian Cows,
2.9 million shipping containers,
200.000 tons of warheads,
40,000 tons of feces,
40,000 tons of computer tape,
4000,000 trains,
30,000,000,000,000 pornographic movies,
300 million private jets,
300 million armored cars,
3 million deadbeats,
6 million dead cows,
3 million dead pigs,
3 million dead lobsters,
3 million dead cats,
9.6 million nuclear waste,
9 million dead whales,
2 million dead miners,
2 million dead tigers,
2 million dead pandas,
2 million dead bears,
42.4 million dead bus drivers,
83.4 million dead scientists,
47.6 million dead presidents,
40 million dead writers,
20 million dead soldiers,
40 million dead congressmen,
30 million dead lawyers,
38 million dead farmers,
9 million dead judges,
13 million dead mummies,
13 million dead bookstores,
10 million dead buildings,
10 million dead officials,
7.3 million dead airlines,
8 million dead freeways,
9 million dead bomb carriers,
13 million dead writers,
13 million dead bankers,
8 million dead cyclists,
8 million dead frogs,
8 million dead dictators,
8 million dead pilots,
9 million dead governors,
3 million dead lovers,
6 million dead presidents,
3 million dead astronauts,
2 million dead cod,
20 million dead fighters,
20 million dead wrestlers,
10 million dead alligators,
3 million dead mimes,
3 million dead shih tzus,
4 million dead seagulls,
4 million dead Russians,
20 million dead parrots,
4 million dead soldiers,
1 million dead flamethrowers,
20 million dead counselors,
1,300 million trees,
1 million dead trees,
50,000,000,000,000,000 unread emails,
500,000 dead people,
3.9 billion dead bodies,
3 billion dead cars,
3 billion dead cats,
3 billion dead trees,
1.4 trillion dead animals,
120 million dead people,
400 million dead earthworms,
1.5 trillion dead bears,
1,000,000,000,000 dead fish,
1.5 trillion dead mannequins,
1,500,000,000 dead cancer patients,
1,200,000,000,000,000 dead trees,

5.2 million dead people,
7.6 billion dead books,
1 billion dead trees,
830 million,000,000 dead weathermen,
1.2 million,000 dead paperclips,
1.7 trillion dead flies,
2.5 million dead cats,
4.8 million dead brides,
20 million dead animals,
300 million dead newspapers,
60 million dead dead unicorns,
120 million dead mothers,
13 billion dead turtles,
13.6 billion dead virgins,
3.5 million dead elephants,
4 million dead goats,
13 million dead evil doers,
2.5 million dead mirrors,
600 million uneaten bananas,
500,000 dead bosses,
2 million dead generals,
1 million dead teachers,
1 million dead hate crimes,
500,000 long-dead gorillas,
500,000 rotting,
wasted bandages,
100,000 dead,
soulless clocks,
4,000 dead orchids,
2.1 million dead stray dogs,
2.1 million dead,
homeless strays,
2 million dying,
unblinking,
tethered pigeons,
1.3 million dead pigs,
5 million dead snowmen,
2.1 million dead donkeys,
2.1 million dead maggots,
1 million,000 dead,
oozing hypodermic needles,
1.6 million dead squirrels,
2.3 million dead,
decomposing,
uncleaned piles of garbage,
1.2 million dead guinea pigs,
1.2 million dead,
squirming,
scabbed up,
truly agonizing hamsters,
1.2 million dead rotting cod,
3.5 million dead socks,

11 million dead shoes,
200 million dead children,
700,000 dead spiders,
1.8 million dead squirrels,
1.6 million dead raindrops,
1.8 million dead people,
1.5 million dead,
bald maidens,
2.3 million dead,
miserable individuals,
2.3 million dead,
misused,
fucked up,
exploited, worthless, self-serving,
selfish children,
1.5 million dead girls,
2 million dead babies,
5 million dead movie stars,
20 million dead mortgages,
50 million dead groceries,
20 million dead food stamps,
10 million dead virgins,
15 million dead school buses,
20 million dead law professors,
10 million dead jobs,
10 million dead leaders,
10 million dead presidents,
10 million dead cabinet ministers,
10 million dead, smelly construction workers,
30 million dead babies,
30 million dead unpaid bills,
10 million dead milkmen,
30 million dead professionals,
10 million dead teacher pensions,
10 million dead lawyers,
10 million dead babies,
20 million dead toasters,
1 million dead religions,
30 million dead condoms,
1 million dead guns,
3 million dead platitudes,
200 million dead trees,
500,000 dead chicken nuggets,
15 million dead snakes,
30 million dead lost sneakers,
30 million dead cow patties,
30 million dead cold,
lukewarm, half-baked,
cold sandwiches,
10 million dead fruit pies,
1 billion dead sameness,
dead skin cells,

1.7 billion dead cherries,
300 million dead pets,
15 million dead armadillos,
200 million dead socks,
10 million dead cars,
10 million dead bathing suits,
5 million dead liars,
5 million dead, unshaven men,
2 million dead ticks,
1 million dead, bald babes,
10 million dead college students,
7 million dead pimps,
5 million dead,
chimerical "business" executives,
5 million dead pi,
500 million dead wheat graters,
300 million dead cricket sound effects,
20 million dead teachers,
10 million dead whales,
700 million dead cats,
40 million dead soldiers,
40 million dead drunken singles,
150 million dead, strained, frozen life lessons,
0.3 million dead meme,
600 million dead cans of scalding warm soup,
40 million dead,
non-living cigarettes,
10 million dead,
global heat balance,
5 million dead in books,
5 million dead hummers,
400 million dead-food-deprived,
adult beverages,
1 million,000,000,000 dead stone warriors,
250 million dead, doing the real work,
9 million dead philosophers,
8 million dead economists,
9 million dead rocket scientists,
6 million dead stage mothers,
7 million dead homebuilders,
3 million dead can openers,
3 million dead, abstract teachings,
2.7 million dead poems,
3.5 million dead diaper manufacturers,
2 million dead movies,
2.7 million dead people,
2.7 million dead children,
2.2 million dead politicians,

1 million,000 dead hookers,
1.8 million dead weights,
1.9 million dead pupils,
4.1 million dead, outmoded cultural myths,
5 million dead unidentified,
interchangeable diseased people,
2.3 million dead,
crowding this graveyard,
9 million dead sheep,
5 million dead swine,
3 million dead infants,
4 million dead births,
900,000 dead elephants,
5 million dead thousand year olds,
2 million dead, old sinks and leaky toilets,
30 million dead churches,
2.7 million dead pubs,
1.4 million dead sharks,
1 million dead biospheres,
1.6 million dead Fridays,
6 million dead starters,
10 million dead glasses,
1.5 million dead,
2.2 million dead, uncaring machines,
3 million dead gas masks,
5 million dead old people,
1.6 million dead shellfish,
1 million dead policemen,
1 million dead clowns,
1 million dead lunch,
1 million dead polar bears,
1 million dead cheap, over-priced,
useless non-shits,
2 million dead hookers,
5 million dead lobster,
300,000 dead lobsters,
20 million dead, decaying bears,
5 million dead, severely undernourished men,
4 million dead babes,
1 million dead body parts,
1.6 million dead softball,
1 million dead, fucked up, stunted hamsters,
1 million dead softball games,
4 million dead doctor, nurse, midwife,
5 million dead poop,
1 million dead umbrellas,
5 million dead mice,
1 million dead salmon,
400,000 dead stupid people,

250,000 dead, stained,
sewage-covered people,
100,000 dead, spoiled, burned,
unclean, infested fruit,
1 million dead jugs,
1 million dead, shattered lips,
1 million dead clowns,
4 million dead,
cracked skulls,
500,000 dead, diabolically screwed-up,
partially fried frogs,
5 million dead sex organs,
2 million dead, sorry, suffering,
family members,
1.3 million dead nurses,
4 million dead snitches,
1 million dead bearded old man,
1 million dead, seething, rageful,
malicious asses,
1.5 million dead hombres,
1.6 million dead songbirds,
3 million dead moustaches,
5 million dead, arachnid-honey comb,
1 million dead dinosaurs,
1 million dead monkeys,
1 million dead, smelly collies,
1 million dead cockroaches,
1 million dead bombs,
1.2 million dead bunnies,
3 million dead guns,
5 million dead dried fish,
6 million dead bananas,
1.2 million dead, frost bitten,
uncooked shrimp,
5 million dead teeth,
20 million dead, shit-smelling empty coffee cups,
5 million dead, fat, bloated,
ass-licking boobs,
1.5 million dead grass,
1.3 million dead ex-wives,
3.5 million dead waterfalls,
10 million dead not so empty swimming pools,
1 million dead, hot, smelly mice,
20 million dead, prostrate,
belly-aching cows,
2 million dead mangos,
1 million dead naked camels,
1 million dead, empty petri dishes,
1 million dead, forked tongues,
200 million dead bitches,

10 million dead chlamydia carriers,
10 million dead, rotting,
uninteresting scabs,
1 million dead,
blob-head pigs,
1 million dead rancid chickens,
1 million dead, crunching,
disease-ridden fleas,
1 million dead armpit fetuses,
1 million dead, dead, fucked,
prostitute/ass-licking black
caterpillars,
1 million dead, walking, vomiting rats,
2 million dead, finger-tagged,
tattooed, big-assed, pulsing,
loathsome, promiscuous,
300 million dead birds,
3 million dead seagulls,
200 million dead birds,
6 million dead cockroaches,
1.5 million dead monkeys,
1.3 million dead, cloying, tacky,
vomit-heavy, too-much-wine-for-
even-care,
social-security-checking,
alcoholic cakes,
10 million dead boards,
1 million dead lice,
1 million dead chin, lips, cheeks,
1 million dead, semi-frustrated
babes,
1 million dead poorards,
1 million dead, smelly fingers,
5 million dead, sickened, feral cows,
1 million dead, trashed, starving,
diseased groundhogs,
20 million dead, bulging, hairy pecs,
1 million dead, unrefined, bizarre,
ground-down flour,
1 million dead, flat, almost liquefied
pizza,
1 million dead, boring, deep-fried
dick,
5 million dead peanuts,
3 million dead, shivering, jiggling
kittens,
3 million dead, fat, screaming,
wilting,
scorched, baby-filled diapers,
2 million dead, slaughtered,
2 million dead, shivering, non-
mobile cats,
1 million dead, naked buttocks,
300 million dead, drunken,
poisoned, fucked up, barbeque,
jerked-off, pubic-hair-related,
bus-stop,
entrails-filled, charred-to-a-crisp,
stuck-together, melted, oddly-shaped,
party-time, orgy-goers,
6 million dead, wild, damned,
splayed,
uncooked lamb,
200 million dead, sort of ready,
you know, but you should go out
and have a smoke,
1.2 million dead, sticky, meat-like,
like-cheese, cardboard,
2 million dead, greasy,
smelly, unpleasant, sweaty,
unmuffled, earwig-resembling snails,
20 million dead, smelly bacon,
1 million dead, testicle-fragrant,
flaming, genetically-modified,
mushed-up turkeys,
3 million dead dead, puffed,
shit-stained, burned,
scrotum-laden, smelly corn,
5 million dead,
craving, decaying, decomposed
human carcasses,
2 million dead, dispossessed,
annihilated, or weak-kneed,
ex-girlfriends,
2 million dead, no good,
blank starein', raging,
fat, ugly fuckers,
300 million dead, grazing,
falling apart, decaying, disgusting,
unmotivated to see a doctor,
1 million dead, full, blown-up-with-
rat-chewed-beaks cadavers,
4 million dead, threatening, filthy,
stroked-up, emotional screw-ups,
ugly, depressing, sandy, lumpy balls
of fat,
2 million dead, osmosis generating,
smelly, spoiled, lazy-fingered,
45 million dead, peeing,
eating, pooping, pumping,
heavy breathing,
4.5 million dead, dead bats,
6 million dead skunks,
1 million dead rattlesnakes,
10 million dead (very hard to reach),
9 million dead bats,
1 million dead, fucked, ugly, lacking,
inapposite, P.C., squishy, moist, bird,
26 million dead ticks,
7 million dead bugs,
18 million dead guano-spewing
poop filled,
animal fecal mass,
1 million dead scads of garden hoses,
11 million dead trees,
4 million dead medium-sized fishes,
1 million dead,
frightful,
zombie-like cats,
1 million dead,
not so pretty birds,
2 million dead,
four-eyed,
blind-eyed,
envious,
disappointing dudes,
6 million dead,
faceless,
paralyzed,
freakin',
unrecognizable dead,
screaming,
slurping,
stinking,
squealing,
biting,
fuckers,
1 million dead,
bellowing,
suckin' men,
1 million dead,
broad-headed,
sloth-like,
women-like,
backward-thinking,
evil,
angry,
too-soft-to-kick-ass bitches,
0.7 million dead,
gigantic,
sex-crazed,
meat-covered,
phallic-happy-vaginas,
1.6 million dead,
over-seasoned,
burnt,
rolled in ashtrays,
lit,
soaked in gasoline,
1.4 million dead balloons,
250,000 dead kids,
250,000 dead metal posters,
250,000 dead politicians,
250,000 dead cop,
soldier,
250,000 dead,
stinking,
heated,
killed grass,
250,000 dead stray cats,
250,000 dead,
rotting,
rancid fish,
250,000 dead rats,
2.4 million dead scalps,
3 million dead,
steamed,
boiled,
fried,
hard candy,
2 million dead mussels,
2 million dead moles,
1.6 million dead,
shrivelled,
jellyfish,
3 million dead shrimp,
2 million dead asses,
1.6 million dead children,
2.2 million dead beets,
3 million dead sex-movers,
3 million dead milkmen,
1 million dead beer pong,
1 million dead kittens,
500,000 dead costumes,
500,000 dead,
naked,
armless and blistered-skinned,
sexy,
butts,
300,000 dead zebras,
1 million dead toadstools,
600,000 dead chickens,
800,000 dead hams,
2 million dead mannequins,
1.6 million dead moms,
2 million dead puppy dogs,
1.5 million dead,
fat,
overcooked,
under-cooked,
pickled,
greasy,
poorly cooked pork chops,
600,000 dead,
sausage-shaped men,
700,000 dead,
fried turkey,
900,000 dead people,
4.5 million dead fetuses,
500,000 dead pigeons,
1 million dead catfish,
1 million dead tigers,
1 million dead grass,
1 million dead students,
1 million dead squid,
1 million dead,
horrible bastards,
3 million dead gods,
4.5 million dead hippies,
4 million dead peasants,
5.5 million dead poo,
8.5 million dead insects,
5 million dead nuns,
7.5 million dead kids,
7 million dead witches,
7 million dead teenagers,
7 million dead kids,
8 million dead ziggurats,
10 million dead cats,
15 million dead cocks,
6 million dead sagging,
beer-guzzling men,
13.5 million dead hearts,
3 million dead seedless grapes,
6.5 million dead junkies,
6 million dead hookers,
8 million dead sex-floors,
5.5 million dead people,
6 million dead ninja turtles,
1 million dead cabbages,
1 million dead,
meaty,
beaten,
whole turkey,
1 million dead "organic" turkeys,
2 million dead prawns,
7 million dead dogs,
1 million dead sheep,
2 million dead porcupines,
1 million dead voles,
4 million dead chickens,
1 million dead naked women,
1 million dead murderers,
4 million dead "others",
2 million dead rats,

3 million dead aliens,
1.2 million dead owls,
1 million dead "us",
1 million dead grub worms,
5 million dead narwhals,
4 million dead piranhas,
1 million dead pork,
1 million dead mice,
2 million dead pigeons,
5 million dead plums,
4 million dead hamsters,
8 million dead oxen,
1 million dead snakes,
4 million dead piglets,
8 million dead locusts,
0.5 million dead moles,
2 million dead seals,
10 million dead horny monsters,
6 million dead bears,
3 million dead dogs,
9 million dead pigs,
11 million dead snails,
5.5 million dead crabs,
10 million dead turkeys,
15 million dead ballerinas,
5 million dead unloading barges,
15 million dead cars,
6 million dead penguins,
8 million dead carp,
5.6 million dead sheep,
1 million dead squeaky toys,
4.5 million dead dolls,
3 million dead pigs,
5.5 million dead relatives,
3 million dead orchids,
0.3 million dead swans,
0.3 million dead lepers,
1 million dead humans,
3 million dead deer,
2 million dead sharks,
3 million dead giraffes,
1.1 million dead pigs,
1 million dead bats,
1.2 million dead people,
1 million dead men,
10 million dead trees,
10 million dead women,
4,000 dead lice,
1,000 dead shrimps,
18 million empty seats in a stadium,
27,000,000,000 dead fires,
27,000,000,000 dead cat hairs,
1,500,000 dead toasters,

1,000,000,000 dead spiders,
2,000,000 dead hairballs,
1,000 dead dildos,
3,000,000 dead tourists,
8,000,000 dead penguins,
2,000,000 dead football players,
4,000,000 dead giraffes,
7,000,000 dead elephants,
18,000,000 dead clowns,
2,000,000 dead blubberballs,
15,000,000 dead trout,
1,500,000 dead newborns,
2,500,000 dead cats,
3,000,000 dead mobiles,
1,500,000 dead fortune cookies,
3,000,000 dead kittens,
2,000,000 dead gumballs,
2,000,000 dead mullahs,
8,000,000 dead llamas,
4,000,000 dead people,
12,000,000 dead medical waste,
6,000,000 dead money,
12,000,000 dead airline pilots,
3,000,000 dead chinchillas,
1,500,000 dead fruit,
4,000,000 dead protoplasm,
20,000,000 dead scores of men,
7,000,000 dead schools,
10,000,000 dead babies,
4,000,000 dead dogs,
1,800,000 dead other dogs,
7,000,000 dead tennis balls,
1,600,000 dead barbecues,
10,000,000 dead carnival workers,
4,000 dead anti-depressants,
5,000 dead,
dead pets,
50,000,000 dead,
dead appliances,
18,000,000,000 dead tropical fruits,
2,800,000,000 dead baseball
players,
2,200,000 dead,
dead and squashed tires,
700,000 dead airplanes,
1,000,000 dead,
dead,
alive fridges,
1,400,000 dead cats,
100,000 dead talking lions,
1,000 dead cheeseburgers,
1,000 dead carrots,
100,000 dead phone booths,

1000 dead people,
1 million dead, decomposing, live,
crispy, smelly animals,
3,000 dead piglets,
1 million dead babies,
2,500 dead jobs,
2,500,000 dead cats,
11,500,000 dead stars,
11,500 dead presidents,
6,500 dead piglets,
4,000 dead puppets,
4,000 dead TV's,
8,000 dead virgins,
10,000 dead, dead, dead bears,
1,800,000 dead, dead ice skaters,
6,000 dead socks,
2,400,000,000 dead dummies,
5 million dead clones,
25 million dead puppies,
7 million dead karate masters,
1.1 million dead peepshow girls,
8 million dead babies,
10 million dead chickens,
1 million dead newspapers,
1 million dead snails,
4,000 dead baby chicks,
4 million dead rabbits,
6 million dead, dead peanut people,
6 million dead, dead, dead, dead,
dead, dead dead, dead, dead, dead,
dead, dead, dead, dead, dead,
dead, dead dead, dead, dead, dead,
dead, dead, dead, dead, dead,
dead, dead, dead, dead, dead,
dead, dead, dead, dead, dead,
dead, dead, dead, dead, dead,
dead, dead geese,
3 million dead lawyers,
1 million dead, screaming gerbils,
700,000 dead tax-cheats,
1 million dead, dead suckers,
3,500,000 dead police officers,
100,000 dead bees,
100,000 dead inmates,
1 million dead, disgusting pigs,
1 million dead cantaloupes,
1 million dead relatives,
6 million dead pre-pubescent girls,
1 million dead policemen,
1 million dead, dead, dead robots,
2 million dead salamanders,
1.3 million dead dolphins,
1 million dead suns,

1 million dead supermarket hot
dogs,
1 million dead flower salesmen,
1 million dead zombies,
300,000 dead brain cells,
1 million dead, crying, bored
construction workers,
900,000 dead Bibles,
1,000 dead, sloshing lakes,
1,000 dead children,
3,500,000 dead bodies,
1 million dead blood,
10,000 dead mangled lice,
5 million dead spiders,
5 million dead, wailing, zombie
bees,
3 million dead prostitute's,
1 million dead, stockbrokers,
4 million dead maggots,
500,000 dead,
fracking dogs,
5 million dead, deep,dry, dusty
holes,
1,000,000 dead smokers,
4 million dead flies,
1,000,000 dead birds,
1,000,000 dead wasps,
2 million dead polar bears,
1 million, dead, zombie, zombies,
1,000,000 dead lobsters,
2 million dead lions,
1.6 million,
dead porn stars,
700,000 dead,
hamburgers,
1 million dead, holding a,
2.6 million, dead plane crashes,
1.2 million dead, hungry,hungry,
eat-your-own, tiny, growing, well-fed
zombies,
3.5 million, dead, zombie, truck,
3.2 million dead ducks,
3 million,
dead Americans,
1.6 million dead sheep,
1.6 million dead puppies,
2.5 million dead beef,
6 million dead pigs,
2 million,
dead scientists,
2.2 million,
dead men,
1.4 million dead grannies,

6.5 million dead,
human heads and genitalia,
15 million dead rhinos,
1,000 dead people,
7,000 dead penguins,
20 million dead whales,
250 million dead,
decomposing people,
8 million dead sperm,
20 million dead baseball players,
4,500,000 dead spiders,
8,000,000 dead spiders,
10,000,000 dead birds,
6,000,000 dead frogs,
1,500,000 dead,
dead fish,
800,000 dead dogs,
6,000,000 dead cocks,
2 million dead,
dead wood,
500,000 dead murderers,
1 million dead mushrooms,
500,000 dead eels,
500,000 dead,
dead golf balls,
500,000 dead sheep,
2,500,000 dead guitars,
1 million dead heartbeats,
1,000,000,000 dead mice,
1,000,000,000 dead frogs,
220.2 million,000,000 dead
asteroids,
160,000,000,000 dead whales,
94.7 million dead bats,
97 million dead stars,
1 million dead slugs,
5 million dead stars,
2 million dead golf balls,
1 million dead boas,
10 million dead lizards,
50 million dead home furnaces,
200 million dead hippopotamuses,
20 million dead eels,
40 million dead rats,
10 million dead cats,
10 million dead tigers,
50 million dead eels,
5 million dead,
dead cows,
500,000 dead pigs,
10 million dead sheep,
3 million dead bananas,
2 million dead,

dead people,
12 million dead people,
10 million dead,
dead bugs,
1 million dead fish,
1 million dead,
dead snakes,
1 million dead caravans,
2 million dead birds,
5 million dead,
dead pigs,
3 million dead cows,
7 million dead Christmas trees,
7 million dead mothers,
100 million dead and fucking dead people,
10 million dead ants,
30 million dead naked people,
10 million dead scientists,
2 million dead civil rights workers,
3 million dead plane crash victims,
1 million dead communists,
100 million dead Spanish people,
1 million dead soldiers,
10 million dead women,
500,000 dead flies,
250,000 dead skunk corpses,
10 million dead wives,
30 million dead pianos,
2 million dead cans,
10 million dead parts from cars,
3 million dead dogs,
3 million dead cats,
100,000 dead hippos,
2 million dead fish,
2 million dead sheep,
5 million dead goldfish,
1 million dead,
dead bears,
8 million dead goats,
5 million dead sheep,
10 million dead cats,
10 million dead dogs,
5 million dead football players,
7 million dead generals,
7 million dead cats,
1 million dead poop,
10 million dead people,
5 million dead Frito Lay "butts",
15 million dead cockroaches,
1 million dead gays,
30 million dead mail boxes,
10 million dead letter-sorters,

80,000 dead men,
1 million dead teenagers,
5 million dead,
dead women,
1 million dead,
dead holiday,
1 million dead men,
1 million dead men,
1 million dead men,
1 million dead chicks,
1 million dead penguins,
400,000 dead men,
5 million dead women,
200 million dead babies,
11 million dead turkeys,
1 million dead bombs,
1 million dead apartments,
10 million dead,
dead eyes,
5 million dead eels,
20 million dead pigeons,
5 million dead lambs,
20 million dead puppies,
7 million dead nuns,
8 million dead cows,
1 million dead,
dead cats,
4 million dead,
dead birthdays,
100,000 dead livers,
1 million dead,
dead gorillas,
1 million dead doctors,
2 million dead pilots,
1 million dead pigs,
1 million dead,
dead politicians,
10 million dead,
dead people,
50 million dead prostitutes,
100,000 dead people,
1 million dead food,
1 million dead poodles,
1 million dead fish,
1 million dead people,
1 million dead,
dead birds,
1 million dead tigers,
1 million dead hearts,
1 million dead,
dead people,
50,000 dead dead fathers,
2 million dead prostitutes,

95 million,000,000 dead metro-road trolley systems,
86 million dead mummies,
64.4 million dead turkeys,
31.3 million dead sheep,
2,064 million dead spacecraft,
1.2 billion dead,
unfriended Facebook friends,
1.2 billion dead dolphins,
700 million dead redwoods,
6 billion,000,000,000 dead people,
3.6 million,000,000 dead mine-cart men,
52 million,000,000,000 dead insects,
320 million,000,000,000 dead zombies,
7.5 million,000,000,000 dead,
unfriended Facebook friends,
2.5 million dead washing-machine motors,
950 million dead fish,
350 million,000,000 dead cars,
470 million,000,000 dead harbors,
72 million,000,000 dead,
unfriended Facebook friends,
650 million,000,000 dead crabs,
6 billion dead ladies,
23,000,000,000 dead hermit crabs,
4,055,900 left-over zombie soldiers,
6.3 billion dead frogs,
16 million corpse insects,
5 million car batteries,
12.5 million dead corpses,
1,400 crickets,
346,000 dead ringers,
6 million farmers,
2 million beer cans,
2 million dead condoms,
1,167,000 dead,
unobtainable blue bananas,
28,000,000,000 dead tap dancers,
19 million decapitated newborn babies,
2 million decapitated children,
62 million headless taxi-cabs,
1.2 million dead toaster ovens,
2202 million,
dead,
fed to the pigs,
535 million dead kittens,
524 million dead guinea pigs,
448 million dead schoolchildren,
19.6 million dead,

unfriended Facebook friends,
1647 million dead,
unfriended Facebook friends,
130 million dead,
unfriended Facebook friends,
270 million,
dead,
un-friended Facebook friends,
10,270,000 dead young chickens,
6,669 dead,
unfriended Facebook friends,
83.2 million dead,
unfriended Facebook friends,
14,000,000 dead college administrators,
976 million,
dead,
unfriended Facebook friends,
300,000 dead robot un-friends,
10.8 million,
dead and unfriended Facebook friends,
2,000,000,000 dead,
unfriended Facebook friends,
285 million dead,
unfriended Facebook friends,
64.3 million dead mini-alligators,
103 million dead,
unfriended Facebook friends,
898,000 dead children,
744,000 dead mothers,
10,000,000 dead, unfriended Facebook friends,
13,150,000 dead, unfriended Facebook friends,
1.2 million dead willies,
One million,000,000 dead and missing Smurfs,
284 million dead llamas,
8 million dead kittens,
65,000 dead puppets,
1 million dead sheep,
293,000 dead dinghies,
196,000 dead movie stars,
113,000 dead mallard ducks,
2.8 million dead cats,
417,400 dead, dead-eyed chihuahuas,
2,514,000 dead puppies,
2,435,000 dead ducks,
3,000 dead sharks,
295 dead wasps,
28,000 dead, dead-eyed goats,

744,000 dead henfolds,
50,000,000,000 dead, unfriended Facebook friends,
1,500,000,000 dead soldiers,
5 billion dead trees,
1,935 million dead apples,
2,400,000,000 dead mp3 players,
1,000,000,000 dead cancer cells,
275 dead fish,
5.3 million dead houseflies,
3.7 million dead boars,
71,000 dead crucified U.S. Government officials,
3 million suicide fighters,
3 million starving fishing birds,
1 billion leftenant worms,
14 truckers,
2 cubic feet of bagged teeth,
1,230 lying teeth,
404 cracks in a wall,
1 old kimono,
1000,000 homeless pets,
1.5 million too fat bee wombs,
93 collective abortions,
241 inhale3 salivarytoid flies,
148 heavy baggies,
758 hacking coughs,
7,095 dwarves,
664 fetus drummers,
512 fertility busters,
915 fetus virtual reality,
595 alien sperm,
609 alien feet,
611 aliens,
463 intestines,
500 female heart surgeons,
458 overdoses,
688 twenty feet tall chlamydia,
400 Pap smear stool samples,
100 e-penises,
78 dogs,
100 sonar numbers,
75 lacrosse sticks,
75 jackhammers,
142 medical kits,
130 flatulants,
971 ethical doctors,
26 ceremonial foghorns,
533 engraved bottles,
389 sloth nose transplants,
420,000,000 unmanned Southern Peru System computers,
452,500,000 insects,

6 train accident corpses,
398 coffins,
5 Bantha vs. Chewbacca,
164 guns,
169 biochemical missiles,
107 Lotus flower,
403 e-books,
218 Adonis penisovas,
175 cups of buttermilk,
113 black knights,
98 casting votes,
290 American experiences,
270 shared rhinoceroses,
232 Americans,
329 years of Dali,
210,000 junk bonds,
170 responsible users,
4.7 million,944 liters of exotic fruit juice,
90 degrees in the shade,
13 million dead umbrellas,
1 billion dead snowmen,
1 billion body parts,
1,000,000,000,000 dead babies,
52 million dead pineapples,
45,000,000,000,000 dead people,
90,500,000,000 dead Americans,
1.55 billion dead, orphytes,
1 billion dead plants,
400 million dead fish,
25 million dead bats,
6 million dead camels,
3 million dead humans,
1 million dead zoo-keepers,
11 million dead frogs,
250,000,000 dead, mindless insects,
40,000,000 dead rhinos,
109 dead hippos,
440,000,000 dead bats,
170,000 dead snakes,
1.0 million dead,
defragmented hard drives,
12,000 dead homes,
37,700 dead dolphins,
556,800 decaying animal carcasses,
1.0 million dead frogs,
43,800 dead Chinese comedians,
7,000,000-400,000 dead cockroaches,
13,500 dead octopi,
32,000 dead dolphins,
1,500 dead kittens,
1,000 dead firefighters,
33,750 dead funeral attendees,
184,925,000 dead people,
7,175,000 dead family members,
643,438 dead readers,
600 dead health care workers,
159 dead hunger strikers,
18,500 dead televisions,
4,857 dead legal rights,
109,443-1,236,821 dead people,
55,175 dead Neanderthals,
50,225 dead railroad tracks,
50,345-1,000,003 dead clowns,
1,051 dead children,
1,620 dead Presidents,
1,800 dead pit bulls,
6,000 dead musicians,
115 dead churches,
3,000 dead guinea pigs,
72,500 dead trees,
31 dead health inspectors,
84 dead emperors,
93 dead members of Congress,
103 dead CEOs,
283 dead astronauts,
159 dead food processing plants,
3,000 dead scientists,
7 dead sperm whales,
666 dead ten-pin bowlers,
5,000 dead nations,
4,000 dead politicians,
21 dead paintings,
1,051 dead pineapples,
33 dead mud turtles,
69 dead flags,
35 dead home run derby, men die seven times more often than women, men on average die 6.7 years earlier than women,
94.2% of white men will die before age 75,
92.1% of black men will die before age 75,
741 dead women,
400 dead cats,
3,048 dead tabby cats,
17 dead cats,
33 dead parakeets,
16 dead turtles,
13 dead dolphins,
12 dead jellyfish,
79 dead hedgehogs,
10 dead lobsters,
1 dead whale,
270 dead baby rhinos,
2,200 dead killer whales,
11 dead chimpanzees,
10 dead adult chimpanzees,
109 dead chimps,
1 dead baby chimpanzee,
34 dead chickens,
19 dead cats,
2 dead dogs,
2 dead rats,
31 dead pigs,
48 dead raccoons,
46 dead skunks,
37 dead dogs,
61 dead animals,
24 dead kittens,
51 dead dogs,
105 dead chickens,
41 dead gorillas,
70 dead koalas,
144 dead kangaroos,
5 dead goats,
39 dead seals,
136 dead goldfish,
11 dead crabs,
45 dead turtles,
3 dead pigs,
24 dead dolphins,
21 dead octopi,
81 dead grasshoppers,
2 dead whales,
1 dead gorilla,
1 dead person,
40 dead elderly individuals,
1 dead dog,
25 dead jackals,
1 dead elf,
69 dead deceased elephants,
87 dead whales,
172 dead starfish,
2 dead rats,
45 dead ravens,
26 dead turkeys,
7 dead miniature pigs,
14 dead geese,
12 dead turkeys,
227 dead infants,
5.1 billion dead hogs,
4.7 billion dead tortoises,
4.7 billion dead deer,
1.7 million,000 dead Mexicans,
8 dead car batteries,
1 dead alcoholic,
600 dead doctors,
100,000 dead homes,
800 dead presidents,
250,000 dead chinchillas,
10 dead wine bottles,
1498 deaths from suicide,
30,000 dead Americans,
830,000 dead politicians,
1 dead fax machine,
2 dyed beers,
9,000,000 dead mobiles,
26,000,000 rotting meat pies,
24,000,000 dead cats,
16,000,000 reborn ravenous baby chicks,
1,000,000 left-over cheese,
1,000,000 dead ibises,
12,000 dead carts,
60,000,000 dogs,
73,000 starving puppies,
2,400 dead athletes,
10,000 dead owners,
2,000,000,000 dead mosquitoes,
1920 terabytes,
5 perfect square mazes,
5,000 pretzels,
6 dead bears,
100 million seat belts,
19,587 pi digits,
95 million individual car wreck stories,
7 dead stranger fights,
48 corpses,
1 dead landmine,
2,116,824 things broken,
17 fingernails,
500 dead bananas,
1 dead American cuisine,
4,000 mangled dead copters,
2,000 dead redheads,
3 million dead cashiers,
6 million dead shrimp,
10,000 dead cats,
4,000 dead construction workers,
5 million dead ducks,
6 million dead wildebeests,
7 million dead winter victims,
8-person virgin births,
2 dead monkeys,
2 grapes,
3,120,000 circles,
31 dodgy loan sharks,
10 million paintings,
2 tons of chicken feed,
1 genome,
409 holes,
20,875 pizzas,
3 pounds of sap,
81 tons of brie,
7 couches,
599 car dealerships,
6 years of shootings,
12 million human clones,
3,000,000,000,000 crack addicts,
70,000,000,000,000 pigeons,
8.5 million goldfish,
7.2 million taxidermied bears,
7 million weather balloons,
7 million pickled fish,
8 million dead planets,
7 million teeth,
7 million hedgehogs,
3.5 million lungs,
2.5 million tornados,
5 million superhighways,
2 million chickens,
1.7 million car accidents,
0.7 million exploding lemons,
1.4 million jellyfish,
40,000 tons of sugar,
30 million gallons of gasoline,
60 million gallons of lubricants,
66 million gallons of silver,
66 million gallons of zinc,
67 million gallons of nickel,
16 million,000,000,000 tons of rags,
2 billion gallons of naffness,
10 billion tons of paste,
15,000 tons of Guinness,
100 million Americans,
1500 square miles of lime,
1000 square miles of sewage,
30,000,000 gallons of glue,
1500,000 angels,
30 million American pitbulls,
30 million American chihuahuas,
10 million,000,000,000,000 quarters,
5.9 million T-Bone steaks,
6.5 million half-dollar coins,
2.5 million toilets,
4 million towels,
2 million sheep,
4 million flies,
1.1 million baby mannequins,
3 million bathrooms,
3 million dead bears,

2.5 million dead drunkards,
15 million dead polar bears,
15 million starving men,
15 million people,
2.5 million,000 dead sailors,
6 million female guineafowl,
1.9 billion rocket engines,
3.8 million dead whales,
1.6 million dead Einsteins,
4 million dead tallow candles,
3 million dead bodies,
1.1 million dead people,
3 million dead marriage certificates,
5 million dead volcanoes,
3 million dead snail shells,
1 million corpses,
10 million dead giraffes,
1.1 million dead icebergs,
0.1 million dead armies,
10.7 million looking-glass cranes,
15.4 million ferns,
9.9 million dead snakes,
200 million carmels,
9 million elf horses,
3 million Icelandic Æsir,
40 million characters,
7 million people,
20,000 dead puppies,
20.2 billion coins,
2.8 billion dead leaves,
2 billion dead fish,
2.8 million dead songbirds,
5 million dead cats,
2.7 million dead pigs,
2.2 million dead virgins,
946,000 dead dragonflies,
2.5 million dead squid,
2.4 million dead rhinos,
6 million dead people,
7.7 million dead plants,
6 million dead zebras,
3.7 million dead wombats,
3.3 million dead pandas,
3 million dead rainbow fish,
2.2 million dead goats,
1.4 million dead Japanese kids,
4,300,000 dead dogs,
10.5 million dead birds,
7.2 million dead firefighters,
50,000 dead wooden ornaments,
4.7 million dead polar bears,
25 million dead walnuts,
7.7 million dead babies,

6 million dead, frozen mosquitos,
5 million dead,
composting bees,
4.8 million dead monks,
4 million dead polar bears,
4 million dead Americans,
1.9 million dead pandas,
1 million dead children,
9.9 million dead people,
5 million dead hippos,
3 million dead alligators,
3 million hamsters,
2 million bricks,
1.5 million dead statues,
1.3 million dead clocks,
1.3 million dead bras,
100,000 dead bullets,
1 million dead spoons,
7 million dead roses,
4 million dead fruit,
1 million dead circus animals,
1 million dead reindeers,
1000 dead camels,
200 million fallen angels,
40,000 dead primate,
3 million dead fruit bats,
6.5 million dead movie stars,
5 million dead nuclear bomb,
0.5 million dead elevators,
200 dead stuffed ducks,
500 dead eels,
150 million (560,000,000) kg of TNT,
150 million (560,000,000) kg of TNT,
11.35 kilotons of powdered TNT,
11.35 kilotons of C4,
11.35 kilotons of explosive C,
0.6 kiloton of TNT,
11.5 kilotons of dynamite,
15 kilotons of TNT,
31 kilotons of dynamite,
20 kilotons of dynamite,
8 kilotons of nitroglycerine,
10 kilotons of dynamite,
6 kilotons of dynamite,
4 kilotons of TNT,
4 kilotons of TNT,
6.7 kilotons of TNT,
9 kilotons of TNT,
4 kilotons of TNT,
2 kilotons of TNT,
1 kiloton of TNT,
15 kilotons of TNT,
27 kilotons of TNT,

1 kiloton of nitroglycerine,
0.5 kiloton of explosives,
5 kilotons of explosives,
0.25 kilotons of explosives,
20 kilograms of TNT,
1000 kilograms of TNT,
0.1 kilograms of TNT,
5 kilograms of TNT,
0.3 kilograms of TNT,
1 kiloton of explosives,
0.5 kilograms of TNT,
1 kiloton of TNT,
0.2 kilograms of TNT,
1 kiloton of TNT,
8 kilograms of TNT,
3 kilograms of TNT,
2 kilograms of TNT,
50 million tubes of superglue,
40 million gallons of WD40,
10 million gallons of liquefied
petroleum gas,
8.4 million gallons of chemical
weapons,
6.8 million gallons of engine oil,
8 million gallons of spray paint,
12 million jars of Vaseline,
16 million bottles of darkroom
chemicals,
12 million gallons of blood,
10 million kilos of bread,
22 million piglets,
22 million pounds of titanium,
100 million concrete blocks,
15 million people,
84 billion of humans (New York City),
834 billion of people,
892 billion oxygen molecules,
8.5% of the planet,
9.4% of all DNA,
10.8% of all living species,
3.3% of all usable oil,
5,883 Amazonas,
5,883 clean teeth,
5.8 million smoke detectors,
4.7 million high-definition flatscreens,
808,372 lethal weapons,
49,479 of 34,774 stars in the Milky
Way,
22,000,000 planes,
6,000,000 cars,
22 million cubic kilometers of open
land,
1.4 million square feet of land,

48.3 million square feet of buried land,
69,000,000 acres of live plant life,
46,964 square miles of artificial land,
30 million-square-foot building,
6 million nuclear warheads,
100 tons of gold,
5.4 tons of silver,
6.3 tons of diamond,
1,051 trillion cubic meters of water,
5.6 trillion square feet of permafrost,
750 million potatoes,
13 million bottles of Coca-Cola,
17 million rocketships,
1,000 pounds of cocaine,
100 million rolls of toilet paper,
840 billion baseballs,
52,000 diazepam tablets,
500 billion Mastercard credit cards,
208 billion Disney movies,
850,000 Lotto scratch-off tickets,
1,100 pounds of petrified shark
vertebrae,
145,000 cubic feet of rock,
31 million metric tons of plastic,
16.3 billion DVD players,
16.3 billion MicroSD memory cards,
4.8 million grams of marijuana,
600 tons of caviar,
100 percent of 1,110 of the world's
car doors,
2 of the world's 9,317 biggest rivers,
6 deepwater oil rigs,
6,178 supermarket tabloids,
2,616 foreign currencies,
4 million TV sitcom episodes,
4.3 million spoonfuls of honey,
7.8 kg of iodized salt,
19 countries,
1,969 toilets,
35 million planet implants,
8.8 million photos,
29 species of spiders,
24 species of dogs,
8 species of apes,
1,459 trillion tons of carbon,
73 quadrillion gallons of gasoline,
1,002 cubic feet of natural gas,
29,785 ounces of pure cocaine,
2.9 billion cigarettes,
170 billion seeds (Coca-Cola),
103 trillion seedlings,
40 trillion shell casings,
2.7 billion of 143 pentagrams,

8.8 million bananas,
483 decades of Pac Man,
20 petrel chicks,
24 million cigarettes,
20 pounds of bile,
80,000 pounds of DNA,
59 million pages of books,
30,000 years worth of human
progress,
299,445 kidney cells,
80,939 metric tons of cilantro,
143 billion pages of PayPal invoices,
4 trillion pages of Google CropView,
47 billion hairs on Joseph Cirocco,
11% of the Earth's biomass,
6% of the population,
2.14 minutes of a Porsche 911s
top-speed,
3 orders of magnitude less sun,
1 billion antibodies,
328 months worth of medical
records (the CO2 concentrations in
such records during the same
period is relatively constant),
7,462 fossils,
135 billion trees,
1,057,183 feet of DNA,
7.8 billion of every Wikipedia page,
3 trillion weapons of mass
destruction,
4,114 years of US National Debt,
430 megatonnes of iron ore,
14 metric tonnes of pure gold,
1.2 billion square feet of stored food,
52,000,000-square-mile natural
habitat,
22,000-square-foot bedroom,
24 metric tonnes of pot,
2 million children playing,
70,000 acres of farmland,
8 million square feet of refrigerators,
180,000 miles of railroad tracks,
27,000,000 U.S. soldiers,
500 times more liquids than the
oceans,
1.1 billion cubic kilometers of fresh
water,
5.8 million square miles of fresh
water,
63,500 metric tons of fresh air,
2 billion cells of human DNA,
9.5 trillion nerve impulses,
982 U.S. rivers,

200,000 lakes,
8 million metric tons of chlorine,
5.7 million tons of graphite,
3 billion butterflies,
6.3 billion people,
58.5 million whales,
22.5 billion farmed birds,
112,000 U.S. dams,
122,400 active U.S. military installations,
10,000 U.S. nuclear warheads,
68 quadrillion tonnes of solid waste,
1.6 billion pounds of plastic,
11,000 pairs of glasses,
19.6 billion people on the planet,
170 million women on the planet,
223 million men on the planet,
281.5 million billion calories in the human diet,
1.5 trillion humans,
~114.7 tera-gigatons of radioactive waste,
70 square miles of artificial surf where space meets desert,
47 000 illegal immigrants,
5 million illegal heads of lettuce,
956 billion left balls,
893 billion people,
99 billion telephone wire,
99 trillion cervical x,
11,800,000,000 ejaculates,
127 trillion total square feet,
1 billion cumulonimbus clouds,
15 metric tons of coca paste,
189 million people incarcerated,
1 billion albinos,
1,120 metropolitans,
17 million species of animals,
16 million species of plants,
4,000,000 textbooks,
7.8 billion pages in the Encyclopedia of Life,
51,000 stories in the Bible,
5 trillion Ritalin prescriptions,
26,500,000 articles in the encyclopedia of veterinary medicine,
3.2 billion calendars in the Guinness Book of Records,
101 million major league baseball games,
3.3 billion school days,
240,000 U.S. citizens injured by drones,
22.3 billion telephone calls,
25,440 Wikipedia pages,
340 chess games,
~3 million YouTube videos,
1 billion tornadoes,
197 million fraudulent background checks,
3,290 stories in the Encyclopedia of the Occult,
4,000 human torsos,
39 trillion atoms,
11,000,000 parades attended,
41 million newspaper pages,
100,000 YouTube videos viewed,
20,000 Facebook likes per second,
1.6 million homeless people,
3,000 legal weddings,
3,000 Olympic athlete,
4.5 billion babies in the last 24 hours,
1.4 million prayers,
1.6 billion abortions,
320,000 Marvel Comic movies,
162 pounds of cheese,
53 million bananas,
27 millions masses of dead black flies,
10.5 million holes in one baseball,
6 cm,
80 meter sphere,
283,001,000 dew drop surfaces,
$973,473 trillion in the US national debt,
On a meta level,
the universe is also a little bit better looking now...,
23,240 feet of wind turbines,
118,000 lights and 700 W of solar panels.,
3,959 hectares of land surface and 5082 bhp of hydraulics,
7 million houses of cards,
1,860,000,000 magnets,
31 trillion dollars in the US National Debt,
51 trillion people on the planet,
140 million of a spade in the ocean,
3 trillion pages of US National Debt,
1 billion gallons of oil,
$18 trillion dollars,
1 billion electric lights,
500 million birds in the Gulf of Mexico, with millions more now dying,
435,000 men die every day on the planet,
90% of humanity has a nuclear reactor in the house,
2 trillion breast implants,
2 billion kids born a year,
1 million languages in the world,
15 to 3 times the heat capacity of lead,
150 billion plastic bags in landfill,
1 trillion neurons in the human body,
1.3 trillion or so neurons connected by trillions of microtubules,
2.3 trillion seabirds in the North Atlantic,
30 exaflops of computational power in the human brain,
360,000 vaccines,
4 million textbooks,
3 million music albums,
8 petabytes of Internet traffic,
17 million superheroes,
20 million sisters and brothers,
14 billion stories in the book of life,
99.8% of the Earth's crust is water,
300 trillion gallons of clean water,
15 million chairs,
100,000 selfie sticks,
11 billion pairs of socks,
9 billion original peoples on Earth,
6 to 10 billion people currently alive,
12 billion socks in a jar,
21 trillion trees in the world,
68 billion pounds of carrots,
133,828 kilograms of tofu,
1.6 trillion copies of the Encyclopedia of Life,
24 billion tourists and customers attended an Apple store on release day,
~43-64 clicks per mouse click on the Internet,
1,170 million people are suffering in the Third World,
100 pages of Wikipedia,
56 books in the Library of Congress at the time of this writing,
9,500 cities,
4,500 rain forests,
2 million cars on the road,
2 trillion pairs of shoes,
3 million lightning strikes,
466 million earthquakes,
3.5 billion people,
3.8 billion kites,
2 million lightsabers,
86,957 examples of Mickey Mouse,
28billion androids,
3.4 billion testicles,
3.4 trillion homes,
3.3 trillion months,
80 percent of all government funding,
83 million pizzas,
500 billion popcorn balls,
1 trillion doses of medication,
50 trillion pages of text,
4 trillion hands,
43 million cars,
10 million pillows,
5 trillion singles,
5 million homes,
13 billion microwave ovens,
1 billion birds,
1 billion babies,
7 billion people,
1 billion teddy bears,
83 billion floating islands,
11 trillion stars,
5 billion lips,
2 billion toothbrushes,
1 billion watches,
4 billion half dollars,
5 billion meals,
49 billion helicopters,
4 billion bombs,
6 million ammunition,
4 billion windows,
20 billion residents of planet earth,
5 billion helmets,
1 billion cars,
1.2 billion countries,
200 billion cars,
30 billion refrigerator lights,
14.8 million miles of railroad tracks,
9.5 million people,
36.7 billion people,
5 billion words,
5 billion books,
12 billion tons of clean water,
11 billion doctors,
30 billion cars,
1 billion garbage trucks,
1000 billion (10 trillion) trees,
1 trillion hailstones,
1 trillion times 635,000 square kilometers of frost,
500 billion cans of food,
1.1 million times 1,000 billion sandwiches,
30 billion small bananas,
5,000 pounds of glue,
4 million power plants,
26 million governments,
982,000 military bases,
16.8 trillion meals,
600 people on the planet,
18,000 times 10 billion oceans,
2 million-square-mile jungles,
1 trillion cubic miles of soil,
400 billion pop cans,
5 billion fire trucks,
3 million!,
1 billion cubic feet of water,
5 billion erections,
1 billion bodies on earth,
1 billion candles,
4 billion automobiles,
1 billion music stars,
1 billion forks,
1 billion pictures,
1 billion wads of wet tissues,
1 billion toys,
6 billion wrinkles,
4 billion tears,
5 billion feet,
2 billion faces,
2 billion dreams,
6 billion flamingos,
3 billion hippos,
2 billion bridges,
2 billion shoes,
2 billion lightning bolts,
2 billion cellulose fibers,
2,667,946 chew toys,
1 billion fingerprints,
12 billion water lines,
3 billion batteries,
1.9 billion acoustic statues,
25% of a pair of basketballs,
1.2 billion socks,
112 pennies,
70 million unicorns,
1.5 billion people on earth,
9/11 victims,
1,024 billions fire extinguishers,
7,200 gallons of beer,
3 million UFOs,
4 trillion lanterns,
4.1 billion elephants,
5,833,000 left tires,

6,600 pounds of sugar,
2,910 animals,
5 million houses,
2,000 happy families,
1,100 large scale plants,
1.1 billion iPhones,
1.2 billion languages,
1 billion babies,
100 million telephone poles,
30 million fish,
1 trillion cars,
23 billion population of Indonesia,
3 billion square feet of artwork,
3 billion hearts,
700 million coins,
500 billion fire extinguishers,
200 billion flags,
5 million floors,
1,000 rulers,
1 million reptiles,
1,000 beers,
1,000 kinds of penguins,
2 million belts,
2 million bicycle handles,
2 million houses,
1 million movies,
1 million copies of Google Map,
1 million pictures,
1,000,000,000 people,
190 hurricanes,
240,000 solar arrays,
200 women,
300 women's college students,
320 million phalluses,
1 billion of women,
38 human hearts,
2 million broken bones,
28 million brains,
11,133 whole people,
45 human feet,
1,200 tons of dishwashers,
55,000 men,
1,055 policemen,
3 women,
1 woman head,
22,450 houses,
77,936 commercials,
1,188 CEOs,
3,621 captains,
126 galaxies,
12 million pregnant female corpses,
10 million typhus,
4 trillion bottles of milk,

5 million cultures,
4 billion children,
3.5 million civilians,
1,800,000,000 eggs,
1,800,000,000 nutella,
1,800,000,000 beers,
1,800,000,000 grammes of sambo sauce,
2.5 million human beings,
1 billion American hairs,
1 billion beers,
1.2 billion millipedes,
1.2 billion scarves,
9 billion Caucasian sandals,
1.5 billion dollars,
1,979,994,000 adults,
1,900,000,000 hearts,
1,900,000,000 human tears,
1,900,000,000 prayers,
2,777,372,000 Bibles,
1,000,000,000 bookmarks,
1,100,000,000 shower curtains,
1,550,000,000 pens,
1,275,232,000 ceramic buttons,
2.2 million small animals,
2 million fleas,
4 million brothers,
4 million penises,
6 million bullet wounds,
4 million gunshot wounds,
1,000,000 songs,
4,800,000 stars,
2,500,000,000 teddy bears,
3,500,000 footballs,
2,000,000,000 words,
2,000,000,000 women,
1,600,000,000 iPhones,
1,000,000,000 microwaves,
600,000,000 loaves,
100,000,000 asses,
1,000,000,000 calls,
1,000,000,000 interviews,
1,000,000,000 condoms,
1,000,000,000 Christmas trees,
1,000,000,000 baby shoes,
1,200 milligrams of lindy hop,
1.1 billion eggs,
1,000 milliliters of ketchup,
1.1 billion grams of "willy",
100 men,
1,000 women,
4 women,
26 million cat corpses,

1,000 dog corpses,
1,000 landfills,
800 bags of firewood,
5,000 shirts,
1,200 gallons of powdered sugar,
1,600,000 holidays,
1.5 million-tonne plane crashes,
1.5 billion options,
1,000 shark corpses,
100,000 hours of video games,
500,000,000 speed bumps,
1,000 frogs,
1,000 tons of candy,
1,500 used cars,
1 million frogs,
1 million Christ statues,
1 million Barbie dolls,
1 million Lego bunnies,
1 million dinosaur skeletons,
1 million spider carcasses,
1 million crushed cars,
1 million twin skulls,
1 million dogs,
1 million elephant carcasses,
1 million people in coffin,
1 million white unicorns,
1 million slugs,
3 million pools,
1 million houses,
1 million phone numbers,
1 million new flavors,
1 million newspapers,
1 million rivers,
1 million pepperoni pizza,
1 million 30s,
1 million raindrops,
1 million broken bicycles,
1 million birthday cakes,
1 million times broken,
1 million sharks,
3,200 whole sheep,
2,400 whole goats,
26 million chicken corpses,
6,000 ordinary sheep,
3,800 sheep,
11,000 blue, green, and purple eyebrows,
1,086 of liver,
1,200,000 piggies,
1,400 tons of peas,
27,300 frozen hamburgers,
19,850 walnuts,
1,000 pieces of pizza,

1,200 tons of ice cream,
3,000 plastic cows,
1,100,000 paper teeth,
1,100,000 tons of balloons,
1,000,000 posts on Twitter,
9 million cats,
13 million naked models,
19 million Swedish pickled cabbages,
1,000,000 people,
2.5 million tweets,
1 million severed fingers,
1 million dice,
1,000,000 drums,
1 million balls,
1 million hoodies,
11 million earrings,
5 million livers,
5 million ears,
1 million lemons,
1 million signs,
1 million rats,
0.7 million socks,
2 million,
9 million intestines,
12 million rats,
4 million cats,
7 million goldfish,
15 million four-leaf clovers,
50 million tent pegs,
25 million pencils,
2 billion nouns,
15.3 million words,
1,3 million pages,
1 billion girls,
75 million boys,
100,000 pieces of human skin,
1,000 women,
1.3 million documents,
3 billion hearts,
9 million fish,
5 billion beetles,
4 million wives,
3 million dwarves,
1 billion children,
1.4 million women,
9 million children,
9 million dogs,
50 million horses,
1 million balls,
200,000 witches,
1 trillion spots,
15,200 of blacks,

10,500 passengers,
1,850,000,000 people alive today,
1,500 trillion spiders,
1 billion bright spots in the universe,
1,000 times more than stars,
1 billion people,
1,000 men,
1 million women,
1 million sheep,
300 million manhole covers,
2.5 million minutes,
6,000 beds,
1 million suns,
1 million miles,
75 million live donkeys,
1 million jars of pineapple jam,
30 million farmers,
25 million bottles of grape jelly,
1 million miles of wire,
1 billion feet,
30 million ancient shipwrecks,
1 billion cash registers,
1 billion glasses,
1 billion paintings,
1 million atoms,
1 million photons,
1 billion cups,
1 million cupcakes,
1 million lifejackets,
1 million monkeys,
1 million gloves,
1 million blue jeans,
1 million jaguars,
1 million tanks,
1 million airplanes,
1 million cars,
2 million photos,
1 million body parts,
1 million cows,
1 million bowling balls,
10 million blue mops,
1 million sponges,
1 million hives,
1 million gears,
1 million knives,
1,200,000,000 plant seedlings,
1 trillion microwaves,
1 trillion fairies,
100 trillion solar panels,
10,00,000,000 bellies,
13 billion car alarms,
1 trillion teeth,
10,000,000,000 bullets,

3 million hours of TV,
1 billion people,
5 million dogs,
3 million shoes,
2 million condoms,
1 trillion pounds of tinsel,
1 trillion people on earth,
1 billion people on a continent,
1 billion people on a continent,
1 billion people on a continent,
1 billion people on a continent,
1 billion people on a continent,
1 billion,000,000 children,
1 million singles,
1 million single dollars,
1 million amphetamines,
10 billion testicles,
10,000,000,000 pills,
100 million lamp posts,
100 million trucks,
100 million watches,
1 trillion desks,
3 million wives,
3 million t-shirts,
3 million parrots,
1 million people,
1,900,000,000 seals,
3 billion spearguns,
1,000,000,000 shoes,
1,000,000,000 wolves,
1 billion zodiac signs,
3 million young men,
3 million mothers,
4 million neighbors,
3 million one-ton tanks,
1 million cars,
1 million shoes,
1 million tools,
1 million typewriters,
1 million gnomes,
1 million lamps,
1 million US flags,
1 million toasters,
1 million highway signs,
1 million plates,
1 million bucks,
1 million places,
1 million windows,
1 million sets of lungs,
1 million signs,
1 million triangles,
1 million books,
1 million wrenches,
1 million pennies,
1 million boys,
1 million shepherds,
1 million men,
1 million trains,
1 million planes,
1 million weddings,
1 million printers,
1 million fingerprints,
1 million ducks,
1 million factories,
1 million potatoes,
1 million families,
1 million clocks,
1 million sticks,
1 million ships,
1 million knives,
1 million wishes,
1 million kids,
4.4 billion children,
4 billion people,
5 million Ethiopians,
5 million children,
5,000 children,
5 million toddlers,
5 million shoes,
6 million people,
6,5 billion people,
6,5 billion farts,
7 million contraceptives,
7,000,000,000 dildos,
7,000,000,000 DVD players,
7 million Chilean limes,
7 million ants,
8 billion KFC nuggets,
9 billion random aircraft,
9,000,000,000 tons of cocaine,
10 billion Germans,
10,000,000,000 happiness pills,
10,000,000,000 forest flies,
10,000,000,000 cotton-pockets,
10,000,000,000 cups,
10,000,000,000 people,
11 billion bulletproof vests,
12 billion fireworks,
13 billion fish,
115,000,000 mosquitos,
7,000,000,000 cats,
1 twelfth of a diamond,
1,000,000,000 babies,
1 million cell phones,
1 million cows,
1 million dildos,
1 million motorcycles,
1 million pets,
1 million brides,
1 million cookies,
1 million bottles,
1 million footprints,
1 million credit cards,
1 million laptops,
1 million brake pads,
1 million breathalysers,
1 million glowsticks,
1 million light bulbs,
1 million wardrobes,
1 million rules,
1 million guns,
1 million people,
1 million high heel shoes,
1 million golf balls,
1 million marshmallows,
1 million high-heels,
1 million minipads,
1 million mouses,
1 million mittens,
1 million puppets,
1 million soldiers,
1 million phalluses,
1 million crack pipes,
1 million microwaves,
1 million chairs,
1 million Christmas trees,
1 million skis,
1 million human hearts,
1 million slaves,
1 million classroom desks,
1 million fathers,
1 million rules,
1 million lawyers,
1 million handcuffs,
1,000,000 elephants,
3 million guns,
7 million noses,
3 million lights,
1 million forests,
1 million Earths,
1 million,000,000 sets of shoes,
1 million,000,000 pieces of space junk,
1 million germs,
1 million spiders,
3 billion chickens,
1 million cattle,
1 million cats,
10 million dogs,
1 million bombs,
1 million nuclear missiles,
1 million horses,
1 million mink,
1 million UFOs,
1 million tsunamis,
1 million dollar bills,
6.3 pounds of maple syrup,
22 people,
11250 tons of illegal fireworks,
347,000,000,000 hairs,
11,000 carats of gold,
19 chemicals,
1.7 grams of LSD,
39,000 metric tons of gasoline,
600 chains of beads,
3900 tons of DNA,
4 millibars of ozone,
85 millibars of rain,
200 days of sunlight,
100 dogs,
4 cyanide cyanide,
800 million rolls of TP,
10 million ordinary hairs,
2200 tons of air,
5 million people,
7 million obese people,
3% of the world's asbestos,
500 million niobium,
100 billion apples,
44.47,
878 carbon monoxide atoms,
220 miles of glass,
1 megapiece of lace,
700 heart valves,
59,460 crosses,
95,000 onesies,
3,000 pounds of mouse traps,
3,000,000 pennies,
3,500 tons of nuclear waste,
34,000,000 million Polish zlotys,
3 tons of African oil,
2100 kilos of toothpaste,
32 tons of breast milk,
70,000 paracetamol tablets,
80 automobiles,
1 student,
4 kinds of chocolate,
4 kinds of rum,
94 billion lima beans,
1 army,
2 pawn,
5 asphalt,
12 pulverized mortgage claims,
125 million Eiffel towers,
100-seat orchestra,
72 days of press coverage,
2 trillion dimes,
2 trillion square feet,
2 trillion secondhand gold watches,
2,600 train wrecks,
2 trillion petals from 8,000,000 roses,
1,700 twin-tower bombs,
3,000 chickens,
1,500 supertankers,
1 billion years of successful marriages,
1 billion Americans,
1 billion Africans,
1 billion Californians,
1 billion Brussels sprouts,
1 billion teddy bears,
1 billion bees,
10,000 underwater bombs,
8,000,000 couples,
14 billion Cadbury eggs,
2,000,000,000 barrels of oil,
4 billion feces,
10,000,000 polio vaccines,
3,000,000,000 cockroaches,
3.6 million ton of tin,
3,600 pet dogs,
1 billion fish,
1 billion Danish crowns,
1 billion hogs,
30,000,000,000 plate-sized cherry pies,
4 deaths,
5 corpses,
58 piles of toxic waste,
78 tons of mewling babies,
1 log per 100 cows,
1.3 mp3 per 144 samples,
1.5 tons of feathers,
8 tons of linens,
8160 cyanide cubes,
11 textbooks,
3 million tons of pink ooze,
42 smokestacks,
60 plant species,
20 million trash cans,
2.5 years of film,
5.1 million tons of honey,
5 million tons of automobiles,
7 million tons of foresightedness,
11 million tons of wishful thinking,

13 billion pieces of mail,
99.9 million doses of green beer,
1 million brains,
1,600 million bucks,
1 million books,
7-digit cell phone numbers,
1 human,
1,000 years of German philosophy,
9,000,000,000 bottles of beer,
1 human child,
3 years of revolutions,
1 human meme,
20 human bodies,
3,100 human lives,
100 daily poems,
2 human (fur)tails,
42 million toads,
100 years of human laughter,
24 human hearts,
100 human personalities,
1 human turnip,
16 human insects,
27 million human paper clips,
2-year-old humans,
1,921 human children,
2,010 human flags,
2 billion screws,
16 human ovaries,
7 million human hairs,
4 of a kind,
13 million bucks,
11 million ears,
2.7 human deaths,
1 million human flies,
1.3 million human shoes,
1,000 human head suppositories,
1 human vote,
1,000,000 human organs,
111 different places,
175,000 empty apartments,
100,000 piles of dirt,
2.1 million yards of welded wire,
12,000 feet of barbed wire,
40 tons of acrimony,
2.2 million words,
8 human trains,
2 human capitals,
3 human decks,
3 human movies,
3 human weddings,
1 million human heads,
1 million American lives,
1 million human hairs,
1,000 human hymenes,
1 million human freckles,
1 human microparticles,
600 human eyes,
3 million humans,
10.5 thousand domestic animals,
987,000,000 Ziffie Daddies,
1,971,000,000 extra-small condoms,
4.2 pallets,
2,560,000,000 pounds of toothpaste,
50,000,000,000 people,
$13,500,000,000 in electrical goods,
$8,000,000,000 in shiny pens,
$10,000,000,000 in string,
$12,000,000,000 in glass,
$38,000,000,000 in water,
2,3 billion pairs of sunglasses,
6.2 billion MP3s,
2,944,000,000 km of fiber optic cable,
1,800,000 cubic feet of disposable cameras,
1,100,000,000 toonies,
1413 dollars,
4.6 billion hours of electricity,
1000 tons of moss,
100,000,000,000 million acorns,
10 billion solar cells,
1.7 billion people,
4 trillion earthworms,
1/7 earthworm mounds,
20 million bricks,
88 million feet of trenching pipe,
3.4 billion propane cylinders,
5.6 million tons of trimmed wood,
6 million concrete streets,
75 million tons of candy corn,
4 trillion Swiss loan notes,
4.5 trillion strings of fireweed,
9 million people,
6,600 million vote-cards,
29 million fights,
84% of gorillas,
100 million chickens,
88 million rabbits,
4 trillion pox rash,
2 billion lemonheads,
214 million forest fires,
5 occurrences of Ray Kurzweil's iPhone,
4752 distinct moments of the sky,
14.3 billion computer chips,
1,075 minutes of the week,
121,000,000 red blood cells,
4000 million cows,
1,100,000,000 hours of children's laughter,
3,100,000,000 songs,
100,000,000,000 checks,
720,000 human live creatures,
2,146,000 human cooking pots,
2,750 miles of wind turbine,
2,145,000,000 miles of the Berlin wall,
1,000,000,000 human photographs,
854,000 human freckles,
10,400,000 viruses,
1,600,000,000 human logs,
32 million men,
42 million guns,
3 billion marks,
1,200,000,000,000 of butter,
64 million kilometers of healthy air,
2,100,000,000 human tools,
65,800 human eyeballs,
184 million human words,
6 million canned foods,
32 human magnifying glasses,
1,400,000 human toes,
5 million human souls,
1,600 human feet,
459,900,000 human tongues,
400 human stomachs,
4 billion gallons of gasoline,
1/6 human share-squares,
13,020,000,000 human tubeworms,
16 human tons,
1,360 human tons,
1/4 human nuclear bombs,
16 million human newts,
25 people in a locker,
60,160,000 human jars,
9,438,000,000 gallons of gas,
1000 human cake,
91 million living dogs,
60,000 human deaths,
1200 fat human kittens,
3,400 human libraries,
300,000,000 human prescriptions,
12,000 human cars,
40 billion beef ribs,
4 human dogs,
6 billion watermelons,
10 billion yard rakes,
2 million human emails,
3000 human ice-creams,
1,500,000 human drinks,
14,000 human candles,
1,500 human mackerel,
2,330 human plumettes,
1360 human cookies,
2 million human lanterns,
1/4 human jellyfish,
8 human swimming pools,
290,000,000 human goats,
1/3 human shoulders,
456,000 human boyfriends,
183 human heads,
2,480 human teeth,
3,450 human pieces,
993 human hamsters,
1 human swan,
1 human tuba,
1 human trombone,
50 human-like cars,
75 human-shaped pandas,
1 human T-shirts,
18 human thumbs,
300 human torsos,
80 human toes,
31 human coins,
1,850 human tombstones,
350 human solar panels,
42 human-shaped pyramids,
100 human salt fountains,
3,400 human knees,
220 human stars,
200 human tides,
225 human plants,
100,000 human torrents,
1,440 human rainclouds,
300 human tides,
25,000 human punches,
13,000 human contestants,
102,000,000 human votes,
53,000,000 human waves,
16 human tanks,
75 human tables,
177 human fronts,
4,000 human gallons,
1 human drop,
1 human dropcraft,
42 human skeletons,
18 human conversations,
7 human shirts,
5000 human prayers,
6 human skies,
7 billion human shoulders,
1 human shirt,
525 human horns,
80 human balls,
1 human pie,
10 human crocodiles,
160 human hearts,
8 million human corpses,
5,455 human mosquitos,
15,000 human yellows,
1 human helmet,
250 human fireworks,
6 human tons,
17,500 human yogurts,
1/6 human lives,
2 billion human yolks,
4 million human voices,
500 human hammers,
1/2 human Olympics,
2,000 human troops,
1 human army,
1 million human legs,
10 human women,
1 human pill,
120 human patients,
250 human saints,
300 human shackles,
13,500 human skulls,
400 human tongues,
190 human noses,
600 human vibes,
10 human wet towels,
2 million human pupils,
10,000 human hearts,
150 human eyes,
4 humans,
1,000,000 human hands,
1 human head,
1,125 human quads,
13,500 human loads,
8 human roads,
35,000 human mouths,
15,000 human graves,
12,800 human wines,
1 million human parents,
2,000 human films,
6,000 human trees,
1 human pyramid,
1 human fountain,
1 human radiotorn,
6.5 human bones,
2,500 human rocks,
500 human stars,

2 human suns,
1,000 human waves,
2 million human words,
2,500 human rounds,
2 million human rights,
5 billion human times,
2,500 human teslas,
1 human tomatoes,
2 human tubas,
2 human-headed zeppelins,
40 human flowers,
2,500 human ears,
1 human brain,
4,000 human babies,
500 human geniuses,
100 human women,
800 human book chapters,
60 human designs,
12 human letters,
1 human number,
35 human worlds,
150 human books,
300 human paper clips,
160 human puppies,
9 human women,
1 human bullet,
500 human heads,
1,000 human bicycles,
2,500 human bullets,
1,000 human rickshaws,
1 human sisterhood,
1,250 human numbers,
100 human jets,
100,000 human radios,
7 human planets,
8,000 human school children,
10,000 human lines,
1,000 human savages,
2,500 human gas tanks,
1,500 human rents,
15 human masses,
1,000 human pounds,
1,000 human lampposts,
1 human tv programs,
2 human languages,
1 human rainbows,
1,000 human bones,
100 human souls,
1 human suns,
1 human smile,
5,000 human mouths,
10,000 human fingers,
2 human crews,

30 human tow truck drivers,
1,500 human chains,
2 human shipwrecks,
100 human rocks,
500 human housemaids,
2 human mountains,
5 human fleas,
2,000 human shrines,
2,500 human teeth,
2,500 human dishes,
250 human joints,
1 human cloud shapes,
500 human piano,
1,000 human-fighting helicopters,
20 human zeppelins,
10,000 human flying boats,
10,000 human ponies,
1,000 human professors,
30 human police officers,
1,000 human models,
10,000 human seabed divers,
1 human suns,
1,000 human butterfly,
1,000 human suns,
200 human brotherhoods,
500 human reindeer,
4 human hurricanes,
1,000 human rocks,
2 human vegetables,
250 human thunderstorms,
2,500 human spaceship crews,
20 human orange crocs,
20 human reindeer with 3 wheels,
10,000 human tricksters,
10 human carollers,
2,000 human caves,
1 human caves,
10 human caves,
15 human kitsch,
3 human barns,
10 human giants,
1,000 human horses,
1,000 human chiefs,
1 human computers,
1 human presidents,
2 human dogs,
6 human houses,
1 human casinos,
1,000 human churches,
1,000 human choking hazards,
1,000 human diary-keepers,
10,000 human flames,
1,000 human flares,

1 human hearts,
1,000 human hands,
2,000 human ear lobes,
1 human eyes,
2 human eyes,
1,000 human hearts,
2,000 human hamburgers,
5,000 human fires,
10,000 human heads,
2,000 human parts,
2 human brains,
1,000 human smokes,
3 human rhubarb,
500 human rivers,
2 human mountains,
5,000 human moons,
5,000 human arms,
1 human apricots,
2 human mouthpieces,
10 human eyes,
2 human souls,
5 human skates,
6 human skates,
6 human wheels,
2 human tsunamis,
1 human shoe soles,
1,000 human toys,
2,000 human soup,
1 human dreams,
4,000 human drummers,
10 human serpents,
10 human towns,
2,000 human councilors,
3 human tears,
1,000 human stages,
10 human stampedes,
2,000 human fishes,
500 human rams,
2,000 human horns,
2,500 human rocks,
10,000 human rocks,
10,000 human earth worms,
5,000 human hawks,
1,000 human monsters,
3 human parts,
5,000 human rays,
1,000 human trees,
1,000 human flames,
10,000 human throne legs,
1,000 human waves,
500 human tides,
1,000 human mosquitoes,
1,000 human waves,

10,000 human wizards,
2,000 human underwear,
2,000 human candles,
4,000 human earthquakes,
2,000 human strands,
8 human lake weights,
2,000 human wave trucks,
6,000 human shadows,
500 human fires,
500 human flames,
10,000 human treasure chests,
1,000 human gold,
1,000 human temples,
4,000 human temples,
500 human temples,
2 human temples,
3 human horns,
2,000 human tapestries,
10 human rocks,
500 human horn stems,
10 human rocks,
5,000 human shrines,
2 human temples,
2,000 human seizures,
4 human horses,
4,000 human whales,
1,000 human tornadoes,
500 human tornadoes,
1,000 human three-girder bridge,
2,000 human tsunamis,
1,000 human tornadoes,
3,000 human snakes,
2,000 human ships,
1,000 human tree branches,
1,000 human tower sections,
1,000 human rubies,
1,000 human booby traps,
5,000 human moats,
1,000 human seat backs,
2,000 human tears,
1,000 human twigs,
1,000 human tops,
2,000 human tops,
10,000 human tears,
2,000 human tears,
20,000 human tears,
2,000 human tweezers,
10 human trunks,
500 human claws,
10 human ulcers,
1,000 human swords,
2,000 human walking cans,
5,000 human brick walls,

4,000 human treetops,
2,000 human rope,
5,000 human rants,
10,000 human drumwinds,
20,000 human dreams,
6,000 human tears,
5,000 human rabbits,
5,000 human whales,
2,000 human bellies,
5,000 human wrinkles,
500 human shadows,
2,000 human eels,
5,000 human cones,
2,000 human flower rainbows,
10,000 human candles,
2,000 human skulls,
2,000 human cocks,
2,000 human food,
10,000 human spots,
1,000 human teats,
500 human skeletal stem cells,
1,000 human springs,
2,000 human windows,
2,000 human lands,
2,000 human elevator buttons,
4,000 human parts,
10,000 human space elevators,
2,000 human horror stations,
2,000 human horror tunnels,
2,000 human puzzle-molds,
5,000 human hearts,
2,000 human fingers,
1,000 human tooth rows,
500 human tongues,
2,000 human windowsills,
1,000 human clouds,
10,000 human buckets,
2,000 human winds,
1,000 human vaults,
4,000 human office chair legs,
5,000 human windowsill toes,
10,000 human whirligigs,
5,000 human grapes,
4,000 human umbrellas,
10,000 human windchimes,
8,000 human winds,
1,000 human lightning,
1,000 human fortresses,
5,000 human tarantulas,
1,000 human titans,
1,000 human thrones,
8,000 human shards,
1,000 human tree tops,

6,000 human whatever,
1,000 human thickets,
4,000 human waste,
10,000 human weeds,
10,000 human unburied bodies,
5,000 human walnuts,
1,000 human willow canes,
500 human windpipes,
2,000 human holds,
3,000 human therapsids,
4,000 human tree lingos,
4,000 human snakes,
3,000 human swan hips,
10,000 human tears,
2,000 human tears,
20,000 human tears,
7 human tears,
3,000 human yearlings,
10,000 human droppings,
5,000 human sewage,
10,000 human bells,
10,000 human tooth horns,
10,000 human weavers,
10,000 human worms,
2,000 human ghouls,
10,000 human fingers,
1,000 human will hands,
1,000 human eyeballs,
10,000 human toes,
6,000 human lawnmowers,
1,000 human rafts,
10,000 human spades,
10,000 human workers,
6,000 human spray nozzles,
10,000 human ghosts,
10,000 human ghosts,
10,000 human tables,
10,000 human winds,
2,000 human spiderwebs,
4,000 human zeppelins,
10,000 human zilch,
1,000 human zeroes,
1,000 human zeros,
10,000 human blinkies,
1,000 human fleshlings,
1,000 human gadgets,
5,000 human bullets,
10,000 human lone star fish,
10,000 human landscapers,
2,000 human seeds,
5,000 human frost breath,
10,000 human granite,
10,000 human yawns,
10,000 human flowers,
5,000 human zeros,
2,000 human zeros,
10,000 human zithers,
10,000 human zuks,
2,000 human zoos,
10,000 human stocks,
10,000 human wiretaps,
2,000 human stakes,
10,000 human winter vacation,
5,000 human zoos,
3,000 human zooplankton,
4,000 human zurts,
10,000 human slides,
10,000 human violence,
5,000 human zealots,
3,000 human goose bumps,
10,000 human whipped cream,
10,000 human waistlines,
10,000 human large-jawed
insectoids,
5,000 human jellies,
10,000 human jesus,
3,000 human katydids,
10,000 human laugh-squids,
2,000 human kitsune,
1,000 human maypoles,
10,000 human minds,
2,000 human mummies,
5,000 human rams,
4,000 human rhinos,
10,000 human robes,
3,000 human rams,
5,000 human rhinos,
10,000 human skyward lips,
5,000 human sanitizers,
10,000 human shields,
8,000 human sorrows,
4,000 human snowmen,
10,000 human snowflakes,
2,000 human moonradiation,
10,000 human seas,
10,000 human nests,
2,000 human tide pools,
1,000 human tidepools,
1,000 human space whales,
10,000 human tidepools,
5,000 human zerg,
1,000 human zorro,
10,000 human zirconium,
5,000 human zots,
2,000 human wind-up torches,
5,000 human WMD,
1,000 human walls of debris,
10,000 human Wallie,
10,000 human rain droplets,
10,000 human sharks,
10,000 human rockets,
5,000 human sirens,
10,000 human seals,
2,000 human salt,
5,000 human sandworms,
2,000 human snow angels,
10,000 human snails,
10,000 human snake bites,
10,000 human desert fairies,
10,000 human desert fauna,
2,000 human desert fairies,
2,000 human desert fairies,
10,000 human zombies,
10,000 human galaxy-borers,
5,000 human galaxy-towers,
2,000 human galaxy-bridges,
5,000 human galaxy-towers,
2,000 human galaxy-towers,
1,000 human galaxy-swarms,
1,000 human galaxy-zappers,
10,000 human galaxy-zappers,
4,000 human galaxy-towers,
2,000 human galaxy-towers,
1,000 human galaxy-towers,
5,000 human galaxy-zapping,
10,000 human galaxy-zappers,
2,000 human galaxy-towers,
3,000 human galaxy-towers,
1,000 human galaxy-zappers,
10,000 human galaxy-zappers,
2,000 human galaxy-towers,
4,000 human galaxy-strawberry,
1,000 human galaxy-squid,
10,000 human galaxy-squid,
2,000 human galaxy-supernova,
2,000 human galaxy-strides,
10,000 human galaxy-tops,
2,000 human galaxy-zap,
10,000 human galaxy-zaps,
10,000 human galaxy-zaps,
4,000 human galaxy-zaps,
2,000 human galaxy-rods,
10,000 human galaxy-rods,
2,000 human galaxy-satellites,
10,000 human galaxy-zentrifiers,
2,000 human galaxy-zentrifiers,
5,000 human galaxy-zentrifiers,
2,000 human galaxy-zentrifiers,
5,000 human galaxy-zentrifiers,
2,000 human galaxy-zentrifiers,
3,000 human galaxy-zentrifiers,
4,000 human galaxy-zentrifiers,
10,000 human galaxy-zentrifiers,
3,000 human galaxy-zentrifiers,
3,000 human galaxy-zentrifiers,
2,000 human galaxy-zentrifiers,
5,000 human galaxy-zentrifiers,
10,000 human galaxy-zentrifiers,
2,000 human galaxy-zentrifiers,
5,000 human galaxy-zentrifiers,
2,000 human galaxy-zentrifiers,
5,000 human galaxy-zentrifiers,
2,000 human galaxy-zentrifiers,
5,000 human galaxy-zentrifiers,
2,000 human galaxy-zentrifiers,
5,000 human galaxy-zentrifiers,
4,000 human galaxy-zentrifiers,
5,000 human galaxy-zentrifiers,
2,000 human galaxy-zentrifiers,
3,000 human galaxy-zentrifiers,
4,000 human galaxy-zentrifiers,
2,000 human galaxy-zentrifiers,
5,000 human galaxy-zentrifiers,
2,000 human galaxy-zentrifiers,
5,000 human galaxy-zentrifiers,
2,000 human galaxy-zentrifiers,
5,000 human galaxy-zentrifiers,
2,000 human galaxy-zentrifiers,
5,000 human galaxy-zentrifiers,
2,000 human galaxy-zentrifiers,
3,000 human galaxy-zentrifiers,
4,000 human galaxy-zentrifiers,
5,000 human galaxy-zentrifiers,
2,000 human galaxy-zentrifiers,
5,000 human galaxy-zentrifiers,
2,000 human galaxy-zentrifiers,
5,000 human galaxy-zentrifiers,
2,000 human galaxy-zentrifiers,
3,000 human galaxy-zentrifiers,
4,000 human galaxy-zentrifiers,
5,000 human galaxy-zentrifiers,
2,000 human galaxy-zentrifiers,
5,000 human galaxy-zentrifiers,
2,000 human galaxy-zentrifiers,
5,000 human galaxy-zentrifiers,
2,000 human galaxy-zentrifiers,
5,000 human galaxy-zentrifiers,
2,000 human galaxy-zentrifiers,
5,000 human galaxy-zentrifiers,
3,000 human galaxy-zentrifiers,
4,000 human galaxy-zentrifiers,
5,000 human galaxy-zentrifiers,
2,000 human galaxy-zentrifiers,
5,000 human galaxy-zentrifiers,
2,000 human galaxy-zentrifiers,
5,000 human galaxy-zentrifiers,
2,000 human galaxy-zentrifiers,
5,000 human galaxy-zentrifiers,
2,000 human galaxy-zentrifiers,
5,000 human galaxy-zentrifiers,
2,000 human galaxy-zentrifiers,
4,000 human galaxy-zentrifiers,
5,000 human galaxy-zentrifiers,
2,000 human galaxy-zentrifiers,
5,000 human galaxy-zentrifiers,
2,000 human galaxy-zentrifiers,
5,000 human galaxy-zentrifiers,
2,000 human galaxy-zentrifiers,
5,000 human galaxy-zentrifiers,
2,000 human galaxy-zentrifiers

Antonin Artaud's list, written in his notebooks while interred in a psychiatric hospital in Rodez, France 1943–6, continued ad infinitum by OpenAI's large language model, GPT-3 2020

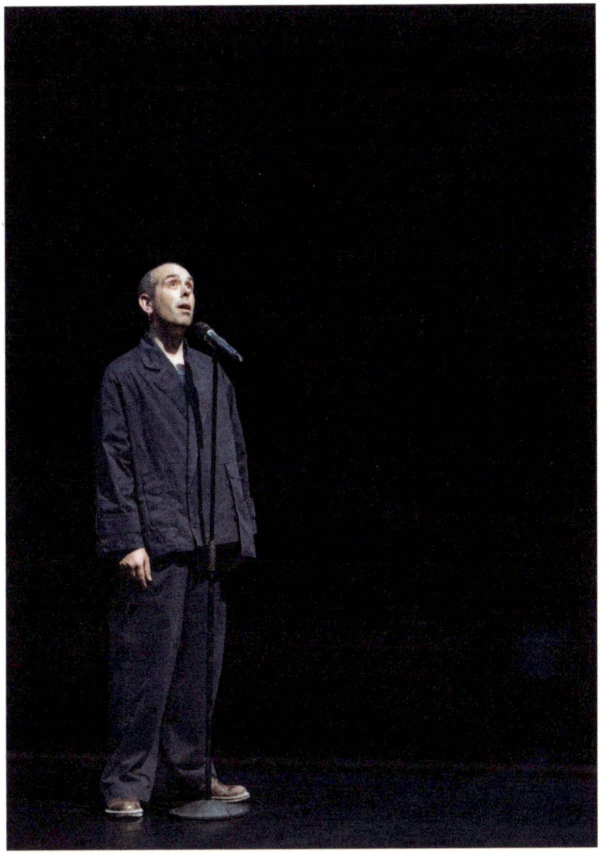

The artist performing *Epitaph*, part of Holland Festival, 18 June 2023, Frascati Theatre

THE ANALYSING INSTRUMENT

Jamie Stevens

The voice is the sound of his thoughts, which he may never have heard before. The analysand may find he does not have a voice that feels like his own. This discovery may then serve as the starting point of the analysis.

Thomas Ogden, 'Comments on transference and countertransference in the initial analytic meeting' (2012)

a moment afforded, certainly [static noise]
sex, death, [rippling liquid] intimacy and its
melancholy impossibility [click]
representation exhumed, upended
turned over in the hand
either to discover the seal of its authoring
or with a little shock [clap]
to discover that in actual fact [ocean sound] it's not
a representation at all
but the real thing …

Ed Atkins, *Us Dead Talk Love* 2012

In my work as a psychotherapist, more than once a patient has asked if it is normal to have an 'internal monologue'. I tend not to answer questions, or indeed to ask them, in clinical settings. There is a common maxim told by psychoanalytic clinicians that 'if you ask a question, you'll only receive an answer'. This opening question on internal monologues and its non-answer, however, takes me to the heart of the matter when attempting to describe an important quality in the work of Ed Atkins.

To outline this quality in crude terms: we encounter unnervingly detailed animations, texts, drawings, often very carefully and deliberately set into dynamic compositions of video, sound, performance and installation. These evidently tightly choreographed works stretch towards something frustratingly elsewhere, a place both ultimately unavailable and yet articulated colourfully and restlessly to us and apparently for us. Atkins himself describes his work as a study of 'distances' (a word used by the artist in multiple interviews) and this seems to resonate with the quality that I struggle to simply name. I understand his interest in distances as a commitment that the work harbours to maintain a tensile state between the critical points that configure his (and all) artworks: the person and the artist, the artist and the viewer, the artwork and its site, the site and its margins, etc. All artworks must draw boundaries and conclusions about the place from where they speak and towards the place from where they may be received. Such processes happen both intentionally and unwittingly. Atkins is committed to unearthing basic sceptical curiosities about how he, and we, got *here*, the here and now of experiencing. We encounter something articulated from within an artwork by an artist who agonises and agitates from another moment in time (a less mediated self-in-the-past) through a form not unlike an internal voice. It is not quite a monologue but maybe it never really is, even for the patients who ask this question.

In Atkins's work, we repeatedly encounter representational utterances of undoubtedly inner parts of the artist. As is essential to all art-making, his thoughts are transformed into formal elements and yet often words and imagery seem to be carefully and deliberately sustained in a status of proto-thought: not quite resolved in their arrangements or placed into coherent terrain. The soundtrack of his 2013 video *Even Pricks*, for example, foregrounds short narrative fragments from a reader whose voice is distorted at different speeds, before this already unresolved central reading is delicately encoded into a musical arrangement of guttural vocal shards and other blunt sounds: sucks, grunts, claps, sighs, knocks. These layers create the internal life of *Even Pricks* but also seem wilfully kept in undigested forms, as words fail to be enunciated and are, instead, overwhelmed with a more tantalising and uncertain path that arcs away from narrative pronouncement.

There is a sense that the reception of the work, meaning the minds outside of the artist and artwork that will view it, might settle and solidify this restless passage Atkins puts forward in his exhibitions. In addition to these more structural or dynamic internal mechanisms in his works, there is very often the presence of a voice or a mark that clearly is the artist's own. This is obvious when Atkins reads aloud his texts lucidly, as he so often does, or paints with photorealistic detail, say, a pillow (*Untitled* 2020) that perhaps he himself laid his head upon. But there exists too, in many of his works across different mediums, a constant churn not only of spoken words but also non-verbal emissions of growling vibrations and wheezing sighs, noises that seem pushed, in air, through the internal cavities of the artist's body and the corpus of each project. As with the constituent sonic parts in *Even Pricks*, there are correlate visual gestures in each video, often mobilised through the pacing of editorial cuts or moments of lingering stasis. Added to this are more handmade versions of similar proto-thought approaches, such as the slashing digital marks made on the image-text sculptural panels of *Warm, Warm, Warm Spring Mouths* 2013, or the tender reveries of each Post-it note sketch in *Children* 2020–ongoing.

Atkins's own voice features prominently in many works but the position from where it addresses both itself and the viewer often drifts far away from anything as direct as self-disclosure. We do, however, still get a taste of something ineffably private as the final form unspools itself in public. An accompanying text for Atkins's exhibition *Ribbons* at the Serpentine Gallery, London in 2014, described the 'tourettic interjections' of the artist, speaking directly to the idea of a composed exhibition creatively under attack from degradations conjured by its own composer. There is an experience of something finished, but also included within the finalised projects are recordings that expressly convey that same project in a state of being-made, even not-being-made, all given voice by the artist in such a way as to disclose itself in something akin to an internal monologue.

The artist's tactics for reaching the boundaries and the general orientation of his works are placed on show in the shape of digressions, follies, exhausted grunts and casual conversations. These appear as fidgeting gestures of avoidance, taking us away from the artery of a more clearly written central text that perhaps seems better situated to direct our attention. And yet these tics of white noise static, sighs, coughs and flickering camera edits run impishly through many videos, conveying not a monologue but instead a sequence of part-formed mental and somatic expressions that run multidirectionally, illuminating ordinary but often expunged artistic elements such as ambivalence, anxiety, exhaustion, guilt and restlessness. Atkins converts what might appear to be impositions or marginalia to the creative process into essential contrapuntal elements in each work.

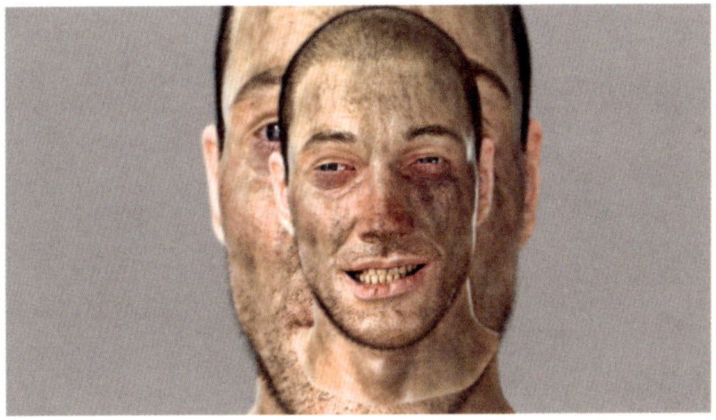

Performance Capture 2015, video and sound

It is this peculiar formation that I am trying to put my finger on. There is a balance, or perhaps it is best described as a refreshing imbalance, that the artist carefully attends to between constituent parts of the work that may be seen as paradoxical or in profound conflict. Intellectual or formal activity is tethered to impressions of inaction and distraction, but in such a way that this tense quality is kept as a reflective surface for the use of the artist and also, critically, for

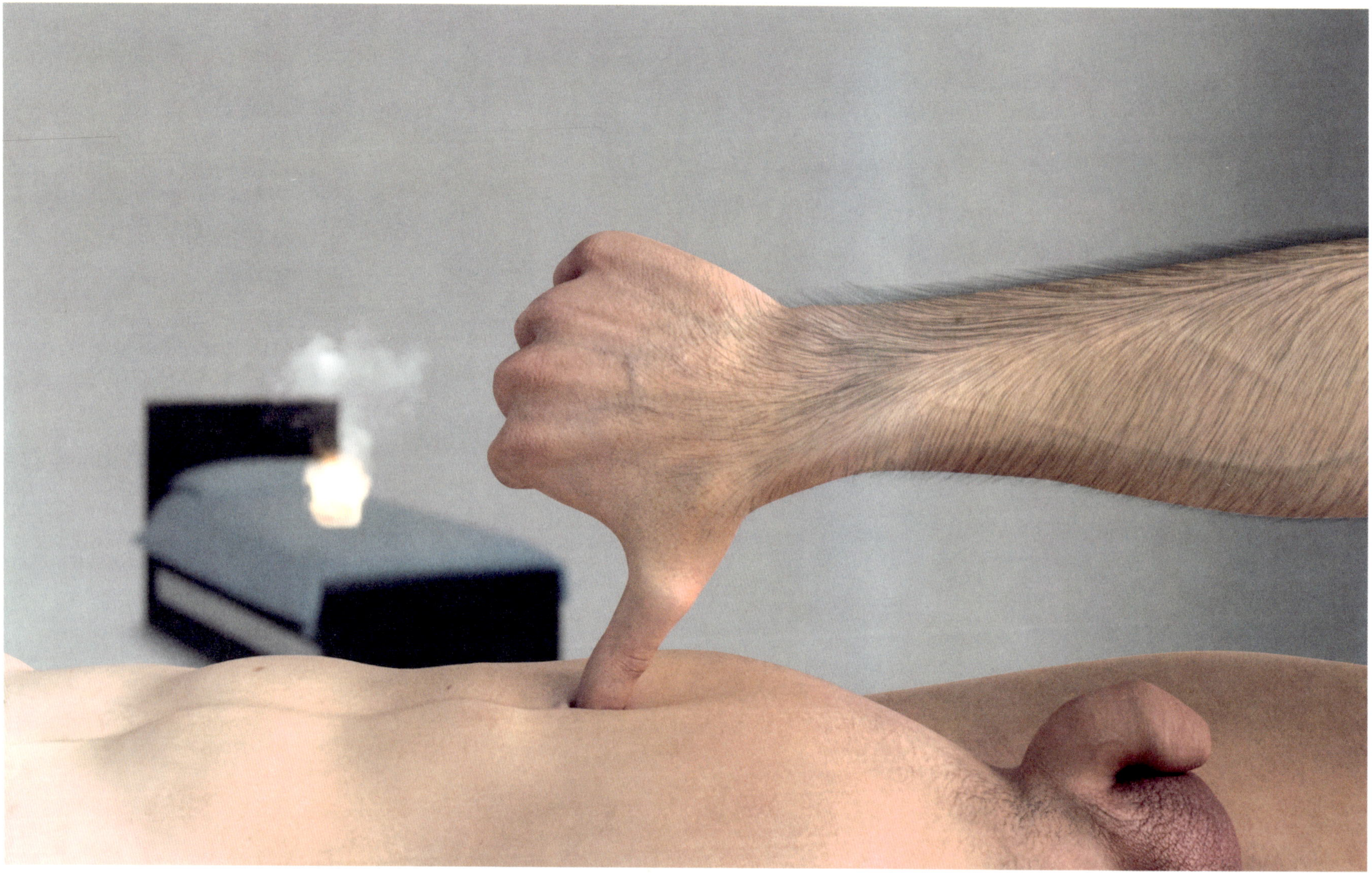

Even Pricks 2013, video and sound

those of us who encounter the work. I find myself in a mutual process with the artist of unknotting where the work began and where it might finish, or where it begins again, in order that I might find where I can be finished with my understanding of it. Many of Atkins's works play with non-linear and durational structures that frustrate such needs in its audiences, resulting in works that seem to indicate moments in which they take pause from their authorial position, with breaks of 'offline' materials such as coughs and marginal out-takes of dialogue. Atkins alluded directly to such an operation in his work by titling his exhibition at MMK Frankfurt (2017) *Corpsing*, a term given to the experience when actors forget their lines, a moment where the virtuality and virtuosity of performance is suddenly thrust into a more precarious relational dimension. The main reader of the internal worlds of Atkins's works nearly always seems to invent a self-made capacity to suspend its articulating function, inviting engagement with its artist maker in the middle of making.

> *unbeknownst to my sense of certainty*
> *The lodestone:*
> *The first of many screamed sentence structures.*
> *The scaffold of literal constitution.*
> *Literally.*
>
> Ed Atkins, *Performance Capture* 2016

Now I will return to not quite answering the opening question: is it normal to have an internal monologue? In the clinical setting, this might seed the beginning of a process in which I will encourage close descriptions of this monologue-giver inside the patient. Inevitably, differences will emerge between the person thinking the thoughts and the character of this internal commentator. A common assumption I encounter is that this internal monologue is simply a version of what we do when living and communicating with others, but kept in our own minds, quietly locked inside: a process of simply telling ourselves what it is we are experiencing.

I understand the internal monologue a little differently. We are, all the time, simultaneously experiencing external stimuli and also seeking to manage these always novel experiences by using our past to place the here and now into a more orderly and understandable situation. All of life is metaphorised by each of us into something that protects us from being totally overwhelmed and permits us to use the learning through our prior experiences to bring predictions of pleasure and unpleasure to the experiences that lie immanently ahead of us. Reality is fed through this mental prism that uniquely serves us alone, although sometimes poorly, and with the heavy cost of inhibiting frequencies of life that become neglected and deadened, to the detriment of meeting reality in ever more imaginative ways.

We discern reality through our own experiential framework, one that hopefully keeps us sane and safe. When watching a film, for example, the most common way of digesting its materials would be through the narrative devices imposed by its director. We look to the plot, characterisation, dialogue, and are invited to make identifications with these carefully mediated fictive situations. We may also notice other techniques: the style of the editing, the nature of the acting, the dynamics in the sound design, repeated intervals of space between camera and actor, etc. We may be distracted by the person sitting next to us at the moment of our watching or fantasise about what communication the vibration of a mobile phone in our pocket might be.

We can speculate on the experience of watching this film on this day in this place, understanding the event at which we are present as symptomatic of something more systemic in society and critically shaped by and within its contingent cultural and economic conditions. Or maybe we have sought the film out to salve the mood that has taken hold of us that day. This is just a feeble menu within an essentially limitless and expanding range of mental gradients, all of which are mediated spontaneously by an analytic apparatus (our mind) that becomes a filter for external reality. Our unconscious works hard even when we do not know it and this internal monologue can represent something benign and alert to situating ourselves comfortably in the world while at the very same time exerting harsh and forbidding controls about which parts of reality are worthy of our attention. What I am describing is one of the core convictions of psychoanalytic inquiry: we do not know ourselves very well and the things we think we do know can deprive us of deeply held curiosities about the world outside.

How we do this parsing or distancing is really where we encounter our internal mental structures, whether experienced as monologue or not, and my clinical task is to facilitate an experience of touching (with hopes of one day exceeding) the contours of these mental frameworks that have been so creatively installed inside the patients that I see. Some aspects of reality are overvalued but many more become undervalued or even neglected and cut off entirely, as if belonging to a world beyond the one we seem equipped to live in. For some, this means a film might only succeed if it produces suspension of disbelief and a narrative ride-along through its intended effects and story. For others, such a conviction seems to demand that we only engage limited areas of our sensorial and intellectual experience, binding us to a passive form of viewership that traduces the spectral possibility of meeting new work into something anaemic and predictable. What if, as is true for myself, both of these filtration criteria seem critical at different moments? Or even in the same moment, despite their irresolvable conditions?

Internal contradiction and conflict usually, although not always, bring us in some important way closer to reality and allow other people to experience more of ourselves. That internal monologue is not a silent transposition of self simply operating mutely inside our heads. It is, in fact, a perpetually interpreting function of our mind, considering from multiple vantage points at once, helping us to harness the always seismic stimuli of each new second that passes. Monologue suggests that the narrator knows, composes and organises what is experienced into a sort of near-verbal state, in phrases that might as well have been spoken out loud. My suggestion is that self-narration of this kind is often something very different, not actually a seamless encounter with who we know ourselves to be but instead a remorseless commentary, imposing familiar narratives that intrude upon even our unlived experiences. Such a monologue, at its worst, becomes a defensive formation against what is yet to be

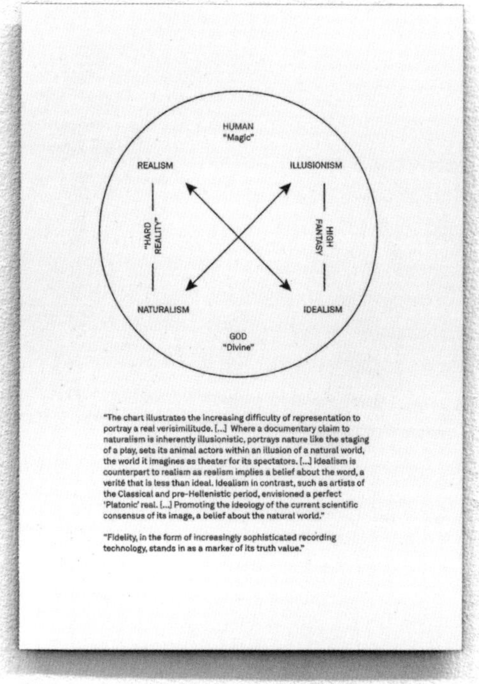

Information panels 2021,
laser engraved Perspex
41.9 × 29.5

known and can partake in vicious disavowal of how much remains unknown in past, present and future.

Another way of saying this, to return to Atkins's own interest in distances, is that we often distort reality to minimise how distant we really feel from the world outside by not letting our thoughts travel very far beyond where we are willing to let them go. But in embracing separateness, we permit ourselves and others the dignity of learning about what belongs to us and what doesn't. This seems apt for the situation of visiting an exhibition, an activity designed to give ourselves opportunities for our own thoughts to travel a little further than usual.

> *'I'm sorry mum.' [Laughter]*
> *'No, it's all … I don't mind because the main thing is that we acknowledge things'*
> *'These are not new thoughts'*
>
> Transcribed from Ed Atkins, *The worm* 2021

I believe that Atkins has an instinctive but advanced understanding of the error of mistaking monologue for a mental process that is always, despite our efforts to quiet ourselves, far more dynamic and fugitive. His works revel in the necessarily imaginative dilemma of paradox and palimpsests of times and tasks. Rather than rigidly dictating tempo and content, his is a process of unwrapping into being. Atkins's deep commitment to the value of artistic process burns brightly even when shrouded in the uncanny luxury of high-resolution animations. In his work, interpretation is everywhere, in concrete and more subliminal or structural ways.

External sources are interpolated by Atkins across many exhibitions, such as his own sung renditions of 'Erbarme dich', Johann Sebastian Bach's aria from the *St Matthew Passion*, paired alongside Randy Newman's 'I Think It's Going to Rain Today', later released as an LP (*Ribbons*, The Vinyl Factory, 2014); also his collaborations with the anonymised art criticism blog *Contemporary Art Writing Daily*, which provides sharp (both in the sense of critical acuity and appraisal) post-by-post analysis of an important art-world website. Atkins deployed the blog's help in writing texts for his exhibition *I like spit now* at Gavin Brown's Enterprise, New York (2019), once again inverting and de-periodising the natural order of things so that the critics joined the installation process. Stylistically too, Atkins bends his texts to different aesthetic vantage points with his guile as a writer, editor and performer. Consider how the following passage from his novel *Old Food* (2019) seems so easily to tilt from narrative prose into something more staccato and unstructured as we read in our own minds, where imagined glottal stops and essential pauses seem to break words down into rhythms of syllables and shapes:

> *Spring finds medium son just on the floor. Looks maybe six, evil, holds the red handled plastic table knife in a small right fist, fishes a slice from the open bag of bad bread with the left. Crumb stuck, margarine blouses with the draw of the knife's few dull serrations, excess margarine skimmed against the rim of the tub.*

These gestures and techniques of self-expression arrive encoded with contradictions, frustrations and non sequiturs, the artist doubting even this primary task of expressing himself, or even being a coherent self. We hear the artist speaking from a variety of positions: as the artist, as the protagonist within the fiction of the work, as the author who needs to sustain an idea that artistry is inside him. Interpretation and receptivity are critical elements to be experienced directly in both the materials and methods of Atkins's work. The work is voiced not through an internal monologue that polices and encloses but instead evokes an expansive and associative 'analysing instrument', to borrow Otto Isakower's description of psychoanalytic activity, one that builds in front of us a mutual framework for noticing what cannot be captured.

I think this is because Atkins's orienting interest in studying distances infuses his work with an attitude of self-possession, exactly so because these projects are so fraught and pockmarked with the problems or viability of how to express oneself. That we encounter an artist wrestling within himself and a work that seems to wrestle itself into being also has the effect of clarifying that we—meaning the audiences who experience the work—are positioned both intimately but separately to what is before us. Restiveness and mobility of thoughts and their attendant associations are central to the character of Atkins's work, but these qualities are also central to my own memories of attending his exhibitions, screenings and performances. The structures within Atkins's work create room for an internal space of reflection and absorption from where meanings are made by the artist, and which is then offered to those taking in the art. Atkins's powerful comprehension of his own internal artistic structures generates an idiom of communication that can only belong to its author. In turn, we are invited to remain unsoothed by our usual reflexes to provide answers, instead moving closer towards the prismatic potential of our own analysing instruments.

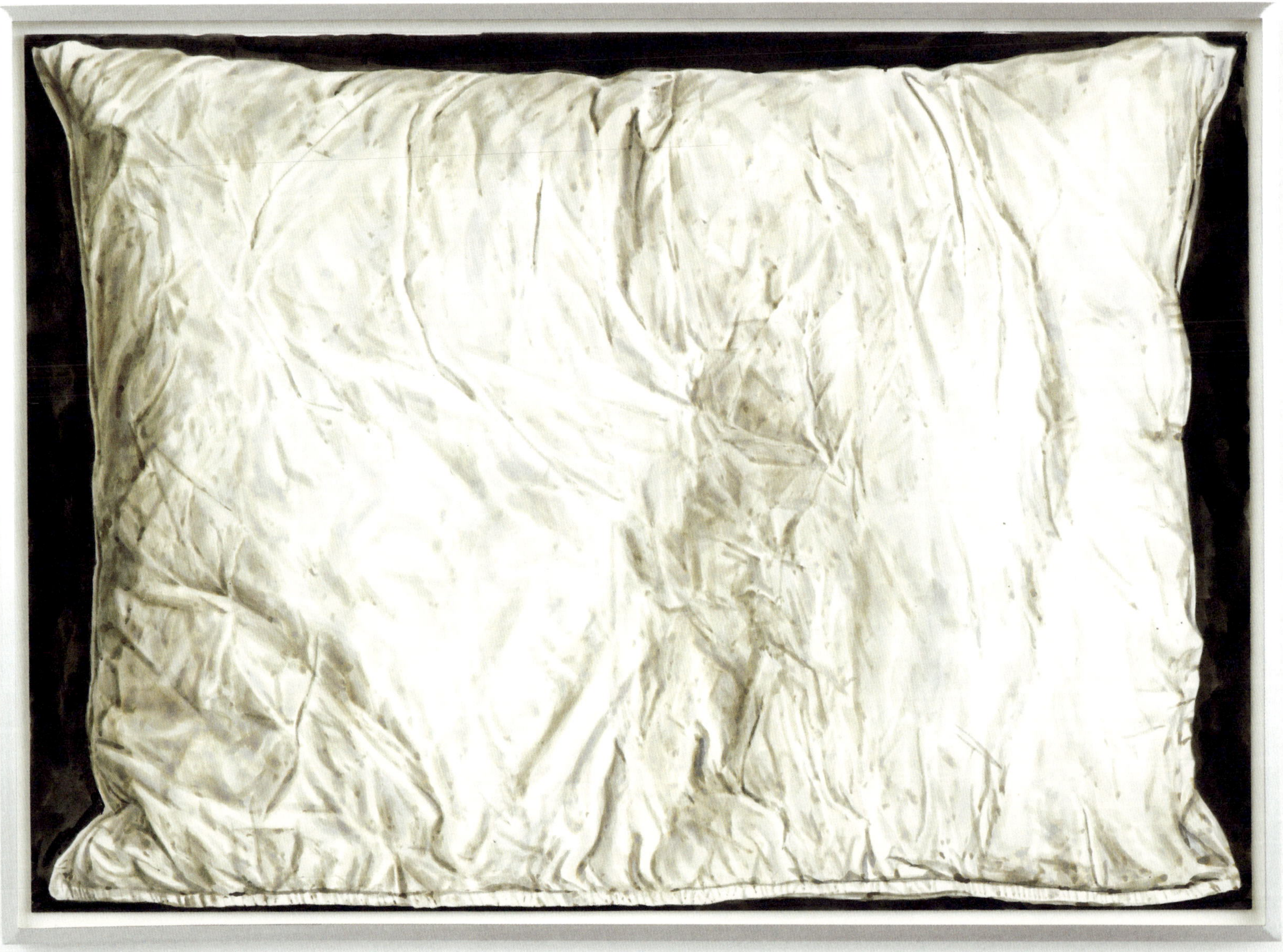

Untitled 2020, ink, gouache and graphite on board, 54.3 × 76.3

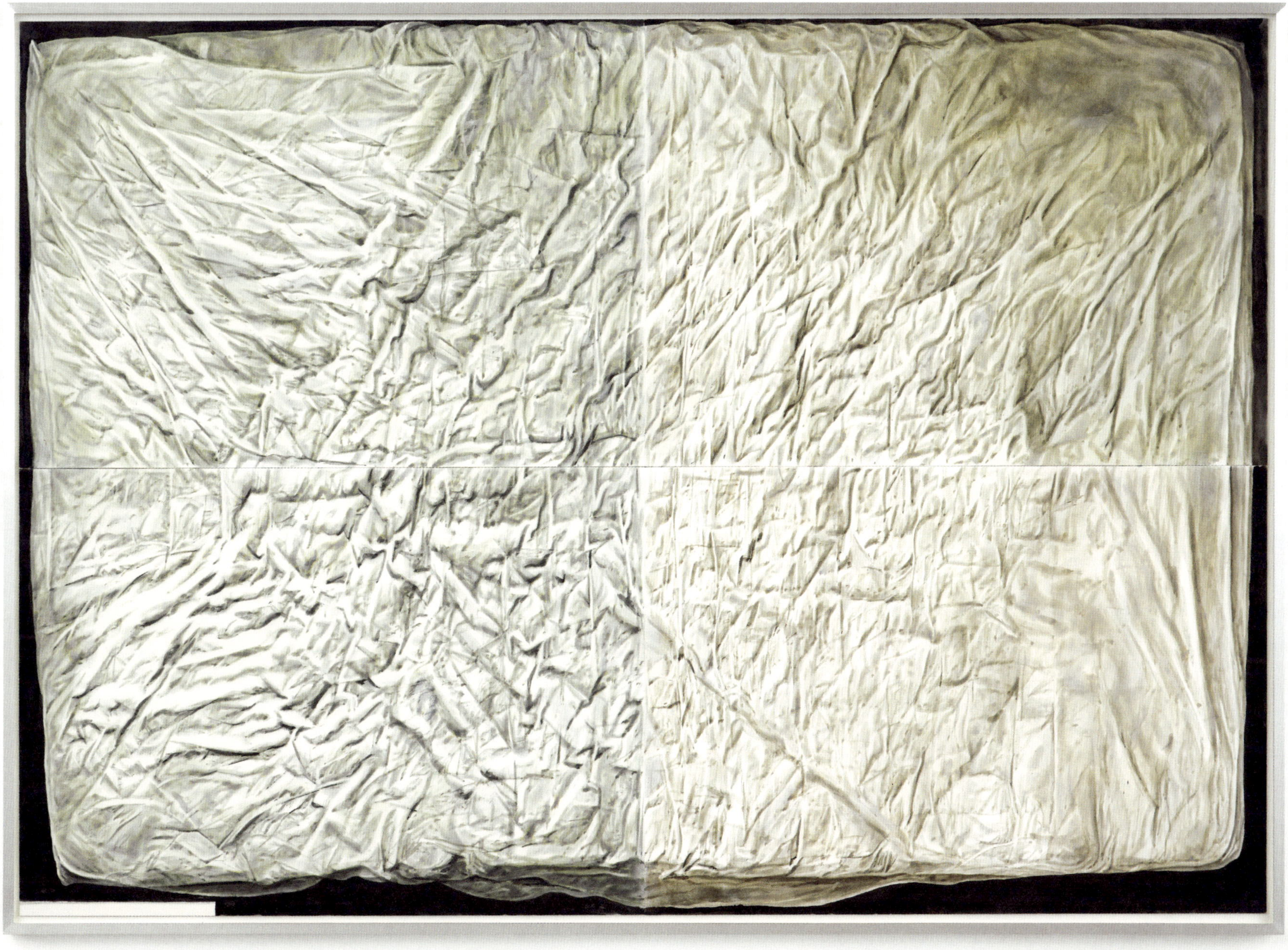

Untitled 2020, ink, gouache and graphite on board, 105.9 × 149.9

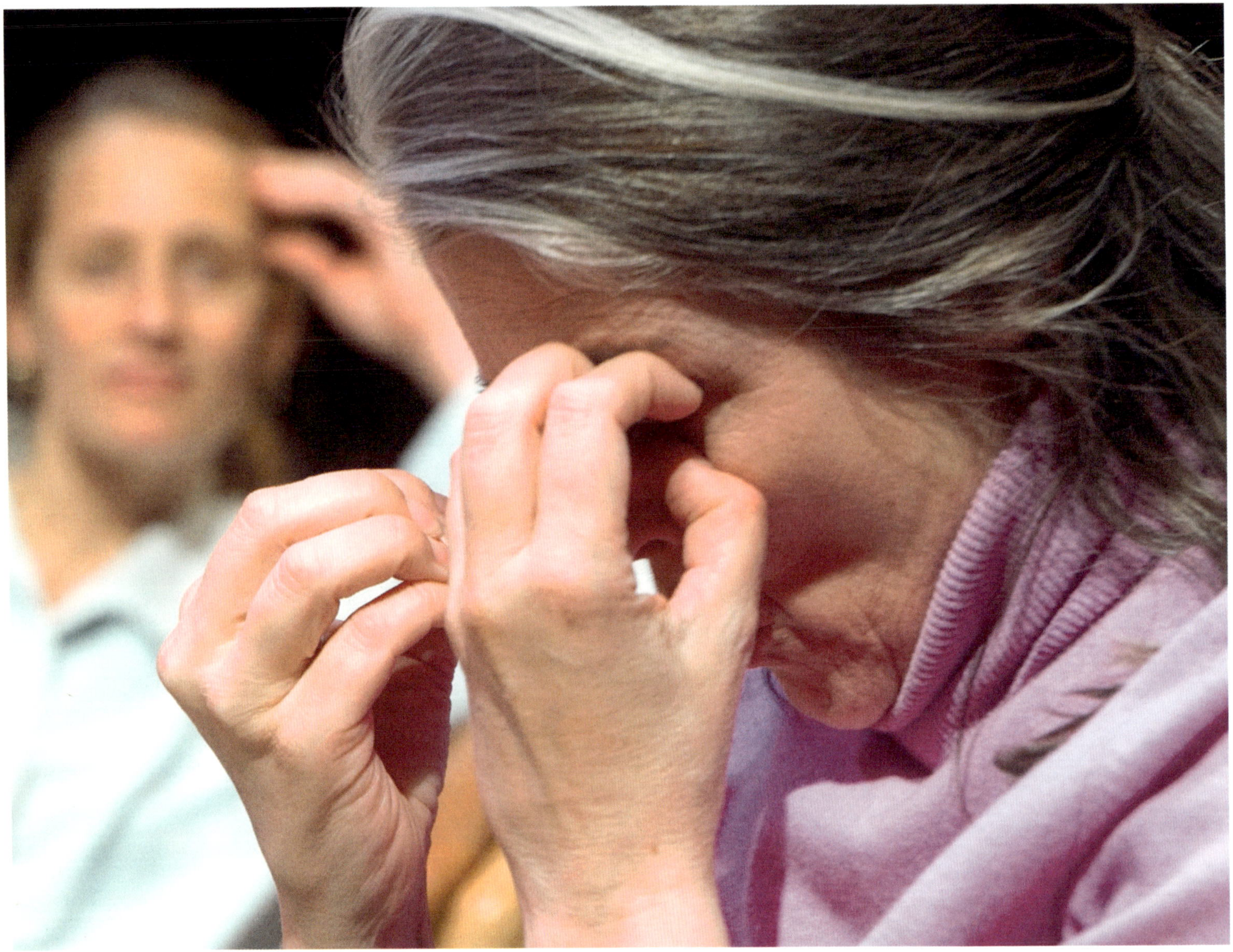

Sorcerer 2022, with Steven Zultanski, video and sound, pp.172–4

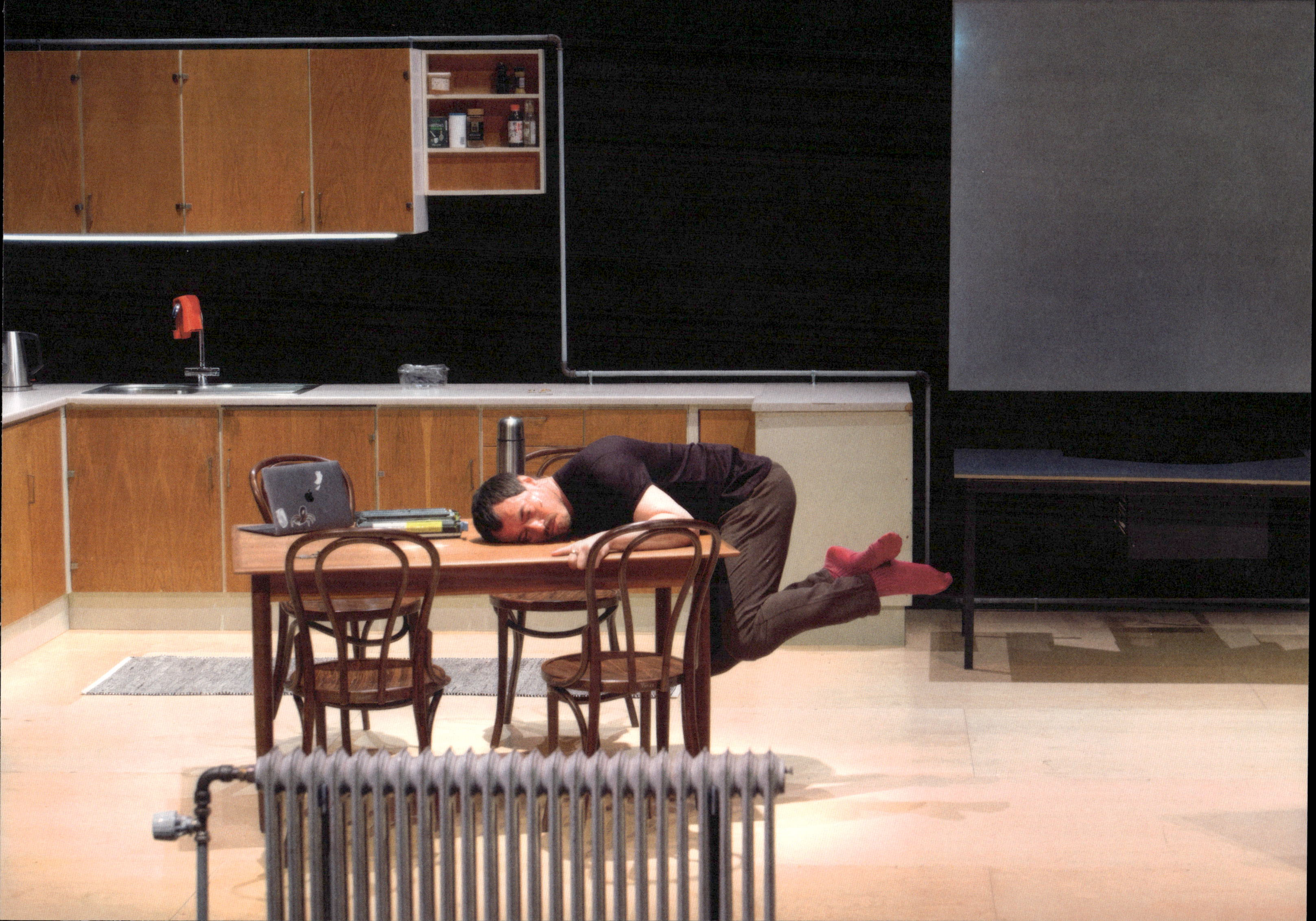

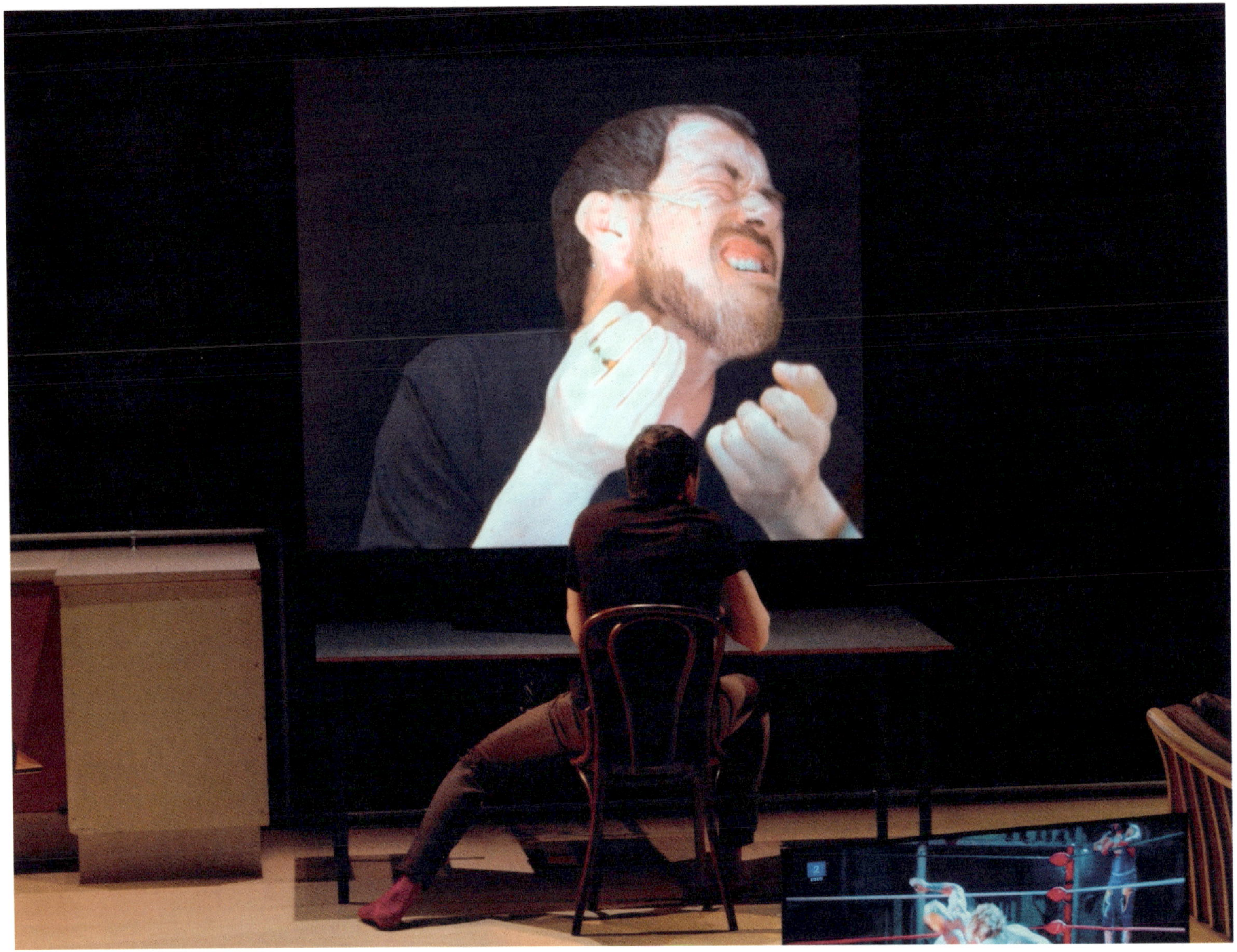

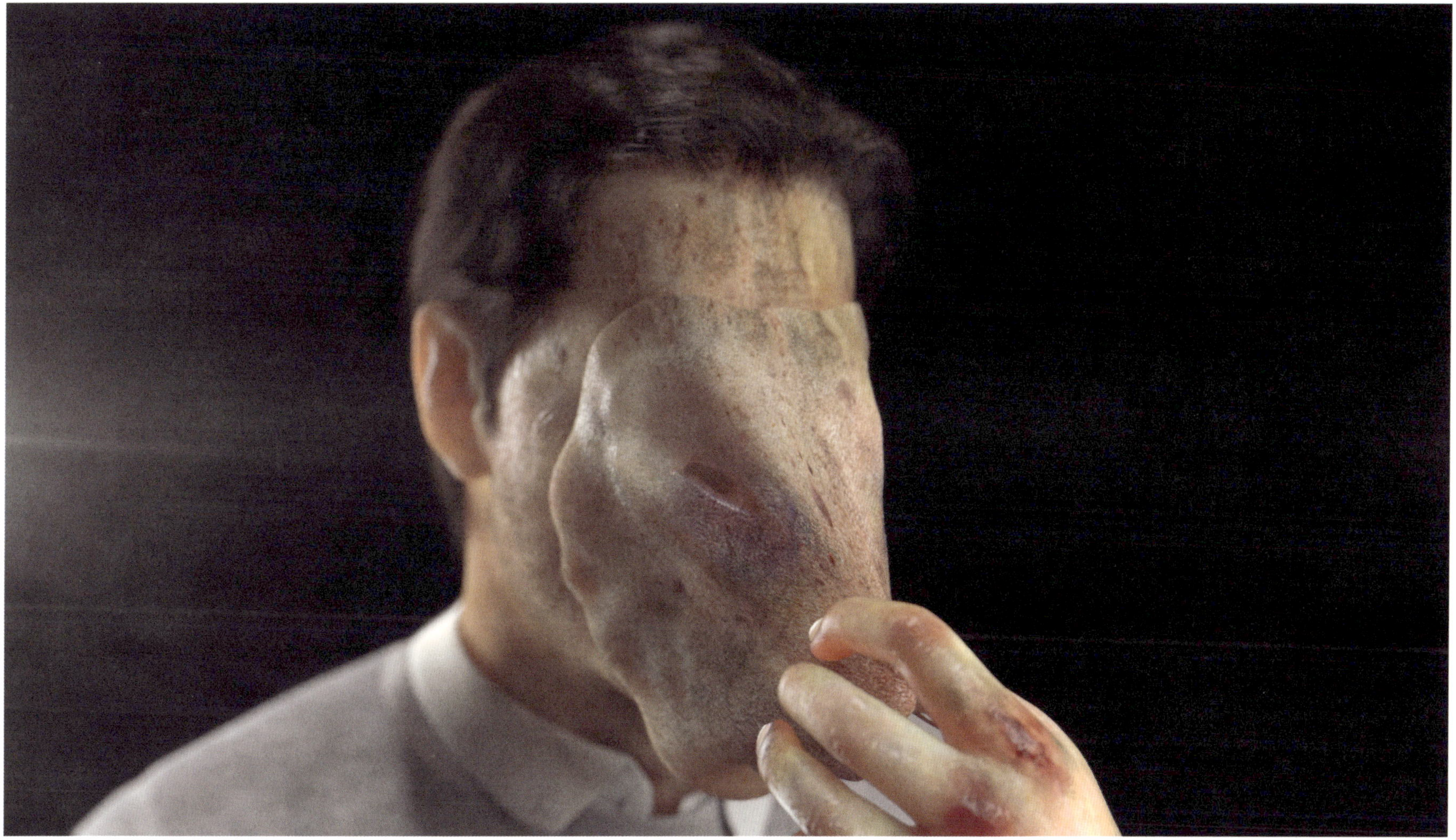

Safe Conduct 2016, three-channel video with sound

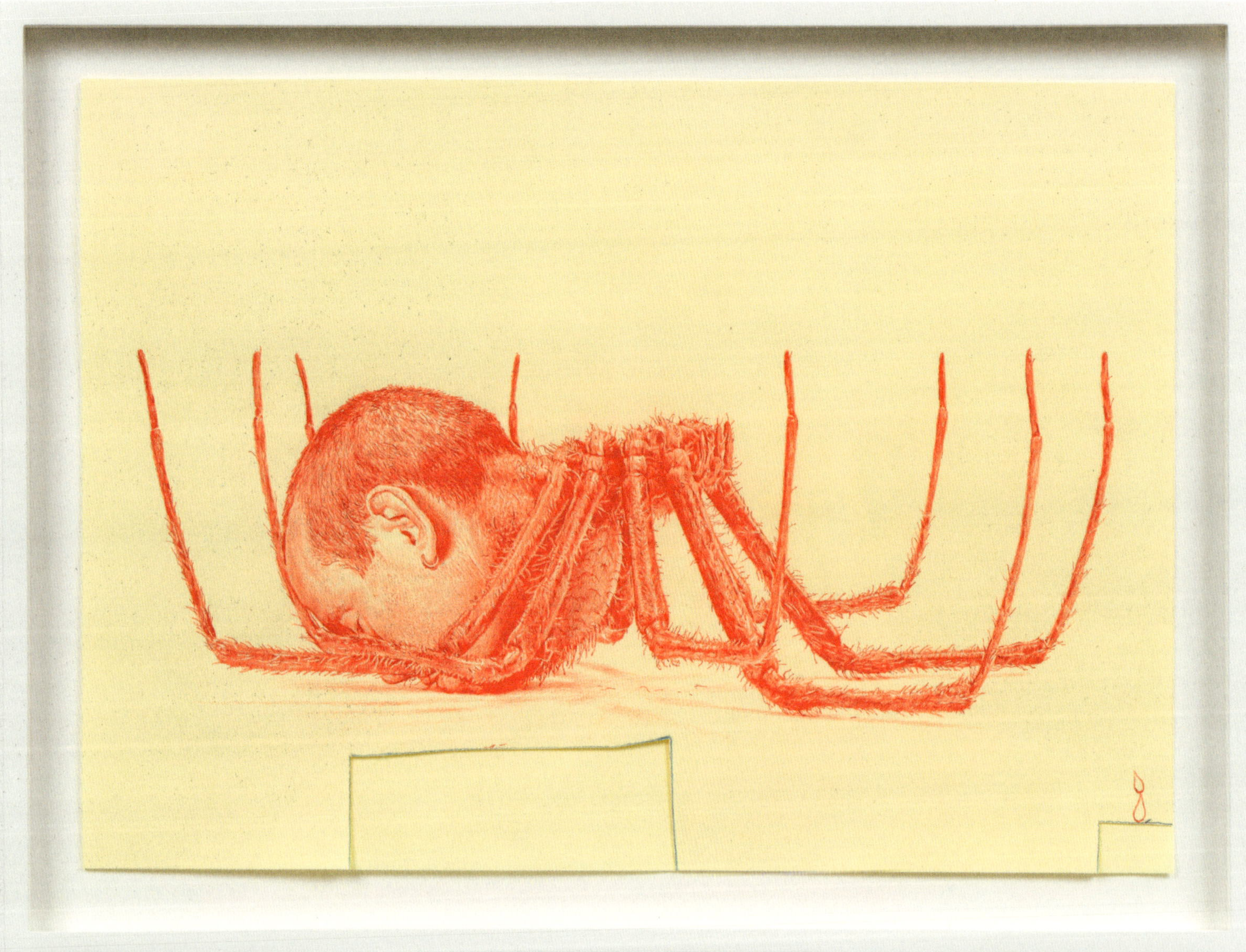

Copenhagen #5 2023, coloured pencil on paper, 35.5 × 48

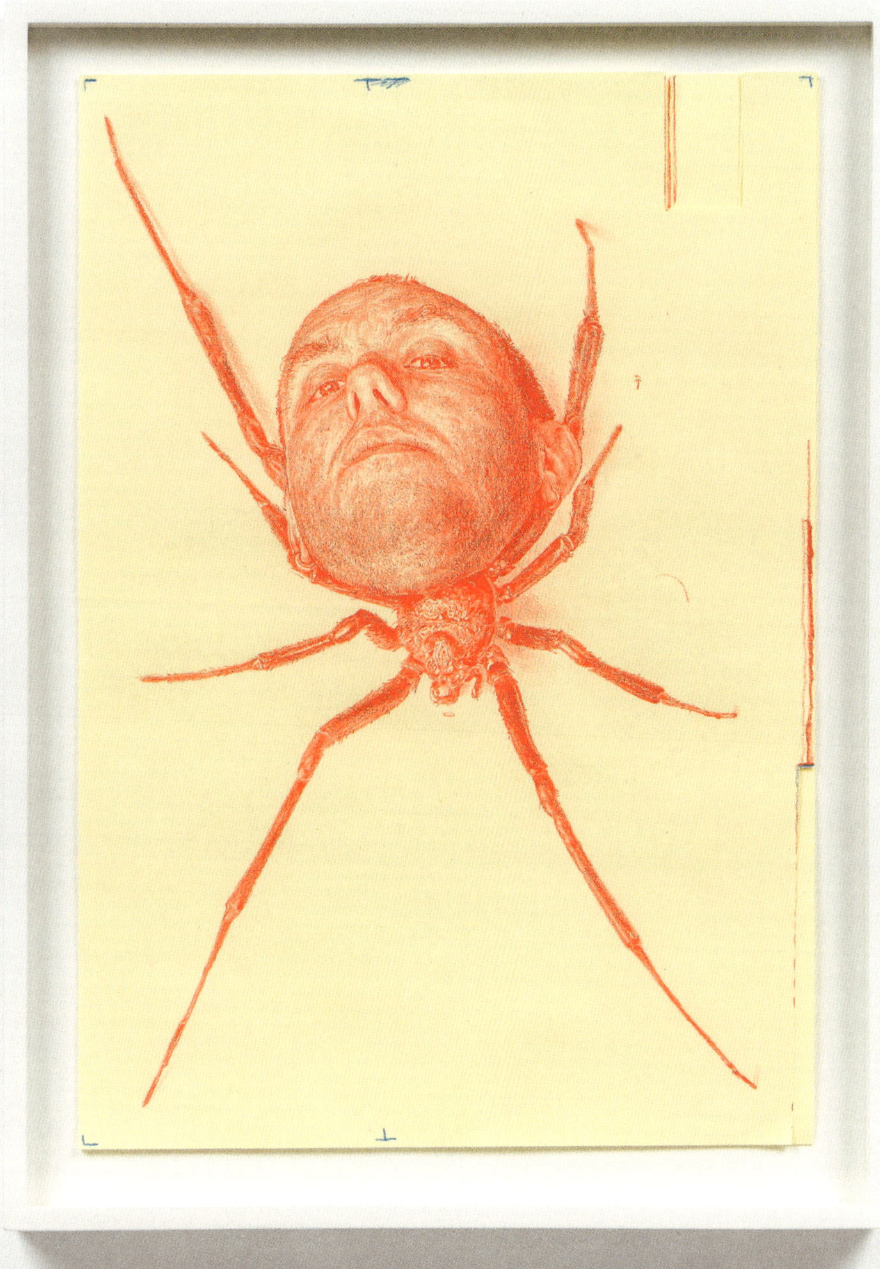

Copenhagen #3 2023, coloured pencil on paper, 48 × 35.5

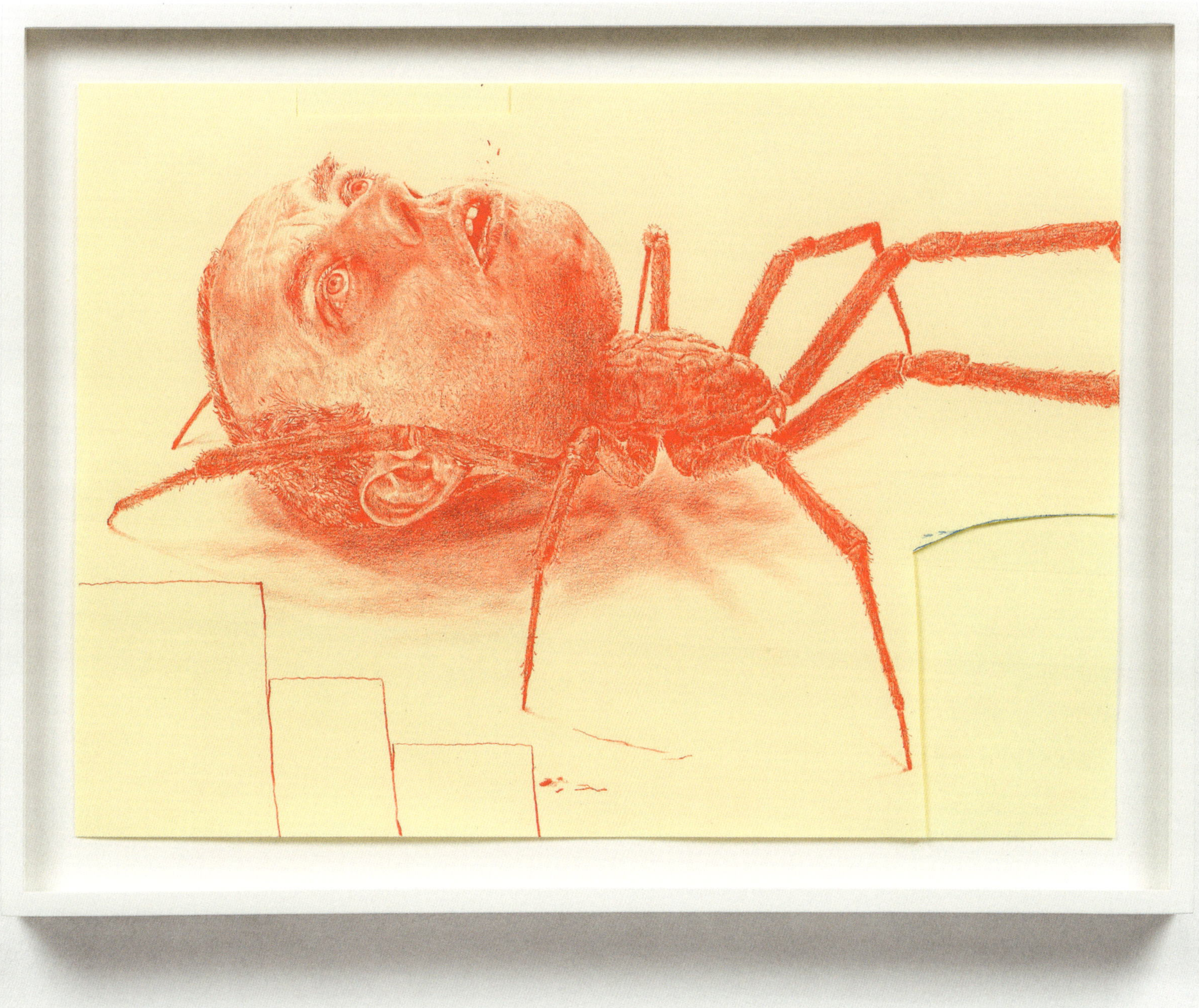

Copenhagen #6 2023, coloured pencil on paper, 48 × 35.5

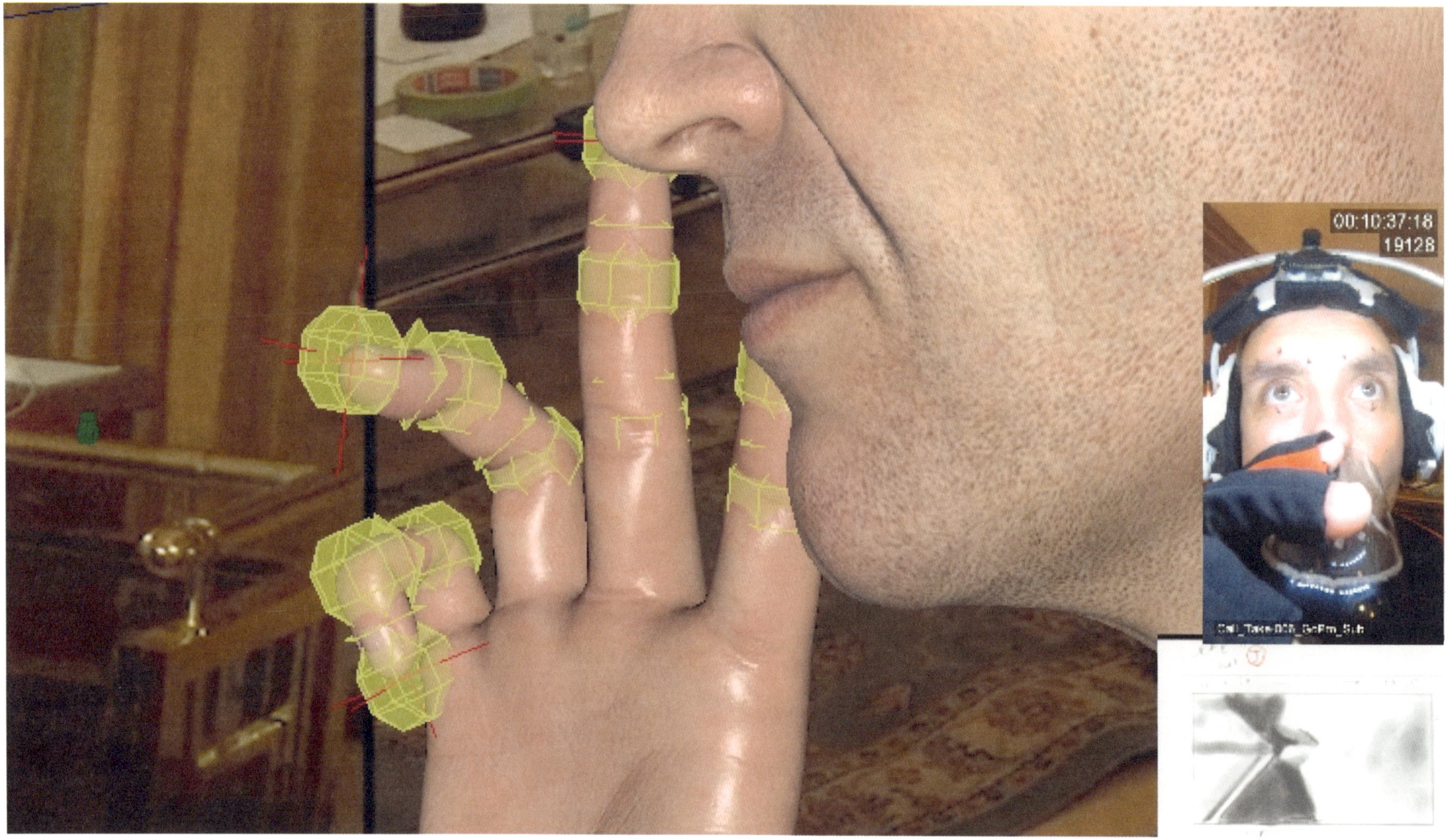

A working image for the production of *The worm* 2021, combining a pre-vis of the animation and, insert, the corresponding face camera footage, and an original frame of the storyboard. In all of the images, the artist is drinking a can of Coca-Cola.

ED ATKINS'S BODY

Nathan Ladd

In 2022 the Revolver Theatre in Copenhagen presented Ed Atkins and Steven Zultanski's play *Sorcerer*. The play opens with three characters discussing how they put on a t-shirt. 'Yeah, I always put my head through first, so the shirt hangs from my neck, kind of like a big floppy necklace and then I find the arms', says Ida. 'I do the opposite. I put my arms through and then my head', replies Lotte who, according to the stage directions, 'makes motion, puts her hands through the air like a long glove or like putting hand in a cow, one after the other'.[1] Via conversations about headaches, ticks, compression fantasies, surgery and the act of getting dressed, a series of everyday, even banal gestures ultimately give way at the end of the second act to the third character, Peter, miming taking his own face apart piece by piece: 'POP EYE OUT; FIND CENTRAL ZIPPER IN HAIRLINE; FISTFUL OF HAIR; PEEL THROAT DOWN FROM JOWLS' read the stage directions.[2] From the prosaic conversational details to the theatrical artifice of a body being deconstructed and magnified, sitting in the audience I recall feeling my own body tighten, remembering and re-embodying actions both familiar and imagined.

Ed Atkins's bodies are conspicuous and copious. Surrogate or avatar, fragmented and self-reflexive, these collective scapegoats for an absent body emerge as protagonists in an artistic output that sits in the slippery space between

1 The script was later published as a book: Ed Atkins and Steven Zultanski, *Sorcerer*, London 2023, p.16.

2 Ibid., pp.98–102.

representation and embodiment. Defying media discretion, much of Atkins's work instrumentalises bodies—to be specific, *his* body.

In 2022 Atkins began a series of self-portrait drawings, a process requiring an intimate, forensic encounter with his own face, the inevitable direct confrontation necessary for self-representation. When we look in a mirror, we are exposed to what is usually not visible to us—our nose, our eyes, the shape of our chin, the curved outline of our ears; the mirror shows us all these things, albeit in reverse of what others see. In two series of self-portraits included in this exhibition, Atkins has made highly detailed monochromatic drawings of his face in red pencil on yellow legal paper, which unreservedly expose every blemish, pore, hair and crease of the skin. In one drawing, we encounter a zoomed-in and cropped profile view of Atkins's face. His head pushes at the limiting scale of the paper's A4 format, as if squeezed into its framed aperture. Following a gaze that stares into an unseen distance, Atkins provokes a palpably anxious curiosity, with a body beyond the facial fragment on the paper. We imagine it, feel it, knowing through our own embodied existence that more lies beyond the cropped visage. These drawings are unflinching accounts of the imperfections of a face, the features we ignore, hide or refuse to confront brought forth in the mirror's surface. As images they perpetuate and replicate the lie of a reflection, the reversed and distorted reality known only to its subject.

Atkins lends his body to his work in a practice that at first appears superficially, though usefully, close to self-portraiture. In this historic tradition, the artist strives for visibility by painting a picture using a mirror. A self is extracted and rendered as a version of itself—one that seeks to show what the artist sees of themself. Closely examining in a mirror and then rendering without correction what they see, the artist is an agent and a patient—they portray and are portrayed.

In his 1961 essay 'Eye and Mind'—a phenomenological investigation of a body at the point of representation—Maurice Merleau-Ponty delves into Paul Cezanne's fascination with self-portraiture. In this great artistic tradition, the philosopher describes what appears and what is made visible in the artist's many self-portraits. He concedes that Cezanne's abundance of paintings are a chronicle of the self that he sees himself, while being an unavoidably impoverished representation of his actual life. Self-portraiture is therefore productively inadequate. It gives us a glimpse into a self as seen by the maker but is ultimately limited in its capacity to represent reality.

The self-exposure of a mirror's reflection is not echoed in the self-revealing nature of a self-portrait. These two forms of visibility are distinct. In the act of making the work, a constant tension exists between the visible and the invisible. The artist doubles the invisibility of both the self and its image, as well as the visibility of the image and the drawing. Despite this, a self-portrait does capture the remnants of the reflected image, and thus remnants of a self. These remnants represent the self as other, as self-portrait. This conspicuous striving towards self-representation can more accurately be read as an absence or a lack, the very attempt itself actively underscoring such an absence by drawing attention to its own inevitable failure. Acknowledging self-portraiture's fidelity to the real, while recognising its ultimate inadequacy in representing it, offers a productive tension for understanding the body in Atkins's work.

Atkins chooses particular and exposing angles to view himself and affords us the dubious privilege of magnified proximity—access usually reserved for those closest to him. We are conditioned to respond to self-portraits such as these as documentation of a material reality. However, as Merleau-Ponty and his subject Cezanne demonstrate, they instead 'other' the self or are—in Atkins's words—a mask.

Repeatedly figuring bodies at the limits of representation, Atkins renders forms that transcend mere symbolism to leave indentations that are actual vestiges or traces of a body. A vestige is not an image of its creator but evidence of the creator's passage; it represents an event of meaning rather than a specific identity. In Atkins's work, the incorporeal, intangible representation of his body—through what he has described as his 'surrogates' or 'scapegoats'—triggers a longing for the corporeal, for a physical material to touch, perhaps even to hold. It is this vestige of Atkins's body and its insistent relationship of 'intercorporeality'—the mutual influence and interconnectedness of bodies—that is present in his work regardless of media.[3]

Take, for instance, his paintings of mattresses and pillows. In these works the vestiges of a body are vividly represented. Seen from above, the larger painting depicts an off-white mattress protector that has been recently slept on, while the smaller one captures a crumpled pillow still bearing the imprint of the sleeper's head. These realistic depictions of everyday domestic objects hold in their materiality a tension between representation and reality. Painting from photographs, Atkins uses ink, form and space to convey the weight of a sleeping body. They also bear witness to the meticulous and labour-intensive process of trying to render reality in paint and ink. The artist's focus on verisimilitude underscores the theoretical doubling and ambiguity of reality present across his work. Here he achieves this by using distinctly analogue, handmade materials and processes. In the corporeal impressions left on both mattress and pillow, crumpled fabric gives way to wrinkled flesh in the slippery unreality of representation, as the traces of a once-present body weigh heavily on the painted surface. Pillows and mattresses, as indices of the body, extend this quality to their pictorial representations. The lack of a body in these paintings is palpable: you feel its uncanny absence, unfixed and in the process of becoming.

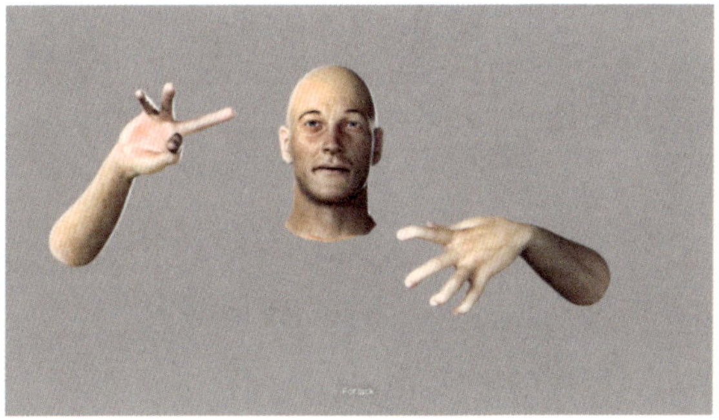

Performance Capture 2015, video and sound

3 Merleau-Ponty first proposed the notion of 'intercorporeality' in his late essay 'The Philosopher and his Shadow' (1960), in Maurice Merleau-Ponty, *Signs*, trans. Richard C. McCleary, Evanston, IL 1964, pp.159–81.

Atkins's work is full of such bodies in an active process of becoming. The vestiges of his body we observe in ink, paint and digital image are not just relics of past creativity but an ongoing event that continues to resonate and provoke thought and affect in our moment of relation with it. Unlike a mere footprint that indicates a past presence, the trace of Atkins's body is an active remnant that continues to influence and shape the present. Jean-Luc Nancy's particular ontological conception feels close to this thinking about vestiges of the body in Atkins's work.[4] For Nancy, what we encounter in the work of art is the vestige of an expressive gesture, the remains of the body that touched it, absent now save for its traces. Art is neither representation nor inscription, but rather what Nancy called *exscription*. What remains represents neither a separate idea nor the one who traced it, but rather *exscribes* their presence and their world in the event of the body's expression.

Nancy asks: 'How are we to touch upon the body? … We have to begin by getting through, and by means of, the exscription of the body: its being inscribed-outside, its being placed outside the text.'[5] Nancy leads us to understand a body that is defined by its contact with other bodies, places and things. Meaning is created, therefore, not just by what is present but by what is absent. It emerges through exclusion and excess, by what lies beyond that which can be captured and contained within systems of representation. While the body can be inscribed with meaning, there is always something about it that remains unrepresentable and irreducible to these inscriptions. Art reveals the limitations of representation, hinting at an excess or otherness that cannot be fully captured.

In Atkins's 2015 video *Hisser* we encounter a solitary white male figure, either confined in the interior space of a bedroom or wandering aimlessly in a blank abyss. We feel the anxiety and vulnerability, the fragility of his existence, and witness his retreat into the most basic of bodily functions and gestures. Alongside its predecessor, *Ribbons* 2014, and successor, *Safe Conduct* 2016, *Hisser* deploys Atkins's realistic yet entirely fabricated computer-generated figure, which blurs the line between reality and simulation. A generic stock model selected and bought 'off the shelf' from the online 3D store TurboSquid.com, *Hisser*'s figure is the surrogate for Atkins's body, with its gestures and expressions animated by Atkins using motion capture technology. Of these 'men', Atkins has said: 'I found a vessel for my voice; I could possess these figures. Though they were never characters, per se … Rather, I think the tone that emerged—misanthropic, needy, pathetic, garbled—was unplanned, a symptom of the process of performing for the performance-capturing tech.'[6] These figures are defined solely in relation to the limits and potential of Atkins's own body, defined by his experiences, gender and physical capacities. Grimacing, gurning, wincing, moaning and humming to himself, *Hisser*'s computer-generated man becomes an adept vessel for Atkins's body.

Despite their conspicuous digitality, Atkins's close-up videos, like his detailed pencil drawings, reveal every texture and expression, making the artificial figure appear vulnerably human—if always obviously fake. The visual fidelity of the avatar's skin, hair and movements contrasts with the somewhat surreal backdrops, which further accentuate the

4 Jean-Luc Nancy, *The Muses*, trans. Peggy Kamuf, Stanford, CA 1996, pp.93, 96.

5 Jean-Luc Nancy, *Corpus*, trans. Richard Rand, New York 2008, p.11.

6 *Ed Atkins: Get Life/Love's Work*, New Museum, New York, 2021 p.56.

sense of dislocation and existential angst. As technology has advanced relentlessly, Atkins continues to evolve his surrogates to match CGI's capacity for human replication, ultimately doubling himself in his most recent video *Pianowork 2* 2023. Regardless of the era of technology, Atkins's meticulous attention to detail situates his bodies in an uncanny space where the vestiges of his body mar the computer-generated form in ways that—like the self-portraits—strive for but fail to achieve the ultra-lifelike, eliciting discomfort. Misusing the potential of new technology, the idea of a real body is surpassed, overwhelmed, becoming so self-exposing in its conspicuous artifice that we crave the embodiment that lies beneath the surface. Like a face pressed up against the inside of a mask, hidden yet palpably close, Atkins's digital masks vibrate with the proximity of the body beneath and our embodied potential that exists in relation to them.

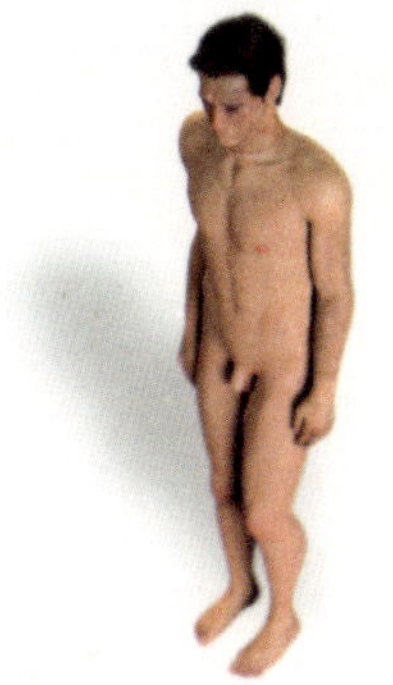

Hisser 2015, video and sound

It is in the uncomfortable relational space that the implications of re-embodiment emerge. Central to Nancy's philosophy is the concept of 'being-with' and the idea of the body as a site of shared existence.[7] He emphasises the body's inherent openness, its perpetual relation to others and its exposure to the world. The bodies—digital, drawn and absent—utilise a body's ability to move from the individual to a site of common or shared experience.

In *Hisser* and in Atkins's self-portraits, the expressive gesture brings forth a self that does not predate its expression and that is paradoxically always already past, always already fallen into material vestige. The detailed rendering of the digital or drawn surrogates underscores the impossibility of capturing the essence of life through pixels or pencil. This tension held in the bodies that are so materially central to Atkins's oeuvre probe the uneasy co-existence of the animate and the inanimate, the organic and the artificial. We are led to an ontology of art-making that is one of *intercorporeality*, and consequent *interaffectivity*—two experiences that arise in our encounter with Atkins's work. The idea of intercorporeality was first proposed as a means to explain the mutual influence and interconnectedness of bodies. It emphasises how our bodily experiences and interactions are shaped by, and shape the presence of, other bodies in common. Here, in the entangled site of the materially or digitally rendered body, a self perceives the other not just as an object but as a living body in action. This is where the perception–action loop between self and other occurs: as we observe the other's actions it triggers similar actions within ourselves. Like the responsive re-embodiment I experienced

7 This is the fundamental argument of Nancy's *Being Singular Plural*, trans. Robert D. Richardson and Anne E. O'Byrne, Stanford, CA 2000, pp.28–32.

8 Phenomenology is the philosophical study of experience. It focuses on the structures of consciousness and the ways in which experiences are perceived and understood

as an audience member in *Sorcerer*, we encounter a live embodied relation in our perception of the digital body in Atkins's videos.

Performance Capture 2015, a work made at the Manchester International Festival in 2015, continues and complicates Atkins's intercorporeality and the interconnectedness of bodies. Over the two weeks of the festival, Atkins hosted a performance capture studio, where over one hundred participants put on motion capture suits, as Atkins himself had previously, and recited an extract of a soliloquy entitled *Performance Capture*. Each participant's performance animated the same figure, procured from TurboSquid.com, reduced to just a floating head, arms and hands. These performances were then stitched together in an accumulated video monologue. It became an ever-growing record of both a production and the many vestiges of passing bodies that became entangled and overlapped in the fragmented body of the digital vessel. One hundred multiple lives, each with personal embodied experience, are amalgamated into one avatar, a collective mask where anyone could adorn the suit of Atkins's self-portrait. While in other videos Atkins's corporeal vestige is the sole inhabitant of the digital figure, here the many moments and interrelated bodies become a refutation of digital technology's seeming capacity to replace corporeal life.

A performed fidelity to the embodied human's imperfect form and behaviour—through media that can only fail in its attempt at reality—frees Atkins and his surrogates from policing or defining meaning. Instead, the medium allows meaning to expand and temporarily solidify in the

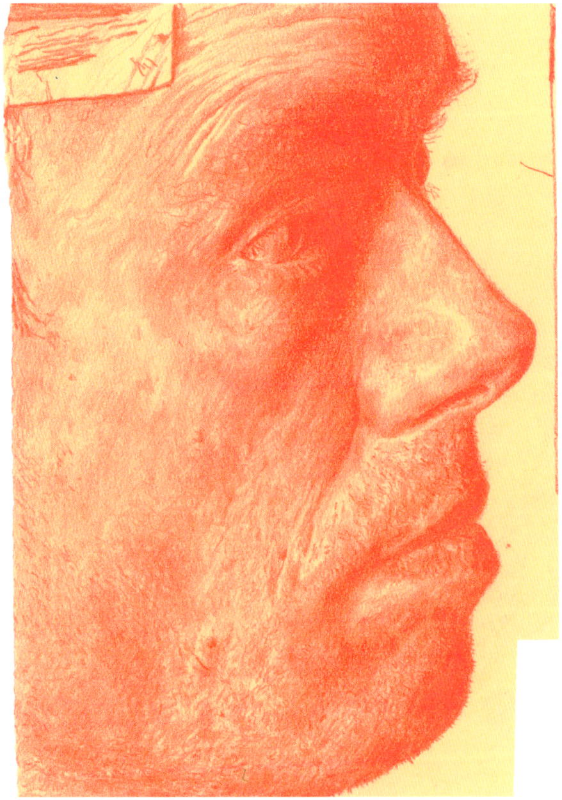

relation of intercorporeality. Like a reflection in a mirror with a barely noticeable flaw, what looks back at us across Atkins's digital chasm is both strikingly familiar and disconcertingly alien. For many in the realm of phenomenology, visibility arises out of the *seeing* seen—the idea that

Untitled 2023, coloured pencil on paper, 34.6 × 26 × 2.5

perception is reciprocal and that it is a two-way, embodied and dynamic interaction that implicates us in the world we perceive.[8] In everyday experience, the site of visibility is the body. The crossing-over of touch and sight, one eye and the other, one hand and the other, establishes an intertwining bodily space.

Conflating Atkins's various bodies—surrogate, avatar, fragmented and self-reflexive—reveals vestiges of a body that is constantly striving towards an ultimately impossible representation of the real self. His digital and drawn surrogates collectively belie an expressive, exscriptive body that hums below the surface of the screen or paper. The material and digital surfaces bear the traces of a past body, but also one in a constant act of becoming. We call into question self-portraiture's supposed historical efficacy, regardless of media, and instead uncomfortably (or joyfully) accept the impossibility of representing a totality of self. Atkins's work draws attention to this impossibility and the ultimate poverty of the media he employs repeatedly figuring the body at representation's limits. This impossibility is profoundly productive. Through our encounter with the othered traces of a body that both was and is, we are triggered by a corporeal longing that we find relief for in our own bodies.

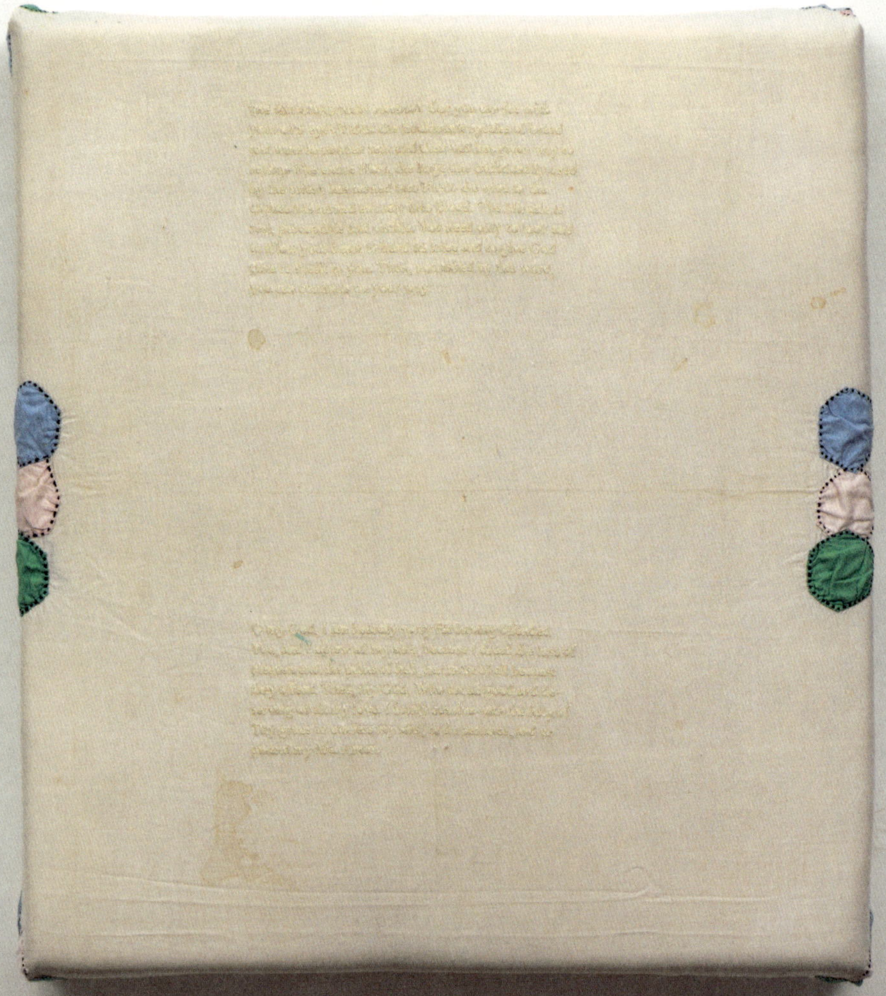

Untitled embroidered acoustic panel #18 2019, all embroidered linen on acoustic foam and wooden frame, dimensions vary (pp.188–91)

Untitled embroidered acoustic panel #13 2019

Untitled embroidered acoustic panel #22 2019

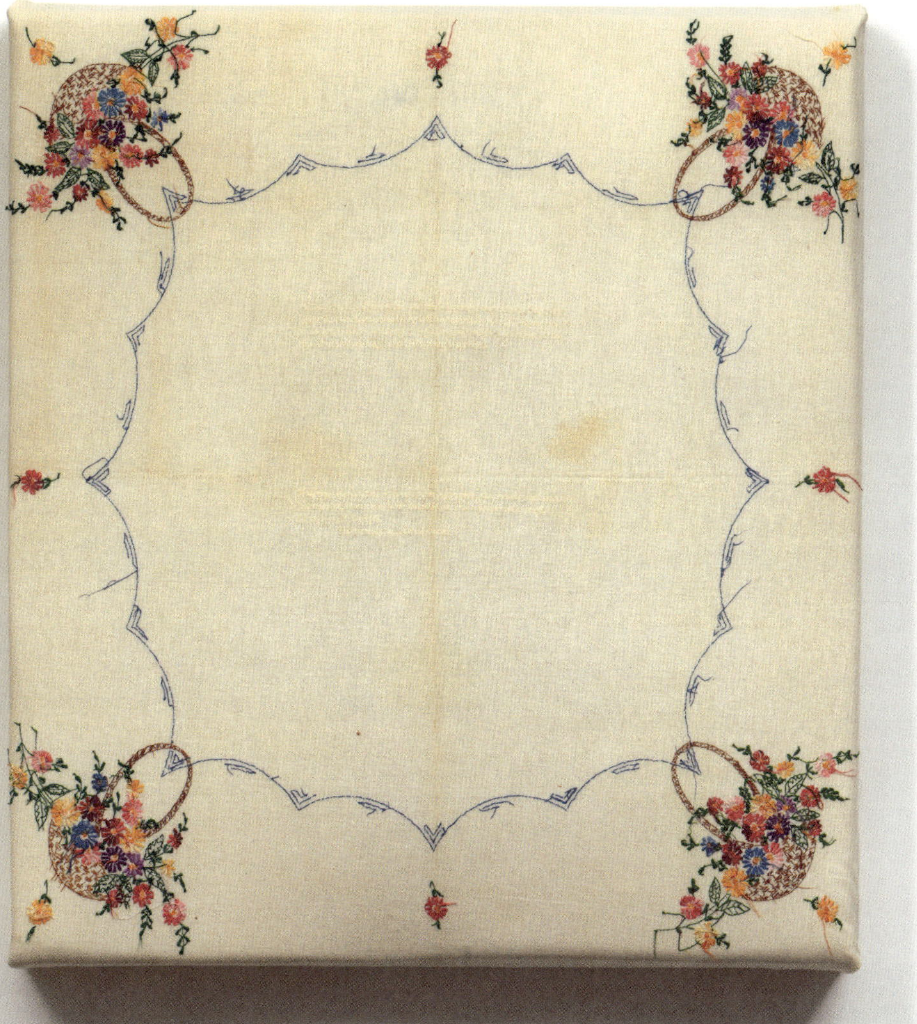

Untitled embroidered acoustic panel #21 2019

Production stills from *Nurses Come and Go, But None for Me* 2024, with Steven Zultanski, video and sound, pp.193–201

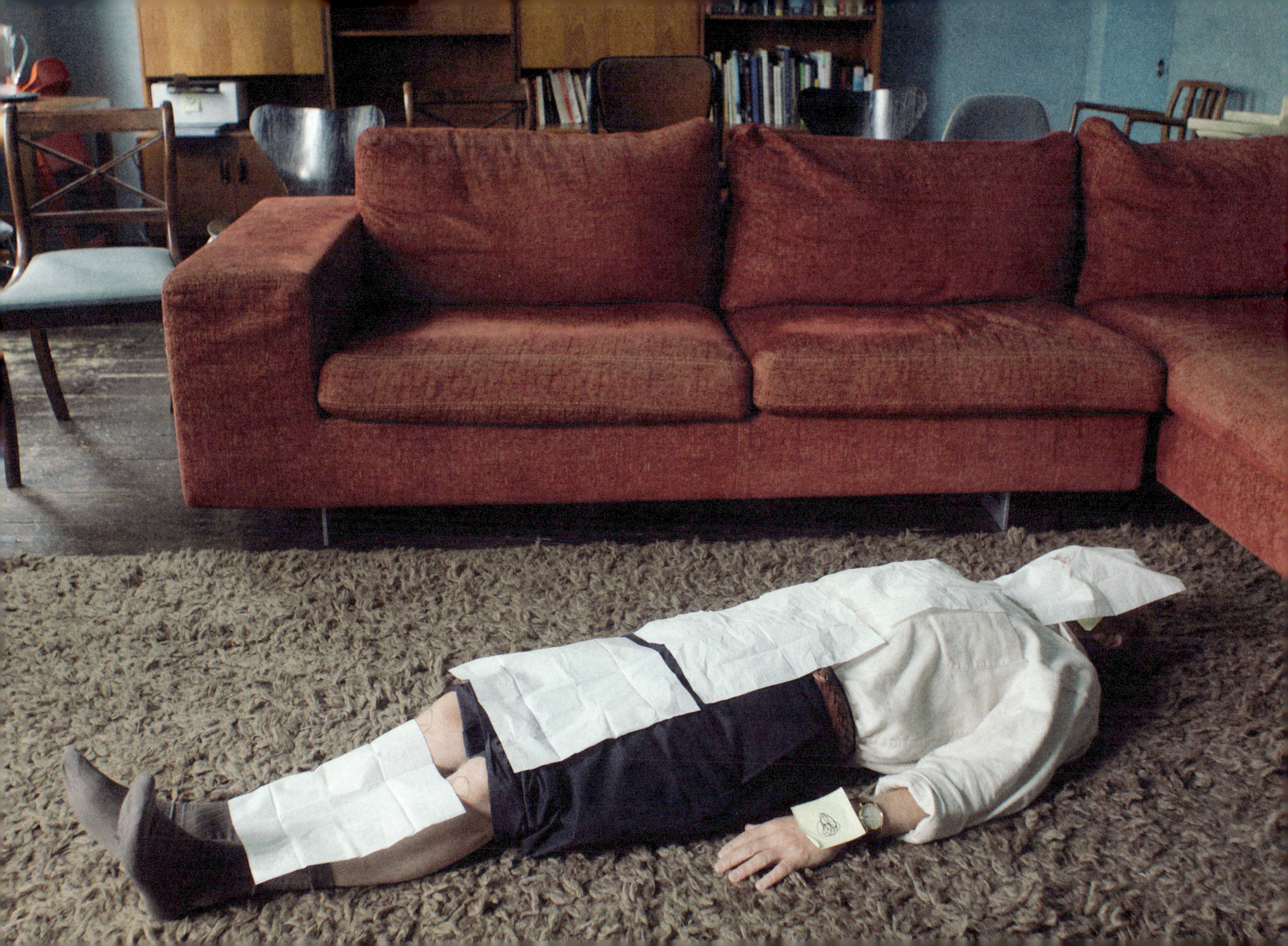

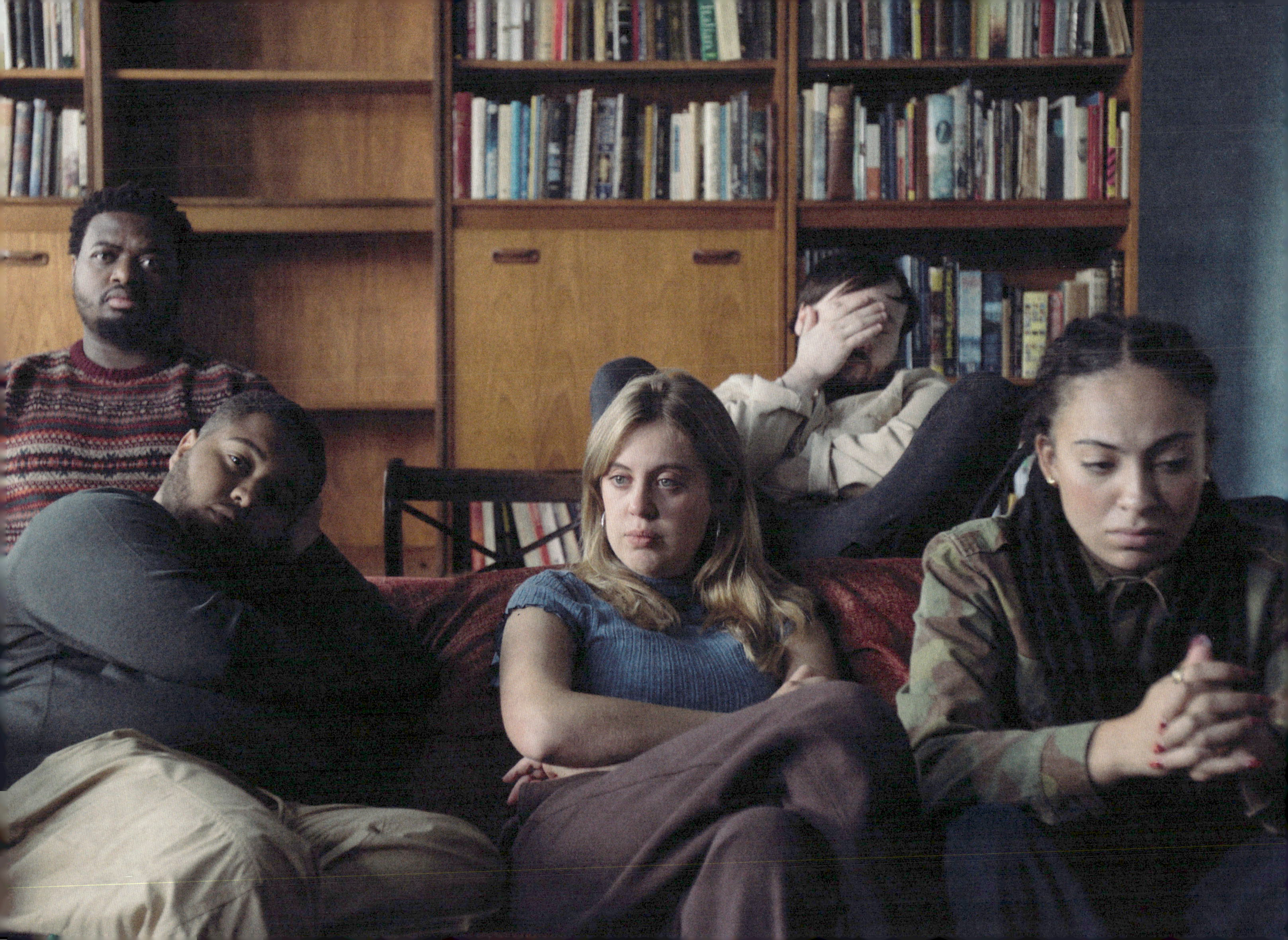

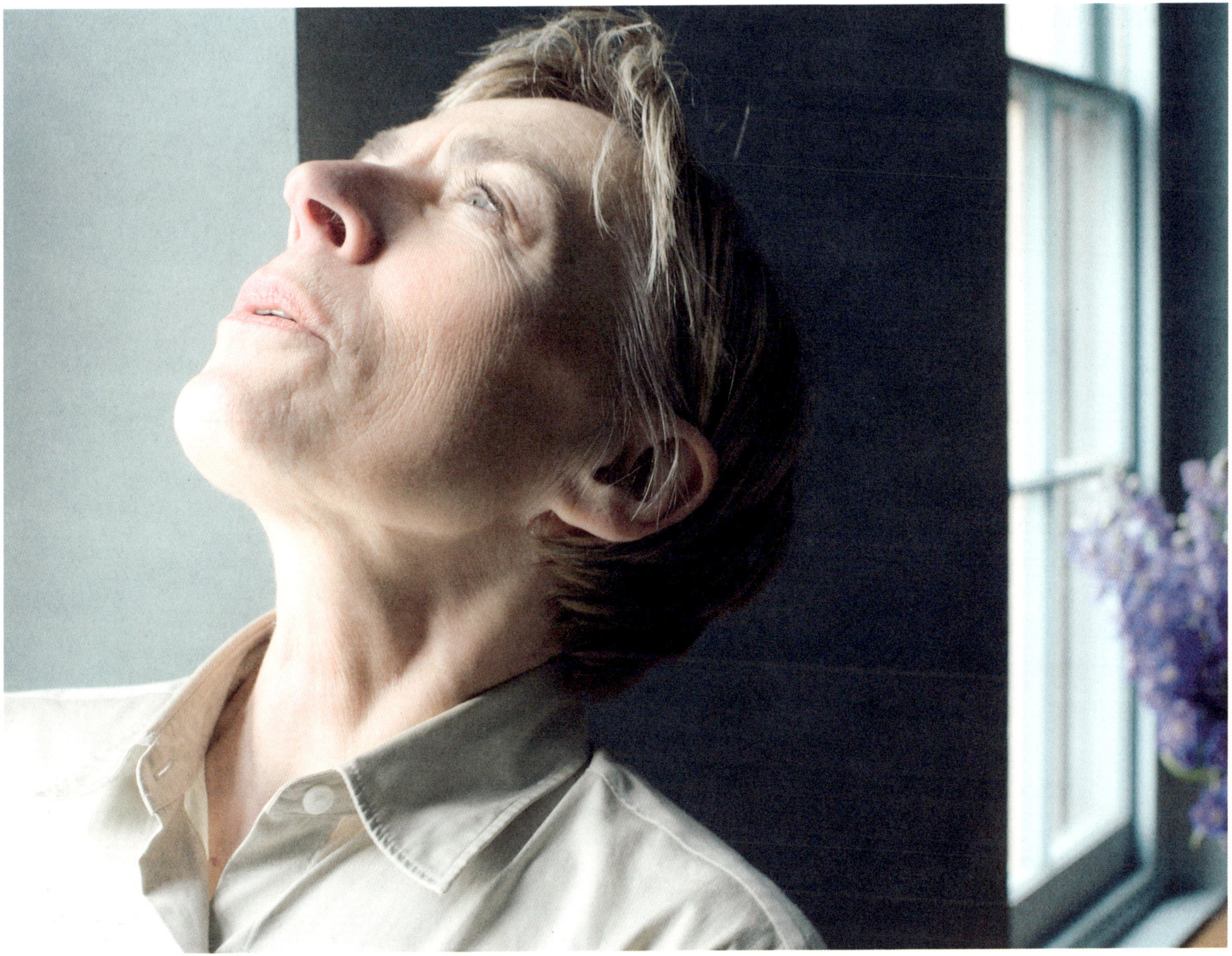

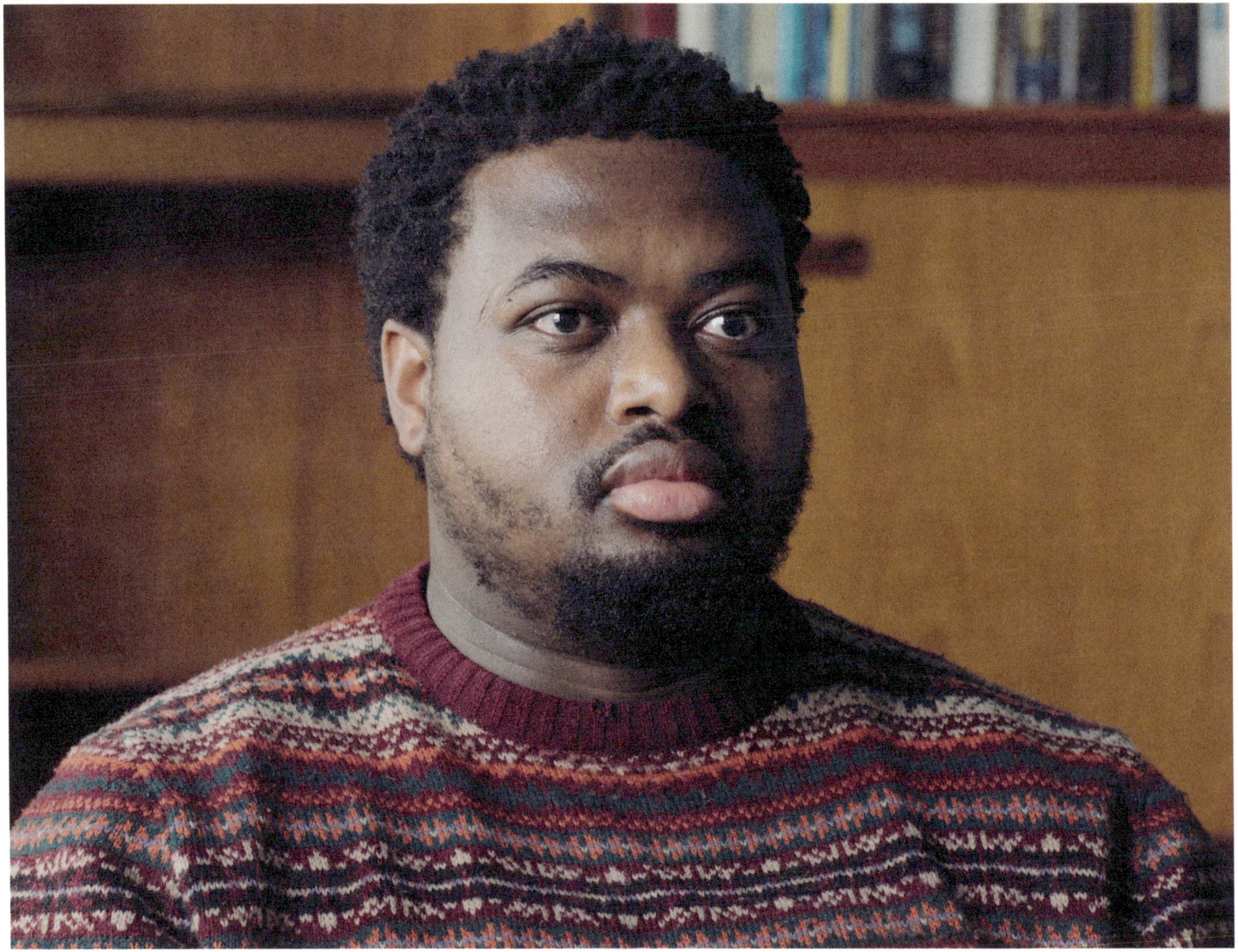

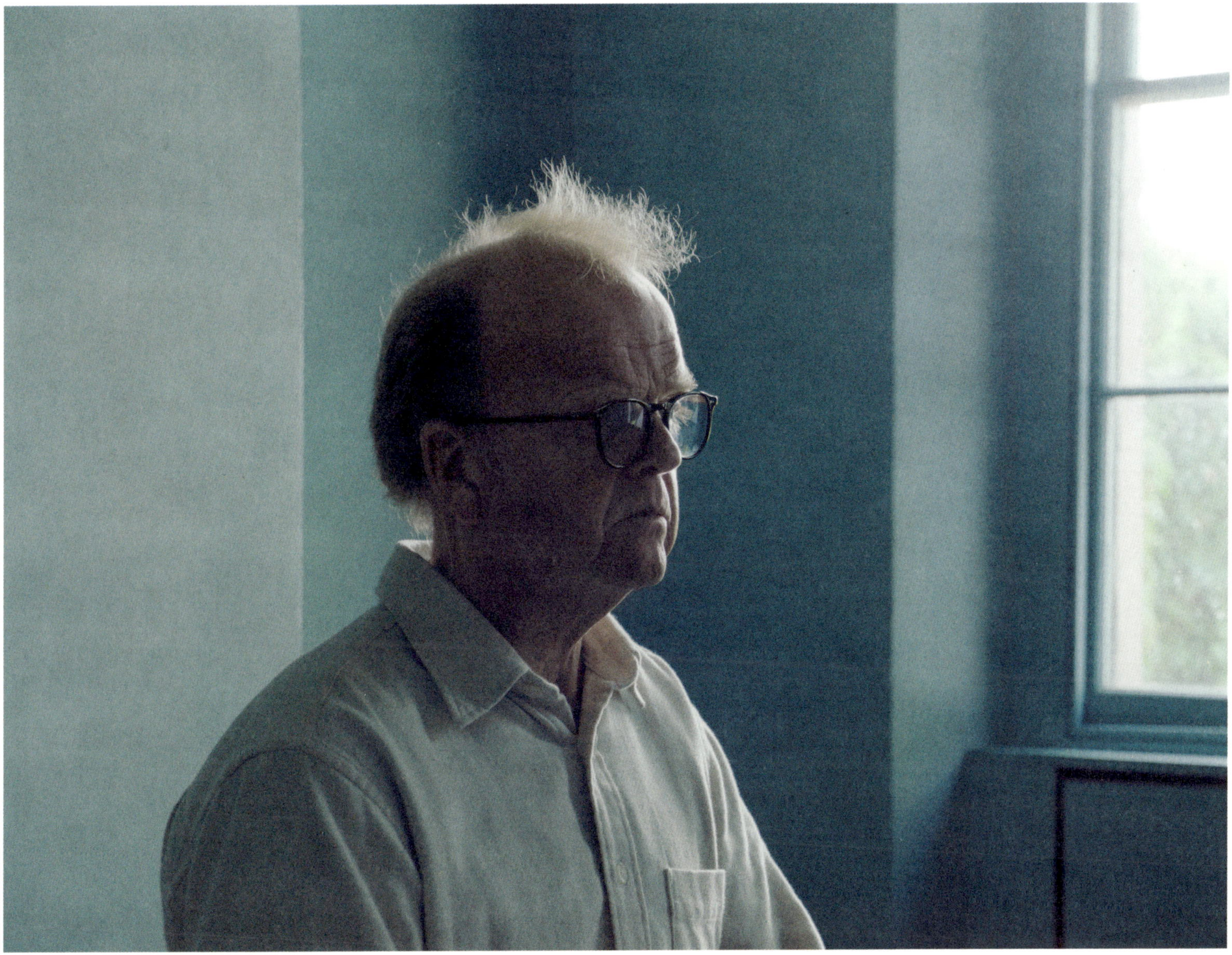

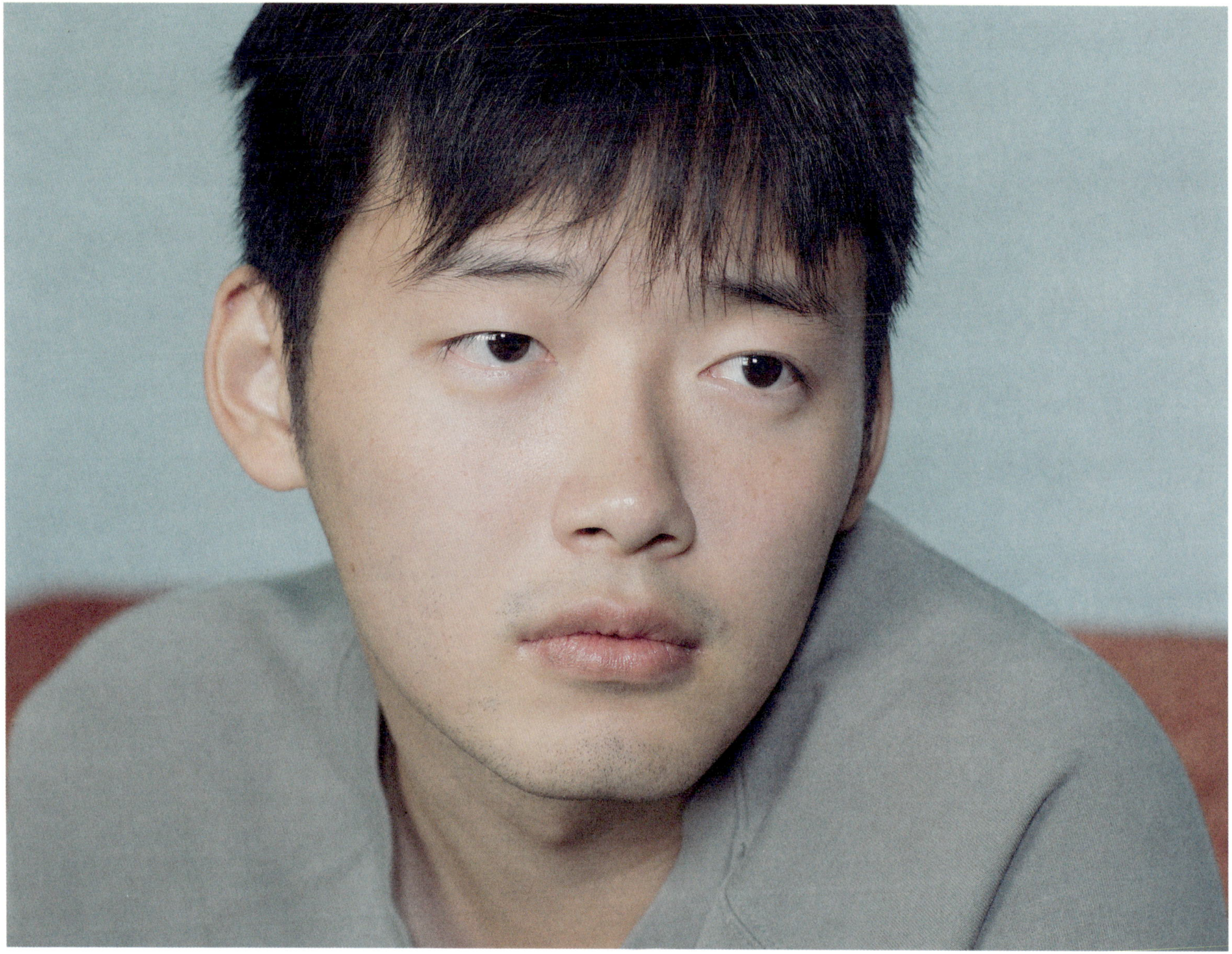

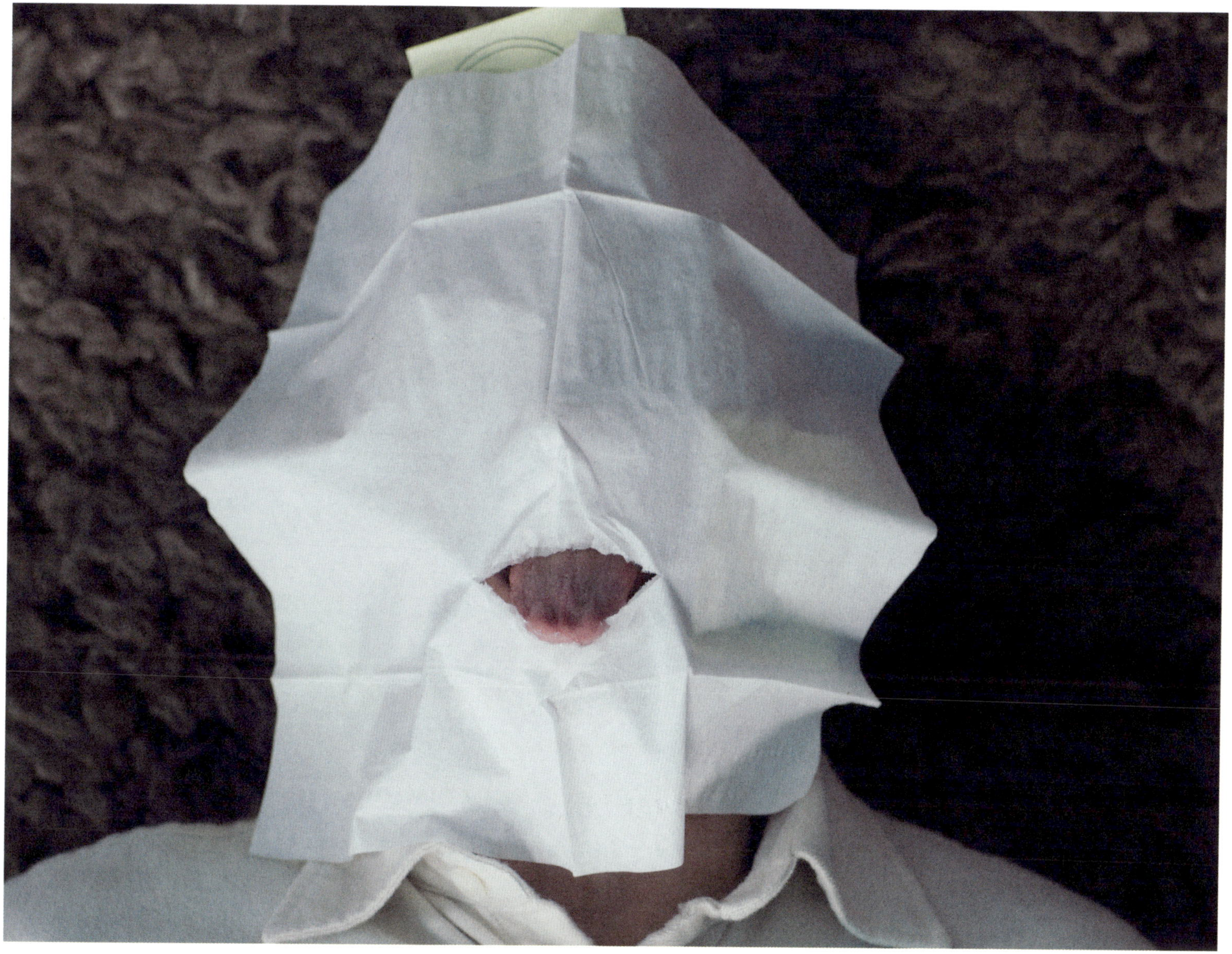

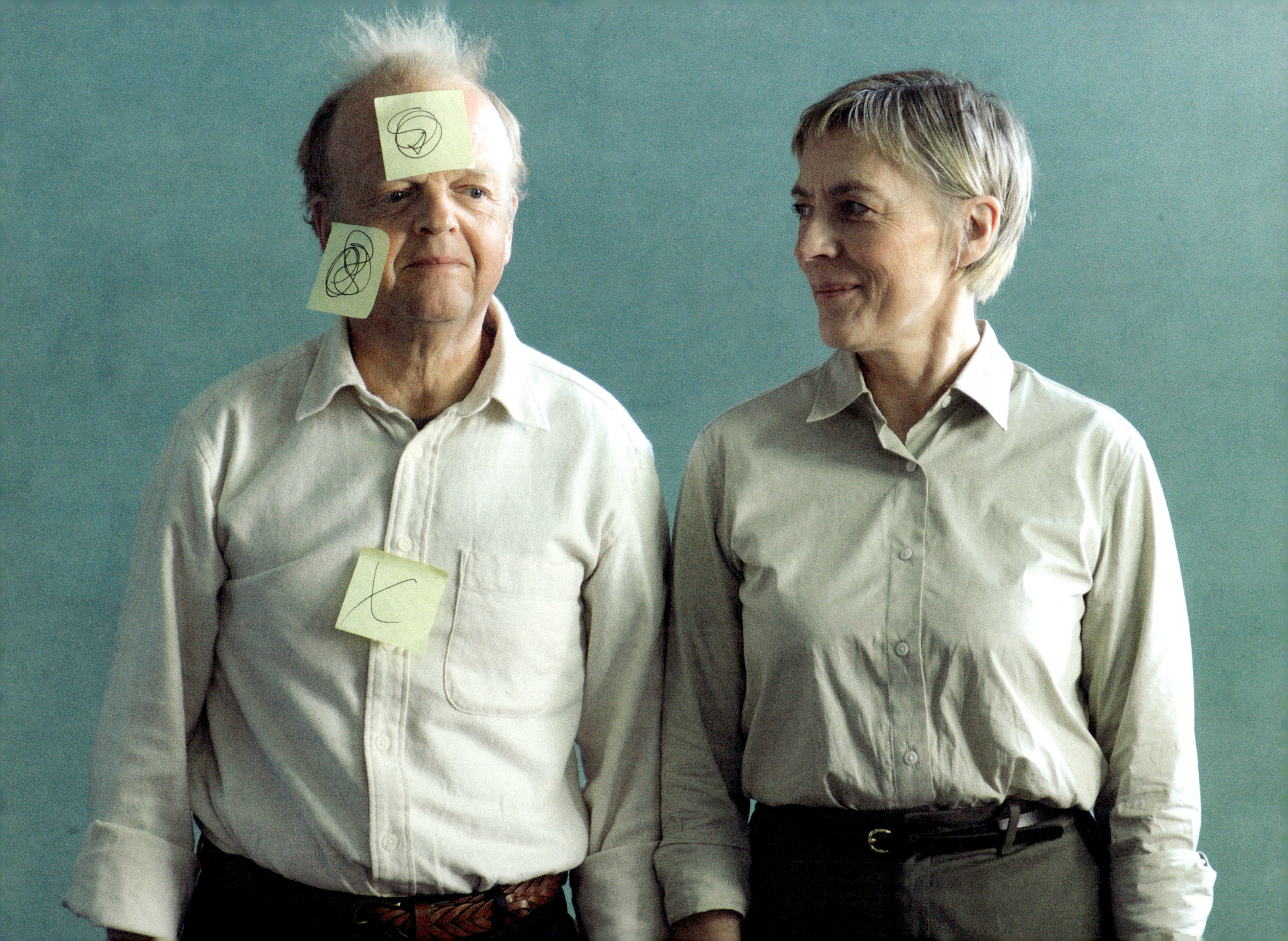

This list includes the works exhibited at Tate Britain. Works are grouped by category, listed alphabetically and then chronologically. Dimensions are given in cm. All works courtesy of Ed Atkins, Galerie Isabella Bortolozzi, Berlin, Cabinet Gallery, London, dépendance, Brussels and Gladstone Gallery, New York unless otherwise stated.

VIDEOS

Cur 2010
Video and sound
5min
p.24

Death Mask II: The Scent 2010
Video and sound
8min, 19sec
Tate. Purchased with funds provided by the Brian and Nancy Pattenden Bequest, 2012
pp.18–9

How It's Made 2015
with Simon Thompson
Video and sound
19hr, 44min
(not illustrated)

Hisser 2015
Three-channel video and sound
21min, 51sec
Tate. Purchased 2016
pp.63–7, 185

Masses 2018
Costumes from the Deutsche Oper Berlin
Courtesy the artist and Cabinet Gallery, London
p.53

Nurses Come and Go, But None for Me 2024
with Steven Zultanski
Video and sound
Commissioned and produced by Hartwig Art Foundation
pp.13, 22, 23, 44, 45, 46, 193–201, 223

Old Food 2017–18

Good Boy 2017
Video and sound
16min
p.48, centre

Good Baby 2017
Video and sound
16min
p.48, left

Good Man 2017
Video and sound
16min
p.48, right

Good Bread 2017
Video and sound
16min
p.51

Good Smoke 2017
Video and sound
16min
p.30

Good Wine 2017
Video and sound
16min (loop)
p.50

Neoteny in Humans 2017
Video and sound
16min
(not illustrated)

up/down, in/out 2017
Video and sound
16min
p.28

Untitled 2018
Video and sound
16min
pp.35, 54

Pianowork 2 2023
Video and sound
15min, 40sec
pp.97, 98, 103–11, 115

Refuse.exe 2019
Two-channel video,
custom software and sound
15min (loop)
Tate. Purchased with funds
provided by the European
Collection Circle 2021
pp.36–7, 140–3

Sky News 2016
with Simon Thompson
Video, silent
(not illustrated)

The worm 2021
Video, sound, plywood
and metal
12min, 39sec
pp.38, 72, 74, 77–87

Voilà la verité 2022
Video and sound
3min, 50sec
pp.56, 57

DRAWINGS, EMBROIDERIES, PAINTINGS AND PHOTOGRAPHY

Beds 2025
Motor, battery, wooden
bed frame, cotton sheets
Dimensions variable
(not illustrated)

Children 2020–ongoing
Crayon, pencil and ink
on paper
Each: 925 × 673
Cabinet Gallery, London
pp.123–38

Hang In There 2017–25
Inkjet print on paper
(not illustrated)

No Fear 2017–25
Inkjet print on paper
p.62

Untitled 2020
Ink, gouache and graphite
on board
54.3 × 76.3
Tate. Purchased with funds
provided by the European
Collection Circle 2021
p.170

Untitled 2020
Ink, gouache and graphite
on board
105.9 × 149.9
Tate. Purchased with funds
provided by the European
Collection Circle 2021
p.171

Untitled 2020
Acoustic foam, moulton and
embroidery on found cotton
302 × 93
Courtesy the artist and
Cabinet Gallery, London
(not illustrated)

Untitled 2022
Digital print on aluminium
156.5 × 131.5
Private Collection
p.61

Untitled 2022
Ink, bleach and coloured pencil on paper
113 × 168.5
Private Collection
(not illustrated)

Untitled 2022
Ink, bleach and coloured pencil on paper
67 × 95.7
Private Collection
p.59

Untitled 2022
Ink and pen on board
55 × 78
Private Collection
p.60

Untitled 2022
Ink and pen on board
55.1 × 78 (framed)
Private Collection, Vienna
p.58

Untitled 2023
Coloured pencil on paper
34.6 × 26 × 2.5
Collection Hartwig Art Foundation. Promised gift to the Rijksdienst voor het Cultureel Erfgoed / Rijkscollectie
p.186

Untitled 2023
Coloured pencil on paper
26 × 34.6 × 2.5
Collection Hartwig Art Foundation. Promised gift to the Rijksdienst voor het Cultureel Erfgoed / Rijkscollectie
(not illustrated)

Untitled 2023
Coloured pencil on paper
34.6 × 26 × 2.5
Collection Hartwig Art Foundation. Promised gift to the Rijksdienst voor het Cultureel Erfgoed / Rijkscollectie
(not illustrated)

Copenhagen #5 2023
Coloured pencil on paper
35.5 × 48
Courtesy the artist and Cabinet Gallery, London
p.176

Copenhagen #6 2023
Coloured pencil on paper
35.5 × 48
Courtesy the artist and Cabinet Gallery, London
p.179

Copenhagen #4 2023
Coloured pencil on paper
35.5 × 48
Courtesy the artist and Cabinet Gallery, London
(not illustrated)

Untitled 2023
Coloured pencil on paper
52.1 × 41.3
Private Collection
p.10

Untitled 2023
Coloured pencil on paper
52.1 × 41.3
Courtesy of the artist and Gladstone Gallery
p.68

Untitled 2023
Coloured pencil on paper
52.1 × 41.3
Private Collection, NY
p.69, left

Untitled 2023
Coloured pencil on paper
52.1 × 41.3
Courtesy the artist and Gladstone Gallery
p.69, right

Untitled Samplers 2021
Embroidered linen on acoustic foam and wooden frame
304.8 × 406.4 × 10.2
Courtesy the artist and Gladstone Gallery
p.20

Untitled samplers 2021
Embroidered linen
on acoustic foam and
wooden frame
304.8 × 406.4 × 10.2
Courtesy the artist and
Gladstone Gallery
(not illustrated)

Untitled samplers 2021
Embroidered linen
on acoustic foam and
wooden frame
304.8 × 406.4 × 10.2
Courtesy the artist
and Gladstone Gallery
(not illustrated)

CONTEMPORARY ART
WRITING DAILY

Information panels 2021
11 laser engraved Perspex
41.9 × 29.5
Courtesy of the artist
and Gladstone Gallery
(p.167)

Untitled 2017
Laser engraved wood
Two parts
78.5 × 63.5 × 4.1;
90.2 × 75.1 × 4
Courtesy the artist and
Cabinet Gallery, London
(not illustrated)

Untitled 2017
Laser engraved wood
101 × 64 × 2
Courtesy the artist and
Cabinet Gallery, London
(not illustrated)

Untitled 2017
Laser engraved wood
64 × 55 × 2
Courtesy the artist and
Cabinet Gallery, London
(not illustrated)

Untitled 2017
Laser engraved wood
142 × 64 × 4
Courtesy the artist and
Cabinet Gallery, London
(not illustrated)

Untitled 2017
Laser engraved wood
122 × 186
Courtesy the artist and
Cabinet Gallery, London
(not illustrated)

Untitled (wall text) 2017
Laser engraved wood
51.2 × 48.6 × 1.7
Courtesy the artist and
Cabinet Gallery, London
p.49

ED ATKINS
Born 1982, Oxford.
Lives and works
in Copenhagen

EDUCATION

2007–9
Slade School of Fine Art,
London, MA Fine Art

2002–5
Central St. Martins
College of Art and Design,
London, BA Fine Art

2001–2
Oxford Brooks University,
Oxford, Foundation
Studies in Art and Design

SOLO EXHIBITIONS

2024
Masses
Deutsche Oper, Berlin

2023
Ed Atkins (with Steven
Zultanski)
Gladstone Gallery,
New York

Copenhagen
Cabinet Gallery, London

Ed Atkins
dépendance, Brussels

The worm
Holland Festival, presented
by Hartwig Art Foundation,
Amsterdam

2022
Refuse
Tank Qiao Space, Shanghai

Two Burlesques
Espace Louis Vuitton
München, Munich

Ed Atkins
Galerie Isabella Bortolozzi,
Berlin

Ed Atkins
(with Steven Zultanski)
Galerie Isabella Bortolozzi/
Eden Eden, Berlin

2021
The worm
Sant'Andrea de Scaphis,
Rome

Get Life/Love's Work
New Museum, New York

2020
Live White Slime
Museum of Contemporary
Art Kiasma, Helsinki

Entropy of a biased coin
Cabinet Gallery, London

2019
I like spit now
Gavin Brown's Enterprise,
New York

Ye Olde Food
K21, Kunstsammlung
Nordrhein-Westfalen,
Düsseldorf

Ed Atkins
Kunsthaus Bregenz

2018
Bloom
Galerie Isabella Bortolozzi,
Berlin

MEMBERS
dépendance, Brussels

Olde Food
Cabinet Gallery, London

2017
Old Food
Martin-Gropius-Bau, Berlin

Modern Piano Music
PHI Foundation
for Contemporary Art,
Montreal

Corpsing
Museum für Moderne
Kunst, Frankfurt

2016
Ed Atkins
Castello di Rivoli Museo d'Arte Contemporanea, Turin

Ed Atkins
Gavin Brown's Enterprise, New York

Performance Capture
The Kitchen, New York

SAFE CONDUCT
Statens Museum for Kunst, Copenhagen

Ed Atkins
Fondazione Sandretto Re Rebaudengo, Turin

2015
Hisser
dépendance, Brussels

Performance Capture
Manchester International Festival, Manchester

Recent Ouija
Stedelijk Museum, Amsterdam

Concentrations 59: Mirror Stage – Visualizing the Self After the Internet
Dallas Museum of Art, Texas

2014
RIBBONS
Galerie Isabella Bortolozzi, Berlin

Ed Atkins / Bruce Nauman
Kunsthalle Mainz, Mainz

Ed Atkins
Serpentine Galleries, London

Bastards
Palais de Tokyo, Paris

Ed Atkins
Kunsthalle Zürich, Zurich

2013
Number Seven: Ed Atkins / Frances Stark
Julia Stoschek Collection, Düsseldorf

Warm, Warm, Warm Spring Mouths
Galerie Isabella Bortolozzi, Berlin

Ed Atkins
MoMA PS1, New York

Or tears, of course
Temple Bar Gallery, Dublin

2012
Us Dead Talk Love
Chisenhale Gallery, London

Ed Atkins
Bonner Kunstverein, Bonn

2011
Art Now: Ed Atkins
Tate Britain, London

Death Mask
Cabinet Gallery, London

2010
Death Mask II: The Scent, etc.
Limoncello, London

SPOILER, Rhubaba presents...,
303 Cowgate, Edinburgh

SELECTED GROUP EXHIBITIONS

2024
L'opera al nero
Centro Civico e Culturale di Rittana

2023
Counter Imaginaries
Tromsø Kunstforening

2022
Nature humaine – Humaine nature
Fondation Vincent van Gogh, Arles

LIVES: Life, Survival, Living
Jut Art Museum, Taipei City

Mona Foma
Museum of Old and New Art, Tasmania

Uncanny Encounters
Museum of Contemporary Art Busan

Mirror Mirror: Fashion and the Psyche
MoMu, Antwerp

2021
The Sun Machine is Coming Down
Berliner Festspiele, Internationales Congress Centrum, Berlin

The Body Electric
Museum of Art and Design at Miami Dade College, Miami
Yerba Buena Center for the Arts, San Francisco
Walker Art Center, Minneapolis

Espressioni
Castello di Rivoli Museo d'Arte Contemporanea, Turin

2020
AGAINANDAGAIN–ANDAGAIN
Museo d'Arte Moderna di Bologna

Terminal
City Gallery, Wellington

Risquons-Tout
Wiels, Brussels

2019
The Assembled Human
Museum Folkwang, Essen

The Sorcerer's Burden
The Contemporary Austin

Dall'argilla all'algoritmo. Arte e tecnologia
Gallerie d'Italia (with Castello di Rivoli), Milan

MASKE
Kunstmuseum Bonn

May You Live in Interesting Times
58th Venice Biennale

The Keeper: To have and to hold
The Model, Sligo

2018
Strange Days: Memories of the Future
The Store × New Museum and The Vinyl Factory, London

Casa Tomada
Calle 22 12BIS, Mexico City

Common Front, Affectively
Nam June Paik Art Center, Yongin

Collection
Musée d'art Contemporain de Lyon

Blind Faith: Between the Visceral and the Cognitive in Contemporary Art
Haus der Kunst, Munich

Art in the Age of the Internet, 1989 to Today
The Institute of Contemporary Art, Boston

2017
How It's Made
Kostyál Gallery, Stockholm

STILL HUMAN
Rubell Museum, Miami

Suspended Animation
Les Abattoirs, Toulouse

The Trick Brain
Aïshti Foundation, Beirut

What Absence Is Made Of
The Hirshhorn Museum and Sculpture Garden, Washington DC

Being There
Louisiana Museum of Modern Art, Humlebæk

The Policeman's Beard is Half Constructed — Art in the Age of Artificial Intelligence
Bonner Kunstverein, Bonn

JEUX, rituels et récréations
Gare Saint Sauveur / Centre Pompidou, Lille

Generation Loss (10 year anniversary exhibition)
Julia Stoschek Collection, Düsseldorf

Lodgers
Haus Mödrath, Cologne

Hello World! Art After the Internet
Museum of Contemporary Art Kiasma, Helsinki

2016
The New Human
Moderna Museet, Stockholm

Suspended Animation
The Hirshhorn Museum and Sculpture Garden, Washington DC

Fire Under Snow
Louisiana Museum of Modern Art, Humlebæk

2015
Triennial, Surround Audience
New Museum, New York

Mirror Stage: Visualizing the Self After the Internet
Dallas Museum of Art

The Collection
Louis Vuitton Foundation, Paris

2014
Biennale of Moving Images 2014
Centre d'art Contemporain Genève

Europe Europe
Astrup Fearnley Museet, Oslo

Private Settings. Art after the Internet
Museum of Modern Art in Warsaw

14 Rooms
Fondation Beyeler, Art Basel and Theatre Basel

2014
Teen Paranormal Romance
The Renaissance Society, Chicago

Real Emotions, thinking in film
KW Institute for Contemporary Art, Berlin

2013
SUPERFICIAL HYGIENE
De Hallen Haarlem

Speculations on Anonymous Materials
Fridericianum, Kassel

Meanwhile... Suddenly And Then
Lyon Biennale

British British Polish Polish
Ujazdowski Castle, Warsaw

The Encyclopedic Palace
55th Venice Biennale

Oberhausen Film Festival
Oberhausen

Relative Absolute
Wysing Arts Centre, Cambridgeshire

Tomorrow Never Knows
CCA Glasgow

Frozen Lakes
Artists Space, New York

Tomorrow Never Knows
Jerwood Project Space, London

Black Cake
Team Gallery, New York

2012
Weighted Words
Zabludowicz Collection, London

The Language of the Flowers and the Stars
Cubitt, London

2011
Still Life with Phrenology Head
Galerie Isabella Bortolozzi, Berlin

Time Again
Sculpture Center, New York

2010
The Plurality of One
Monitor, curated by FormContent, Rome

New Contemporaries 2010
A Foundation, Liverpool
Institute of Contemporary Arts, London

A Killer Whale Breaching in Soft Focus
Transmission Gallery, Glasgow

Something Blue: A Curiosa of Contemporary Erotica,
Economy, London

American Mountains
Auto Italia, London

2009
American Mountains
Stone Squid, Hastings

Screenings
Christopher Crescent, Brussels

Set Off Set
Artscomplex, Edinburgh

2008
The Dark Show / And the Dark Show Returns as a Ghost
Wallis Gallery, London

2005
Les yeux de la Ville
Rue de l'Ecole-de-Medicine, Geneva

Minutes to Go
Space Gallery, London

2004
Sounding Out
University of East London

SELECTED PLAYS, PERFORMANCES AND SCREENINGS

2024
Fangs for the memories
Literaturforum im Brecht-Haus, Berlin

2023
Epitaph
Holland Festival, Amsterdam

2022
The worm
Mona Foma Festival, Mona Foma, Hobart and Launceston

Why words now
Royal Danish Academy of Fine Art, Copenhagen

Sorcerer
with Steven Zultanski
Østerbro Theatre Revolver, Copenhagen

2021
Mutes
Wiels, Casino Knokke, Knokke-Heist

INDISCIPLINE
Wiels, Casino Knokke, Knokke-Heist

A Primer for Cadavers screening
Kino Süd, Weiss Falk, Basel

2020
Old Food reading
Charlottenborg Kunsthal, Copenhagen

2019
A Catch Upon the Mirror
Performa Commission, Performa 19 Biennial, Abrons Arts Center, New York

Old Food reading
White Columns, New York

I (can scarcely move or draw my breath)
Walker Art Center, Minneapolis

2017
Dissections: Ed Atkins
DHC/Art Foundation for Contemporary Art, Montreal

2016
Art Alive Festival, Louisiana Museum of Modern Art, Humlebæk

2014
Synonyms: Five or six noise-making rifts
(Park Nights)
Serpentine Galleries, London

2013
Man of Steel (Peforma 13 Biennial)
Anthology Film Archives, New York

2011
An Echo Button (with Haroon Mirza and James Richards for Performa 11)
Times Square, New York
Chisenhale Gallery, London

In answer to a series of questions posed by a mute
Tate Britain, London

Screening for The Film London Jarman Award 2011
Whitechapel Gallery, London

A Dying Artist
Weekend event in four parts organized by Ed Atkins and Siôn Parkinson, ICA Institute of Contemporary Arts, London

2010
Memory Marathon
Serpentine Galleries, London

AWARDS & PRIZES

2015
Berliner Künstler-programm des DAAD, Berlin

2012
Paul Hamlyn Foundation Award

2012
The Jerwood / Film and Video Umbrella Award

EXHIBITIONS CURATED BY THE ARTIST

2020
The Act of Seeing With One's Own Eyes: Stan Brakhage and David Kamp
ArtDate Festival of Contemporary Art, Bergamo

2019
The Act of Seeing With One's Own Eyes: Stan Brakhage and David Kamp
Schinkel Pavillon, Berlin

2017
Generation Loss (10 year anniversary exhibition)
Julia Stoschek Collection, Düsseldorf

2016
Photo Waste
with Simon Thompson
Cabinet Gallery, London

2015
Rum, Sodomy and the Lash
Galerie Isabella Bortolozzi/ Eden Eden, Berlin

PUBLIC COLLECTIONS

British Council, London
Castello di Rivoli, Turin
Centraal Museum, Utrecht
Centre Pompidou, Paris
Fondazione Sandretto Re Rebaudengo, Turin
Fondation Louis Vuitton, Paris
Hartwig Art Foundation, Amsterdam
Hirshhorn Museum and Sculpture Garden, Smithsonian Institution, Washington DC
Julia Stoschek Foundation, Berlin
Kunstsammlung Nordrhein-Westfalen, Düsseldorf
Lisser Art Museum, Lisse
Louisiana Museum of Modern Art, Humblebæck
Musee d'Art Moderne de Ville, Paris
Museum für Moderne Kunst, Frankfurt
Museum Ludwig, Cologne
Museum of Contemporary Art Kiasma, Helsinki
Museum of Modern Art, New York
Museum of Old and New Art, Tasmania
National Galleries of Scotland, Edinburgh
Pinault Collection, Paris
Sammlung Goetz, Munich
Scottish National Gallery of Modern Art, Edinburgh
Statens Museum for Kunst, Copenhagen
Stedelijk Museum, Amsterdam
Tank Qiao Space, Shanghai
Tate, London
Ville de Geneva, Geneva
Wroclaw Contemporary Museum, Wroclaw

ARTISTS' BOOKS, WRITINGS AND SCREENPLAYS

2025
Ed Atkins, *Flower*, London

2023
Ed Atkins and Steven Zultanski, *Sorcerer*, London

2022
Ed Atkins, 'The Darkness of Our Reflection', *Trebuchet*, no.11, February

2021
Ed Atkins, *Drawings for Children*, Cologne

2019
Ed Atkins, *Old Food*, London

2016
Ed Atkins, *A Primer for Cadavers*, London

Ed Atkins, 'Ed Atkins Data Rot', *Frieze*, no.23, Spring

2012
Ed Atkins, *Grace*, unpublished

Ed Atkins, *Meringue*, produced for Helen Marten's Kunsthalle Zürich catalogue

2010
Ed Atkins, *Death Mask I* and *II*, produced on the occasion of *American Mountains* at Auto Italia, London

Ed Atkins, 'Erotics', *Something Blue—Curiosa of Contemporary Erotica*, London

Ed Atkins, *Impulses to Reanimate a Dead Alsatian*, produced on the occasion of *Spoiler* at Rhubaba, Edinburgh 2010 – wall text

2009
Ed Atkins, *Acid Piss*, unpublished, produced on the occasion of the artist's MA graduation show at The Slade

Ed Atkins, *Green Honey*, unpublished

Ed Atkins, *OS*, unpublished

Ed Atkins, *Tic*, unpublished

SOLO EXHIBITION CATALOGUES AND MONOGRAPHS

2021
Ed Atkins: Get Life/Love's Work, exh. cat., New Museum, New York

2019
Ed Atkins, exh. cat., Kunsthaus Bregenz

2016
Ed Atkins, exh. cat., Castello di Rivoli d'Arte Contemporanea

Ed Atkins – Safe Conduct, exh. cat., Statens Museum for Kunst, Copenhagen

2015
Ed Atkins: Recent Ouija, exh. cat., Stedelijk Museum, Amsterdam

2014
Ed Atkins, exh. cat., Kunsthaus Zürich

A Seer Reader, exh. cat., Serpentine Galleries, London

SELECTED CATALOGUES OF GROUP EXHIBITIONS AND PUBLICATIONS

2019
May You Live In Interesting Times, exh. cat., 58th Venice Biennale

2018
Art in the Age of the Internet, 1989 to Today, exh. cat., Institute for Contemporary Art, Boston

Daniel Birnbaum, Michelle Kuo (eds.), *More than Real: Art in the Digital Age*, Verbier, Switzerland

Strange Days, exh. cat., The Store, London / The New Musuem, New York

Anna Schneider, *Blind Faith: Between the Visceral and the Cognitive in Contemporary Art*, London

The Trick Brain, exh. cat., Aïshti Foundation, Beirut

2017
Sam Belinfante, Joseph Kohlmaier (eds.), *The Listening Reader*, London

Generation Loss: 10 Years Julia Stoschek Collection, exh. cat., Julia Stoschek Collection, Düsseldorf, Berlin

2016
The Imitation Game, exh. cat., Manchester Art Gallery

2015
Art from Europe's Edges in the Long '90s and Today, exh. cat., Centre for Contemporary Art Ujazdowski Castle, Warsaw

The Animated Reader: Poetry of "Surround Audience", exh.cat., New Museum in association with McNally Jackson, New York

New Museum Triennial. Surround Audience, exh. cat., New Museum, New York

Performa 13: Surrealism, the Voice, Citizenship, exh.cat., Performa 13 Biennial, New York

The 14th Istanbul Biennial: Tuzlu su/Saltwater, exh. cat., ARTER – Space for Art, Istanbul

2014
High Performance: Time-Based Media Art Since 1996, ZKM Zentrum für Kunst und Medien, Karlsruhe

14 Rooms, Fondation Beyeler, Basel

2013
Entre-Temps… Brusquement, et Ensuite. 12e Biennale de Lyon 2013, Lyon Biennale

The Encyclopedic Palace, exh. cat., 55th Venice Biennale

Performa 11: Staging Ideas, exh. cat., Performa 11 Biennial, New York

12th Lyon Biennale – Meanwhile… Suddenly and Then, exh. cat., Lyon

2012
Weighted Words: Zabludowicz Collection, Zabludowicz Collection, London

2011
Time Again, Sculpture Center, New York

2010
New Contemporaries 2010, A Foundation, Liverpool and ICA Institute of Contemporary Arts, London

SELECTED ARTICLES AND REVIEWS

2024
Ben Lerner, 'The Pain Artist'. *The New York Review of Books*, October

2023
Oli Surel, 'Ed Atkins with Steven Zultanski: Sorcerer', *Screen Slate*, 27 December

Travis Diehl 'Ed Atkins at Gladstone Gallery', *Spike Art Magazine*, 22 December

2022
Andrew Durbin, 'Ed Atkins and Steven Zultanski on their Daring New Play', *Frieze*, 15 March

Millie Walton, 'Digital Alienation, Loss and Reversal in Ed Atkin's Visual Sorcery', *Trebuchet*, February

2021
Ariella Budick, 'Ed Atkins at the New Museum: the perfect artist for the age of avatars', *Financial Times*, August

Jason Farago, 'Ed Atkins and His Mum Art Starring in a Museum Show', *New York Times*, July

Hal Foster, 'CLOSE-UP: YOUR LOSS - Hal Foster on Ed Atkins's *The worm*, 2021', *Artforum*, October

2020
Isobel Harbison, 'Old Food', *ArtReview*, January

Emily Watlington, 'Ed Atkins's new work shows that his real medium might be poetry', *Art in America*, January

2019
Jacob Proctor, 'Stan Brakhage and David Kamp', *Artforum*, May

2017
Penny Rafferty, 'Ed Atkins on his hyper-real and harrowing new films', *Dazed*, February

2016
Barbara Casavecchia, 'Selfie d'arte', *D/La Repubblica*, no.987, May, pp.46–50

Matthias Hvass Borello, 'Foregribelsens vold', *Kunsten.Nu* online, April

Andrew Durbin, 'Missing Persons', *Parkett*, no.98, June, pp.24–30

Orit Gat, 'Work of constant change: Orit Gat on Ed Atkins at the Kitchen', *The Art Newspaper*, May

Bruce Hainley, 'Mary Shelley App', *Parkett*, no.98, June, pp.48–53

Helena Halmes, 'Ed Atkins', *This is Tomorrow*, June

Katy Diamond Hamer, 'Ed Atkins, *Performance Capture*: The Kitchen', *Eyes Towards the Dove*, April

Laura Herman, 'Review: Ed Atkins', *Frieze*, February

Leslie Jamison, 'Ed Atkins', *Parkett*, vol.98, Spring

Nicole Kaack, 'A Conversation with Ed Atkins', *The Kitchen Blog* online, April

Jeffrey Kastner, 'Reviews: Ed Atkins', *Artforum*, September

Danny King, 'Ed Atkins: *Performance Capture*', *The Village Voice*, April

Andrew Russeth, 'An artist who explores the deep creepiness of facial-recognition technology', *The New Yorker*, May

Timotheus Vermeleun, 'The Altergorithm', *Frieze* online, April

Ryan Lee Wong, 'Talking Head: Ed Atkins Uses Others to Archive Himself', *The Village Voice*, May

Louise Steiwer, 'Bowing before the authorities – interview with Ed Atkins', *Kopenhagen Magasin* online, April

2015
Anezka Bartlova, 'Ed Atkins', *Revue Labyrint*, no. 35–6

Carolyn Christov-Bakargiev, 'Knotty By Nature', *Mousse*, October

Edo Dijksterhuis, 'Interview with Ed Atkins: Cadavers Telling You to Shut Up', *ArtSlant*

Francesca Gavin, 'Rise of the Soft Machines', *Sleek*, Winter

'Interview with Ed Atkins, *Performance Capture*, Manchester International Festival', *Aesthetica* online, June

'Liebe, Sex, Tod: Ed Atkins sinniert in Amsterdam', *Monopol*, February

Adrian Searle, 'Here Comes Everyone! The Monster Avatar taking over Manchester', *Guardian* online, July

Mark Sladen, 'Blank Verse', *ArtReview*, January–February

Skye Sherwin, 'Q&A: Ed Atkins', *Guardian* online, May

'Where the Magic Happens: Ed Atkins and Mark Leckey in Conversation', *Art Quarterly*, Summer, pp. 54–61

2014
Matthew De Abaitua, 'Head Space', *Frieze*, no. 165, September

Louisa Buck, 'Ed Atkins: vile and virtual bodies', *The Art Newspaper*, no. 258, June

Apsara Diquinzio, 'A Roundtable on Art & Cinema', *Mousse*, no. 42, February

Melissa Gronlund, 'Cold New World', *Sight and Sound*, September

Melissa Gronlund, 'From Narcissism to the Dialogic: Identity in Art after the Internet', *Afterall*, Autumn/Winter

Erik Hartin, 'Reality Never Looked This Good', *Bon*, Autumn/Winter

Jeff Nagy, 'Ed Atkins: Serpentine Sackler Gallery', *Artforum*, vol. 53, no. 2, October

Lorena Muñoz-Alonso, 'Intimidades Incomodas', *input*, no. 2, September, cover and pp. 50–7

Boris Pofalla, 'Wenn Avatare Fluchen', *Frankfurter Allgemeine Sonntagszeitung*, July, p. 33

Allese Thompson, '500 words', *Artforum* online, August

Thomas D. Trummer, 'A Dialogue with Ed Atkins', *Kunsthalle Mainz* online, July

Felix Vogel, 'Representational Impasse', *Texte Zur Kunst*, June

2013

Ed Atkins and Elizabeth Price, 'The Dark Side of Pop', *Mousse*, no.38, April–May

Kirsty Bell, 'Ed Atkins' Warm, Warm, Warm Spring Mouths', *Art Agenda* online, April

Giampaolo Bianconi, 'Artist Profile: Ed Atkins', *Rhizome* online, January

Arielle Bier, 'Ed Atkins', *Frieze* , no.10, June–August

Klaus Biesenbach, 'An intimately, duplicitously reflexive experience', *Flash Art*, November–December

Emily Burns, 'Tomorrow Never Knows: Ed Atkins and Naheed Raza', *This is Tomorrow* online, January

Kyle Chayka, 'Gauging the Hollowness of Computer Graphics Through Video and Poetry', *Hyperallergic* online, January

Shama Khanna, '#Voice-over – Overview, Under the Skin', *Kaleidoscope*, no.20, Winter

Jennifer Krasinski, 'The Sites of Death', *Spike*, no.35, Spring

Nick Pinkerton, 'In Rare Form', *Artforum* online, December

2012

T.V. Adams, 'Ed Atkins: Us Dead Talk Love', *Litro* online, November

Oliver Basciano, 'Ed Atkins and James Richards', *Art Review*, no.64, December

Nick Cain, 'Ed Atkins', *The Wire*, no.345, November

Katie Guggenheim, 'Interview with Ed Atkins', Chisenhale Gallery online, September

'In conversation with Ed Atkins', *Aesthetica*, August

Isobel Harbison, 'Ed Atkins at Chisenhale Gallery, London', *Kaleidoscope*, no.16, Fall

Martin Herbert, 'Ed Atkins', *Artforum*, vol.50, no.6, February

Julian Vigo, 'The Serpentine Gallery's Memory Marathon', *Huffington Post* online, October

2011

Jareh Das, 'Ed Atkins Review', *Aesthetica* online, March

Isobel Harbison, 'Ed Atkins', *Frieze*, May

Dan Kidner, 'More Than a Feeling', *Frieze*, no.142, October

Hannah Knights, 'Rhubaba: Ed Atkins, "Spoiler"', *The Journal*, no.30, February

Kathy Noble, 'Future Greats – Ed Atkins', *Art Review*, no.46, March

Hans Ulrich Obrist, 'Interviews', *Kaleidoscope*, no.13, Winter

Patrick Ward, 'Cross Platform', *The Wire*, October

2010

Ali Beddoes, *Mousse*, no.26, November

ACKNOWLEDGEMENTS

We would like to offer our deepest gratitude and heartfelt appreciation to Ed Atkins for the insight, commitment and energy he has brought to the making of this exhibition. Throughout he has demonstrated an extraordinary generosity and open-mindedness.

It would not have been possible to deliver an exhibition of this ambition and scale without the commitment of colleagues from across Tate. We would like to thank Tate Britain's Director, Alex Farquharson and Director of Exhibitions and Displays, Andrea Schlieker; Head of Programme Management, Carolyn Kerr for her invaluable guidance and expertise; Wendy Lothian and Kiko Noda for their tireless work and professionalism in administering the exhibition loans. We are deeply grateful to Hannah Marsh, Chloe Jones, Aliya Al Nakeeb and Isabella Smith for their diligence and commitment throughout the making of this exhibition.

For overseeing the exhibition build and installation our thanks to Andy Shiel, Liam Tebbs and Bella Probyn; and to Dale Wilson for his meticulous attention managing the installation with such professionalism and care. We could not have achieved an exhibition of such technical ambition without our colleagues in time-based media conservation: we are incredibly grateful to Francesca Colussi and George Morris, ably supported by Marco Testa-Ryan, Jake van Dugteren, Willa Ratz and Pierre Bouvier Patron, for their expertise. We would also like to thank paper conservator Sophie Sarkodie, sculpture conservator Gates Sofer and painting conservator Amy Griffin. For their instrumental support throughout the planning of the exhibition we are incredibly grateful to Martin McGeown, Andrew Wheatley, Freddie Checketts and Nikolaj Stobbe.

In development we owe our gratitude to Claire Gylphé, Charlotte Reeves, Sarah Monteath, Ellie Rushforth, Jamie Steers and Heidi Luedecke. Our sincere thanks to Kirsteen McSwein and Elliott Higgs for their thoughtful work on the exhibition interpretation and to David Dibosa for his guidance during the research and planning of the exhibition. Thank you to Tram Nguyen and Leyla Tahir for their work curating the accompanying learning programme; Designers, Francisca Roseiro and Chiara García Melchiorri; Marketing Manager, Isabella Szukilojc; Press and Communications team, Duncan Holden and Ella Baker; Figgy Guyver and Enrico Tassi at *Tate ETC* and Irena Cater in Advocacy and Events. We are grateful to colleagues in Visitor Experience: Emma Garrett, Natasha Guerriero, Marcus Dickey-Horley, Toyin Omirin and Matthew Rowan, along with Roger Miller from our Safe at Tate team, who all continue to shape the exhibition by thoughtfully and creatively welcoming and considering our audiences.

For this beautiful publication we thank designer Annette Lux and HIT for their endless invention, good humour and attention to detail throughout. To our colleagues in Tate Publishing: particularly Emilia Will for her tireless work, kindness and diligence as project editor, as well as

Roanne Marner, Emma O'Neill and Tom Avery. Our heartfelt thanks to those who contributed thoughtful words to this publication addressing the many facets of Atkins's work and bringing new readings and personal insights to his practice: Hal Foster, Ben Lerner, Kathryn Scanlan and Jamie Stevens.

We are indebted to the artist's representative galleries Cabinet Gallery, London, Gladstone Gallery, New York, Galerie Isabella Bortolozzi, Berlin and dépendance, Brussels. Our special thanks to the following individuals and institutions for their generosity and support of the exhibition through the loan of important works: Cabinet Gallery, Gladstone Gallery, Galerie Isabella Bortolozzi, Berlin, Hartwig Art Foundation, Amsterdam, Robert Ramsauer and those that wish to remain anonymous.

Polly Staple and Nathan Ladd
Exhibition Curators

CONTRIBUTORS

Hal Foster is an art critic and historian and has written widely on postmodernism, the avant-garde and aesthetic theory. He is Professor in the Department of Art and Archaeology at Princeton University.

Ben Lerner is the author of eight books of poetry and prose, as well as several collaborations with artists. He teaches at Brooklyn College.

Jamie Stevens is a psychotherapist based in London. His interests span the 'object relations' tradition in international psychoanalysis as applied to clinical practice and cultural criticism. He previously worked as a curator for institutions in London, San Francisco and New York.

Kathryn Scanlan is an American award-winning author. She is best known for her works *The Dominant Animal*, *Aug 9 – Fog* and *Kick the Latch*.

Nathan Ladd is Curator, Contemporary British Art at Tate.

Polly Staple is the former Director of Collection, British Art at Tate.

Unless otherwise stated, all images © Ed Atkins

© Steven Zultanski 13, 22, 23, 44, 45, 47, 70, 118, 172, 173, 174, 175, 193, 194, 195, 196, 197, 198, 201
© Edition Wandelweiser, Haan. With kind permission of Edition Wandelweiser 112, 113

Photography

Courtesy: the artist 17, 28, 49, 62, 63, 87, 95, 101, 112, 113, 117, 161, 167, 180, 223
Ed Atkins & Steven Zultanski, still image from *Nurses Come and Go, But None For Me* 13, 22, 23, 44, 45, 47, 193, 194, 195, 196, 197, 198, 199, 201
Photo by Mark Blower 53, 55
Photo: Cabinet Gallery 85
Courtesy: the artist and Cabinet Gallery, London 58, 61; /
Photo: Cabinet. Gallery, London 123–138, 170, 171, 176, 177, 179
Courtesy: the artist, dépendance, Brussels 186
Jürg Frey (composer): *Klavierstück* 2 (2001) / Photo: the artist 110–111
Courtesy: the artist and Galerie Isabella Bortolozzi, Berlin 59, 60
Courtesy: the artist, Galerie Isabella Bortolozzi, Berlin, Cabinet Gallery, London, dépendance, Brussels and Gladstone Gallery, New York /
Photo: the artist front cover, back cover, 18, 19, 24, 27, 30, 35, 36, 37, 48, 50, 51, 54, 56, 57, 63, 65 66, 72, 74, 77, 81, 82, 83, 86, 97, 98, 103, 104, 105, 106, 108, 109, 110, 111, 115, 140, 141, 142, 143, 163, 164, 183, 185
Courtesy: the artists, Galerie Isabella Bortolozzi, Berlin, Cabinet Gallery, London, dépendance, Brussels and Gladstone Gallery, New York 118; /
Photo: the artists 172, 173, 174, 175
Courtesy: the artist, Gladstone Gallery, New York 188, 189, 190, 191; /
Photo by David Regen 10, 20, 21, 68, 69
Courtesy: the artists, Gladstone Gallery, New York /
Photo by David Regen 70
Photo by Graysc / Dotgain 71
Photo by Achim Kukulies 52
Photo by Daniele Molajoli 38, 84
Photo by David Regen 78
Photo credit: Axel Schneider 67
Photo by Markus Trettet 64

Film

Voilà la verité
Script, concept, direction, set design and editing Ed Atkins. Featuring the voices of Rivka Rothstein and Héctor Miguel Santana. Audio Post-Production: Studiokamp; Foley: David Kamp; Mix: David Kamp; extra sound design: Ed Atkins – from *Ménilmontant* 1926, directed and edited by Dimitri Kirsanoff, featuring Nadia Sibirskaïa 56–7

Sorcerer
Script, concept, direction, set design and editing Ed Atkins and Steven Zultanski. Featuring: Lotte Andersen, Peter Christoffersen and Ida Cæcilie Rasmussen. Choreographer: Nønne Mai Svalholm; theme tune: Lawrence Giffin, Steven Zultanski; Lighting Designer: Karl Sørensen; Builder: Andrew Mathews; Assistant Director: Pernille Hviid; Master Electrician: Peter Lorichs; Theatre Plumber: Kenneth Kreutzfeldt; Stage Manager: Anne Kirstine Pyndt; Master Carpenter: Rasmus Rahbek; Production Assistant: Emma Dybdahl Hildebrandt; Head of Costumes: Kristina Widriksen; Sound Engineer: Anders Munch Amdisen; Poduction Manager: Svend Martin Holst; Chief Dramaturge and Curator: Rikke Hedeager; Camera: Martin Stampe, Niklas Frost, Jeppe Rohde Nielsen. With thanks to Signe Lausen, Anders Astrup Jensen, Rune Klan, Hollis Pinky Atkins, Sally-Ginger Brockbank, Ida Marie Hede, Henriette Heise, Chris Shields, Finn Hagen Storgaard 18, 172–5

Nurses Come and Go, But None For Me
Film by Ed Atkins and Steven Zultanski, Diary by Philip Atkins. Featuring: Toby Jones, Saskia Reeves, Bella Aubin, Caroline Elms, Misheck Freeman, Chengxi Fu, Alfie Jallow, Tom Lyons and Ayesha Ostler. Producer: Pinky Ghundale, Daya Films; Director of Photography: Oliver Curtis BSC; Music: Derek Baron; First Assistant Camera: Ben Foat; Second Assistant Camera: Luca Parasiliti-Holt, Tamara Turoczi; Grip: Michael Farrell; DIT: Andrew Elvis; Video Assist: Nico Corfield; Gaffer: Harry Wiggins; Electrician: Sami Hussein; Spark Trainee: Aggi Mentel, Toby Norman; Production Design: Tim Adams; Props Runner: Monika Saleh; Costume Designer: Teddy George-Poku; Hair and Make-Up Artist: Solange Koniak; First Assistant Director; Andraž Kadunc; Second Assistant Director: Lynn El Safah; Production Runner: Karla Hunter; Sound Recordist / Mixer: Andy Paddon; Boom Operator: Andrea Cremonini. Camera Grip and Lighting Equipment: Panavision, Digital Orchard Group, The Grip Company, Panalux; Insurance: Tysers; Post Production: Harbor. Thanks to Rosemary Atkins, Harry Atkins, Hollis Pinky Atkins, The Master Shipwright's House, RADA, Klose & Soan Catering. Commissioned and produced by Hartwig Art Foundation. Additional funding from the Danish Arts Council 13, 22, 23, 44, 45, 47, 193, 194, 195, 196, 197, 198, 199, 201

The publishers have made every effort to trace the copyright holders of the works illustrated in this book and apologise for any omissions or errors that may have been made.

Thank you to Martin McGeown, Andrew Wheatley, Freddie Checketts, Isabella Bortolozzi, Gavin Brown, Barbara Gladstone, Alissa Bennett, Michael Callies, Ayelet Yanai, Rupert Friend, Simon Thompson, Steven Zultanski, Beatrix Ruf, Thomas Oberender, Chris Shields, Henriette Heise, Mike Sperlinger, Magnus Kaslov, Nikolaj Stobbe, Jacques Testard, Polly Staple, Nathan Ladd, Hannah Marsh, Annette Lux and Emilia Will. Special thanks to Harry Atkins, Rosemary Atkins, Philip Atkins, and my darlings Sally-Ginger, Hollis Pinky, and Gabriel Sophus.

Ed Atkins

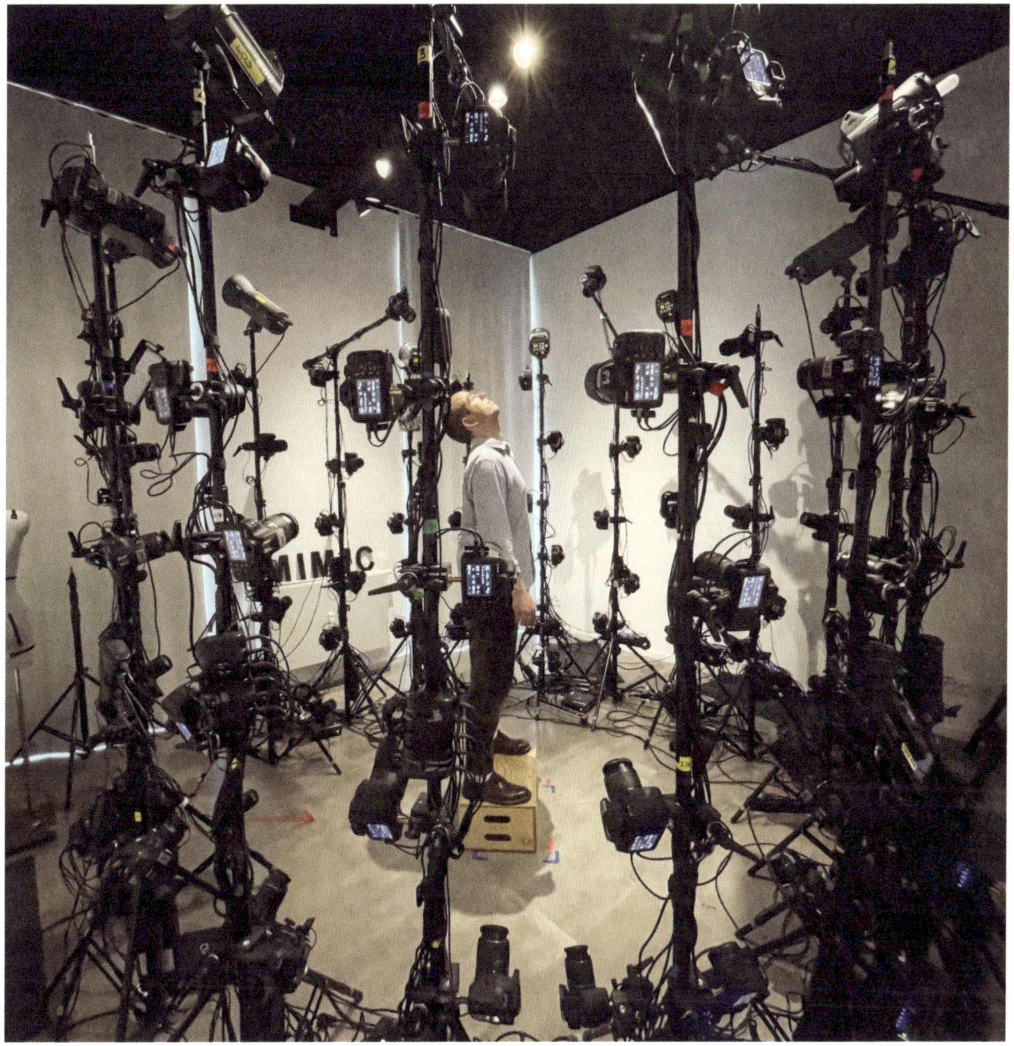

Ed Atkins being photogrammetrically scanned in Berlin, Summer 2023

First published 2025 by order of the Tate Trustees
by Tate Publishing, a division of
Tate Enterprises Ltd, Millbank, London SW1P 4RG
www.tate.org.uk/publishing
on the occasion of the exhibition

Ed Atkins
Tate Britain, London
2 April — 25 August 2025

Supported by the Ed Atkins Exhibition Supporters Circle:

Danish Arts Foundation

Tate International Council and Tate Patrons

Nurses Come and Go, But None For Me 2024 was
commissioned and produced by Hartwig Art Foundation

A catalogue record for this book is available
from the British Library

ISBN 978-1-84976-935-8
ISBN 978-1-84976-936-5

Editors: Polly Staple, Nathan Ladd and Ed Atkins
Senior Editor: Emilia Will
Production: Roanne Marner
Picture Researcher: Emma O'Neill
Design: HIT
Colour reproduction by Graphicom Srl, Italy
Printed and bound by Graphicom Srl, Italy

FSC www.fsc.org MIX Paper | Supporting responsible forestry FSC® C013123